# THE FAITHS OF THE

# POSTWAR PRESIDENTS

George H. Shriver Lecture Series in Religion in American History No. 5

# The Faiths of the Postwar Presidents

FROM TRUMAN TO OBAMA  ⌁ David L. Holmes

The University of Georgia Press    Athens and London

© 2012 by the University of Georgia Press
Athens, Georgia 30602
www.ugapress.org
All rights reserved
Designed by Mindy Basinger Hill
Set in 11/15pt Adobe Jenson Pro
Printed and bound by Thomson-Shore
The paper in this book meets the guidelines for
permanence and durability of the Committee on
Production Guidelines for Book Longevity of the
Council on Library Resources.

Printed in the United States of America
12  13  14  15  16  C  5  4  3  2  1

Library of Congress Cataloging-in-Publication Data

Holmes, David L. (David Lynn)
The faiths of the postwar presidents : from Truman to Obama /
David L. Holmes ; introduction by Martin E. Marty.
p.     cm. — (George H. Shriver lecture series
in religion in American history ; no. 5)
Includes bibliographical references and index.
ISBN-13: 978-0-8203-3862-0
ISBN-10: 0-8203-3862-1
1. Presidents — United States — Religion.
2. Presidents — United States — Biography.  I. Title.
BR516.H63 2012
973.92092'2 — dc23                    2011029959

British Library Cataloging-in-Publication Data available

*To James C. Livingston*

# CONTENTS

# PREFACE

No president's story is complete until his death — and even then, reevaluations frequently occur. In the case of a sitting or recent president, assessments are especially subject to change. In certain ways, a book or chapter on such a president resembles a first draft.

This book went to press in the summer of 2011. In the months since, more than a dozen works on the postwar presidents have appeared. None changes in any significant way the evaluation of any president's religious faith given in these pages. In September 2011, for example, the Kennedy Library released tapes of interviews conducted with Jacqueline Kennedy several months after her husband's assassination. Although her words would have provided color and detail, they support the revisionist interpretation of John F. Kennedy's Roman Catholicism found in this book.

My thanks to the following alumni and students of the College of William and Mary who assisted in preparing this publication during the half-dozen years of its research and writing: Katelyn R. Browne, Jack E. Cohen, Leah R. Giles, Ann E. Glennie, Andrew E. Jungclaus, Jarrett W. Knight, Anna L. Krause, Susan M. Metallo, Wistar W. Murray, Hannah R. Perry, and Maggie E. Southwell. Additional thanks go to the staffs of the Swem Library at the College of William and Mary, the Alderman Library at the University of Virginia, and the nation's presidential libraries.

# INTRODUCTION

The founders of the United States, both its leaders and ordinary citizens, had a problem: what to do about religion in the new republic. Those who had immigrated from Europe, remembering everything from corruption to holy wars, knew that in the hands of civil authorities religion could by force of law be used, and that rulers had used it. Heads of state might employ preferred faiths to endorse their own selfish policies, show favoritism in the public, or penalize those who dissented from officially approved creeds. The American colonists, now republicans, had just "killed [off] the king" in the Revolutionary War, so monarchs and governors could play no legally legitimated role in determining the civil place of religion. The thirteen former colonies differed among themselves in polities and policies. Some retained the establishment of religion with all the legal perquisites that went with it, while others fought for disestablishment and thus attempted to give a place for dissent against the favored faith. What should the citizens of 1787 and 1789 do?

It has been well said that the founders solved the problem of religion by not solving it. They drafted and approved the First Amendment to the Constitution with its classic clause barring Congress from making laws respecting the establishment of religion or prohibiting its free exercise. Earlier, in Article VI of the Constitution itself they had assured that "no religious test" should have any part in qualifying or disqualifying anyone from public office. But they did not go so far as to spell out the details, and they did not include anything about the religious role of the executive branch in the person or through the agency of the chief executive. That left a vacuum to be filled in a society of whose citizens President Dwight Eisenhower was to say, "We are a religious people." He overshot in a second phrase, claiming on slight grounds that the nation's laws presupposed belief in a supreme being.

This people—"religious" and "nonreligious"—has shown through the decades that the majority favors religious expression from the president. Willy-nilly, the president serves a kind of priestly role. When a spaceship explodes, when terrorists attack or enemies bomb, when publics need to employ someone with a voice to prod or to console, it falls on the president to resort to both rhetoric and example that sound and look religious by most definitions of that term.

David Holmes, who is so familiar with the sources that he sounds as if he is on speaking terms with the post–World War II presidents, serves us well by showing how each of them—again, by rhetoric and example—summoned the support of citizens. Sometimes they turned their rostrum into a bully pulpit, and sometimes they all but bullied people "in the name of God" to support their policies. Doing both of these in the role we have called priestly has been a bipartisan endeavor in which chance, accident, serendipity, and brutal design—its partisan enemies always call this "hypocrisy"—have left generous records of religious-sounding rhetoric.

Fortunately, while Holmes does not trumpet the claim that he is nonpartisan or bipartisan, as each president's rhetoric usually is advertised, he finds that the gestures and sounds of the president cannot help but lean one way, the president's way, and against all others. Reading histories of the responses to those gestures and that rhetoric, as Holmes does here often enough, provides illuminating access to the minds of the presidents as they tried to make history or live creatively with events occurring around them. While Europeans often call America secular and many Americans ruefully join them in that assessment, it has certainly been easier for chief executives to respond to religious interests or to try to impose them than it has been to remember the founding impulses. Holmes sorts these out.

Having had adult experience during all the tenures described in this book, and having written extensively on their era, I will stress that Holmes has chosen well from the sources on which he forms his narrative or makes his case. There are surprises, especially when presidents transcend partisan interests for a suprapartisan common good or when presidents having little formal theological training come up with theological interpretations of citizen action. Holmes's manners are too controlled to permit him to propagandize, overstate cases, or lose his way in the maze of presidential politics, so he comes across as an intelligent, fair-minded, and reliable guide.

It is no surprise that Baptists Jimmy Carter and Bill Clinton could cite chapter and verse from the Bible better than could Catholic John Kennedy, but it is a surprise (amid the cultural biases back when Kennedy was elected in 1960) to see how elegantly he tailored his approach and opinions to the means and ways of then-still-Protestant America. It is a surprise that friend-of-evangelicals Ronald Reagan—who could court Bible-believing, Jesus-is-the-only-way-to-salvation constituencies with considerable elegance and appeal while not losing evangelical followers—could also populate heaven with religiously diverse astronauts who, he assured all citizens, had gained heaven. No one expects or should expect consistency among presidents who had to court diverse and sometimes partly contradictory constituencies.

One among many delights of the book shows up in Holmes's probing and sometimes tender accountings of the parental home-life, the settings and experiences in various locales, and the events in the lives of young presidents-to-be. It is helpful to read what he adduces to show how candidates became winners with the aid of religion; how religion transformed each of them; and how as office holders, they transformed religion. The reader of these accounts through sixty years of presidencies is not likely to find grounds to foresee a decline of religious interests in putatively secular America's coming years.

Interest groups, churches, voluntary agencies, and others who favor a candidate for office often publish and distribute what they call "voters' guides" that are full of propaganda. They would do better to help voters gain perspective to make decisions by providing fair historical backgrounds, beginning with this book by David Holmes.

*Martin E. Marty*
PROFESSOR EMERITUS, THE UNIVERSITY OF CHICAGO

# THE FAITHS OF THE

# POSTWAR PRESIDENTS

# Harry S. Truman

*1884–1972* ⟶ PRESIDENT FROM 1945 TO 1953

In 1907, when Harry Truman was working on the family's farm in Grandview, Missouri, the rector of the Episcopal church in nearby Independence led a systematic canvass of his city's religious membership. According to this survey, the population of Independence that year fell into the following religious categories:

- 1,031    Mormon
- 482    Christian Church (Disciples of Christ)
- 464    Methodist
- 462    Presbyterian
- 414    Baptist
- 245    Roman Catholic
- 59    Episcopalian
- 20    German Evangelical Church
- 11    Christian Scientist
- 9    Lutheran
- 4    Seventh Day Adventist
- 25    "Scattered"
- 1,337    "No Church"[1]

Inevitably, the survey raises questions. Are African American churches omitted, or are they included in the Baptist, Methodist, and perhaps other categories? Is the Jewish population listed under "Scattered" or "No Church," or is it entirely disregarded? Regardless of the survey's accuracy, it shows that Harry Truman was raised in a churchgoing, largely Protestant environment. In 1907, Independence had two and a half times more church members than persons who listed no church affiliation. Mormons represented the largest religious group, for Joseph Smith Jr. had declared that the second coming of Jesus would occur in Independence. In 1860, his son Joseph Smith III had formed the headquarters of the Reorganized Church of Jesus Christ of Latter-Day Saints (today renamed the Community of Christ) in the town.

Although Harry Truman is identified historically with the town of Independence, the Trumans were actually country people—their family farms encompassed hundreds of acres. But farming went bad just when Truman graduated from high school, so for him college became an economic impossibility.

The first of three children, Truman grew up a Baptist. Forty years before he was born, the major Baptist denomination in the United States divided over the issue of slavery, resulting in two factions: Northern Baptists, later renamed American Baptists, and Southern Baptists. In Truman's home state of Missouri, the churches generally affiliated with the Southern Baptists.

In 1867, Truman's maternal grandfather, Solomon Young, donated land adjacent to the family farm in Grandview (roughly twenty miles outside Independence) for a church. Despite this generosity, Young never officially belonged to a denomination. According to family lore, the donated church was initially a "union" church, one that rotated services among various Protestant denominations. All of the denominations that used the church "wanted to arrive at the same place," Solomon told his young grandson, "but they had to fight about it to see who had the inside track with the Almighty."[2] In time, the church became Baptist. Truman attended the church in Grandview frequently, and in 1950 he returned as president to lead the dedication of the new church building.[3]

On both sides, Truman's family displayed a distrust of religious pretension. Truman noted more than once that his maternal grandfather "used to say that when he heard his neighbor pray too loudly in public he went home and locked his smokehouse."[4] He noted that his paternal grandfather, Anderson Truman, "felt the same way—but thought that the Baptists had the best chance to arrive at happiness beyond the grave."[5]

Martha Young, Truman's mother, grew up in the church that met on her father's farm. Raised during a period when Baptists emphasized women's education, she spent two years at the Baptist Female College in Lexington, Missouri. In later years, Truman's mother claimed to be a "Lightfoot Baptist"—that is, a Baptist who was not averse to dancing, card playing, or other behaviors frowned upon by more pietistic believers.[6] Just as Martha's father—who never affiliated with a church—influenced her outlook on such matters, so she also clearly influenced her son's religious views.

In 1881 Martha married John Truman, a Baptist. Subsequently, the family moved from Grandview to Independence. Though Harry Truman later recalled that neither of his parents were especially active churchgoers, he remembered that his mother left the Baptist church in Grandview because she believed it contained "too many liars and hypocrites."[7] In Independence, she enrolled Harry in the Sunday school of the Presbyterian church. Presbyterianism was perhaps the most prestigious denomination in Independence, but Martha Truman's decision seems to have been based on the fact that it was the closest church to the new Truman residence.

The change in denominations was only temporary, and after a few years the Trumans returned to the Baptist tradition. Baptists do not baptize children, only converted adults who have accepted Jesus Christ as their lord and savior. In keeping with their interpretation of the New Testament, they administer baptism in the manner that John the Baptist baptized Jesus, by immersion. At the age of eighteen, Truman was baptized in the Little Blue River, which ran by his grandfather's farm and its church.[8]

During his school years, Truman sometimes joined his cousins at Independence's First Baptist Church (where his sister Mary Jane was baptized), but he never officially joined the congregation.[9] After relocating to Kansas City in 1903, the Trumans periodically attended Benton Boulevard Baptist Church. The family moved back to the Grandview farm in 1906, but Harry did not formally join the Grandview Baptist Church for another ten years. He would then belong to that church for the rest of his life.

Truman was a loyal and generous member of his congregation. In 1949, while president, he not only contributed more than twenty thousand dollars toward the building of a larger church (the equivalent of almost two hundred thousand dollars today), he also brought the pastor and one of the deacons to the White House to discuss the building plans. When Truman purchased the previous church building, he sold it to a Pentecostal denomination to assure that it would remain a place of worship rather than be demolished.

As a Baptist, Truman was his own man. Just as his family distrusted inordinate emotionalism in worship, he disliked it as well. Baptists require a conversion experience or marked heightening of faith before baptism, but

Truman did not fall into the born-again tradition. Throughout his life, he rarely spoke of Jesus as a savior who died on the cross at Mount Calvary to pay the penalty for human sins. Billy Graham told him that believing in the ethics of the Sermon on the Mount and the Golden Rule was not enough to gain salvation. He needed to personally accept Jesus Christ as his savior. While in no way denying the divinity of Christ, Truman disagreed with Graham's theology. Thus he should not be viewed as an evangelical.[10]

Instead, Truman's Christianity was based on both the moral code of the Ten Commandments and the ethical teachings of the New Testament. From childhood on, he was a great reader. Truman later declared that he had read his mother's illustrated Bible three times by the age of fourteen.[11] As a child, he learned moral guidelines directly from the Bible and from his parents.

In later years, biblical references filled Truman's correspondence and public addresses. Throughout his life, he thought that the Bible—especially the Ten Commandments, the Sermon on the Mount, and the Golden Rule—contained the solution to every human problem. "If a child is instilled with good morals and taught the value of the precepts laid down in Exodus 20 and Matthew 5, 6, and 7," he told his wife, "there is not much to worry about in after years."[12] In his fiftieth year, he wrote that he was "still of the opinion that there are no other laws to live by, in spite of the professors of psychology."[13] When president, he once expressed the hope that "we can make Stalin realize that we believe in [the] Sermon on the Mount and that as a realist, he ought to do as he would be done by."[14]

Ultimately, Truman was a Baptist because that was the religious tradition in which he was raised. He attended services at other churches, went briefly as a young child to a Presbyterian Sunday school, and married an Episcopalian. Thus he had ample opportunity during his life to change denominations. But he seems to have chosen to remain a Baptist because of that denomination's democratic form of government, its lack of priestliness and hierarchy, its simple worship, its unadorned sanctuaries, and its overall lack of pomp and circumstance. "I'm a Baptist," he once wrote,

> because I think that sect gives the common man the shortest and most direct approach to God. I've never thought that God gives a damn about pomp and circumstance, gold crowns, jeweled breastplates, and ancestral background.

Forms and ceremonies impress a lot of people, but I've never thought that the Almighty could be impressed by anything but the heart and soul of the individual.[15]

Truman prayed regularly. When his mother was dying, he knelt by her bed daily with the pastor of the Grandview Baptist Church. According to his testimony in 1950, he had said the following prayer each day from high school on:

Oh! Almighty and Everlasting God, Creator of Heaven, Earth and the Universe:—

Help me to be, to think, to act what is right, because it is right; make me truthful, honest and honorable in all things; make me intellectually honest for the sake of right and honor and without thought of reward to me. Give me the ability to be charitable, forgiving and patient with my fellowmen—help me to understand their motives and their shortcomings—even as Thou understandest mine!

Amen, Amen, Amen.[16]

Despite this evidence of religiosity, some Americans did not perceive Truman to be a religious man. He drank bourbon with his political associates and with his Episcopalian wife, played poker, did not object to dancing or theater, and used profane language in private and sometimes in public. When Baylor University, a Southern Baptist institution, announced shortly after Truman assumed the presidency that it would confer an honorary doctorate on him, the 4,500 "messengers" to the Texas Baptist General Convention expressed firm opposition. "No Baptist school," declared the chairman of that convention's Civic Righteousness Committee, "should confer a degree on a man who likes his poker and drinks his bourbon. I know that we all agree that no man—even the President of the United States—could be a good Baptist and drink his liquor."[17] Despite the opposition of the delegates to the state convention, Truman was awarded the degree.

During his presidency, Truman's sporadic church attendance only contributed to this perception. Although he attended church more frequently than the public knew, his opposition to making church a spectacle caused him frequently to avoid it both in Washington and Missouri. His papers in the Truman Library contain numerous notes to the minister of Washington's First Baptist Church expressing regret that he would be unable to attend that Sunday. In one note written shortly after he became president, he declares that "I won't be able to go anywhere tomorrow . . . it now requires so many people to get me around there is no pleasure in going anywhere."[18]

"I don't want people to come to church to see the President," Truman told his pastor at Grandview Baptist. "They ought to go there to worship God." In the same conversation he cited the experience of Calvin Coolidge, who regularly attended the First Congregational Church of Washington, D.C. Knowing that Coolidge would be there, visitors came to the church each Sunday, "practically," in Truman's description, "crowd[ing] out" the church's regular members. "Then when he ceased to be president they quit," Truman concluded, "and it almost killed the church."[19]

While vice president and president, Truman neither went to church regularly nor indicated publicly ahead of time when or where he was going. To minimize the distraction, he always tried to arrive immediately before the start of a service. In Washington and while vacationing at his regular retreat in Key West, he tended to alternate churches. He was always accompanied by the Secret Service and usually by reporters and photographers. He found that he caused less of what he termed a "spectacle" when he attended chapel services at such places as Walter Reed Hospital, Bethesda Naval Hospital, or the submarine base in Key West. The mass of reporters and photographers could not follow him into military installations. "I am going to the 1st Baptist Church today, quietly if I can," Truman wrote to his mother and sister several months after assuming the presidency. "I've been to both the Army and Navy chapels, and to the big Methodist Church, so I have to give my own crowd a chance to gawk and stare—so I'll do that today."[20]

Truman objected when the pastors of churches publicized his visits. "He made a real show of the occasion," Truman wrote about the pastor of Foundry Methodist Church after worshipping there in 1948.[21] "I'll never go back. I do not go to church for show. I hate headline hunters and showmen as a class and individually."[22]

Another such "headline hunter" in Truman's view was Billy Graham. Graham began his evangelistic career during Truman's presidency. In 1950, after Truman agreed to a request for a meeting in the White House, Graham advised him that America needed God during the Korean War and suggested a national day of repentance and prayer. When reporters asked what he and the president had discussed, the inexperienced Graham, then only thirty-one years old, told them about his suggestions. He then posed for photographs kneeling in prayer on the White House lawn.

An indignant Truman decided Graham was a phony. Throughout his presidency, he ignored the evangelist's continued efforts to contact him and even refused an invitation to attend Graham's Washington Crusade in 1952. In 1967, Graham traveled to Independence and apologized to Truman for the episode at the White House. Although Graham succeeded in befriending eight presidents during his career, Truman was not one of them.[23]

In contrast, Truman liked the attitude of the Reverend Welbern Bowman, pastor of his home church in Grandview. In addition, he appreciated the way the Reverend Edward Pruden of Washington's First Baptist Church treated him "as a church member and not as the head of a circus."[24] For that reason, Truman attended First Baptist—located eight blocks from the White House—more often than any other church during his presidency.

In Pruden's description, Truman preferred to attend the smaller family service on Sunday mornings, rather than the main service at 11:00 a.m. The president was aware that fewer "tourists and other visitors who might be looking for him" would be at the earlier service. In addition, Pruden remembered, Truman preferred worshipping in a service where "parents and their children came together."[25]

On one occasion Truman showed up unannounced for the 9:30 service and was informed by the pastor that he might rather wish to attend the main service that day, for the earlier service was a graduation ceremony for Sunday school children who were moving from one age group to another. When Truman declared that he was "fond of children and would enjoy the proceedings," Pruden impulsively asked if he would address the children. Truman agreed to do so, walked down the aisle at the appropriate time, stood before the communion table, and spoke to the awed children "about how fortunate they were . . . to grow up in a democracy where the principles of the Christian faith were known and taught, and where each person could worship God according to the dictates of his own heart."[26] Pruden invited Truman to transfer his membership to First Baptist Church, but Truman responded by saying that he belonged to the Baptist church in Grandview for over thirty years and wished to remain a member.[27]

In 1953, Truman retired to Independence, but he continued to find attending public worship an ordeal. As his popularity grew in the years after his presidency, visitors flocked to Independence. In his autobiography, written in his seventies, Truman declared that he still

> could not appear regularly in church either in Grandview or in Independence without feeling like a showpiece or someone on exhibit, so I do not go as often as I want to. People ought to go to church to worship God and not to see some mortal who is there.[28]

This or some other reason may explain why Truman did not attend church at Independence's First Baptist Church, located just two blocks from the house he inherited after his mother-in-law's death in 1952. Some, or many, of its members were dismayed. "He walked past this church many times," an elderly volunteer whose husband attended the local Masonic lodge with Truman told an inquirer. When asked again if Truman had even once attended services there, she repeated, "He walked past this church many times."[29]

Truman's daughter Margaret once described the religious composition of Independence. For women, she wrote,

> life in Independence revolved around culture, the family, and the church. The so-called best people were Presbyterians. Next in quality were the Campbellites, now known as the Christian Church, who boasted one of the most famous preachers in the country at the time, Alexander Proctor. Farther down the scale were the Baptists, the Mormons and the Catholics. The Episcopalians were so few in number they were scarcely noticed.[30]

Though he first met her when they were both pupils in the Presbyterian Sunday school, Truman's wife—the former Elizabeth Virginia "Bess" Wallace (1885–1982)—ultimately became an Episcopalian. Born and raised in the "snobbish little town" of Independence, Bess came from one of the leading local families.[31] Her mother, Madge Gates Wallace, was a distant, imperious woman. Her father—in an incident that was rarely mentioned—committed suicide when Bess was eighteen. During the early 1900s, Bess left the Presbyterian Church and with other members of her family joined the town's Trinity Episcopal Church.[32] She was confirmed in 1903.

Truman courted Bess for many years. Her mother disapproved of her daughter's association with someone she considered unpromising. Bess finally accepted Truman's marriage offer in 1917, immediately before he left for France with the Missouri National Guard. During the war, Truman wanted Bess to come to New York City and marry him in the Episcopal Church of the Transfiguration ("the Little Church around the Corner"), then a popular place for out-of-towners to get married. Ultimately the couple bowed to the family's preference and in early 1919 held the wedding in Independence's Trinity Church. In the years that followed, the couple occasionally went to services both at Trinity and at Grandview Baptist.

In 1924 Bess gave birth to a daughter, Mary Margaret. When her husband became a senator in 1934, she decided to continue to raise Margaret in Independence rather than in Washington. According to Margaret, her mother rarely attended church in the decades before her father became president. Thus Truman grew concerned about the religious education of their only offspring, being too distant from Independence to assure it. "I am sure hoping you get the daughter properly started on her religious education," he wrote to his wife in 1937 from Washington:

> I don't care whether she's an Episcopalian or a Baptist but she ought to be
> one or the other and the sooner she starts the better. . . . I've tried to give you
> a free hand in this and I hope you are going to get started.[33]

In response, Bess enrolled the thirteen-year-old Margaret in the Episcopal church's choir, an experience her daughter enjoyed.[34] When she was seven, her mother had enrolled her in Trinity's Sunday school. But as she later wrote,

> I complained so loudly that she accepted my offer to a compromise. If I went
> to church with her and sat absolutely still, I could abandon Sunday school.
> Since she seldom went to church (her mother never went) this was tanta-
> mount to an escape clause. Now, in response to Dad's prodding, she enrolled
> me in the Episcopal choir, which I enjoyed. I was beginning to think I

wanted to have a career as a singer. 'I hope she'll get interested in the church end of it,' Bess added in a later letter. This was as far as she could do on my religious education.[35]

In 1956, Margaret, just like her mother, married a Baptist at Trinity Episcopal Church in Independence.

Bess became a more regular churchgoer later in life. When in Washington she occasionally attended an Episcopal church. After permanently returning to Independence in 1953, she attended Trinity Episcopal Church nearly every Sunday and became a member of its altar guild — the organization of parish women who maintained the appearance of the altar and its ornaments.[36] In the 1970s, after her husband died and Bess became unable to attend services, the rector of Trinity Church sometimes brought Holy Communion to the Truman home.[37]

When Truman became involved in Missouri politics, his long association with Thomas Pendergast, boss of the political machine that ran Kansas City at that time, brought him into a Roman Catholic world. Born to an Irish American family in St. Joseph, Missouri, the Roman Catholic Pendergast moved from a Kansas City saloon to the city council and finally to the leadership of the Democratic Party of the surrounding county. The political machine he formed drew upon extensive family relations and business connections, and as a result, favoritism, patronage, and bribes characterized the Democratic politics in Missouri.

Almost all of the men in the National Guard battery Truman captained in France were Roman Catholic. They included Mike Pendergast, brother of "Boss" Pendergast.[38] As early as 1921, the machine identified Truman, who was then operating a failing men's clothing store (or haberdashery) in downtown Kansas City, as a potential candidate for county judge. Truman's potential enticed Pendergast, for he saw in him a Protestant of high morality and a strong work ethic. Moreover, the well-known Protestant editor of the Kansas City *Independence Examiner* — a man whose endorsement was key to running on the Democratic ticket — backed Truman for public office.[39]

In the campaign to follow, the local Ku Klux Klan — virulently anti-black, anti-immigrant, and anti-Catholic — opposed Truman, tarring him as "the errand boy of Catholic machine politicians."[40] But they failed to convince the electorate, which knew of Truman's Protestantism, Masonic membership, and rapport with fellow "Great War" veterans.[41] Truman was elected county judge—the equivalent of today's county commissioner—in 1922.

For the next eighteen years, Truman's fortunes depended upon the Pendergast machine. In the words of one writer, he came from the "traditional way of the machine politician—a road overseer, farm-tax collector, a bridge-mender, a drainer of dirt roads after heavy rains, then a postmaster, a club organizer, the tedious nights learning enough law to justify his election as a county court judge."[42] As his political career progressed, accusations of corruption trailed him everywhere. Because he believed it impossible to succeed in Kansas City politics without some Pendergast associations, Truman was never afraid to be known as "a Pendergast man." His opponents would have declared that the ethical cost of such political "success" was too great.

Although he held public office in what one writer called "a state festering with political corruption," Truman carefully distanced himself from the inner workings of the Pendergast organization.[43] He quickly gained a reputation for independence, fair-mindedness, and honesty.[44] In the meantime, Pendergast viewed Truman's religious commitments as advantageous in elections, for he believed they helped to offset the Roman Catholic stigma that encumbered his machine in a Protestant state. His political instincts were accurate: Truman's Baptist affiliation and his wife's Episcopal membership attracted a number of mainline Protestant Republican votes.

Pendergast's machine collapsed after his 1939 conviction and fifteen-month imprisonment for tax evasion charges. When the discredited Pendergast died in 1945, Truman defied his advisers and flew on an army bomber to attend the funeral Mass and burial in Kansas City. He had been inaugurated as vice president of the United States only nine days earlier. "He was photographed coming and going and paying his respects to the family," Truman's leading biographer writes, "all of which struck large numbers of people everywhere as outrageous behavior for a Vice President—to be seen honoring the memory of a convicted criminal."[45] But as Truman told his advisers, Pendergast gave him his start in politics. He was not about to shun his funeral simply out of fear of negative publicity.

Truman held mixed views of Roman Catholicism. During World War I, he befriended his unit's chaplain, Father L. Curtis Tiernan, who remained in military service after the war. Tiernan was a Jesuit, and Truman liked not only his intellect and breadth of information but also his kindliness, political views, and sense of military bearing. During his presidency, Truman invited Tiernan to become the U.S. ambassador to the Vatican.[46] While serving in France, Truman wrote to Bess, "I believe in [sic] all churches even the Roman Catholic can do a man a lot of good."[47] In 1945, when Tiernan was chief of U.S. Army Chaplains in Europe, Truman—by now president—attended a Mass the priest led in Berlin.[48] While president, Truman considered Pope Pius XII a friend, though the relationship of the two leaders was confined to correspondence.[49]

In 1960, a fellow Mason, concerned about the presidential candidacy of John F. Kennedy, wrote Truman to ask if a member of their fraternal order could vote for a Roman Catholic. The retired president found the question peculiar. "You will find that tolerance," he responded tartly, "is one of the most important things under the Constitution of the United States. . . . No Scottish Rite Mason ought to encourage any such an approach to the Government of the United States."[50] In a letter to Bess on the eve of World War II, he had exhibited the same tolerance when he expressed no concern over a nephew's decision to marry a Roman Catholic and perhaps to convert.[51]

But the qualifying word "even" that Truman had used during World War I in his letter to Bess is significant. Truman was tolerant of Roman Catholicism, but he was too much of a Baptist to be comfortable with it. "When you go to Rome, be very careful," he wrote to Margaret prior to her trip to Europe in 1951 that included a private audience with the pope:

> Your dad's a Baptist, the most democratic of religious organizations and sometimes the most bigoted. You'll see the head of the most autocratic of religions. He's a great man, but he stands for autocracy in the minds of men where the worship of God is concerned.[52]

Ecclesiastical pretension so concerned Truman that he devoted additional sentences to this warning. His letter to his daughter continues:

> Remember "that where two or three are gathered together for worship of God, there He will be," whether Pope, Bishop, Priest, or Rector is present. So, don't be taken in by the glamour of the Archbishop of Canterbury, the

Bishop of Rome, or any other self-appointed Vicar of the Prince of Peace. Just be the great daughter that you are, of a Missouri farmer, Grand Master of Masons, and . . . Baptist.

In 1959, during the national discussion of whether a Roman Catholic such as John F. Kennedy should be president, Truman expressed to an interviewer his discomfort about the governance of the Roman Catholic Church. Although he would campaign for Kennedy the following year, he conveyed concern in the interview about the church's intolerance when it was united with a nation's government:

> Well, the main difficulty with that situation has been that the hierarchy of the Catholic Church wants always to control the political operation of a government. That's the reason they've had trouble in France. That's the reason they've had trouble in Italy. That's the reason they've had trouble . . . for the Reformation, which Martin Luther, the great Martin Luther, gave them the best attitude that man could give them on that subject, and I have no feeling at all about the morals and dogma of the Catholic Church, but when the Catholic Church gets to a point where it's in control, the government is always against the little people, and tolerance is not considered. That's true in Spain. That's true in Colombia, in South America. In Spain, a Baptist can't be buried in daylight and can't be buried anywhere but in plowed ground.
>
> Well, now, I wonder what would happen if this great United States of ours would prevent Catholics from being buried in daylight and force them to be buried in plowed ground. We don't feel that way here, but whenever a religious organization gets control of a government of a country, you'd better look out. You're in trouble — it doesn't make any difference whether it's Protestant, Catholic, or Jew.[53]

Despite his dislike of pretension, Truman joined the Masons, an organization that wore special garb and used such titles as "worshipful master" and "grand sword bearer." In 1940, he was elected grand master of Missouri. Especially in local politics, membership in the Masons served him well.

Although Truman could accept the rituals of Masonry, he had mixed reactions to his wife's Episcopal Church — the most ritualistic of the Protestant denominations. He was married in an Episcopal church, raised his daughter Episcopalian, and occasionally attended Episcopal services with Bess and Margaret. In Washington, too, Truman moved in circles of Episcopalians. Not only were Franklin and Eleanor Roosevelt members of that denomination, but also Secretary of State George Marshall, his successor Dean Acheson (whose father was Episcopal bishop of Connecticut), and a large number of cabinet members, senators, justices of the Supreme Court, and high-ranking military officers.

But Truman never became an Episcopalian. The principal reason may be that the American branch of the Church of England contained too much medieval ritual and structure for him. In addition, Episcopalians at that time occupied the highest social and economic levels of American society. Even Bess sometimes felt out of place when she worshipped at a socially prominent Episcopal church. Truman's egalitarianism, his belief in the democratic structure of Christianity, and his impatience with what he once described in his diary as "high bishops Episcopal" undoubtedly caused him to remain a Baptist. Significantly, when he went to church alone, it was almost always to a Baptist church.[54]

A number of controversies enveloped the Truman presidency, including the use of nuclear weapons to end World War II, the partition of Palestine and establishment of Israel, and the anti-Communist campaign of Senator Joseph McCarthy. In each case, religion played a role.

The small number of people who worked on or knew about the atomic bomb remained divided over its potential effects. Ethical and moral questions abounded. Two months before the bombs were dropped, the ongoing debate among Truman's advisers—coupled with the departure of Bess and Margaret for Independence—drove the president to seek solace in adjacent St. John's Episcopal Church. He quietly joined the parishioners in worship, unannounced. In his diary he noted that he found the service "rather dull," but declared that he appreciated "the chance to do some thinking . . . the time wasn't wasted."[55]

In the days that followed, Truman's moral quandary dissipated. After meeting with Stalin and Churchill at Potsdam in July 1945, he approved the use of the weapon. When the bombs were dropped on Hiroshima and Nagasaki on August 6 and 9, stunned clergy immediately telegrammed the president. The general secretary of the Federal Council of the Churches of Christ in America—the leading organization of mainline American Protestantism—wired:

MANY CHRISTIANS DEEPLY DISTURBED OVER USE OF ATOMIC
BOMBS AGAINST JAPANESE CITIES BECAUSE OF THEIR NECESSARILY
INDISCRIMINATE DESTRUCTIVE EFFORTS AND BECAUSE THEIR USE SETS
EXTREMELY DANGEROUS PRECEDENT FOR FUTURE OF MANKIND.

To this telegram, Truman firmly replied:

I was greatly disturbed over the unwarranted attack by the Japanese on Pearl Harbor and their murder of our prisoners of war. . . . When you have to deal with a beast, you have to treat him as a beast. It is most regrettable but nevertheless true.

Initially, Truman had approved the use of atomic bombs on several grounds, but principally because they would save American lives. His military advisers had predicted that American forces would experience between two hundred fifty thousand and a half million deaths if they invaded the Japanese islands. That figure roughly equaled the number of all American forces lost through that point in the war. Viewing the bombs as "probably . . . the only way the Japanese might be made to surrender quickly," he chose to drop the bombs. For Winston Churchill, the issue was clear. The bombs would "avert a vast, indefinite butchery . . . bring the war to an end . . . [and] give peace to the world." The decision, Churchill declared, "was never even an issue."[56]

In reality, Truman was as troubled by the bomb's devastating effects as his critics. The reports he received of Japanese deaths—approximately one hundred fifty thousand, mostly of civilians—exceeded the predictions of his advisers. After the leveling of Nagasaki, he canceled any further use of the bomb without his express permission. According to one cabinet member, Truman found the prospect of destroying another city and killing "all those kids" agonizing. Nevertheless, in the face of moral censure from Christians, he defended his initial use of the weapons.[57]

Three years later, faced with strife between Arabs and Jews in Palestine, Truman confronted a thorny decision over whether or not to recognize a Jewish state. Scholars have reached ambivalent and somewhat contradictory conclusions concerning his views of Jews and Judaism.

On the one hand, the young Truman grew up in Independence next to Orthodox Jewish neighbors. One historian suggests that he first tried "kugel, matzoh, and gefilte fish" in their home. He helped out the family on the Saturday Sabbath, or Shabbat, running errands they could not.[58]

When Truman opened his haberdashery in Kansas City, his partner was Eddie Jacobson, a Jew who had served with him in France. The two men remained close. In 1943, Truman spoke at a large rally in Chicago calling for relief for European Jews. Before an audience of twenty thousand, he chastised anyone who believed the Germans were incapable of committing antisemitic atrocities.[59] Finally, in 1948 Truman defied many of his advisers—including Secretary of State George C. Marshall, whom he otherwise greatly admired—and decided to recognize Israel. He cried when the chief rabbi of Israel told him that he was placed in his mother's womb to give the Jewish people a homeland.[60]

On the other hand, Truman's background displayed some anti-Semitism. He once noted that no Jew had ever been in his home in Independence (the former Wallace home), because neither Bess nor her mother allowed it.[61] In 1918, just before embarking for Europe from Manhattan, he sent a letter to Bess referring to New York City as "Kike town." Writing her from France, he referred to Jacobson as his "Jew clerk"—a description intended to praise Jacobson's intelligence.[62] In June 1945, he wrote in his diary that "the Jews claim God Almighty picked 'em out for special privilege. Well I'm sure He had better judgment. Fact is I never thought God picked any favorites."[63]

One participant remembered a 1946 cabinet meeting about the Palestinian crisis. After receiving a deluge of telegrams from Jewish leaders, an exasperated Truman said: "If Jesus Christ couldn't please them when He was here on earth, how could anyone expect me to have any luck?"[64] Writing to a Jewish congressman in 1948, Truman declared, "I don't think there has ever been any more lobbying and pulling and hawing than has been carried on by the Jews in this Palestine difficulty."[65]

In 2003, the National Archives released a previously unknown portion of Truman's diary from 1947, recently discovered in the blank pages of a book on real estate. The diary included numerous important entries, but the one more publicized consisted of Truman's anger at the lobbying of Jews for the recognition of Israel. "The Jews, I find," Truman wrote,

> are very selfish. . . . [W]hen they have power . . . neither Hitler nor Stalin
> has anything on them for cruelty or mistreatment to the underdog. Put an
> underdog on top and it makes no difference whether his name is Russian,
> Jewish, Negro, Management, Labor, Mormon, Baptist he goes haywire.[66]

He wearied of the Zionist lobbyists that swamped the White House, finally
shutting them out altogether.

Although Truman's comments seem to reinforce previous charges of anti-
Semitism, Jewish sources were relatively unperturbed by them. Various Jewish commentators noted that Truman "was irritated at the moment"; that
his correspondence contained the use of similar epithets for blacks, Italians,
and Asians; and that he had been above all "the first world statesman to
recognize the State of Israel, a scant eleven minutes after its creation." The
writer concluded that "the establishment of the State of Israel . . . owed much
indeed to one man from a prejudice-ridden small town in the Midwest."[67]

In the view of a leading scholar, Truman's deep knowledge of the Old Testament (rooted in his Baptist faith), as well as his sense that Jews deserved
their own homeland, tipped the balance toward recognizing Israel. Truman's
familiarity with the Bible and sense of Christian justice—more than concerns
about domestic affairs, foreign policy, or politics—shaped his decision.[68] "For
Truman," David McCullough writes, "Palestine was never just a place on the
map."[69]

Fueled by the cold war, an anti-Communist climate swept up American
politicians during Truman's presidency. First, the House Un-American Activities Committee (whose members included Congressman Richard M.
Nixon) gained national attention by investigating not only the American
Communist Party but also Communist influences in Hollywood. By 1950,
Senator McCarthy had emerged with his charges that hundreds of Communists had infiltrated not only the U.S. State Department but also the
Truman administration and the U.S. Army. Anti-Communism suffused
domestic politics.

Although Truman rarely shifted with the winds of public opinion, he
was not immune to these trends. One way that he responded to McCarthy

involved connecting the future of American democracy to the religiosity of the founding fathers. In a 1951 speech Truman asserted that the basic strength of the United States was spiritual, being founded on religious principles by Christian men who entrusted the new nation to the protection of divine providence. While Senator Joseph McCarthy was accusing numerous Americans of Communist activities, Truman strongly suggested that McCarthy and his supporters had strayed from the Christian moral principles they claimed to represent.[70]

When Truman died in Independence on December 26, 1972, his simple funeral reflected the religious practices he engaged in over his life. Largely Episcopalian in structure because of the influence of his wife and daughter, it remained simple and unadorned because of Truman's faith. After reading the army's advance plans for a five-day funeral called "Operation Missouri," Truman joked, "It looks like a damn fine show. . . . I just hate that I won't be around to see it."[71] In the end, the ceremonies were scaled back to two days.

Truman decided against lying in state or having a second funeral service in Washington. In Independence, a hearse took the president's body from the funeral home to the Truman Library on a route lined by thousands of servicemen. More than seventy-five thousand mourners, including former presidents Richard Nixon and Lyndon Johnson, filed past Truman's body, which lay in state through the night.[72] Assisted by a Methodist chaplain in the Missouri National Guard, the rector of Trinity Episcopal Church presided over the service that followed. At Truman's request, it included neither hymns nor a eulogy.

The next day, the private interment in a plot adjacent to the library began with a speech by the grand master of the Masons of Missouri. Led by Canon John Lembcke, the ceremony that followed was adapted from the Episcopal Book of Common Prayer.[73] The retired pastor of the First Baptist Church in Independence offered the concluding prayer.[74]

Harry Truman once described his first jobs "as a window washer, bottle duster, floor scrubber in an Independence, Mo., drugstore, [and] as a timekeeper on a railroad contract gang." He continued that he had served "as an employee of a newspaper, as a bank clerk, as a farmer riding a gang plow behind four horses and mules, as a fraternity official learning to say nothing at all if good could not be said of a man, as [a] public official judging the weaknesses and shortcomings of constituents, and as President of the United States of America."[75]

During the seven years he was president, he declared, "I am not Roosevelt! I am not from New York. I am from the Middle West. I must do what I think is right."[76] "Some people think that public relations should be based on polls," he said at another time:

> That is nonsense. I wonder how far Moses would have gone if he had taken a poll in Egypt? What would Jesus Christ have preached if He had taken a poll in the land of Israel? Where would the Reformation have gone if Martin Luther had taken a poll? It isn't polls or public opinion alone of the moment that counts. It is right and wrong.[77]

Forthright, modest, unpretentious, honest, and stubborn, Truman was—as his staff knew—a religious man. While president, he often invoked the name of God. He not only knew the Bible thoroughly but also continued to read it into his old age. Although he regularly used the Bible for guidance on moral issues, his interest in religion was sufficiently strong that he even perused the Koran and the Book of Mormon.

Until the end of his life, he prayed openly. "Boys," he said to the Senate pages when he assumed the presidency following Roosevelt's sudden death, "if you ever pray, pray for me now."[78] Five days later, Truman closed his first presidential address to Congress with the words attributed to King Solomon in I Kings 3:9: "Give therefore thy servant an understanding heart to judge thy people, that I may discern between good and bad; for who is able to judge this thy so great a people?"[79]

Truman believed that morality lay at the heart of religion; he thought that the Ten Commandments, the Sermon on the Mount, and the Golden Rule contained the basic precepts of Christianity. "I think religion is something one should have on Wednesday and Thursday as well as Sunday," he once wrote to Bess.[80] In another letter to her, he declared, "I don't think any church on earth will take you to Heaven if you're not real anyway. I believe in people living what they believe and talking afterwards."[81]

Truman's upbringing by his parents instilled in him a deep concern for character. Although they raised him as a Baptist, he declared more than once that he was a "Lightfoot Baptist" just as his mother had been.[82] Because he believed that character was at the heart of Christianity, he was suspicious of elaborate denominational structures. Ecumenical in his religious outlook, he attended churches of other denominations. He maintained his membership in the Baptist church, however, and he attended Baptist churches far more than churches of any other denomination. His interpretation of Christianity was very Protestant, though it lacked the emphasis on Christ as savior.

Truman's reliance on character served him well throughout life. His initial greeting from Boss Pendergast was a baffled question as to why everyone liked him so much. Virtually everyone who worked closely with him held him in high regard. Expecting to be a sergeant in his National Guard battery in World War I, Truman (who had previously served in the Guard from 1905–1911) found instead that his peers elected him their first lieutenant. "No man can be that good," a general commented after reading an evaluation of the then Lieutenant Truman.[83] When Democratic insiders became convinced that Franklin Delano Roosevelt might die before the end of World War II, they selected Truman to serve as vice president because they knew he was honorable, honest, and competent.

When Truman left office in 1953, he departed with an exceedingly low approval rating and was under attack by political opponents. The accusations of corruption that had followed him since his days with the Pendergast machine only increased during his presidency. Any citizen who had been termed "the senator from Pendergast" remained open to serious question when president.

Republicans and editorial writers across the country came to describe the Truman administration as "the mess in Washington." Among other things, that "mess" included cronyism; wheeling and dealing by Truman's principal military aide; serious criminal activity by high officials in the Internal Revenue Service and the Justice Department; and influence peddling, questionable loans, and kickbacks in federal agencies. Inflation, postwar shortages, the "Loss of China," McCarthy's attacks, Truman's firing of national hero General Douglas MacArthur, and a long, costly, stalemated war in Korea only heightened the criticisms.

To describe America's thirty-third president, Truman's opponents coined such phrases as "to err is Truman." They constantly cited his inability to keep even his small haberdashery from failing. One of the principal commentators of the time used such terms as "worse than unimpressive" and "inept" for Truman and his administration. On the day before the 1948 election, a leading British journal published an article titled "Harry S. Truman—A Study in Failure."[84]

In contrast, Truman's Republican opponent in the election, Governor Thomas Dewey of New York, promised "a firm hand on the tiller" and "a rudder to our ship of state"—aspects of government that many citizens believed were absent from Truman's administration.[85] On election night, the *Chicago Tribune* published an edition whose large headline famously declared, "DEWEY DEFEATS TRUMAN."

But Truman won a surprising victory, receiving approximately two million more votes than Dewey and 57 percent of the electoral vote. He did so, even though his views on civil rights and those of the majority of his party caused the formation of a States' Rights party, led by the then governor of South Carolina. Carrying four nominally Democratic southern states, this "Dixiecrat" party jeopardized Truman's chances of reelection. On the left, he faced the new Progressive Party, formed by liberals who strongly objected (among other things) to his resolute opposition to the Soviet Union and Communism.

Even if the charges of minor corruption and administrative ineptness brought against Truman are accurate, the achievements of the Marshall Plan, the Berlin Airlift, and the integration of the armed forces belong to him. The Truman Doctrine ("to support free peoples who are resisting attempted subjugation by armed minorities or by outside pressures") ended the peacetime isolation that had characterized American foreign policy in the 1920s and 1930s.[86] To stop the Communist invasion of South Korea, Truman secured combat and medical units from almost two dozen members of the United Nations. During his presidency, he advocated national healthcare and civil rights legislation. He attempted to form a global crusade of spiritual forces against what he viewed as godless Communism. Above all, Truman remained intent on avoiding World War III, for he believed the Communist world would ultimately self-destruct. The dissolution of the Soviet Union in the closing years of the twentieth century and the growing influence of capitalism in China may vindicate Truman's policy. It may also discredit the view of Gen. Douglas MacArthur that the United States should have ended the global conquest of Communism immediately through military force in the 1950s.[87]

Many of these initiatives stemmed directly from Truman's Christian beliefs. For him, two passages in the Sermon on the Mount (Matthew 5-7) were paramount: the Golden Rule ("Therefore all things whatsoever ye would that men should do to you, do ye even so to them") and the seventh Beatitude ("Blessed are the peacemakers: for they shall be called the children of God"). These quotations come from the King James Version, the Bible on which Truman was raised and which he generally read.

Two months after the end of World War II, Truman told an audience: "Though we may meet setbacks from time to time, we shall not relent in our efforts to bring the Golden Rule into the international affairs of the world."[88] In 1949, addressing an assembly of Anglican bishops, he said that he and they should work "to mobilize the moral forces of the world for a reawakening of the things that originate in the Sermon on the Mount."[89] Interviewed in the same year about his political philosophy, Truman directed a White House correspondent to read the Sermon on the Mount. When he called for nations to coexist peacefully, he emphasized the seventh Beatitude. Those who knew Truman well knew that he saw himself as a peacemaker.

Since the early 1960s, American historians have ranked Truman among the top ten American presidents. His first major appearance as an Allied leader occurred at the conference with Churchill and Stalin at Potsdam, Germany, shortly after the surrender of Nazi Germany but before the surrender of Japan. At that conference, U.S. Chief of Naval Operations Ernest J. King whispered to Lord Moran, Churchill's physician:

Watch the President. This is all new to him, but he can take it. He is a more typical American than Roosevelt, and he will do a good job, not only for the United States but for the whole world.[90]

In the closing months of Truman's presidency, Winston Churchill told him:

The last time you and I sat across a conference table was at Potsdam. I must confess, Sir, I held you in very low regard. I loathed your taking the place of

Franklin Roosevelt. I misjudged you badly. Since that time, you, more than any other man, have saved Western civilization.[91]

Using words that would have disturbed many Americans at the time, a Washington political commentator declared of Truman, "I am not sure he was right about the atomic bomb, or even Korea. But remembering him reminds people what a man in the office ought to be like. It's character, just character."[92] As in religion, so as in politics, Truman stood his ground. Writers have tended to neglect the role faith played in his life. Harry Truman's faith shaped his character, and his character shaped his politics.

# Dwight D. Eisenhower

*1890–1969* ⌐ PRESIDENT FROM 1953 TO 1961

As a general and as a president, Dwight David Eisenhower worked to keep the religious side of his childhood private. He and his brothers succeeded so well that some of what biographers have written about the family's religious heritage is either inaccurate or incomplete.

Eisenhower did not join a church until he was sixty-three years old. His religious background in the River Brethren, in the Jehovah's Witnesses, and in the nondenominational Protestantism of the United States Army seems to explain the delay. Four decades after his death, these aspects of his religious upbringing still remain little known.[1]

Born in Denison, Texas, Eisenhower grew up in a small frame house in Abilene, Kansas. The center of Kansas Populist politics, Abilene was the terminus not only of the Chisholm Trail but also of a major railroad line. On both of his parents' sides, Eisenhower was of German American descent.[2] He was the third of seven sons, one of whom died in infancy. He had no sisters.

Dwight Eisenhower's father, David, came from a well-to-do abolitionist farming family. In the nineteenth century only a small percentage of Americans went to college, but David attended Lane University in Lecompton, Kansas. A small church college with the somewhat grandiose name of "university," it was established by the United Brethren in Christ, a German American denomination. In the twentieth century it merged with the much larger Methodist Church to form the United Methodist Church. After a brief period of study, he left Lane to marry another student, Ida Stover. David's father gave the newly married couple 160 acres of farmland and several thousand dollars—a large sum at the time—to run it, but they chose instead to operate a general store in nearby Hope, Kansas.

In many ways, life proved a disappointment for Eisenhower's father. Family legend asserts that David and his wife lost their store in 1888 because of an unreliable partner and a greedy lawyer.[3] In reality, the store closed because a long drought prevented farmers from paying their bills. Following the store's failure, David worked on the railroad in Texas, where his third son, Dwight David, was born in 1890. When David moved to Abilene less than two years later, he took a position as a manual worker at a creamery owned by his church, the River Brethren. Eventually, he obtained slightly more lucrative work, first at a gas plant and subsequently at a utility company.[4]

Hot-tempered and a strict disciplinarian at home, David carried a certain embitterment and a sense of the precariousness of life throughout his working days. "Dad was held as a bugaboo," Dwight's brother, Edgar, remarked. "He went about whipping us in a very businesslike manner."[5] But the Eisenhower boys saw little of their father; he was usually absent from the house for twelve or more hours a day, and when he came home, he spent most of his time alone with a book.[6]

In personality, Ida Stover Eisenhower was a contrast to her husband. More of an influence on the family than her husband, she was patient, self-controlled, and resilient. Born into a German abolitionist family in the Shenandoah Valley of Virginia, she was raised in the Lutheran church in the town of Mount Sidney. Its Sunday school still lists her accomplishment of memorizing over 1,300 biblical verses in six months.[7]

Quietly adventurous, Ida moved to Kansas (which, unlike Virginia, had coeducational schools) at age twenty-one after inheriting a sum of money from her father. There she attended Lane University, where she met her husband and excelled academically.[8] After becoming a mother, she had high expectations for her sons, especially in terms of their education and behavior.

Dwight Eisenhower attended the public schools of Abilene. At Abilene High School, sports became one of his principal interests. He was a natural athlete, especially adept at football. Academically, he was superior in such fields as history and geometry while mediocre in others. The high school's yearbook prophesied that he would become a professor of history at Yale and that his brother Edgar, a member of the same class, would be a two-term president of the United States.[9]

When Dwight and Edgar decided to continue their education, they planned to alternate years at college. One would attend college while the other worked to pay the costs, and vice versa. But Dwight had a special love for military history, and the U.S. military academies provided full funding to all cadets admitted. Despite his religious background in two denominations that taught conscientious objection, he decided to seek an appointment to the U.S. Naval Academy in Annapolis. Placing second of the eight Kansans who took the military's competitive examination, young Eisenhower ultimately gained an appointment not to Annapolis but to the U.S. Military Academy at West Point.

While growing up, Ike—a common nickname for Dwight—found a supportive environment in his hometown. Not as insular as often depicted, Abilene supported four newspapers. One of the town's editors, Joe Howe, had created a large library (with a pool table) in the back of his newspaper office, which he encouraged students to use. After school the Eisenhower brothers and their friends often spent time there playing pool and reading—not only books but also the news as it came off the paper's teletype.

Thus Abilene provided a broader education for Dwight Eisenhower than some writers have indicated. Ike's circle of friends included Deane W. Malott, later the president of Cornell University. All but one of his brothers graduated from college. Edgar became a lawyer, Roy a pharmacist, and Milton the president of three institutions of higher education, including Johns Hopkins University. Earl received a bachelor's degree in electrical engineering, worked in that field, and then became the general manager of an Illinois newspaper; he also served briefly as a member of the Illinois House of Representatives. The only brother not to attend college, Arthur, nevertheless became a high executive of a Kansas City bank.

Dwight himself became a five-star general and the thirty-fourth president of the United States. Thus despite their affiliation with a religious group that believed in the imminent end of the world, Ida and David produced a family of achievers. They also produced the first generation of Eisenhowers in America without a farmer or a minister.[10]

Most books state that Eisenhower was raised in the Brethren of Christ, a "plain-people" Protestant sect popularly known as the "River Brethren." Billy Graham, for example, has so described Eisenhower's background.[11] Similar in outlook to the Mennonites, the close-knit River Brethren were characterized by distinctive clothing; the men wore long beards. Based on their interpretation of the New Testament, they baptized adults only, opposed many of what the world considered amusements, and believed that pacifism was obligatory for Christians. Virtually all members of the extended Eisenhower family in Kansas were active in the church, with some holding significant clerical positions. David was raised in the River Brethren, though in time the extended Eisenhower family came to view him as one of their theological black sheep.

Some of Dwight Eisenhower's religious background remains elusive. Apparently they were not active members, but the Eisenhower parents and their sons sometimes attended the plain, unadorned River Brethren church in Abilene or its Sunday school. Dwight Eisenhower's younger brother Earl remembered the church with affection. "These people are very dear to me," he later recalled:

> Whether you believe what they believe, you have to admire them. They tried every day of their lives — that is, my father and mother and everybody around them — to live life as if they were in church. They never never wanted to hurt anybody.[12]

In Earl's view, the River Brethren had a lifelong effect even on this branch of the Eisenhower family that did not belong to it. "They had a great influence on Dwight and Milton and the rest of the boys and me," he said. "I think that influence, whether we acknowledge it or not, was so ingrained that we can't get over it."[13]

Instead, the Eisenhowers were associated — Ida for over fifty years, David for approximately twenty, the sons involuntarily — with the organization that changed its name in 1931 to the Jehovah's Witnesses. When the Eisenhower parents joined the movement, it carried the names "Bible Students" or "Watchtower Society." In 1944, Ida Eisenhower declared that she had been a member of the movement since 1895.[14]

The year was significant, for in 1895 (when Dwight was five years old) the Eisenhowers' fourth son, eight-month-old Paul, died of diphtheria. After his death, three members of the small Watchtower Society in Abilene comforted Ida and David by asserting their belief that the imminent Second Coming of Jesus would cause the resurrection of the dead and allow them to see their son again on earth. The national leader of the Watchtower Society, Charles Taze Russell, had prophesied that Jesus would descend from heaven to earth in 1914. When he returned to earth, Russell taught, Jesus would raise the dead from their "soul sleep." Grief-stricken, the Eisenhowers found this teaching more comforting than the assurance they received from the River Brethren that they would see Paul again in heaven.

Soon Ida and David Eisenhower began to hold weekly Watchtower Society meetings in their home. Some fifteen residents of Abilene, including the Eisenhower sons, attended. Displaying his new approach to religion, David hung a ten-foot-by-six-foot wall chart of the ancient Egyptian pyramids in the house. Accompanying the illustrations were inscriptions that not only prophesied future events but also taught that Christ would return in 1914. The chart, which remained in the Eisenhower family home into World War II, fascinated the sons as they grew up. Since it was prominently displayed in the living room, they saw it virtually every day.[15]

For David and Ida Eisenhower, the change to the movement that subsequently became known as Jehovah's Witnesses represented an affirmation of some of their beliefs but a significant shift in others. Both the River Brethren and the Watchtower Society agreed that the Roman Catholic, Eastern Orthodox, and Protestant churches had fallen away from many of the truths of the Bible. Both groups declared that seekers could find the true Christian faith in the text of the Bible and not in the creeds drawn up in later centuries by church councils. Both contended that Christians should baptize only converted adults, and not children, and should do so in the New Testament manner by fully immersing the new believer in water. Both taught that the true worship of God is simple and unadorned and rejects ritual or outward show, that congregations should follow the biblically sanctioned practice of "shunning" or "disfellowshiping" wayward members, and that a true Christian refuses to serve in the armed services of a secular nation or to participate in its politics or wars.

But in joining the Watchtower Society (or Jehovah's Witnesses), the Eisenhowers also had to accept some beliefs that distinctly differed from those held by the River Brethren. The Society taught that Jesus was indeed God's son, but inferior in status; in terms of Christian theology, they—like the early Unitarians—fell into the category of "Subordinationists." To them, the Son is subordinate to the Father. The Witnesses also taught that the hallowed Christian doctrine of the Trinity was erroneous and untrue to the Bible.

As if those challenges to orthodoxy were not enough, the Watchtower Society asserted—as do historians—that celebrating birthdays or such Christian holy days as Easter and Christmas were pagan practices in origin. The Society opposed taking blood into the body through the mouth or veins (that is, blood transfusions) on the grounds that doing so violates the laws of God. They told members that Christians should not salute a national flag or pledge allegiance to it, for such national symbols are idols.

In addition, they interpreted Jesus's directive to his followers to make "disciples of all nations" to mean that Christians should proselytize by (in that period before radio and television) evangelizing aggressively door to door. They taught that Satan controlled all other interpretations of religion as well as big business. Finally, they taught that the world had entered its last days, with the Second Coming of Jesus and Armageddon—the final battle between good and evil—close at hand.

Although David left the Society around 1915, when their prophecy about the end of the world proved false, he nevertheless continued to study the Bible daily, keeping a Greek New Testament at his bedside. With his nondenominational approach to Christianity he followed the pattern of a brother who became an itinerant evangelist following a conversion experience and preached from the Midwest to California.[16] Ida, however, remained a Jehovah's Witness until her death in 1946. She was a member throughout her son's military career and even into his period as supreme allied commander.

The Eisenhower boys attended the weekly Watchtower meetings held in their parlor. In 1967, Eisenhower described a typical meeting:

> The usual program of worship included hymns, for which Mother played the piano, and prayers, with the rest of the time devoted to group discussion of a selected chapter of the Bible. The meeting was for serious study and for adults only.[17]

The parents also sent the boys—though how often is unknown—to Sunday school at the River Brethren Church. Each morning and night, the family read the Bible aloud and prayed together.

The overall religiosity of their upbringing had a considerable effect on the Eisenhower boys, but none seems to have grown up accepting the distinctive teachings of the Watchtower Society. In keeping with the Society's rules, neither David nor Ida smoked, drank, played cards, or used profanity. As the years went on, however, the parents tolerated those behaviors from their sons. Following a principle of fostering independent thinking, they may have decided that boys will be boys. "We played cards and smoked in our home," Earl later recalled. "All of the boys did after they were a little older."[18] The Watchtower Society also opposed patriotic activities, serving in the military, and saluting flags, but Dwight spent most of his adult life doing precisely those things.

In later years, the religion of their parents became a sensitive issue for the Eisenhower brothers. When asked about Ida and David's faith, they would generally describe their parents as "fundamentalists" or "Bible Students." The latter term, in fact, was accurate, for Bible Students was the original name of the Witnesses. Because the Watchtower Society did not adopt the name Jehovah's Witnesses until 1931, technically neither the Eisenhower sons nor their father had ever been Jehovah's Witnesses. All left the movement well before its change in name. The brothers' editing of the family past took many forms. When Ida died shortly after the end of World War II, the Eisenhower family home in Abilene contained fifty years of *The Watchtower*, the principal magazine of the Jehovah's Witnesses. According to one biographer, Milton Eisenhower (then president of Kansas State University) "bundled up the fifty-year collection of the presumably embarrassing magazines and got them out of the Eisenhower house and away from the eyes of reporters."[19] When the issue of his mother's religion came up during Eisenhower's 1952 presidential campaign, a staff member declared only that she had indeed "become interested" in the Jehovah's Witnesses. But her interest, the staff member wrote, arose years after General Eisenhower had left home and therefore had no impact on him.[20]

In his autobiographical *At Ease*, Eisenhower himself devotes one page to the movement, describing it as "a local group known as The Bible Class." This group, he explains, was in "a kind of loose association with similar groups throughout the country . . . chiefly through subscription to a religious periodical *The Watchtower*." He then indicates that these scattered groups later drew closer together and "finally adopted the name of Jehovah's Witnesses."[21] Subsequently, Eisenhower once again avoided specifics about his religious background by saying only that "a deep Bible-centered faith has colored my life since childhood. Devout parents, who loved the Bible as dearly as life itself, made sure of that."[22]

In the years since his death, most biographers of Ike or his brothers have used similar language. A typical description reads: "Ida organized meetings of the Bible students of the Watchtower Society which met on Sundays in the Eisenhower parlor." The authors simply omit any indication that the Watchtower Society is better known as the Jehovah's Witnesses.[23] Such biographies obscure the highly sectarian nature of Eisenhower's childhood religion.

Dwight Eisenhower entered West Point in 1911. Although his mother had allowed him the choice of attending a military academy, she broke down and cried after he left for the train. She was, after all, sending a son into a possible military career that would indoctrinate value after value opposed by the Watchtower Society.

At West Point, Eisenhower performed competently but failed to stand out academically. He attended chapel services regularly, for chapel attendance was mandatory at West Point until the 1970s. On Sundays, cadets would form up by company and march to chapel. The "Register of Demerits" in the Academy archives indicates that he received demerits for being tardy to Protestant chapel services during his plebe year.

The Academy yearbook, *The Howitzer*, lists Eisenhower as a member of the Young Men's Christian Association (YMCA). *The Howitzer* does not indicate that he taught in the Academy Sunday school, but a retired general and West Point graduate thinks that he did. "I had lunch with Eisenhower in 1965," General James Golden writes,

> and sat next to him. In preparation, I reviewed what I could find out about things we had in common. I was the Superintendent of the Sunday School that cadets ran for the Post children, and I [was] either told or read that he had taught Sunday School as well.
>
> I did mention that at lunch. I do not . . . recall his response, but he did not say he had not taught Sunday School. If he had said that, I would have been embarrassed and would have remembered.[24]

Following graduation, Eisenhower was stationed at Fort Sam Houston in San Antonio, Texas. There he met Mamie Doud, the lighthearted nineteen-year-old daughter of a wealthy Denver meat packer who was spending the winter in the city. The couple married in 1916.

Relatively little is known about Mamie's religious beliefs. Her college-educated father, a descendant of the American Puritans, was Presbyterian. Her mother, a first-generation Swedish American, had been raised in Iowa in a strict evangelical Swedish denomination. Mamie once spoke of the Sunday afternoons when she visited her maternal grandparents' church: "After we'd been in the Swedish church with grandma and grandpa, which of course we couldn't understand, we'd come home and all we could do was sit on the steps and watch people go by. We couldn't play cards. We couldn't do anything. . . . It was awful."[25]

Because Mamie's mother also found her parents' interpretation of Christianity too strict, Mamie never became deeply involved with it. After marriage, she and her husband attended the less strict Presbyterian church in Denver and enrolled their children in its Sunday school.

Death colored Mamie's childhood and later life. All four of her grandparents died by the time she was twelve, and two of her sisters subsequently died while teenagers. Five years after marriage, she and Ike lost their first child, three-year-old Doud Dwight (Ikky) Eisenhower, to scarlet fever.

Though many people turn to organized religion in a time of mourning, Mamie—like her husband—seems to have remained religiously inactive during most of her marriage. The deaths in her family, one writer states, not only "left Mamie with a heightened sense of disaster looming just around the corner"[26] but also did not cause her to believe in God. Eisenhower later recalled that the death of Ikky was the one disaster from which he himself never recovered. "For Mamie," he declared, "the loss was heartbreaking, and her grief, in turn, would have broken the hardest heart."

Relocating more than thirty times in the first thirty-five years of marriage—"I've kept house in everything but an igloo," Mamie once said—Dwight Eisenhower served from the Philippines to Panama.[27] Although he was known for entertaining, for regimental football, and for poker playing, his work ethic and facility for detail increasingly marked him as a future leader. He served under such highly decorated generals as John J. Pershing,

Douglas MacArthur, and George C. Marshall. Gradually, Eisenhower gained a reputation as one of the premier officers in the nation, capped in 1928 when he finished first in a class of 265 at the prestigious Army War College.

Sometimes forgotten today, Eisenhower's brilliance was well known to Franklin Roosevelt and to army chief of staff Marshall. During World War II, he quickly rose to become commanding general of the European Theater, commander in chief of the Allied Forces, and finally supreme commander of the Allied Expeditionary Forces. From 1948 to 1950, he spent a brief and somewhat unsatisfying period as president of Columbia University. Taking leave from Columbia in 1950, he accepted the post of supreme allied commander of the North Atlantic Treaty Organization (NATO) in Paris. After returning to the United States in 1952, he announced his candidacy for the presidency.

Throughout his military career, Eisenhower seems to have "shunned organized religion."[28] He was not known among fellow officers for churchgoing. "I didn't go to church in the chapels in the military," he admitted to Billy Graham early in their relationship. In their first meeting, in fact, Graham found Eisenhower far more profane in his language than anticipated. "He used a lot of army language," Graham said. "It sort of shocked me at the time. I spoke to him a couple years later about that."[29]

Eisenhower's diaries contain only a handful of references to religion or to worship. During World War II, he would astonish his aides by quoting passages from the Old or New Testament on numerous occasions. Yet his letters and speeches almost totally omit references to the Bible, despite the knowledge of it ingrained by his childhood. One Eisenhower scholar has declared that "the several thousand pages" of Eisenhower's published papers display "virtually no references to Biblical phraseology."[30] When Ikky and his younger brother John were infants, the Eisenhowers apparently arranged to have both baptized, presumably by an army chaplain. Their printed letters, however, include no details. Similarly, the existing letters of Dwight to the Doud family about Ikky's death fail to mention the consolations of religion. Although a military chaplain undoubtedly officiated at services held for Ikky, the principal biography of Mamie mentions only the mourning and burial.

The same omission of religious references occurs in other Eisenhower family documents. Although people do not always mention religious services in their letters, the correspondence of Mamie and Dwight seems to omit the subject completely. During Eisenhower's first campaign for the presidency, his staff typically responded to inquiries about Mamie's religious faith by saying that "Mrs. Eisenhower has always been active in church work on Army bases and is a Presbyterian."[31] Whatever the accuracy of this statement, the letters Mamie wrote home to her family on Sundays usually discuss only social occasions on the military post; they make no references to church attendance. Of the many photographs included in her principal biography, none contain an army chapel or civilian church, and none depict a church pageant or similar church ceremony connected with her children.

Because of his background in the River Brethren and in the Jehovah's Witnesses, two churches that baptize only believing adults, Eisenhower entered the U.S. Army unbaptized. More than three decades later, he retired from the army still unbaptized. Although a strong Episcopalian culture existed at the time among high-ranking officers in the army—including Generals Pershing, Marshall, MacArthur, and Patton—Eisenhower never took part in it. His lack of church affiliation seems to have had no effect on his career.

Despite his apparent lack of attendance at church services or participation in religious activities, Eisenhower may have preserved a degree of religious belief during the war. In the words of a leading writer on presidential faith, "Eisenhower had to make extraordinarily difficult strategic decisions and order hundreds of thousands of soldiers to risk and often sacrifice their lives" throughout World War II. This grave responsibility, the author declares, prompted the supreme allied commander "to reexamine his purpose in life and deepen his relationship with God."[32]

Seven years later Eisenhower said to a journalist, "Do you think I could have fought my way through this war, ordered thousands of fellows to their deaths, if I couldn't have got down on my knees and talked to God and begged him to support me?"[33] During and after the war, a story circulated that Eisenhower had knelt in fervent prayer when the Allies began their invasion of Sicily amid problematic weather.[34] Reflecting on the success of the D-Day invasion of Normandy despite similar weather conditions, Eisenhower later declared that "if there were nothing else in my life to prove the existence of an almighty and merciful God," then the success of these two invasions proved it.[35]

On the other hand, Eisenhower's letters to Mamie neither place the war in a religious context nor seem to mention attending church. A writer has described Eisenhower's close associate in the war, Winston Churchill, as an "optimistic agnostic." Churchill once described himself as "not a pillar of the church, but a buttress—I support it from the outside."[36] Yet in his speeches Britain's leader took a much more biblical and religious approach to World War II than did Eisenhower.

Generals commonly invoked God. In the Pacific Theater, Douglas Mac-Arthur followed his famous statement "I have returned" with the words "by the grace of Almighty God, our forces again stand on Philippine soil." He ended the speech by asserting that the "guidance of Divine God points the way. Follow in His Name to the Holy Grail of righteous victory." When MacArthur delivered his farewell address to Congress, he referred to himself as "an old soldier who tried to do his duty as God gave him the light to see that duty."[37]

But Eisenhower's formal statements during World War II invoke no such moods. To be sure, his communiqué of some 230 words to the Allied forces assembled on D-Day calls the invasion a "Great Crusade." It speaks of "the hopes and prayers of liberty-loving people everywhere" and ends by beseeching the "blessing of Almighty God upon this great and noble undertaking."[38] After the war, he also used the word "crusade" in the title of his memoirs, *Crusade in Europe*.

Although this is religious language, few assessments of Eisenhower as supreme commander would dwell on his religious character. In the words of one scholar, the evidence indicates "that he and Mamie rarely attended religious services, even during the war."[39] More than one writer has wondered if Eisenhower was a philosophical Deist during his military career. In fact, Eisenhower's faith might be more accurately described by another of Winston Churchill's self-descriptions. Churchill once declared that he had made "so many deposits in the bank of Religion" as a youth that he had been "confidently withdrawing from it ever since."[40]

Eisenhower's religious bank account, however, began to grow once he became president in 1953. "He felt . . . that as president he should provide leadership and an example," one biographer has noted. "Moreover, he was well aware of the power of civic religion as a central gelling force within American society."[41] Thus Eisenhower's inaugural address to the nation began with words of a type he had not used while supreme commander:

My friends, before I begin the expression of those thoughts that I deem appropriate to this moment, would you permit me the privilege of uttering a little private prayer of my own. And I ask that you bow your heads.

Almighty God . . . my future associates in the Executive branch of Government join me in beseeching that Thou will make full and complete our dedication to the service of the people in this throng, and their fellow citizens everywhere. Give us, we pray, the power to discern clearly right from wrong, and allow all our words and actions to be governed thereby, and by the laws of this land.

Especially we pray that our concern shall be for all the people regardless of station, race, or calling. May cooperation be permitted and be the mutual aim of those who, under the concepts of our Constitution, hold to differing political faiths; so that all may work for the good of our beloved country and Thy glory. Amen.[42]

Letters poured into the White House asking for a copy of the text of this inaugural prayer. It had "none of the poetic magic that suffuses Christian ceremony with beauty," one historian wrote, "rather, it suggested George F. Babbitt before a session of the local Rotary. . . . [But] it sparkled with the earnest sincerity that was Eisenhower's own personal magic."[43] By 1957, the prayer had not only been set to music but also performed in Washington by the Howard University choir accompanied by the National Symphony Orchestra.[44]

Prior to the inauguration, the leading figures of the incoming Eisenhower administration—amounting to almost two hundred persons—worshipped together at the National Presbyterian Church.[45] This occasion, one writer notes, marked "the first time an entire official family attended church services with an incoming President."[46] Less than two weeks later, the thirty-fourth president, now sixty-three, was privately baptized and received into membership in the Presbyterian Church in the United States of America. Earlier in the day he had made a confession of faith before the ruling elders (or "session") of the congregation.

On the same day, Eisenhower took the Lord's Supper—perhaps for the first time, since the overwhelming majority of Jehovah's Witnesses never receive that ordinance. Mamie Eisenhower recommitted her faith at the same service. Although the understanding was that the National Presbyterian's pastor, Edward L. R. Elson, would keep the baptism confidential, to Eisenhower's embarrassment and anger he did not.

Eisenhower's decision to become a regular churchgoer dated to spring of 1952. Two early supporters of Eisenhower for the Republican nomination—Henry Luce, publisher of *Time* and *Life*, and his wife, the prominent writer Clare Boothe Luce—traveled to France to discuss obstacles to the general's candidacy.[47]

At a preliminary meeting, Eisenhower's chief assistant told the Luces that the principal obstacle to Eisenhower winning the nomination seemed to involve his "religion, or rather his lack of religion."[48] The aide continued:

He goes right through the roof when people ask him what his denomination is, what church he belongs to. We've tried to discuss it with him, and he bawls us out and says it's none of our damn business, [because] religion is an absolutely private matter.[49]

At the subsequent meeting, Mrs. Luce did raise the question of religious affiliation. In her words, the general "jumped to his feet, [and] got red to the roots of his hair." Declaring that "a man's faith is a matter between himself and God," Eisenhower said that he "couldn't live a day of my life without God." But people did not ask him about God, he complained. Instead, they kept asking, "What is my church?" Yet he had been raised, Eisenhower said, with the understanding that no one needed to join a church to be a faithful Christian. Finally, Eisenhower said, he would have "nothing but contempt" for himself if he joined a church simply to gain the Republican nomination.

Despite Eisenhower's passion, Luce turned out to be persuasive. Rather than viewing church membership as hypocritical, she argued, Eisenhower should view it as a constructive and necessary thing to do for the sake of the rising generation as well as for his own contemporaries. After all, she noted, presidents serve as role models for a nation's youth. If Eisenhower continued to avoid church, she declared, children could tell their parents: "Why do I have to go to church? The President of the United States has never gone to church and refuses to go to church."

In Luce's account, Eisenhower immediately replied, "Oh, boy, I never thought of that." He then agreed with the suggestions that he not only join the denomination in which his wife had been raised but also begin attending church the next Sunday. From that point on, Luce recalled, Eisenhower went to church every Sunday in Paris.[50]

Believing that he had been elected to lead a national spiritual renewal, Eisenhower spearheaded a national religious revival during his two terms in office. He put himself squarely on the side of organized religion. While in office, he created a staff department and gave it the specific tasks both of dealing with religious issues and of corresponding with leaders of religious traditions. He directed that his cabinet sessions begin in prayer. He began the now-hallowed prayer breakfasts on Capitol Hill. Like the colonial governors and some early presidents, he proclaimed days of prayer for the nation. The words "pray for peace" appeared on canceled mail. In 1954, Congress added the words "under God" to the Pledge of Allegiance. Two years later, Eisenhower approved the addition of "In God We Trust" to U.S. paper currency.

During his presidency, Eisenhower delivered many important speeches at religious gatherings. He also included references to the spiritual dimension of American life in speeches that dealt with other topics. In 1958, he dedicated the Manhattan headquarters of the National Council of Churches, then a highly influential organization in American life. In 1967, he laid the cornerstone for the new National Presbyterian Church in the nation's capital. Generally more active on behalf of mainline religious groups, Eisenhower was cautious about becoming too involved with organizations he viewed as extremist.

In addition, Eisenhower invited many religious leaders to the White House. He was rarely too busy to receive visiting church delegations. He maintained a respectful relationship with the Roman Catholic bishops of America. He furthered the career of the young Billy Graham, being the first of many presidents for whom Graham became a spiritual adviser. Though separated by age, the two men had several important characteristics in common, especially their mutual desire for a spiritual revival in the nation.

Throughout his presidency, Eisenhower worshipped regularly. According to one writer, he went to church on thirty-three Sundays in 1956, "twenty-three of which were at the National Presbyterian Church."[51] Eisenhower's 1957 presidential appointment book indicates his attendance at services of worship on at least twenty-nine Sundays or holidays.[52] Although the appointment book even lists the names of Eisenhower's bridge and golf partners, it lacks entries for some Sundays. Thus, the president may have attended church more often than indicated.

In 1957 Eisenhower usually attended Presbyterian services—most often at his home National Presbyterian Church but also at the Presbyterian church in Gettysburg and, on four Sundays when playing golf at Augusta National Golf Club, in Presbyterian churches in Georgia. He attended Protestant services in military chapels three times, the American Episcopal Cathedral in Paris once, and the opening celebration of the Theodore Roosevelt Centennial at a Reformed church in Washington once. The military services included worship on the deck of an American cruiser en route to a meeting in Bermuda with the British prime minister. According to the appointment book, Eisenhower spent Sundays when he did not go to church practicing golf, walking "around the Farm inspecting the horses and the shrubbery," or spending "a quiet day."

Eisenhower was known to grumble at times about going to church when tired, but he was also known to rush from his helicopter to get to services on time.[53] While at Camp David in September 1959, he invited visiting Soviet Premier Nikita Khrushchev to attend worship with him. After traveling twenty-five miles to attend the Presbyterian church in Gettysburg, Pennsylvania, Eisenhower told the pastor, "I offered to bring Mr. Khrushchev to church, but he declined. He said it would be a shock to his people."[54]

The Eisenhower boys came from a background in the River Brethren, which tended to view the major denominations as having compromised with the world and its evils.[55] They had participated in their parents' Watchtower faith, which taught that "religion is a snare and a racket."[56] Given this background, it is not surprising that the sons broke with the Christianity of their childhood.

What may be more surprising is that most of the Eisenhower brothers later joined mainline Protestant denominations. Two—Milton and Roy—became Episcopalians, thus moving far from their religious roots. Eisenhower's brother Edgar once declared: "We boys are all religious but we don't go around saying [it]."[57] Whether Dwight Eisenhower would have become a practicing Christian if he had not run for president is unknowable. While some evidence indicates that he would have remained unaffiliated, it is significant that four of his brothers did not.

In a discussion with Billy Graham, Eisenhower once declared that he respected the way his parents had raised him in religious matters. But he commented, "I've gotten a long way from it."[58] In his study of the Eisenhower administration, Ira Chernus wrote that "the evidence for direct influence" of the River Brethren and Jehovah's Witnesses on Eisenhower "is so slim and inconclusive that it does not seem worthwhile to speculate on it. . . . The Christian influences on Eisenhower do not bear the marks of any particular denomination."[59]

These assessments may be only partially true. When Eisenhower entered West Point, he entered into the world of a professional soldier, an occupation whose purpose went completely against the pacifist views of the River Brethren and Jehovah's Witnesses. But his refusal to join any denomination until age sixty-three and his negative words to his secretary about the "trappings of religion" seem to show traces of his upbringing in antiestablishment interpretations of Christianity. The independence he proudly maintained in his religious views also parallels the independence of his father and of his paternal uncle. He did strongly identify with Protestantism, at one point describing himself to an interfaith group of chaplains as a "fanatic Protestant" and at another encouraging the idea of a national shrine to Protestantism in the nation's capital.[60] But when he officially joined a church after becoming president, he did so to set a good example for the nation.[61]

When Dwight Eisenhower formally became a Christian, he joined a middle-of-the-road denomination, the Presbyterians. One writer describes his adult religion as "moderate and tolerant, simple and firm."[62] Similarly, in other areas of life he tended to be a moderate man, avoiding his father's overt passion and his mother's quiet ardor. His brand of politics, though tilted to the right, has typically been labeled "moderate Republicanism."

Most presidents hold a public and a private religion. Sometimes few glimmers of the private religion emerge, but in Eisenhower's case readers have at least one such example. In 1953, the president's personal secretary, Ann Whitman, wrote to her husband that "the President preached religion at me all the day long." The final pages of this letter are missing, but in the portion that exists, Mrs. Whitman said that Eisenhower told her: "An atheist is a stupid person. He is one who won't think." She goes on to say that the president stated that

He could accept the theory that the Earth was created by fiery volcano, but we had always been taught scientifically that intense heat destroyed life—how then [do we] account for the beginnings of life, [because] the first protoplasm must have come from somewhere. He said he did not conceive of God as any being—that he abhored [sic] the trappings of the church as much as anyone—but . . .

The remaining words in the letter are lost.[63]

In the two decades after World War II, church membership in the United States rose to nearly two-thirds of the nation's population. Roman Catholics baptized approximately one million babies a year. Methodists reported their largest growth spurt since the 1920s. Jewish, Roman Catholic, and Protestant theological seminaries overflowed with students. Only a small percentage of Americans did not identify with a religious tradition.[64]

On one level, it seems surprising that a man previously uninvolved with organized religion would lead a revival of religion in the United States after World War II. Before his presidency, formal religion had played little or no role in Eisenhower's adult experience. Even in positions of authority, he had displayed no inclination to invoke ceremonial religion.

But in another sense, Eisenhower's leadership of the revival was fitting. For him, mainline religious affiliation was a longstanding American tradition. America's major opponent in the cold war, Soviet Russia, was officially godless. The Soviet Union advocated communism, opposed democracy, and stifled personal and religious freedom. In Eisenhower's arsenal of democracy, religious participation provided another weapon against communism. "Our form of government," he told an audience, "is the political expression of a deeply felt religious faith."[65]

The Eisenhower-led religious revival also fostered a middle-of-the-road atmosphere in which extremism found no real place. The staid 1950s did exhibit many forms of extremism. Religious fundamentalism was bursting forth on radio and TV. The John Birch Society and Senator Joseph McCarthy stood out on the religious and political right. The Pentecostal revivalist Oral Roberts moved his healing ministry to television. But for Eisenhower, centrist organized religion represented the best of mainstream American values.[66]

Eisenhower's sense of moderation extended to his view of the Supreme

Court's decisions under Chief Justice Earl Warren. The Warren Court's decision on church-state issues disturbed him. He came to view the Court as biased against churches and organized religion. Believing that the public schools of the United States should offer children basic religious instruction, he opposed the Court's prohibition of school-sponsored Bible reading. "There is no reason for Americans," he declared, "to raise their children in a communist type school that denies existence of a God."[67]

Because he had experienced firsthand the cataclysmic results of the accommodation most of European Christianity made to fascism, Eisenhower supported the involvement of churches in politics. "Based on his own experience," one writer notes, Eisenhower "questioned whether religious, moral, and political questions could be divorced from one another without sacrificing all morality in politics."[68] During the Vietnam era, however, college students began displaying civil disobedience and resisting the draft. In this case Eisenhower felt they and the clergy who assisted them had gone too far. In the words of a grandson who was a student during the period, he became "truculent" in his opposition.[69]

The atmosphere of the times was ripe for a religious revival. The return of the World War II veterans, their marriages, and the subsequent baby boom led to a renewal of family values, which have traditionally included religious faith. After the sufferings of the Depression and the destruction of World War II, the American public desired a return to normality. Place, home, and dwelling—in the analysis of one sociologist of religion—dominated American spirituality in the 1950s.[70]

In the decades just after the war, culminating in the Cuban Missile Crisis of 1962, many Americans also experienced a sense of helplessness at the thought of atomic war with the Soviet Union. In 1954, a Gallup Poll asked respondents to explain why the United States was currently experiencing a religious revival. Slightly more than 40 percent cited fears of war with the Communist world and general uncertainty about the future. Another 40 percent named such matters as "realization of God as Supreme Being" and "need for more faith."[71] One pollster of the time said that rarely in American history had more citizens craved tranquility and moderation.[72] In such an atmosphere, regular church or synagogue attendance fostered a needed sense of purpose and security.

Dwight Eisenhower's religion does not appear to have been deep or reflective. His piety and the revival of organized religion he championed had its major detractors. "Uncritical products of the culture accepted it," one critic wrote of religious membership in the 1950s, "just as they accepted practically everything else in an increasingly standardized society. Religion belonged to decent American living; any other thesis was unpatriotic."[73] Reinhold Niebuhr, the Protestant theologian whose writings would later influence Barack Obama, declared: "I wouldn't criticize the whole revival. I've criticized the revival wherever it gives petty and trivial answers to the great and ultimate questions about the meaning of life. . . . When an evangelist says, for instance, 'We must hope in Christ' without spelling out what this means in our particular nuclear age, this is irrelevant."[74]

Nevertheless, Eisenhower presided over a major religious revival in the United States. Unlike the evangelical and charismatic revival of recent decades, the revival of the 1950s occurred in mainstream Judeo-Christian traditions. Every religious group that occupied the approximate American religious center—Judaism, Eastern Orthodoxy, Roman Catholicism, and mainline Protestantism—grew. It was an unexpected legacy for a president who was raised in the extreme left wing of American religion.

Eisenhower's commitment to religion continued beyond his presidency. After retiring to his farm in Gettysburg, he and Mamie regularly attended Gettysburg Presbyterian Church, whose young minister Eisenhower held in especially high regard.[75] During the winter months, when he and Mamie went to California, they worshipped regularly at Palm Desert Community Presbyterian Church. David Eisenhower, who was closely associated with him during that period, remembers that his grandfather displayed a "resistance to fads and passing ideas common in church life" and "disliked dramatic and cathartic conversions."[76]

Eisenhower never lost his attachment to profanity. It regularly came out when he was playing golf in Gettysburg. According to David Eisenhower:

> Grandad never threw clubs or pounded them shapeless after poor shots. Instead his face would wrinkle up . . . his body would shudder then stiffen as he bellowed an oath. His anger was always directed at himself, but with such ferocity that it struck fear in anyone playing with him. . . . He was

mercurial. . . . One afternoon he shocked my mother for eighteen holes with unpredictable and terrifying outbursts of wrath, agony, and self-reproach.[77]

According to Eisenhower, his grandfather's Washington minister, Edward L. R. Elson, believed that President Eisenhower "had only a dim awareness of the chilling effect his outbursts on the golf course had on others."[78]

Prior to leaving the presidency, Eisenhower had suffered two heart attacks. When he experienced a third heart attack in April 1968, he was flown to Walter Reed Hospital. There, Eisenhower suffered his fourth heart attack. The many visitors to his hospital bed included Billy Graham.[79]

Eisenhower would never leave Walter Reed. Surrounded by his family, he died of congestive heart failure on March 28, 1969. His last words were "I want to go; God take me."[80] The dean of Washington National Cathedral presided over a brief service for the immediate family.[81] After the body lay in state at the cathedral, President Richard M. Nixon delivered a eulogy in the Rotunda of the Capitol. "He was probably loved by more people in more parts of the world," Nixon declared, "than any President America has ever had."[82]

The next day, a full Presbyterian service was held in the National Cathedral. Thousands lined the streets during the funeral procession. Thousands more gathered at railroad stations as Eisenhower's funeral train traveled toward Abilene. In one town, "when it became apparent to the crowd that the general's coffin would not be seen, the hum of expectant conversation died and voices were lifted in 'The Battle Hymn of the Republic.'" The train pulled away just as the crowd finished singing "The Star-Spangled Banner."[83]

Eisenhower's final funeral service occurred on April 2 at the Eisenhower Presidential Library in Abilene. He was buried in the library chapel beside his firstborn son, Doud Dwight. After the funeral, Mamie Eisenhower continued to live in Gettysburg and to worship in its Presbyterian church. After her death in 1979, she was buried beside her husband and son.

When a longtime aide visited Eisenhower at Walter Reed, the former president told him he did not expect to leave the hospital alive. "How can I complain," he then added, "when all the daydreams of my youth have been fulfilled?"[84]

# John F. Kennedy

When John Fitzgerald Kennedy was a candidate for president, his religious affiliation made a great deal of difference to many Americans. The question of Kennedy's Roman Catholicism animated the 1960 election. It provided an analog to such elections as those of 1800 and 1928, when the religions of Thomas Jefferson and Al Smith played a crucial role. In 1960, many Americans voted for or against Kennedy simply because he was a Roman Catholic.

Several years after the election, a journalist named Jim Bishop published a book entitled *A Day in the Life of President Kennedy*.[1] Its cover contained a photograph of President Kennedy, Jackie Kennedy, and their two young children, Caroline and John, standing in front of Joseph Kennedy's estate in Palm Beach, Florida (which had a chapel), following a private service on Easter Sunday. Since Bishop's book dealt with a typical weekday in President Kennedy's life, the inevitable implication was that formal religion and the institutional, worshipping church mattered so much to Kennedy that he regularly attended daily Mass, as his mother, Rose Kennedy, did.

Both of John F. Kennedy's parents came from affluent and influential Irish American families. Born in Boston in 1890, his mother, Rose Fitzgerald Kennedy, was the daughter of the colorful Irish American politician John F. "Honey Fitz" Fitzgerald, a three-term congressman and three-term mayor of Boston. His father, Joseph ("Joe") Patrick Kennedy, came from a similarly well-to-do Boston background. Operating saloons and other businesses, he rose to positions of influence in the Irish American community and in the Democratic Party of Massachusetts.

Conducted in the private chapel of Archbishop William Cardinal O'Connell, the marriage of Joe and Rose in 1914 displayed the status of the Kennedy and Fitzgerald families. Ultimately, the couple had five daughters and four sons, with John F. Kennedy as the second child. Although concerns about Kennedy's religion clouded his presidential campaign, a wide range of Roman Catholic practice and belief actually characterized his family.

Both religiously and politically, the dominant force in the family was Joe Kennedy Sr., a graduate of Boston Latin School and Harvard College. While he achieved some acceptance at a college whose students were overwhelmingly Protestant, he also encountered the prejudice against Irish Americans then so common among the old families of New England. In the words of one writer, Joe Sr. graduated from Harvard "with two burning desires: to become a millionaire by the age of thirty, and to show up the Protestants who had snubbed him."[2] He achieved both, rising as of 1969 to a net worth of $400 million and producing a son who became president.

After graduation Joseph Kennedy began to build up his wealth through shipping, banking, investing in the stock market, producing Hollywood films, and even bootlegging. Assisted by his wife, he also became intent upon building an American Roman Catholic dynasty. Not only money and politics but also religion would play a central role in this dynasty, for loyalty to Roman Catholicism then characterized Irish Americans. As the patriarch, Joe attempted to assure that the Kennedys would be perceived as one of the preeminent Roman Catholic families of the United States. They would be a caste apart, a Roman Catholic parallel to the Protestant Brahmins of Boston.

Since Joe Kennedy contributed millions of dollars over the years to Roman Catholic causes, a succession of archbishops of Boston viewed him as a financial pillar of their church. Patronized by and frequently photographed with bishops, he wielded considerable influence in church affairs. In 1936, Cardinal Eugenio Pacelli (later Pope Pius XII) was a guest at the Kennedy home in Bronxville, New York. Three years later, the Kennedy family had a private audience with the pope at his coronation. On the following day, their son Teddy received his First Communion from Pius XII.[3]

In his recent autobiography, Senator Edward Kennedy declares that his father was "deeply religious." He reports that the family "prayed together daily and attended Mass together at least weekly."[4] But little evidence exists that Joe Sr. was particularly devout or observant. Although he insisted that his wife and children attend Mass regularly, his own attendance was less regular. "For Joe," a writer observed, "the Catholic Church was like the Democratic

Party—an institution that he was born into and that he used as he saw fit—but he had no more deep faith in one than the other."[5]

Character was not Joseph Kennedy's strongpoint. Nothing if not ambitious, he was viewed by opponents as sly, arrogant, and manipulative. "I think the world outside his house was war for Mr. Kennedy," a friend of Jack Kennedy later speculated. Essentially friendless, Joe Sr. "regularly left people feeling small and miserable."[6] Although he complained about the "snubbing" he received at Harvard, his personality undoubtedly caused other students to avoid him. Ethically, he aged poorly. "He was completely amoral," declared Arthur Krock, the Washington bureau chief for the *New York Times* who knew Kennedy well. Krock, who was Jewish, said, "I think only a Roman Catholic could possibly describe how you could be amoral and still religious. That is, how you can carry an insurance policy with the deity and at the same time do all those other things. Yes, he was amoral. Sure he was."[7]

Despite the strict teachings of his church about marital fidelity and the strong opposition to adultery in Irish American circles, Kennedy maintained sexual relationships over the years with numerous models and society women. During one affair, he traveled with Hollywood actress Gloria Swanson to Europe. Cardinal O'Connell even met privately with Miss Swanson, who was also married, in an effort to get her to end the affair.[8] So well known was Kennedy's womanizing that a London newspaper exposed it when he served during World War II as American ambassador to the Court of St. James. Rose Kennedy, whose own father had extramarital affairs, was fully aware of her husband's extensive philandering, but she focused her attentions on her children and her religion.

Of the Kennedys, Rose was clearly the most religious. Teddy Kennedy calls his mother "the most devout and persistent believer I have ever known."[9] As a high school student, she declined admission to largely Protestant Wellesley College at the strong suggestion of her father and Cardinal O'Connell. Instead, she attended Boston's strict Convent of the Sacred Heart. In later years, she considered that the convent college provided her with the religious foundation for her life. But when asked at age ninety to describe her "greatest regret," she declared with some bitterness to a surprised historian that it was not attending Wellesley.[10]

Until age intervened, Rose attended Mass not only daily but often twice a day. "If God were to . . . leave me but one gift," her autobiography declares, "I would ask for faith." Her three "special spiritual inspiration[s]," she also wrote, were the rosary, the stations of the cross, and John Cardinal Newman's *Meditations*.[11] As these devotions suggest, her faith tended to be private. Neither she nor Joe became part of the parish life at churches they attended. In the words of one writer, Rose "would go to Mass, say her prayers, receive communion, and leave."[12] In 1951, Pope Pius XII named her a "papal countess," an honor shared by only five other women in American history.[13]

The Kennedy children were raised in this atmosphere of traditional Roman Catholicism. "I urged my children and grandchildren to embrace this faith bequeathed to them," Rose asserted, "to foster it, to try to strengthen it by prayer, reading, and study, seeking information on dogma that they cannot understand."[14] Unsurprisingly, the five Kennedy sisters—Rosemary, Kathleen, Eunice, Patricia, and Jean—followed their mother's religious practices more closely than their brothers. Quietly devout, Jean seems to have been the most religious. Eunice valued the formal elements of their church and attended Mass frequently.[15] Patricia, however, may have been less tied to the family church. She married a Protestant, the British actor Peter Lawford, who agreed to raise their children Roman Catholic. Ultimately she divorced him and never remarried.

Although Kathleen Kennedy never officially left Roman Catholicism, she was the sister most willing to rebel against her religious heritage. When Kathleen lived in Washington at the start of World War II, her steady date was John White, a journalist and nonpracticing Episcopalian. He later remembered that "she was wavering about the Catholic religion."[16]

While working for the Red Cross in 1944 in London, Kathleen married William J. R. Cavendish, Marquess of Hartington, despite the great opposition of her family to the union. Because the Anglican Cavendish refused—unlike Lawford—to raise their children in the Roman Catholic Church, the ceremony occurred in a civic office in England. Cavendish died in action in Belgium four months after the wedding.

In 1948, Kathleen became engaged to Peter Wentworth-FitzWilliam, 8th Earl FitzWilliam, an Anglo-Irish Protestant in the process of divorcing his wife. In May, the couple flew from London to Cannes where Joe Kennedy was staying to secure his blessing for their marriage. The plane crashed en route, killing all occupants. Kathleen was then buried beside her husband in the Cavendish plot in an Anglican churchyard. The trip to Cannes had been an effort to secure reconciliation between Kathleen and her father. Joe Kennedy became the only Kennedy to attend Kathleen's funeral. Throughout her life, Rose remained reluctant to discuss her fourth child's marriage to a Protestant.[17]

The religious profile of Rosemary, the oldest sister, is difficult to determine. As a child, she seemed relatively uninterested in religious ceremonies.[18] Possibly bipolar, she experienced increasing mental and emotional stress. After a lobotomy arranged by her father when she was twenty-three caused permanent disability, Rosemary was placed in the care of nuns in rural Wisconsin for the rest of her life. The family rarely talked about her.

The four Kennedy brothers—Joseph Jr., John F. ("Jack"), Robert ("Bobby"), and Edward ("Teddy")—tended to model themselves on their father. Unsurprisingly, most exhibited less religiosity than their mother or sisters.

Of the four, Bobby was clearly the most religious. Bobby "never misses Mass," Jackie Kennedy once declared, "and prays all the time."[19] The American writer Gore Vidal, who knew the Kennedys through Jackie, described the future attorney general as "rigidly Catholic."[20] Bobby was the only one of the brothers who knew the lives of the Roman Catholic saints and their feast days. When Rose once commented that "Bobby has taken his religion seriously," one writer viewed this comment, probably correctly, as a suggestion that the other males in the family treated the Roman Catholic faith "more as a family ritual than as a system of personal belief."[21]

Although Bobby's religious views broadened in the years following his brother's assassination, he remained a staunch member of his church for most of his life. Raised in a devout and zealous Roman Catholic family, his wife Ethel had considered becoming a nun. Of the Kennedy wives, she was the most like Rose Kennedy. Like the senior Kennedys, she and Bobby produced the large family (eleven children) typical of Roman Catholic marriages of the time.

For some years Rose hoped that the youngest son, Teddy, would become a priest.[22] Instead, like his brothers, he entered politics. In 1962, when he ran for Senate, the Roman Catholic voters of Massachusetts viewed him, in the words of his Republican opponent, as "a Prince of the Church." The opponent, an Episcopalian, continued, "The identification of the Kennedy family with the Catholic church is so great. . . . You can't lay a glove on him."[23]

The inexperienced thirty-year-old Kennedy won that election by almost 200,000 votes. Despite marital infidelity, a divorce, serious incidents connected with alcohol, and a clearly lukewarm faith, he remained popular in Massachusetts. In 1992 he married another divorced Roman Catholic, Victoria Reggie. Both secured annulments of their prior marriages from an archdiocesan court.

By the time Joe Kennedy Jr. died at age twenty-nine, the degree of his piety had not become entirely clear. During his training as a naval pilot, however, he seems to have stood out to the chaplain for his devoutness. "Joe Jr.," one writer declares, "was far more religious than Jack."[24] When he was killed in a midair explosion during World War II, however, he was in love with an Englishwoman who was not only Protestant but also a twice-divorced mother. Joe Jr. not only supported his sister Kathleen's decision to marry a Protestant but also gave his sister away in the civil ceremony. The death of Joe Jr. in 1944 caused Joe Sr. to focus his political hopes and grooming on his next-oldest son.

Born in May 1917, John Fitzgerald Kennedy was baptized the next month in St. Aidan's Catholic Church in Brookline, Massachusetts. He was raised not only in that church but also in churches at the family's additional homes in Bronxville, Palm Beach, and Hyannis Port. At age ten he was confirmed in Boston by Archbishop William Cardinal O'Connell.

Kennedy studied for two years at a public school in Brookline, for three years at a nonsectarian private school in Boston where Roman Catholics were uncommon, for three years at a secular country day school in the Riverdale section of the Bronx, and for one year at a Catholic preparatory school in Connecticut. He then spent four years at the Choate School in Connecticut. The preparatory school maintained a close relationship to the Episcopal Church and for most of the twentieth century had ordained Episcopal clergy as headmasters. After spending a semester at Princeton, Kennedy continued his college education at Harvard.

Thus Kennedy was educated only for one year in Roman Catholic schools; even Barack Obama received three years of Roman Catholic education. Throughout Kennedy's schooling, his classmates were largely Protestant,

Jewish, or secular—and often they were Episcopalian. This pattern of disengagement continued in Kennedy's later life. Although politically he remained an Irish American Democrat, economically and socially he moved in largely Protestant and secular circles.

If Kennedy attended Mass at the family church or at town churches while in preparatory school, little evidence exists about his church attendance in college. Between his freshman and sophomore years at Harvard, he toured Europe with his friend Kirk LeMoyne "Lem" Billings, an Episcopalian. The diary he kept during the trip indicates that he attended Mass regularly on Sundays wherever they were. Paraphrased, a typical entry for a Sunday reads, "Got up, went to Mass, went to the beach."[25]

While at Harvard, Kennedy belonged to the St. Paul's Catholic Club. With uncertain substantiation, one biographer adds he "consistently attended Sunday Mass."[26] Years later, a Harvard classmate who thought Kennedy "less than pious" remembered expressing surprise that he was going to Mass on a holy day of obligation. The classmate remembered that Kennedy "got this odd, hard look on his face and replied, 'This is one of the things I do for my father. The rest I do for myself.'"[27]

By the start of his senior year at Harvard, Kennedy had clearly become skeptical about the faith in which he had been raised. After returning to the United States from a tour of Europe and the Middle East in 1939, Kennedy asked a Roman Catholic priest:

> I saw the rock where our Lord ascended into Heaven in a cloud, and [in] the
> same area, I saw the place where Mohammed was carried up into Heaven
> on a white horse, and Mohammed has a big following and Christ has a big
> following, and why do you think we should believe Christ any more than
> Mohammed?[28]

Following this conversation, the priest urged Joe Kennedy to get his second son doctrinal "instruction immediately, or else he would turn into a[n] . . . atheist."[29]

In his years at Harvard, Kennedy focused on dating, on being selected by the right club, and on gaining new friends. Although his IQ when tested at age thirteen was 119 (above average but unexceptional), he was known by others at Harvard for his quick mind, sense of humor, intellectuality, and interest in ideas.[30] As is often the case with college students, he became a more serious student in his junior and senior years. After graduating cum laude in June 1940, Kennedy spent the fall semester auditing classes at Stanford University's Business School.

By this time, he was apparently experiencing even more serious doubts about his faith. "We talked about it a lot," Henry James, a Stanford classmate who had been raised Roman Catholic, told a writer in 1991. "He found great difficulty in believing most of the tenets of the Catholic faith. Church bored him! He hardly ever went. Religion didn't interest him. He was all for being au courant, very much up to date with the things that were going on at the time, but not eternal verities."[31]

In the interview, James attributed much of Kennedy's indifference to the Roman Catholicism of his parents. "I think Jack was wary of his mother because of her strong religion," James declared in an interview.

> She was one of those fanatics who . . . went to Mass every day of her life, I think. And Jack wasn't having that! . . . He talked to her . . . but he certainly wouldn't ever tell her anything about his personal actions. . . . He kept her at arm's length because he was just ill at ease with her strong brand of Catholicism—and because, as I say, Jack had made it very clear to me when we had talks about religion that he found great difficulty in believing most of the tenets of the Catholic church.[32]

James also remembered that Kennedy viewed his father as "a political and public Catholic." In Kennedy's view, James recalled, Joe Sr.

> was not a Catholic in any of his practices. He committed adultery, flagrantly. He didn't obey the teaching of the church—unless it's the Irish concept, which is that everything is forgiven . . . by just going to confession. . . . Jack was smart enough to see that his father was brazenly two-faced about it. . . . And so, in Jack's case, if anything was to go, *religion* was to go—not the other. Jack's libertine ways were what he wanted to keep.[33]

During the three years of naval service that followed Stanford, only snippets exist about Kennedy's religious activity. Some information comes from his relationship with a Danish journalist and former Miss Denmark in Washington. Blond, blue-eyed, and Protestant, the multilingual Inga Arvad had already been married twice, though she was separated from her second husband. As a correspondent for a Danish newspaper in Germany, she had interviewed such Nazi leaders as Heinrich Himmler, Joseph Goebbels, and Hermann Goering. Since beauty tends to be its own calling card, she had also sat in Adolf Hitler's private box in the 1936 Berlin Olympics. But because the FBI was convinced she was a Nazi spy, she was "harassed, bugged, and burglarized" during her stay in Washington.[34] Kennedy appeared in the FBI reports, because of the many hours he spent with her. And those reports indicated that he went to confession on at least one occasion.

The affair, which ended in the spring of 1942, became so serious that Kennedy indicated he might marry the "sprightly spying Scandinavian" (Torbert Macdonald's description).[35] When Joe Kennedy reportedly objected, "Damn it, Jack, she's *already* married," Kennedy's reply was that he did not care.[36] His parents strongly opposed the relationship. "A non-Catholic divorcée," as one writer declares, "was hardly what Joe and Rose would find acceptable as a mate for any of their sons."[37] Ultimately the affair caused Joe Kennedy to secure his son's reassignment from Washington. Possibly paid off by Kennedy Sr., Inga secured a quickie divorce in Reno, Nevada, and married an old acquaintance in New York.

Shortly after the end of the affair, White recorded in his diary that Kathleen believed that Jack was "on the verge of renouncing his Catholic religion."[38] Kennedy may have viewed such a decision as retaliation for his parents' opposition to his relationship with Inga. Seemingly connected is another snippet of information, which relates that Kennedy's superiors asked him to conduct a Bible class on Sundays with sailors. In a letter that seems to indicate a continuing questioning of his church, Kennedy then asked his mother if Bible study was "un-Catholic." "I have a feeling that dogma might say it was," he wrote,

> but don't good works come under our obligations to the Catholic church.
> We're not a completely ritualistic, formalistic, hierarchical structure in which
> the Word, the truth, must only come down from the very top—a structure
> that allows for no individual interpretation—or are we?[39]

Ultimately serving as commander of a patrol boat in the Pacific, Kennedy became known as a war hero for his life-saving actions after the boat was sunk. Discharged from the navy as a lieutenant in 1945, he soon entered politics. When he sometimes used a cane or crutches in later years, the public assumed that he did so because of these wartime injuries.

Throughout Kennedy's political career, voters remained unaware that he had been prone to illness almost since birth. Poor health caused him to drop out of Princeton during his freshman year. Initially failing the physical exam both for the army and the navy, he was unable even to acquire life insurance. He was inducted into the navy only after the intervention of his father. As one biographer notes, Boston's Naval Medical Board ignored "Jack's calamitous case history of maladies and hospitalizations over the past twenty-four years."[40]

"Maladies and hospitalizations" plagued Kennedy throughout his life. He suffered not only from the endocrine disorder called Addison's Disease but also from thyroid deficiency, osteoporosis, colitis, and infections that apparently stemmed from venereal disease. Back pain caused Kennedy to wear a corset, to sleep on special mattresses, and at times abruptly to leave events because of pain. His back stiffened when he flew; even on short flights his Secret Service detail "kept a close eye on him" when he disembarked because of their "concern that he'd fall down the stairs."[41] When he lived in the White House, he swam in a pool heated to 90 degrees and watched films from a special bed placed in the building's home theater. During his term as president, he was using up to twelve drugs. He was also the patient of a Manhattan society physician known as "Dr. Feelgood" because of the amphetamine shots (or "uppers") he administered to his patients.[42] Had the public been aware of Kennedy's physical condition, he might have been less successful in politics.

In 1946, Kennedy was elected to Congress. In 1952, following three terms in Congress, he won the U.S. Senate seat previously held by the Brahmin Episcopalian Henry Cabot Lodge Jr. Although Kennedy's service in the Senate was relatively undistinguished, he won the Pulitzer Prize in 1957 for his best-selling *Profiles in Courage*. The book (to which his aide and speechwriter Theodore "Ted" Sorensen substantially contributed) focused on eight U.S. senators who exhibited honor and integrity in their support of unpopular positions.

In the meantime, Kennedy had married. He once told a friend that out of all the good-looking women he had met, he could only marry one—and that he married her.[43] With Cardinal Cushing officiating, the highly publicized wedding took place in 1953 at St. Mary's Church in Newport, Rhode Island. In Jacqueline Lee Bouvier, Kennedy found a wife who captured national attention in a way similar to noted past first ladies, such as Dolley Madison and Eleanor Roosevelt, and future first ladies such as Betty Ford and Hillary Clinton.

Born in 1929, Jackie was the daughter of Janet Lee Norton and John Vernou Bouvier III, a stockbroker and graduate of Yale. Charming, flamboyant, and handsome, Jackie's father was a roguish alcoholic who had a series of mistresses and squandered much of his family fortune. When Jackie was eleven and her sister Lee was seven, a New York tabloid printed photos of Bouvier with his girlfriend.[44] By the later years of his life, Bouvier was so embittered and troubled that Janet did not want him to participate in Jackie's wedding to John F. Kennedy. Thus her second husband, Hugh Auchincloss, gave Jackie away.

A decisive woman from a well-to-do Irish American family, Janet graduated from fashionable Miss Spence's School in Manhattan and briefly attended Sweet Briar and Barnard colleges. Insisting that French be spoken at the dinner table and minimizing (as Jackie also did) her Irish American ancestry, she maintained a strong sense of decorum and propriety that carried over to her elder daughter. "She was raised correctly," French prime minister Charles de Gaulle said after meeting Jackie Kennedy.[45] Janet took her two daughters to Mass every Sunday at the Jesuit-operated Church of St. Ignatius Loyola on Park Avenue in Manhattan.

Two years after divorcing Bouvier, Janet married Hugh Auchincloss. Auchincloss lived on a historic estate in Fairfax County, Virginia, and owned a second home in Newport, Rhode Island. A Yale-educated stockbroker, he was a bibliophile and lawyer of inherited wealth. For Janet's two daughters, he provided the stable home and financial security that their father could not give them. Jackie and Lee kept their last name of Bouvier, but the generous Auchincloss—in the words of one writer—"financed Jackie's many advantages and earned her loyalty with his sturdy dependability."[46]

Despite being married twice before, Auchincloss remained an active Episcopalian. Although Jackie and Lee continued to attend Mass following their mother's remarriage, Janet—who subsequently had a son and a daughter by Auchincloss—began going to the Episcopal church with her new husband. In 1962, when the Auchinclosses moved from the estate in McLean to a historic home in Georgetown, they lived on Thirty-first Street across from Christ Episcopal Church and attended its services. Ultimately Janet became an Episcopalian.[47]

But the Bouvier sisters did not follow their mother's example and remained loyal Roman Catholics. More conventionally attractive than her sister Jackie, (Caroline) Lee Bouvier frequently traveled abroad with her sister and later became very much part of the background of the Kennedy administration. Ultimately married three times, Lee received Roman Catholic annulments of her first two marriages. She secured an annulment to allow her to marry "Prince" Stanislaw Radziwill in a Roman Catholic ceremony, just as Radziwill secured an annulment of his previous marriage in order to marry. Before Jackie Kennedy married Greek shipping magnate Aristotle Onassis in 1968, Lee was his frequent companion.

From her teen years on, Jackie Bouvier enchanted people with her beauty. She possessed a whispery voice that reflected her upper-class New York upbringing. A graduate of the fashionable Miss Porter's School in Connecticut, she studied for two years at Vassar and spent her junior year in France. Deciding in Paris that she preferred an urban atmosphere for learning, she finished her degree in French literature at George Washington University.

Although Jackie had flaws—she could be rude and incredibly extravagant—she displayed traits of gentleness and kindness, possessed an enthusiastic girlish side, and was a good friend to others. Intensely personal, she disliked campaigning and preferred to stay out of the spotlight. "She had a great appreciation for the arts," one observer recalled, "a deep love for animals, and was intent on making sure her children grew up as unspoiled as possible."[48]

But Jackie also experienced her share of sorrows. She not only lived through her parents' untidy divorce but also suffered a miscarriage, a stillborn baby, and the loss of a newborn baby. She lost both a husband and brother-in-law to assassins, and she eventually died of cancer. On the night before her husband's funeral, she said to the auxiliary bishop of Washington, "I really believe in God, I believe in heaven, but where has God gone?"[49] Some months later, she told British Prime Minister Harold Macmillan that she struggled with her religious beliefs and wondered if "there was just nothing afterwards—or some great vague peace."[50]

Jackie and her sister Lee had been raised in the observant but somewhat casual form of Roman Catholicism often found among the affluent. Clint Hill, the Secret Service agent assigned to Jackie at the White House, described her to another agent as "devout."[51] But the Bouvier daughters did not exhibit the fervent piety of Rose Kennedy. "Jackie could always be on a horse," Janet Auchincloss once told a friend, "but not necessarily at Mass."[52] Educated through her first two years of college at schools with overwhelmingly Protestant student bodies and faculties, Jackie's religious education seems to have been limited to lessons from the Baltimore Catechism then required of Roman Catholics prior to their first communion and confirmation. Yet she read widely. At Vassar, one of her classmates remembered her as an "ardent defender of her church whenever it was criticized."[53]

"She wasn't a religious person, not really," her friend and Washington hostess Joan Braden said.

> Mostly, I think, Catholicism was, for her and most of the Kennedys a family
> ritual rather than a true belief system. But in the years after Jack's death,
> she found strength where she least expected it, within. She told me that she
> felt that God was most certainly pulling her through the ordeal, "sometimes
> kicking and screaming all the way," she said, laughing.[54]

When John F. Kennedy and Jackie married in 1953, Gore Vidal—a stepson of Hugh Auchincloss—commented, "Of the available Catholic women in the country, [Jackie] was about the most glamorous and [the Kennedys] regarded it as a big step upwards and an ongoing victory over the WASPS."[55] The couple had two children. Caroline was christened by Archbishop Cushing at St. Patrick's Cathedral in New York City. John Jr. was baptized by the pastor of Washington's Holy Trinity Catholic Church in the chapel of Georgetown University Hospital. After her husband's assassination, Jackie continued to attend Mass and to raise her children as Roman Catholics.

In 1956, Kennedy narrowly missed winning the Democratic nomination for vice president. After easily winning reelection to the U.S. Senate in 1958, he announced he was running for president early in 1960. His candidacy was enormously controversial, for in the years following World War II the Roman Catholic Church had experienced vast growth as a cultural and political force in the United States. Because it viewed itself as the True Church, Roman Catholicism considered itself as entitled to a religious monopoly. At the time, official Roman Catholic teaching asserted its firm belief in

> the state's obligation to make public profession of religion, recognition in principle of the Catholic religion as that of the state; toleration of religious dissidents only if it were practically unavoidable . . . [with] the underlying principle . . . [being] that "error has not the same rights as truth."[56]

Meeting in Rome from 1962 to 1965, the Second Vatican Council rescinded this centuries-old dictate. But in the postwar years leading up to the 1960 election, American Protestants and Jews experienced a "real tension between an authoritarian, centralized, hierarchical church and the spirit of an open, pluralistic, democratic society."[57] Many viewed Roman Catholicism as an international movement that could end religious pluralism and freedom in America, as it already had in such countries as Spain and Portugal. This tension was seen in the anti–birth control legislation kept in place by Roman Catholic voters in Massachusetts and Connecticut and in the opposition to public support for welfare agencies that operated birth control clinics. The Roman Catholic objection to the passage of liberal divorce laws in states, the church's efforts to influence public hospitals to accept Catholic practice in obstetrics, and the continued arguments and lobbying by Roman Catholics for public support of parochial schools did nothing to help matters.

But Kennedy, as his longtime speechwriter Ted Sorensen wrote, had "no reservations about the wisdom of separating church and state."[58] Essentially he won the Democratic nomination over rival Hubert Humphrey, a practicing Protestant, by declaring his independence from both the pope and the bishops of his church. "I am not 'trying to be the first Catholic president,'" he declared in a speech during the crucial campaign in overwhelmingly Protestant West Virginia. "I happen to believe I can serve my nation as president—and I also happen to have been born a Catholic."[59]

One other speech may have helped Kennedy secure the presidency. In September 1960, Kennedy spoke to three hundred Protestant clergy at a highly publicized meeting of the Greater Houston Ministerial Association.

"I believe in an America where the separation of church and state is absolute," he told the clergy.

> I am wholly opposed to the state being used by any religious group . . . to . . . prohibit . . . the free exercise of any other religion. . . . Whatever issue may come before me as president—on birth control, divorce, . . . or any other subject, I will make my decision . . . in accordance with what my conscience tells me to be the national interest. . . . If the time should ever come . . . when my office would require me to either violate my conscience or violate the national interest, then I would resign the office.[60]

By confronting these and other issues directly and by articulating a strong separationist stand on church and state, Kennedy allayed the reservations of many voters who feared a Roman Catholic in the White House. In November 1960 he secured a narrow and controversial victory over Republican Richard M. Nixon.

John F. Kennedy was president for 1,036 days. The invasion of the Bay of Pigs, the Cuban Missile Crisis, the erection of the Berlin Wall, and the ongoing war in Vietnam all occurred during the Kennedy administration. He established both the Peace Corps (originally a proposal of Hubert Humphrey) and the space program and was involved in the struggles over civil rights.

After the stuffy administrations of Eisenhower, Truman, Roosevelt, Hoover, and Coolidge, the Kennedys changed the culture of Washington. "President Kennedy," a Secret Service agent remembered, "preferred to be around people who could make him laugh."[61] The new presidency created a feeling of youthfulness and vitality in the nation. Youth, good looks, and what Kennedy called "vigor" now seemed to be everywhere in the capital—Bobby in the attorney general's office, Teddy in the Senate, fifteen Rhodes Scholars and large numbers of thirty- and forty-year-olds in the administration, young children in the White House, and Jack and Jackie (when not pregnant) staying up hours past midnight at parties.

Kennedy had run for the presidency on the slogan, "Let's get this country moving again." In office he spoke of establishing the "New Frontier"—words that (along with "Camelot") Jackie thought conveyed the magic of her husband's presidency.[62] From 1961 to 1963, "the nation's capital," Arthur Schlesinger

Jr. commented, "seemed engaged in a collective effort to make itself brighter, gayer, more intellectual, more resolute. It was a golden interlude."[63]

Hosting world-class performances featuring internationally known musicians, the Kennedys radiated glamour. Kennedy himself appeared vigorous and at the peak of his manhood. Whenever Jackie appeared with him, the crowds doubled in size. "People just wanted to get a look at her," a Secret Service agent assigned to the Kennedy Detail later remembered. "It was like travelling with a movie star."[64]

Actual Hollywood movie stars, front-page literary figures and artists, guests of high social pedigree, British nobility, and the European jet set attended black-tie, candlelit dinner dances, accompanied by the music of society bands and the songs of Frank Sinatra. The well-publicized entertainments, the Potomac River cruises, and the guests of the Kennedy White House all evoked an American aristocracy. "Does remind you of Scott Fitzgerald, doesn't it?" mused Lady Bird Johnson at one of the dinner dances.[65] In following the president's activities, newspaper readers and television viewers found themselves transported from the White House to Washington's Holy Trinity Catholic Church, to Hyannis Port, to Newport, to Palm Springs, to Virginia's foxhunting country, and to the "Southern White House" in Palm Beach.

When a newspaper compared one of the Kennedys' dinners to the "grandeur of the French court at Versailles," the writer correctly perceived that this worldliness was more suited to the courts of Europe than to the White Houses of previous presidents.[66] Others who attended the Kennedys' entertainments equated their atmosphere to that of "Louis XIV and his court."[67] The columnist Stewart Alsop described the administration as "lousy with courtiers and ladies in waiting—actual or would be."[68] Over it all presided a prince who in the tradition of European royalty wore his Catholic religion lightly.

At times, the Kennedys—almost a royal family—appeared to be on the cover of every magazine. After Kennedy's death, Jim Bishop's *A Day in the Life of President Kennedy* seemed to be on sale everywhere. Customers who stood in grocery lines usually saw pictures of the Kennedys on the front pages of magazines and tabloids at the checkout counter. In the early 1960s, Americans not only became Kennedy watchers but even imitated their dress, with large numbers of American women copying the pillbox hats worn by Jackie. No family of a previous president had received such attention.

Among the Kennedys, no one was more glamorous than Jackie. Had she become first lady immediately after Edith Wilson (the daughter of a Virginia judge and educated in private schools) or Lou Hoover (the daughter of a banker and a well-traveled, multilingual graduate of Stanford), the contrast would have been less stark. Both of these First Ladies not only came from educated and affluent backgrounds but also had lived in sophisticated cities and belonged to the most social of the Protestant denominations—the Episcopal Church. Compared to her immediate predecessors, however—the unpretentious and middle-American Mamie Eisenhower and Bess Truman—Jackie was cosmopolitan and culturally and fashionably sophisticated.

As first lady, Jackie selected a French chef and wore fashions by French designers. She spoke French and encouraged her husband to take French lessons. When she redecorated the White House, she and her committee focused on the early American republic and on the oldest White House furnishings still in existence—those that James Monroe ordered from France or commissioned to refurnish the White House when it was rebuilt after the British burned the capital in the War of 1812. At White House dinners, the menus were often printed in French. "Old-fashioned Washington," one of the city's hostesses declared, "was put on the side. With the Kennedys, the Europeans came to Washington."[69]

This observation provides one key to the Kennedys' mystique. Most of John F. Kennedy's immediate predecessors in the White House were distinctly Protestant, American types. Franklin Roosevelt was the only exception. He was raised in an atmosphere of wealth, Episcopalianism, and a certain amount of British Europeanism. But as a member of a rich and influential family, Kennedy had lived in Europe and traveled both to the Soviet Union and to the Middle East even before finishing college. When he married, he married a woman who emphasized her own French heritage and who—like her mother—was an ardent Francophile. Thus the Kennedys brought not only European culture to the White House but also, to a certain degree, the spirit and practices of European Catholicism.

In addition, President Kennedy brought the European tradition that monarchs and prime ministers can have frequent extramarital affairs while in office. In the days of royalty, European kings had both queens and mistresses. In subsequent centuries European presidents and prime ministers routinely engaged in extramarital relationships. "In Latin countries," a European political scientist writes, "a [prime] minister having a mistress is no news—only a minister without [one] is."[70] During Kennedy's presidency, the prime minister of France, Georges Pompidou, had a mistress. In the same years, high-level French political figures frequented "Madame Claude's" network of call girls. At the funeral Mass for French president François Mitterand, celebrated by the archbishop of Paris, both Mitterand's mistress and his illegitimate daughter sat with the family in Notre Dame Cathedral.

In European countries outside of Britain, mistresses were considered such a normal part of life that they sometimes accompanied the monarch or prime minister to social events. Except for the extreme conservative wing of European Roman Catholicism, citizens of such countries as France accepted the extramarital activities of their national leaders with a shrugged acknowledgement that "men will be men." The French had long excused sexual behavior as outside moral judgment. On his first trip to France, for example, the American founding father John Adams was shocked to discover that it was common, even expected, for French men to take mistresses.

In 2011, Dominique Strauss-Kahn, head of the International Monetary Fund and leading presidential candidate, was charged with the attempted rape of a hotel maid. His arrest raised the question in France of whether "the private lives of the rich, famous and powerful are off limits to public scrutiny." Prime Minister Mitterand thought they were. "Yes, it's true," he answered when asked whether he had a daughter outside his marriage. "And so what? It's none of the public's business."[71]

In the 1960s most Americans—heirs to deep cultural and religious roots influenced by Puritanism and by the Victorian period—were unwilling to overlook such misbehavior. But in Kennedy's case, at least his church did. Although the archbishops of Boston and Washington surely knew of the president's recurrent adultery (a sin their church considered mortal), neither directed his clergy to withhold the Eucharist from him. He remained in good standing in his church. Yet when the widowed Jackie Kennedy married Aristotle Onassis in 1968, the Vatican declared that she had become ineligible to receive the sacraments because she had "knowingly violated the law of the church" by marrying a divorced man whose first wife was still alive.[72]

Throughout the Kennedy administration, voters remained almost totally unaware that John F. Kennedy had continued his father's tradition of womanizing. If what one of his mistresses called his "incorrigible promiscuity" had been known in the 1960s, it would have shocked almost all of the American public.[73] Kennedy's one-night or continuing affairs during his presidency included Jackie's press secretary, the sister of one of Jackie's best friends, a former classmate of Lee Bouvier, a West German of East German background whom the FBI suspected was a spy, a Las Vegas showgirl who was also mistress to a Mafia leader, a bevy of undergraduate students and Washington interns, and two attractive young women designated "Fiddle" and "Faddle" by the Secret Service. Both were supposedly secretaries, but in the words of a former Secret Service agent, "Neither did much work."[74]

A few days before Kennedy had an audience in Rome with Pope Paul VI, he had an assignation with the wife of the principal figure in the Italian automotive industry. He arranged meetings with Hollywood actresses whose beauty he admired, including Marilyn Monroe. A bachelor Secret Service agent assigned to Kennedy's detail recalled being attracted to a flight attendant on the crew of the press plane that accompanied Air Force One. His detail leader told him not to ask her out, for "she's part of the president's private stock."[75]

Kennedy would cruise on the presidential yacht with these paramours or fly with them on air force planes. Sometimes, he met Monroe in a loft located above the Justice Department office of his brother Bobby. The loft contained a bed used by attorneys general whenever they needed to remain overnight because of crises.[76] During Jackie's frequent absences from the White House, Kennedy would take the women into the Lincoln bedroom; in case the first lady's travel plans brought her back to the White House earlier than expected, the president's Secret Service detail kept radio contact with the detail assigned to her.[77] Not just an obsession but also an addiction, women were what some of Kennedy's friends called his "disease."[78] A Washington columnist once observed Kennedy talking to a noted British beauty at a party and looking "rather like a small boy wondering whether to plunge a spoon into a fresh dish of peach ice cream."[79]

Until the mid-1970s—when Judith Campbell Exner, the Las Vegas showgirl, and former White House staffers shared their revelations of the affairs—these extramarital relationships remained unknown to the American public. But Kennedy's brothers and sisters, his friends, foreign heads of state, FBI director J. Edgar Hoover (who regularly sent Bobby Kennedy memos about his brother's "reckless philandering"), Washington insiders, and many journalists—not to mention his staff and the Secret Service—knew of his promiscuity.[80] So did Jackie Kennedy, whose sister once remonstrated with Kennedy about his affairs. Many of Kennedy's mistresses, in fact, knew his other mistresses.

Kennedy's affairs went unrevealed until more than a decade after his assassination largely for three reasons. First, the mainline American press of the time did not reveal private matters about presidents. A *New York Times* columnist remembered a story told by her legendary colleague, R. W. Apple Jr.:

> When he was a metro reporter for *The Times* in 1963, he was assigned to stake out the lobby of a hotel in Manhattan where . . . Kennedy was spending the night. While on the lookout for official visitors, Apple said he saw "a young woman of a Hollywood nature" heading for the presidential suite. He quickly called his editor, who informed him "I was there to report the comings and goings of statesmen, not starlets."

"If that happened now, of course," the columnist reflected, "the only question would be whether Apple could avoid being run over by a crew from TMZ."[81]

Second, most of the press liked Kennedy, which differed from their feelings for such presidents as Nixon, Carter, and the Bushes. To that extent they protected him, just as they protected the private lives of each other. During the early 1960s, CBS president Frank Stanton declared the Washington press was "completely in Kennedy's hands."[82]

Third, the approximately forty Secret Service men assigned to the president and his family did not reveal what they knew. They took seriously the phrase in their credentials that commended them to others as "someone worthy of trust and confidence."[83] Agent Jerry Blaine, who was assigned to Kennedy, remembers that

> Being tight-lipped was a critical part of being a Secret Service agent. . . . Every . . . White House Detail agent had been selected for this elite posi-

tion because he'd proven to be worthy of trust and confidence. Worthy of Trust And Confidence. It was the motto of the United States Secret Service, emblazoned on their commission books and drilled into their psyches . . . so deeply it had become instinctive.[84]

During the twelve years of Franklin Delano Roosevelt's presidency, the Secret Service kept from the American public that Roosevelt was confined to a wheelchair. Yet they were in charge of strapping him to a podium when he spoke publicly. They knew all about Kennedy's extramarital affairs, for they had to stay close to him at all times.

"Take a bullet for the president and keep your mouth shut about the president's personal life," Agent Larry Newman was told when assigned to guard John Kennedy. "Newman and other agents," a chronicler of the Secret Service writes,

> soon learned that [Kennedy] led a double life. He was the charismatic leader of the free world. But in his other life, he was the cheating, reckless husband whose aides snuck women into the White House to appease his sexual appetite.[85]

Had they disclosed the details of what were called Kennedy's "off-the-record" visits, the Secret Service could have exposed a side of the president that would have shocked the nation.[86] "Any one of the Kennedy Detail agents," Blaine notes,

> could have regaled journalists assigned to the White House with dozens of stories that would knock their socks off [and] shoot them straight to the top of their profession. But being tight-lipped was a critical part of being a Secret Service agent.[87]

Kessler observes that Secret Service directors still periodically remind agents that they must not disclose to anyone, especially to the press, what they witness in the White House.[88] Thus many Americans did not know that the president consistently violated his marital vows.

What many Americans did know was that Jack and Jackie Kennedy's social and religious style simply did not fit their stereotype of American Roman Catholics. The last Catholic presidential candidate voters had encountered was Governor Al Smith of New York, a parochial school dropout whose accent reflected his background in the multiethnic Lower East Side of Manhattan. As of 1960, such figures as Mayor Richard Daley of Chicago, former Mayor James Michael Curley of Boston, and kingpin James Farley of the Democratic Party more nearly represented the stereotype of the American Catholic who was active in politics.

If Jack and Jackie fit any religious stereotype at all in the minds of Americans, it was probably that of the worldliest and most ritualistic of the Protestant denominations, the Episcopal Church. Like F. Scott Fitzgerald, whose worldly protagonists often had Irish names but attended Episcopal churches, Kennedy seemed to fit the fashionable Episcopal mold better than the Roman Catholic type. He was an Anglophile, whereas most Irish Roman Catholics of the time were Anglophobes.[89] Many Episcopalians were wealthy; at one time Kennedy's trust funds equaled roughly sixty million dollars. He had graduated from an Episcopal prep school. From "Lem" Billings on (whose experiences with Kennedy varied from visiting a house of prostitution in Harlem to meeting the pope in Rome), most of his friends came from either Episcopal or other Protestant backgrounds.

Only a few of Kennedy's close friends—such as Charles Bartlett, Chuck Spaulding, and Torbert Macdonald—as well as three members of his staff (Dave Powers, Kenny O'Donnell, and Larry O'Brien) shared his Roman Catholic faith. As for Jackie, all of her education had been in private schools with largely Protestant and often predominantly Episcopalian student bodies. Her stepfather and her two youngest siblings were Episcopalian. Her mother had even converted to the Episcopal Church and attended Episcopal worship regularly.

Fifty years later, a reader is struck by the high percentages of WASPs and Jews in the Kennedy circle and administration. They far outnumber the Roman Catholics. Of the ten original members of Kennedy's cabinet, for example, six were Protestants of some kind, two were Jewish, one was Latter-Day Saint (or Mormon), and only one (Kennedy's brother Bobby) was Roman Catholic. Even Secretary of Defense Robert McNamara, the product of a modest Irish Catholic family in California, was Presbyterian. For Kennedy, religious affiliation was no litmus test. According to his principal speechwriter and aide, Ted Sorensen, a Unitarian, he "did not require or prefer Catholics on his staff and neither knew nor cared about our religious beliefs."[90]

But what was John F. Kennedy's religious faith? The truth is difficult to determine. Rarely open about his deeper feelings, he spoke even less frequently about his spiritual views. Thus people tended to see in Kennedy's religion what they wanted to see.

Until the revelations about his private life became known, the assumption that America's thirty-fifth president was a devout son of his church formed part of the Kennedy mythology. Richard Cardinal Cushing of Boston depicted Kennedy as a good and devout Roman Catholic who prayed daily—though the archbishop added a qualification that "if he were still with us, we would not mention a matter so intimate."[91] Dave Powers and Kenny O'Donnell, loyal Roman Catholics who were part of Kennedy's "Irish Mafia," described Kennedy as a "more religious man than he appeared to be or wanted to appear to be."[92]

Others found him more attached to his faith than he displayed in public and testify to Kennedy's appreciation for the ritualistic and sacramental side of Roman Catholicism.[93] An Irish American author who became ambassador to Ireland declared that Kennedy's outlook on human nature, government, and politics reflected the philosophy of St. Thomas Aquinas.[94] Sixteen years after the assassination, one author who had never known Kennedy declared that he "was, and should be remembered as, a Catholic statesman and . . . a man who exemplified the best in the Catholic and American traditions."[95] Cardinal Cushing declared that "President Kennedy . . . felt his religion profoundly. It was as natural for him to be a good Catholic as it was to be a good American."[96]

Others who knew Kennedy personally were more tempered in their views. In an interview forty years after Kennedy's death, Sorensen said, "John Kennedy was a faithful adherent but he did not talk about it."[97] Lem Billings, whose reminiscences usually place his friend in the best possible light, said, "I don't think he was a dedicated Catholic . . . but he was a good Catholic."[98] A Secret Service agent assigned to the president wrote that "Kennedy was not, I believe, an overboard Catholic. Since his whole life was spent in hospitals and periods of extreme pain, I am sure he spent a good bit of time in prayer.

But I did not sense," the agent concludes, "that he was a twenty four hour a day Catholic."[99]

Although such accounts indicate that Kennedy held Christian beliefs, some writers and friends believed that he gradually moved after college into a private Unitarianism or even skepticism. "Is any of my Catholicism rubbing off on you?" Kennedy once asked Sorensen. The man he called his "intellectual bloodbank" replied, "No, but I think some of my Unitarianism is rubbing off on you."[100] Spaulding, a Roman Catholic, once declared: "Jack has traveled in that speculative area where doubt lives."[101] The president's partner on the Washington social scene, *Newsweek* and *Washington Post* editor Ben Bradlee, viewed him as a secular person whose interests focused not on religion but on politics, social life, and women. Kennedy's "cool, ironic demeanor did little to suggest a private piety," two historians write.[102] His detached approach to religion caused one of America's leading Protestant church historians initially to view him as "spiritually rootless and politically almost disturbingly secular."[103]

Today the evidence seems clear that Kennedy possessed what might best be seen as a tribal loyalty to the church into which he was born. For his time, Kennedy was a distinctly atypical American Catholic. He laced his speeches with biblical quotations from the Protestant King James Version, not from the Douay-Rheims Version approved by Roman Catholicism. He neither liked marching in St. Patrick's Day parades nor posing for photographs with nuns and priests. He apparently did not kiss bishops' rings. Schlesinger remembered that Kennedy discussed cardinals, bishops, and other clergy "with the same irreverent candor with which he discussed the bosses of the Democratic party."[104] Sorensen added that Kennedy "showed no awe of the Catholic hierarchy."[105] Part of this distance from his church stemmed from his desire to keep a low religious profile in a country where voters were largely non-Catholic. But it also came from his approach to his religious and ethnic heritage.

Whatever they meant for others, such Roman Catholic devotionals as the rosary, the novena, and the benediction of the blessed sacrament seemed of little interest to Kennedy. When he visited Rome, he found certain of his church's miracles "very difficult . . . to believe."[106] Although he displayed an almost instant bond with members of his staff or Secret Service detail who were Roman Catholic, nothing in his correspondence or conversation indicated that he took any special interest in the history and doctrines of his church or in its popes and saints.[107] Based on their longtime association, Sorensen concluded that Kennedy "cared not a whit for theology."[108] Thus anyone who tried to talk to him about such controversial dogmas as transubstantiation, papal infallibility, or the assumption of the Virgin Mary (proclaimed as infallible dogma while Kennedy served in Congress) probably would have found Kennedy both uninterested and unconcerned.

Unlike Protestants, who believe that Christian institutions can and do err, Roman Catholics believe in the "magisterium"—or divine teaching authority—of their church. When it met in Rome, the Second Vatican Council defined the magisterium in these words:

> The Bishops have by divine institution taken the place of the Apostles as pastors of the church. . . . Whoever listens to them is listening to Christ. . . . The faithful . . . are obliged to submit to their bishop's decision . . . in matters of faith and morals, and to adhere to it with a ready and respectful allegiance of mind.[109]

But the evidence is persuasive that Kennedy did not believe in some of the central teachings of Roman Catholicism.[110] He went through periods of great doubt about his faith. Over his father's objections he wanted to marry a Protestant woman. Ultimately he married a woman who had attended largely Protestant schools and whose mother had left the Roman Catholic Church for the Episcopal Church.

Both before and after marriage, Kennedy's sexual behavior represented the antithesis of Roman Catholic marital teaching. Ralph Dungan has asserted that Kennedy opposed his church's prohibition of birth control.[111] Bradlee remembered that the president was pro-choice on abortion, but that he cautioned him not to print that information.[112] Kennedy also seems to have doubted that he was raised in the one True Church. "He did not believe that all virtue resided in the Catholic Church," Sorensen noted, "nor did he believe that all non-Catholics would (or should) go to hell."[113]

Unless they had a political dimension, Kennedy was essentially uninterested in religious matters. Although Cardinal Cushing declared in his eulogy that Kennedy "was a man of strong religious commitment . . . [with] a faith that was anchored beyond this world, truly in God Himself,"[114] observer after observer asserts that Kennedy, as Lem Billings declared, "never really discussed religion much."[115] In private conversations, he rarely talked about God. "He often discussed his private thoughts with me," Sorensen recalled, "but he never mentioned any explicit hope or fear of an afterlife, or his innermost thoughts on man's relation to God."[116] Sorensen also declared that "not once in eleven years, despite all our discussions of church-state affairs, did he ever disclose his personal views on man's relation to God."[117]

When Kennedy referred to God in his speeches, Sorensen asserted, he seemed to do so more as "a matter of political convention than religiosity," as many politicians did. "I occasionally wondered," Sorensen wrote, "whether there might have been an element of political necessity as well as personal piety motivating him. As to the balance between the two, no one but JFK could know, and he never said."[118]

Yet no one should think of Kennedy as a nominal Roman Catholic who seriously considered leaving his faith as an adult. Although he attended Episcopal schools and had large numbers of Episcopalian friends, no evidence seems to exist that he ever thought of converting to the Episcopal or to any other Protestant form of Christianity. The same seems true of Jackie.

Clearly Lee Bouvier, Jackie's sister, displayed the same unwillingness to leave the church in which she was baptized for any other church. When her second marriage to Prince Stanislaw Radziwill broke up, she could have just let it go. But significantly, she did not. She remained so concerned with staying in communion with her church that she went to great trouble and expense—including one lobbying visit to Rome with Jackie—to secure annulments of her first two marriages so that she could marry under church auspices a third time.

Kennedy had minimal interest in the evangelical Protestantism represented by Billy Graham. Harry Truman had given the young evangelist short shrift, but Graham had become closely associated with the Eisenhower administration. In the 1960 election, he had openly supported and advised Richard Nixon, attended some of Nixon's rallies, and implicitly endorsed him at a national news conference. Following the election, Kennedy played golf with Graham several times, posed for photographs with him at national prayer breakfasts, and secured his help on civil rights legislation. But their meetings were few, and the president never allowed the evangelical Graham to become a spiritual adviser or friend.

Through church attendance, catechetical instruction, and the piety of his mother and sisters, Kennedy assimilated more of the substance of his faith than writers often indicate. He attended Mass, married a Roman Catholic wife in a church ceremony, had his children baptized, and carried a St. Christopher medal money clip given to him by Jackie.

Moreover, various observers speak of Kennedy ducking into a church and lighting a candle for his deceased brother, of attending Mass alone on the morning of his inauguration, or of displaying "a remarkable awareness of the finer points of Catholic dogma" in conversations with clergy.[119] After his unsuccessful meeting with Nikita Khrushchev made nuclear war seem imminent, Kennedy's secretary found a note that he had written to himself. "I know that there is a God and I see a storm coming," the note said, quoting words written by Lincoln prior to the start of the Civil War. "If he has a place for me, I am ready."[120] When a campaign biography described Kennedy as not "deeply religious," he was offended.[121]

From childhood into college, Kennedy regularly attended Mass, though how frequently he attended after college until running for president is unclear. A Roman Catholic on Kennedy's congressional staff asserted that during his years in Congress Kennedy "would go to Mass on Sunday if somebody was watching."[122] When he was a senator, some friends recalled Kennedy's concern as a senator that the spotlight of the presidency would burden him with "Mass every Sunday for four years."[123]

Yet Sorensen, who was closely associated with the president from his senatorial years on, remembered that Kennedy "faithfully attended Mass each Sunday, even in the midst of fatiguing out-of-state travels when no voter would know whether he attended services or not."[124] Agent Gerald Blaine, a member of the Secret Service detail assigned to Kennedy, recalled that

> JFK was a regular church attendee in Washington D.C., Hyannis, Palm
> Beach, Boston and even Middleburg, so I was with him numerous times and
> often sat behind him. . . . President Kennedy always went to the Catholic
> Church unless it involved a funeral service. [He] decided that if he was
> elected as a Roman Catholic that he would carry out all of his obligations.

In the District of Columbia, Blaine recalled, Kennedy's home parish was St. Matthew's Cathedral. He and his advisors selected it not because it was a cathedral but on the basis that it was the closest Roman Catholic church to the White House. On Sundays he attended there, Kennedy would instruct his advance agents to "suggest a short Mass to the priest," Blaine remembered, "and St. Matthew's obliged him."

Upon entering a church for Mass, Kennedy would make the sign of the cross and dip his hand into the holy water at the door. Kennedy did not carry a missal (or Mass book), Blaine recalled, or "any other religious item except his St. Christopher's Medal." The president also did not carry money with him to church. "The agents all learned to have a twenty dollar bill with them," Blaine declared. "President Kennedy . . . would always ask the agent behind him for $20 when the collection plate came around. Evelyn Lincoln [Kennedy's personal secretary] would always reimburse the cash."[125]

As his mother had taught him, Kennedy also said nightly prayers. Cardinal Cushing recalled Joe Kennedy telling him that "there had not been a night since he assumed office when 'Jack' failed to spend some moments on his knees in prayer before closing the long day."[126] His effusive supporter Lem Billings asserted, "I never, never, never remember in my life Jack's missing his prayers at night on his knees." During the Cuban Missile Crisis, JFK not only attended Mass several times but also told a friend that he had spent one day "just listening and praying."[127] One of the president's principal biographers has added a skeptical comment to such recollections: "Kennedy said his prayers in a routine way, and might occasionally have meant them."[128]

In addition, Kennedy went to confession. Billings (though he was often absent from the president's life) declared that Kennedy "always went to confession when he was supposed to."[129] Inevitably, historians know little about Kennedy's use of the confessional, or how often—or even whether—he ever confessed his many adulteries. Apparently, however, he felt no guilt about his promiscuity. "He was very much aware of the rules of the Catholic Church," a cousin who often went to Mass with Kennedy declared. "But like all of us, he was a human being and all of us have failures."[130]

Church historians could employ many terms—'unorthodox Catholic,' "largely free-thinking Catholic,'"detached Catholic," "French Catholic," "practicing non-Catholic," "Deist," or (to use the adjective Harry Truman used for his own faith) "Lightfoot Catholic"—to describe the Roman Catholicism practiced by John F. Kennedy. Some or all of these terms would be accurate. Kennedy's religious beliefs and practices place him outside the magisterium and hence outside anything but the most loose definition of Roman Catholicism.

Like Harry Truman, Kennedy attended his ancestral church but was internally at variance with a number of its doctrines and practices. And like Truman, he never left his church. Kennedy "wasn't going to drop his religion," his friend Henry James said:

> He liked the way it made him special, different in a Protestant world. But otherwise it didn't give him the things people need religion for. And he wasn't going to wrestle with what far brighter, more capable, more feeling people did invest in—"I just don't have time for it" [he said].[131]

Even if Kennedy had wished to move to another denomination, leaving Roman Catholicism would have been tantamount to committing political suicide. Because he was essentially uninterested in religion, however, he lacked either the theological or emotional reasons to change his faith. "He felt neither self-conscious nor superior about his religion," Sorensen summarized, "but simply accepted it as part of his life."[132]

As some of his intimates believed at the time, Kennedy seemed closer in his private views of religion to the American founding fathers than he was to the twentieth-century supernaturalist he was believed to be. The ranks of the founding fathers included orthodox Christians, Christians influenced by Deistic thought, and pure Deists. Although Deism had no creed, most Deists believed more or less in five central points of religion: A God exists; God ought to be worshipped; morality is the best way to worship him; humans ought to be sorry for their misdeeds; and there is a life after death, where the good will be rewarded and the evil punished.

Yet the comparison with the Deistic founding fathers is flawed. At best, Kennedy seems to have believed the first point of Deism, remained lukewarm on the second, and believed neither the third nor the fourth. Whether he believed Deism's fifth point is uncertain.

Yet in one way the comparison is helpful, in that Kennedy's religious life did bear a striking similarity to that of a Deistic president such as James Monroe. Raised Episcopalian, Monroe was strongly influenced by Deism while a student at the College of William and Mary. He married an Episcopalian in an Episcopal service, baptized his children and raised them in Episcopal churches, buried his infant son in an Episcopal churchyard, attended Episcopal worship intermittently, and had an Episcopal funeral. Kennedy did the same things, but in a Roman Catholic context.

The surviving evidence seems to indicate that Monroe was unconcerned about formal religious matters from his twenties on and almost totally focused on this world. Biographical entries list him as an Episcopalian, just as they list Kennedy as a Roman Catholic. Technically, however, both believed relatively little of the doctrine proclaimed by their churches. To be sure, Kennedy's private life bore no similarities to the faultless private life of Monroe, but it did parallel that of the Deistic Benjamin Franklin—another native of Boston who followed French patterns of sexual behavior.

Striking opinions about Kennedy's religious faith came from his family. During the 1960 presidential campaign, Jackie Kennedy, who clearly viewed her husband as a less-than-observant member of the faith, lamented to Krock, "I think it's so unfair of people to be against Jack because he is a Catholic. He's such a poor Catholic."[133] After the election, when someone suggested to Eunice Kennedy Shriver that a book should be written about the president and his Roman Catholicism, she candidly replied, "It will be an awfully slim volume."[134] But the most sweeping of the assessments came from Kennedy himself. "If I had to live my life over again," he wrote to a friend, "I would have a different father, a different wife, and a different religion."[135] As one writer declares, no one had ever accused John F. Kennedy "of being overly pious at any point in his life."[136]

In retrospect, the national debate over whether the pope would control John F. Kennedy's actions if he became president was unnecessary. A religious issue did not exist in 1960 any more than it did during the Jefferson/Adams election of 1800. No major difference existed between John F. Kennedy and Richard Nixon over the role of religion in the nation. The secular and Protestant leaders who expressed a concern that Kennedy might bow to the teachings of his church while in office really had nothing to worry about. If the voting public had known in 1960 what writers now know about Kennedy's religious beliefs and private life, they would have been far more concerned about his personal behavior or medical history than about his church affiliation. His private life alone would have cost him the election.

While riding in a motorcade in Dallas, Texas, on November 22, 1963, John F. Kennedy was assassinated by an ex-marine named Lee Harvey Oswald.[137] At Parkland Memorial Hospital, after "a small army of doctors" worked on the president, the pastor of Holy Trinity Church in Dallas administered the last rites of the Roman Catholic Church.[138] Three days later, after his funeral Mass at St. Matthew's Cathedral in Washington, the forty-six-year-old Kennedy was buried at Arlington National Cemetery. One writer quotes the reaction of presidential aide McGeorge Bundy: "And then it was . . . 'like the fall of a curtain, or the snapping of taut strings.'"[139]

# Lyndon Baines Johnson

1908–1973 ⟶ PRESIDENT FROM 1963 TO 1969

Lyndon Baines Johnson (known as "LBJ" during his political career) never made a public display of his religion. "He was always very reticent about his version of Christianity," one biographer wrote. "This caused many to assume he was unmoved by religion."[1] In 1967, however, Johnson's visit to one church occupied national and international news for many days.

During a weekend visit to Virginia's colonial capital of Williamsburg, the president and his wife, Lady Bird, worshipped at historic Bruton Parish Church. Built in 1715, this Episcopal church is located near the center of Colonial Williamsburg. Its rector, or chief minister, in 1967 was the Reverend Cotesworth Pinckney Lewis.[2] An accomplished preacher, Lewis devoted his sermon that Sunday to a criticism of Johnson's conduct of the war in Vietnam. During the sermon, he turned to address Johnson (who was seated in the Royal Governor's Pew across from the pulpit) directly. "We are mystified," he declared,

> by news accounts suggesting that our brave fighting units are inhibited by directives and inadequate equipment from using their capacities to terminate the conflict successfully. While pledging our loyalty, we ask humbly, "Why?"

After the service, Lewis walked the Johnsons to their car. An angry Johnson shook hands with the minister but said nothing. But Lady Bird Johnson, who was raised in the Old South part of Texas, displayed her Southern manners by finding something in the service to praise. "Wonderful choir," she told Lewis.[3]

In the following weeks, this sermon caused a national furor. Gaining international press coverage, it became the topic of discussions on television and in newspaper columns. Williamsburg's mayor wrote to Johnson to apologize.[4] When Lewis himself wrote to the president a few days after the mayor, Johnson responded:

If there were "more persuasive methods," as you put it . . . to explain our goals in Vietnam I would try them. To me, the issues involved in that complex and tragic war are . . . simple and clear: whether an aggressor should be permitted to overcome an unwilling people by force; whether the United States should honor a pledge . . . whether our people have the will . . . to endure a long struggle . . . [in which] men must risk and sometimes give their lives.

No one . . . could be more acutely aware of that than I am. Yet I believe our continued commitment to the war . . . will reduce the number of men, in this and coming generations, who will have to take that risk.[5]

Supporters of the war, including some members of the vestry that governed Bruton Parish Church, viewed the rector as having grossly overstepped his place. "This man," declared Johnson's home pastor at the National City Christian Church in the nation's capital, deliberately prepared a sermon to deliver to the President. I never did this, and [I] never would have done it. . . . I think it was very poor taste for anyone, particularly a minister, to take advantage of the President's presence to preach to him . . . . I think it's very cheap, vulgar, and almost unpardonable.[6]

Yet by the fall of 1967, the number of Americans who opposed the war in Vietnam was steadily increasing. These opponents praised Lewis for having the courage to speak out against what they saw as an unjustified and destructive war. In the library of the College of William and Mary, where he deposited his papers upon retirement, Lewis's correspondence for 1967 and 1968 displays substantially more letters of support than opposition for his sermon.

Across the nation, clergy divided on the propriety of the sermon, but many rallied behind Lewis on theological grounds. Pointing to the story of Micaiah and Ahab in the Hebrew Bible, they contended that God created the office of prophets to serve as an ethical checkmate against tyrannical kings. In the Judeo-Christian tradition, religion was not intended to be all sop and sweetness. Those who spoke for God were to be something other than yes-men for royal policies.[7] But the leader of a nation who held services of worship in his official residence would rarely hear a contrary or challenging word.

Thus the ministerial fellowship of the Williamsburg area—which included moderates, conservatives, and liberals—voted to support the theological appropriateness of Lewis's questioning of the president.

What relatively few people realized was that the Episcopal cleric's criticism of President Johnson came from the political right rather than from the political left. A Republican, Lewis actually supported an intensification of the war; in 1967, most Republicans generally favored more, not less, military involvement in Vietnam. Although the content of his sermon made that viewpoint clear, most of the press and the critics of Lewis assumed that he was an opponent of the war, or a "dove." In many ways a gifted pastor, Cotesworth Lewis was also well known in the Williamsburg community as a person of high ambition, with an ego to match.

Few religious acts of an American president in recent years have received more press coverage than Johnson's visit to this colonial Episcopal church. The coverage paralleled that given in 2008 to the Reverend Jeremiah Wright's "God damn America" sermon delivered at Barack Obama's church in Chicago.

But within the year after his visit to Williamsburg, Johnson's conduct of the Vietnam War precipitated his downfall. He raised the number of U.S. military in Vietnam from 16,300 in the year he took office to more than 500,000 by 1968. Although estimates of deaths in the war vary widely, at least 40,000 American military and over 500,000 South Vietnamese military and civilians died. Among the Viet Cong and North Vietnamese, the deaths numbered over 1,000,000.

In addition to the immense loss of life, the war created massive federal deficits and undercut Johnson's reputation. American history may remember Lyndon Johnson better for the Vietnam War than for his vision of a Great Society. Presidential scholars, however, increasingly believe that the landmark legislation Johnson passed will ultimately demonstrate that he was much more than a failed president.

The oldest in a family of five children, Lyndon Baines Johnson was born in 1908 in a small farmhouse in semiarid central Texas. The farmhouse was on his grandfather's ranch, which Johnson subsequently purchased and incorporated into his own LBJ ranch. His family, who had been in Texas for generations, was instrumental in establishing nearby Johnson City. LBJ's father, Samuel Ealy Johnson Jr., was a Texas farmer, businessman, and state representative who fell into substantial debt after losing his legislative seat in 1924. Unable to find a permanent job, he lost the family farm. Thus LBJ grew up in a family always short of money. By the 1930s, the Johnsons were living at the poverty level.[8]

LBJ's mother, Rebekah Baines Johnson, came from genteel Texas stock and graduated from Baylor University. Her background included several generations of Baptist ministers. Her grandfather is credited with leading president Sam Houston of the Republic of Texas to Christian belief. During his Washington years, Johnson used to brag that "my ancestors were teachers and lawyers and college presidents and governors when the Kennedys in this country were still tending bar."[9]

Although LBJ gave idealized descriptions of his mother, a close political adviser who came to know her declared that "a more accurate description would include such adjectives as tough, stern, unyielding, obstinate, domineering. She was an unrelenting snob ... [about] ... her ancestry."[10] Although Rebekah was influential in LBJ's life, most biographers believe that he gained more of his temperament and attributes from his father, Sam Ealy Johnson Jr.

Religiously—like many Texans—Johnson came from largely Baptist stock on both sides of his family. But his paternal grandfather, Sam Ealy Johnson Sr., left his Baptist heritage and joined the Christadelphians, a small sect of lay Christians who practice foot-washing, attempt to follow the practices and beliefs of earliest Christianity, and reject the doctrine of the eternality of hell. That the question of hell troubled Lyndon Johnson for most of his life may have stemmed from discussions on this subject with his father, who occasionally attended Christadelphian meetings.

In later years, Johnson remembered his mother, who remained ardently Baptist, as a "highly religious person" who gathered up the children for Sunday school, taught a Bible class, and never missed church. "Every summer," he remembered, "she, all the kids, aunts, uncles, and grandparents would go to the camp meetings."[11] Prevalent throughout the South and Midwest from the nineteenth century on, camp meetings were evangelistic gatherings held outdoors or in a tent featuring preaching and exhortation.

But LBJ's father was not an active churchgoer. "Daddy didn't go to church very often, practically never," LBJ's brother Sam Houston Johnson wrote in 1969. In that way, LBJ's father differed from many Texans of his time. He also differed by opposing prohibition, believing in Darwinism, and voting for the Roman Catholic presidential candidate Al Smith.[12] At times he attended the Christian Church (also called the Disciples of Christ [DOC]) in Johnson City. Lyndon Johnson would later join this church.

Emerging from Pennsylvania and Kentucky during the early nineteenth century, the DOC sought to end denominationalism and to unite all Christians in one body. Viewing the Bible much as nineteenth-century Americans viewed the Constitution, the church operated according to two mottos: "Where the Scriptures speak, we speak; where the Scriptures are silent, we are silent" and "Bible names for Bible things." The first motto meant that the movement rejected "manmade" creeds and attempted to teach only what the New Testament explicitly taught. The second motto caused its churches to use such Biblical terms as "Lord's Supper" and "elder" and to shun such later terms as "reverend" and "sacrament."

Young Lyndon spent his childhood and youth largely in Johnson City. "Homogeneous white, Anglo-Saxon, Protestant," the town had three churches: the Baptist (to which half of the residents belonged), the Methodist, and the Christian Church. Similar in most of their teachings, the three churches often shared a common service.[13]

A biographer describes Johnson City in LBJ's childhood as "hard-shell, hellfire, revivalist, fundamentalist, Old Testament religious."[13] Most residents neither drank alcohol nor danced; they also did not gamble or play cards. Children often played games based upon the Bible. As a boy Johnson often won at "Swords," a game that involved memorization of Scripture. When the children played "Church," a sister recalled that Johnson always insisted on being the preacher.[14]

Despite the predominance of Baptists in the area and his mother's devout faith, Johnson was never strongly attracted to the Baptist church. Although he thought his mother a saintly woman, he followed instead the religious path of the males who were most influential in his life.

Like camp meetings, revivals were part of the religious and social fabric of rural Texas. In Johnson City, the Baptists and the Methodists were revivalistic, but the Christian Church was less so. Although it sponsored revivals, its evangelism aimed more for an intellectual assent from unbaptized persons than for an emotional conversion experience.

In keeping with its interpretation of the New Testament, the Christian Church taught that church membership required a person to go through five stages: acceptance of Jesus as Messiah and son of God, repentance of personal sins, baptism by immersion, and remission of sins, followed by the gift of the Holy Spirit. Because the church also believed (as did the Baptists) that early Christians did not baptize infants, it only baptized adults or young adults who could make the necessary intellectual assent. Thus the DOC concluded their occasional revivals by immersing (the New Testament and early Christian method of baptism) all adults or young people who publicly accepted these teachings.

At the end of one such revival in Johnson City in July 1923, the adolescent Lyndon Johnson confessed his belief in Jesus Christ as his Lord and Savior and was immersed. Exactly where he was baptized is unclear.[15] Family tradition also differs on whether Johnson joined the Christian Church because he was impressed by the arguments of evangelists at the revivals, or whether he chose to be baptized because (as his mother apparently believed) he was trying to impress a young lady he had escorted to the revivals every night.[16]

What is clear is that while the Baptist, and to some extent the Methodist, churches in the Johnson City area featured extensive talk of hellfire, the Christian Church was more subdued on the topic. In later years, Johnson declared that most of the local preachers would convince hearers they were "goin' to hell in a hack. . . . I got to believin' it pretty deep."[17] But from adolescence on, Johnson seems to have preferred a faith that did not emphasize fire and brimstone. In general, he was also never comfortable with born-again theology.

Thus apparently on his own and without family consultation, the fourteen-year-old chose the least evangelical and most ecumenical of Johnson City's three churches. He became a member of the First Christian Church (DOC) of Johnson City and remained officially a member for the rest of his life. Johnson's later political model of "Come now and let us reason together" — a quotation taken from the first chapter of the Book of Isaiah — applies also to the way the DOC approaches matters of theology, worship, and churchgoing.[18]

Prior to his baptism, Johnson had not been particularly religious. Becoming a member of the Christian Church seemed to cause little change in his lifestyle. He drank alcohol with friends, got into fights, and did not excel academically. When he graduated from Johnson City High School at the age of fifteen, he ended his schooling against his mother's wishes.[19]

After high school, Johnson went to California and worked for a time as an elevator operator and in other miscellaneous jobs. Returning to Johnson City, he did road construction. When he decided to go to college in 1926, he borrowed $75 (the equivalent in 2010 of roughly $1,000) and began his freshman year at Southwest Texas State Teachers College at San Marcos, now Texas State University–San Marcos. "When he was going to college in San Marcos," longtime aide to Lady Bird and to LBJ Liz Carpenter commented in an interview, "I bet he showed up at church. He enjoyed going to class and anywhere there were people." Dropping out for a year to teach at a Mexican American grade school, Johnson worked his way through school and graduated in 1930. After an additional year of teaching, he went to Washington to work for a Texas congressman.

In 1934, while visiting his home state, he met Claudia Alta Taylor (1912–2007), who in childhood had gained the name of "Lady Bird." The descendant of prominent families, Lady Bird came from a varied denominational background. Raised a Methodist, she was interested in religion and devoted some of her private reading to it. Her father was sufficiently affluent that he paid the full salary of the pastor of the Methodist church the family attended.

Lady Bird's family sent her as a boarding student to Dallas's elite St. Mary's Episcopal School. She attended the obligatory Episcopal services and subsequently converted to the Episcopal church. According to LBJ's brother, Johnson asked her to marry him on their first date. Ten weeks later, she and Johnson were married on short notice in St. Mark's Church in San Antonio, Texas, by an Episcopal rector she had never met. The couple were wed with a ring Johnson had bought at a department store for $2.50.[20] At the end of the service, the pastor—who had been unable to hold premarital conferences with the couple because of the rush—was heard to say, "I hope this marriage lasts."[21]

The marriage did last, but only because Lady Bird chose to remain in it. In the words of one biographer, Johnson's "abusiveness" toward Lady Bird became "sort of a matter of legend . . . not only because of his affairs, which were carried out sometimes very openly, but because of the way he would . . .

talk, and yell at [her] in front of other people. . . . Every woman sympathized with her."[22] As the years went on, Lady Bird became a successful business-woman through the ownership of radio and television stations in Texas.

Lady Bird once called herself "a great advocate of going to church."[23] She believed in saying grace before meals and maintained an interest in spiritual-ity that continued until her death in 2007. Sam Houston Johnson, Lyndon's brother, once asserted that Lady Bird's consistent church attendance influ-enced that of LBJ. Preferring Episcopal services to those of other Christian denominations, she introduced her husband to this form of worship.

Johnson's Christianity remained nominal and somewhat perfunctory dur-ing his congressional years. But the couple attended—Lady Bird regularly, LBJ less often than Lady Bird wished—Episcopal, Christian (DOC), and other churches both in Washington and at the LBJ Ranch in the Texas Hill Country outside Austin. Prior to 1963, Lady Bird preferred to attend the Washington National Cathedral when the couple was in Washington. Usually Johnson did not accompany her.[24]

Johnson's surge in religiosity came after he assumed the presidency in November 1963. Becoming president did not change his personality, but to some extent it humbled him. "He was always awed by the position," a biographer states.[25] Two months after Kennedy's assassination, Lady Bird noted in her diary that Johnson was now attending church regularly each Sunday. "I am not going to say how glad I am about all this for fear it might somehow evaporate," she wrote, "but I have a feeling it's not going to." She also noted that Johnson now asked that grace be said every evening at dinner— "a custom," Lady Bird noted, "I like and have tried to foster for 29 years."[26]

From 1963 on, Johnson joined the ranks of regular churchgoers. In Johnson City, his home church was the First Christian Church; in Wash-ington, D.C., it was the National City Christian Church. But he attended churches of other denominations, raised his two children Episcopalian, and never made a public display of his church attendance. His state funeral, however, was held at the National City Christian Church.[27]

Lyndon Johnson was a man of enormous appetites. Thus when he became a regular churchgoer, he needed a buffet of churches rather than one or two. In the words of an aide, he liked "to church hop."[28] When overseas, John-son generally went to a principal church in the city he was visiting. During the 1964 presidential campaign, he visited his opponent Barry Goldwater's hometown of Phoenix, Arizona, on the pretext "that they've got a mighty fine preacher at the First Presbyterian Church here."[29] If the numbers were totaled, he may have attended more churches of other denominations during his presidential years than he did services of the Christian Church (DOC).

When at the LBJ Ranch in Texas, Johnson worshipped at a half dozen churches spread over a wide area, usually insisting on driving to them himself. Occasionally he went to one of the churches founded by German immigrants in the Hill Country. After the nineteenth- and early-twentieth-century novelist Karl May created a fascination with the American West among millions of readers, Germans settled in Texas and in other southwestern states. In Johnson's time, some of this German heritage remained in the Johnson City area. Thus when Chancellor Ludwig Erhard of West Germany visited the LBJ Ranch during the Christmas season of 1963, LBJ and Lady Bird took him to Trinity Lutheran Church, located in Stonewall, a tiny town roughly three miles from the ranch. Its pastor, with whom Johnson and Lady Bird occasionally had dinner, conducted a large part of the service in German, and a male choir sang "Stille Nacht."[30]

On other Sundays—or sometimes on the same Sunday—he worshipped at St. Francis Xavier Church, a small Roman Catholic mission church in Stonewall. From the mid-1950s on, Wunibold W. Schneider, a native of Germany, served as its priest. Initially, Johnson tended to visit the church when he accompanied Roman Catholic guests to Mass. "I am not a Catholic," Father Schneider remembered Johnson telling him in their first meeting:

> But I come to your church occasionally, especially when I have friends staying with me from Washington or New York, people who are Catholic. They want to go to church and I go with them because I want to make them feel at home. It's better if I go with them than if I send them off on their own.[31]

When Johnson was vice president, Chancellor Konrad Adenauer of West Germany—a devout Roman Catholic—arrived in Texas with his daughter. Though it was a Sunday, the Adenauers' schedule had prevented them from attending church earlier. Johnson arranged with Schneider's bishop in Austin for a special afternoon Mass (something Roman Catholicism then did not generally permit). The priest not only preached in German but also had the congregation sing German hymns.[32]

Johnson's interest in Roman Catholicism grew after he became president, and Schneider gradually became one of his spiritual advisers. Johnson felt so much a part of the mission church that he once chided the priest for not giving him Holy Communion—which Roman Catholic doctrine of the time did not allow a Protestant to receive. He frequently invited Schneider to dine at the ranch and took him to Adenauer's funeral Mass in Cologne. In 1967 Johnson intervened with Schneider's bishop to prevent the priest's routine transfer to another church.[33]

Sometimes Johnson attended the Episcopal church closest to the ranch—the 130-seat St. Barnabas Church in Fredericksburg—with Lady Bird and his daughters. In the late 1950s, Lady Bird rushed home from the beauty parlor upon hearing that St. Barnabas would be opening and instructed her husband, "We're going to [St. Barnabas] church on Sunday!"[34] Lady Bird remained a member of the church until her death at the age of ninety-four.

Johnson often attended his small home church in Johnson City. A newsman once described it as "a neat, white-painted structure, down a dusty side road, with a notice in the front saying: 'First Christian Church. Welcome.'"[35] The same journalist wrote a vivid description of Johnson worshipping in that church during his presidency:

Even if he wished to worship there unnoticed . . . the President could not do so. When he arrives with his motorcade he is swallowed up outside the church by a crowd of locals, gaping tourists, reporters, police, and television cameras.

Inside, however, Johnson for once is cut off from the trappings of the Presidency. ". . . And the Spirit and the bride say, Come," intones the minister. "And he that heareth, let him say, Come. And he that is athirst, let him come; and whosoever will, let him take the water of life freely." He pauses, and there is absolute silence in the church except for the low drumming of the air conditioning, a gift of the President.

Then the spruce boy at the piano strikes up the rousing old-time tune of "Sowing in the Morning," and as the rumbling voice of the President joins the rest of the congregation—the men ill at ease in their unfashionable suits, the old ladies proud under their elaborate hats—the atmosphere in the church seems suddenly much closer to the vanished frontier than to present-day Washington.

When the minister . . . deliver[s] his sermon, the connection between the President and the church seems still more plain, for the art of preaching the word of God and the art of political oratory are, in the West, allied. The big man wedged into the pew and the bespectacled minister, a row of pens in his breast pocket, both employ comparable techniques: the same beseeching, the same use of rambling stories from rural experience to make a point, the same wide-arm gestures, the same intense personal appeal to "each and every one of you."

One of the preacher's constant themes is the search for Christian unity; it is conceivable that this central tenet of the Disciples of Christ . . . is connected by subterranean wiring to the President's own constant advocacy of the need for "consensus."

However this may be, there is no doubt that the President, on these churchgoing occasions . . . feels himself to be an intimate part of the small local community. "Ah was *looking* for you," he says to an old man after the service, gripping him above the elbow, and asks a small boy, "Are you Linda's brother?"

Then, waving and smiling, he gets behind the wheel of his station wagon and leads his motorcade back to the ranch, the helicopters, and the decisions.[36]

On some Sundays Johnson did not leave the ranch to go to church. Instead, he would invite a pastor from a Protestant denomination to conduct a private service for the family and guests. Sometimes Billy Graham officiated at the services. According to a member of the press assigned to cover LBJ, one clergyman—probably Episcopalian—failed to bring a sufficient number of wafers for the service of Holy Communion. The reporter wrote that Johnson became so furious that he did not invite the minister, as was his custom, to stay for lunch.[37]

In Washington, Lady Bird and their school-age daughters, sometimes accompanied by LBJ, seemed to have initially attended the Washington

National Cathedral on Sundays. Subsequently, they attended St. Mark's Episcopal Church on Capitol Hill. Its pastor, William Baxter, was the father of one of Luci Baines Johnson's classmates at the National Cathedral School, an Episcopal institution. Johnson worshipped in the church infrequently prior to becoming president. On the Sunday after the assassination of John F. Kennedy, however, he chose to attend St. Mark's, perhaps because he knew the press would be expecting him to attend the National City Christian Church and would be present there in force.[38]

Forming a friendship with the rector, Johnson began to attend St. Mark's with some frequency and asked that the church's bulletin be sent to him. He even went to the coffee hour following services, accompanied by an ever-vigilant Secret Service contingent who would have been enormously relieved if their charge had stayed away from church coffee hours. When Rector Baxter participated in the civil rights march on Selma, he notified Johnson that he planned to speak about his experiences on the next Sunday and that Johnson might not wish to attend. Instead, Johnson showed up at the service and brought with him vice president Hubert Humphrey, secretary of defense Robert McNamara, and former presidential candidate Adlai Stevenson.[39]

In the latter part of the 1960s, St. Mark's Church was targeted on Sundays by antiwar protesters. Both the focus of the press on Johnson's worship during services and the quiet opposition of a new rector to the war caused the beleaguered president to discontinue his attendance. With demonstrators milling around the church and antiwar banners prominent, "no one was surprised," one St. Mark's historian declared, "when Johnson simply stopped coming."[40]

The president then redirected his attendance to the architecturally imposing National City Christian Church, his denomination's "national church." During his congressional career, he had rarely come to its services, instead confining his attendance largely to the Episcopal churches of his wife and daughters. But in 1961, when Johnson was vice president, National City church called a new pastor, George R. Davis. Davis's preaching style, liberal evangelical theology, and Texas connections appealed to Johnson. Subsequently, Davis became one of only two prominent mainline clergy in Washington to vocally support the Vietnam War.

From the start of his ministry in the capital, Davis attempted to attract Johnson to his church. For example, he designated a special presidential pew. He also wrote numerous lengthy letters to Johnson, whose cordial but briefer replies suggest that the president was less interested in a relationship than Davis might have wished.

Yet Davis developed a relatively close relationship with LBJ. Writing in her diary in 1966 during the escalation of the Vietnam War, Lady Bird indicated that she and her husband planned to attend services on Sunday at the National City Church. "Dr. Davis is a comfort to him," she wrote, "and I seek out comforts for him like a mother seeking medicines for a sick child."[41]

On weekends at Camp David, the Johnsons continued to attend church. They could not worship in a church within Camp David, for the presidential retreat had no chapel until the administration of George H. W. Bush. Visiting clergy (such as Billy Graham) occasionally conducted services in the presidential living quarters at the camp. But often the Johnsons went to one of the neighboring towns for church, especially to the historic Harriet Chapel (Episcopal) in Thurmont, Maryland.[42]

To a remarkable degree, the churches that Lyndon Johnson attended were what Christianity refers to as "liturgical churches." In Christianity, four churches fall into the liturgical category: Roman Catholic, Eastern Orthodox, Episcopal, and Lutheran. These four churches worship in a more formal way than the churches categorized as nonliturgical—such as the Baptist, Methodist, Presbyterian, Pentecostal, Mennonite, and Johnson's own Christian (DOC). Liturgical churches emphasize the Christian sacraments, follow patterns of worship inherited from centuries of Christianity, and tend to be less emotional and more ritualistic than services in nonliturgical churches.

Growing up in Johnson City, Lyndon Johnson had no liturgical church to choose from. But when he selected a church for membership at age fourteen, he significantly chose the one with the least emotional services of the three churches in the town. In later years Johnson, like his wife and daughters, seems to have preferred to worship in liturgical churches. Although his family clearly influenced him, Johnson also seems to have enjoyed the more formal worship offered in liturgical churches. That his brother, Sam Houston Johnson, also became Episcopalian may be significant.[43]

Although he apparently never considered converting to Roman Catholicism, Johnson's affinity for the most liturgical of the Western churches increased from 1964 on. In that year his daughter, Luci, then seventeen, became engaged. In order to convert to the church of her fiancé, Patrick Nugent, she began to take instructions from a Roman Catholic priest. "She would like to join the Church as soon as the priest thinks she is ready," Lady Bird wrote in her diary in November of that year. The entry continued:

> I feel a sense of separation almost as though I were saying good-by to her—as though she were going off to live in "Timbuctoo."
>
> And yet I have never seen her happier or more radiant.... This decision has been coming on for about five years—it is no flash in the pan—so I can't say "no." How could I make it stick? How would I dare presume I was right?[44]

On July 2, 1964, her eighteenth birthday, Luci was baptized by the Reverend James Montgomery at St. Matthew's Cathedral in Washington and welcomed into the Roman Catholic Church. In June, Lady Bird wrote in her diary that she could not "be happy about it," but conceded that Luci had become much happier as her "earnest search" came to an end. In entries written after the service, she noted with concern that daughter Lynda had left the cathedral "swiftly with tears in her eyes and was down the steps and into the car before the rest of us emerged." Lady Bird's feelings of separation and unhappiness seem to have originated in her sense of having lost a daughter rather than from any sort of anti-Catholic sentiment. "I could not help but think we went in four and came out three," she wrote, apparently believing that Luci's becoming Roman Catholic had affected the cohesion of the family.[45]

Becoming front-page news, Luci's baptism sparked controversy in Protestant circles.[46] Even though an Episcopal priest had baptized her at the age of five months with water and in the name of the Holy Trinity in St. David's Episcopal Church in Austin, Father Montgomery poured water on her forehead during the Mass and said the words of "conditional baptism": "If you have not been baptized, I baptize you in the name of the Father, the Son, and the Holy Spirit."[47]

The conditional baptism was controversial, for it seemed clearly to indicate that Luci's new church viewed Protestant baptisms as potentially invalid. Yet that was not Roman Catholic teaching. During the Catholic Reformation, the sixteenth-century Council of Trent had recognized the validity of Protestant baptisms. Over the centuries, however, many priests had rebaptized all converts "just to be sure."[48] At the time of Luci's rebaptism, the Second Vatican Council was meeting in Rome and seeking ways of promoting Christian cooperation and unity. The assembled bishops displayed no intention of denying the validity of Protestant baptism.

Episcopalians especially protested Luci's rebaptism. The Episcopal bishop of California, James Pike, noted that he had not been rebaptized at the time he converted from the Roman Catholic to the Episcopal faith. He called the rebaptism of Luci "sacrilegious" and a "direct slap at our church." Francis Sayre, grandson of Woodrow Wilson and dean of the Washington National Cathedral, preached a sermon criticizing the baptism as an unecumenical and unnecessary act that insulted the Episcopal church.[49]

Johnson himself reacted angrily not only at the Roman Catholic Church for rebaptizing Luci but also at Pike and Sayre for making a national issue of the matter. What concerned him was the hurt inflicted on his eighteen-year-old daughter, who also received a high number of letters, mostly hostile, about her conversion.[50] "Luci's self-confidence is shaken," Lady Bird wrote in her diary during the controversy. "She is almost hurt and frightened that she should have caused a rift, a disturbance, trouble for her parents . . . between any churches." Johnson's intervention prompted not only the auxiliary bishop of Washington but also Vatican officials to issue a statement declaring that their church had not intended to call Luci's initial baptism into question.[51]

Two years later, in what *Time* magazine called "a semi-monarchical event,"[52] Archbishop Patrick O'Boyle of Washington celebrated a Nuptial Mass for Luci and Patrick. The wedding occurred in Washington's National Shrine of the Immaculate Conception, the largest Roman Catholic church in the United States. Attended by more than seven hundred guests, the wedding was the first ever celebrated in the ornate, still-incomplete cathedral.[53] Johnson had used his great influence to assure that the unfinished cathedral would still be available for his daughter. In 1979, the Nugents divorced, but Luci received an annulment from her church and remarried five years later in a Roman Catholic ceremony at the LBJ Ranch. In 2003, her youngest daughter, Claudia Taylor Brod, who had married into a Jewish family, converted to

Judaism. Luci's sister, Lynda Bird, married Charles S. Robb (later a Virginia governor and U.S. senator) and remains an Episcopalian.

Through Luci and her husband, Johnson came to know several Roman Catholic clergy in Washington. In the years after 1964, he increasingly attended Mass with Luci and Patrick, sometimes accompanied by Lady Bird. In 1967, he attended Mass fourteen times.[54] For Johnson, the Mass was often the second or third service attended on a Sunday.

Although known by the American public for a certain coarseness—he showed scars from an operation at a press conference, for example, and he hoisted beagles by their ears for public display—Johnson was clearly inclined more toward aesthetic and liturgical worship than to the simple low-church Protestant worship he was raised in. As he experienced more and more anguish over the course of the war in Vietnam, he increasingly added attendance at Mass to his Sunday and weekday schedules.[55]

In 1966 Johnson authorized the first air strikes of the oil-pumping and storage facilities around North Vietnam's principal port city, Haiphong, and its capital, Hanoi. The action aroused fears of Chinese intervention and the expansion of the war. "I just know," aide Joseph Califano remembered LBJ telling him on the afternoon of the mission, "that one of our Texas boys, probably from Johnson City, will drop one of those bombs down the smokestack of a hospital or a school and kill a thousand civilians or children."

Following a late evening meeting in that year about the war, Johnson contacted Luci and went with her to pray at Washington's St. Dominic's Chapel, the Roman Catholic church he attended the most frequently. The versions of this account vary in details, but Luci's recollection—written more than thirty years later—reads as follows:

> We went to St. Dominic's Chapel . . . where I joined my father on our knees. I didn't know what Daddy was praying for. I just know that I prayed for him.
>
> When we returned home, my father asked me to stay with him. . . . He climbed onto the bed and lay there sleepless.
>
> Around 3 A.M. he received a call. He answered . . . said "Thank God" and hung up. Only then did he tell me . . . he had sent pilots in to bomb Hanoi Harbor. They had all returned alive. He could sleep now. I could go. . . . The memory today of his angst and relief is as fresh as morning dew.[56]

The account makes no mention of the Vietnamese on the ground.

Of the two other major liturgical churches, Johnson attended Lutheran services from time to time both in Texas and in Washington. He displayed an interest in Eastern Orthodox Christianity, but apparently he did not attend their services. He invited Archbishop Iakovos of the Greek Orthodox Church to give the benediction at his inauguration.[57]

Johnson probably hopped from church to church for a combination of reasons. "He wanted to be free to choose whatever church he wanted to attend that Sunday," said his aide, Jack Valenti.[58] Like most presidents, he was concerned with the effect a large number of journalists, photographers, and tourists had on the worship of a congregation. In addition, eluding the press on Sunday mornings and leaving them lost and confused about what church he was attending undoubtedly amused him. Moreover, in the words of aide Liz Carpenter, "He was always campaigning. . . . He knew it was good politics to vary which church he attended."[59] Finally, his own personality seemed to require moving from church to church.[60]

Thus Johnson varied the churches he attended—Christian (DOC), Episcopal, Roman Catholic, Lutheran, Baptist, and others. Eluding his entourage was more difficult in the urban confines of the District, but even from the White House Johnson occasionally ventured without announcement as far as the Virginia and Maryland suburbs to attend church.

At the LBJ Ranch on Sunday mornings, however, Johnson found his métier. Since he was often at his most expansive after church, the journalists assigned to the ranch knew they could secure lengthy and detailed interviews if they simply followed LBJ to Sunday worship. But following Johnson to church wasn't always easy, for he drove to church at high speed. An Associated Press photographer once declared that he reached 85 miles per hour down Texas back roads and still could not catch up with LBJ on his way to church. The AP's Frances Lewine once drove 200 miles in the Hill Country on a Sunday morning looking for LBJ at church. To track Johnson on Sunday mornings, journalists ultimately set up a walkie-talkie network. "Come on in," Johnson would typically say to reporters who caught up with him at the church. "You need this more than I do."[61]

A man who liked people, Lyndon Baines Johnson was a master negotiator (or what others called a "political arm twister"). He respected intelligence.

Thus he sought out the best people for his cabinet, despite his apprehensions about his own education at Southwest Texas State Teachers College. A genuine sympathizer with the hopes and problems of common Americans, he was dedicated to his Hispanic students as a young teacher. As president, he opposed what he called "preachers and teachers of injustice" and once told the segregationist governor of Alabama to "start thinking 1965, not 1865."

Johnson was one of only three senators from the Confederate states who refused to sign the Southern Manifesto of 1956, which rejected the Supreme Court decision to outlaw segregated schools. He hired the first African American in the position of presidential secretary and integrated a private Texas club by taking her there with him. He was a product of the New Deal, and he continued its expansion in his administration. His boyhood church taught him that Christians should be concerned with the weak and the powerless, and he sponsored powerful legislation that dramatically changed American life.[62]

Yet Johnson also possessed a large but fragile ego. Intensely political from a very young age, he could be as manipulative as any politician. A womanizer, he was accused by evangelist Pat Robertson of "possessing the easy morality and arrogance of [a] Texas wheeler-dealer."[63] A vain man who craved attention, he gave a bust of himself to Paul VI during a visit to the pope in 1967.[64]

Johnson expected his staff to do what he said and to ask no questions. Capable of treating people appallingly, he often undercut his kind and gracious side with vulgarity, dishonesty, and cruelty. He was almost paranoid about the Kennedy family and about what he called "the Eastern crowd." Those feelings about being the first American president to lose a war and what the Kennedys would say may have caused him to continue a war that now-declassified conversations with his advisers show that he and others doubted could be won as early as the mid-1960s.

The enormous death toll and expense of the Vietnam War disproportionately defines Lyndon Johnson's administration. To a significant extent, the war eclipsed his dream of a Great Society. During his five years in office, the initial chant of many Americans of "All the way with LBJ" changed to "Hey, hey, LBJ, how many kids did you kill today?" That Johnson waged a war on poverty and persuaded a recalcitrant Congress to pass such landmark legislation as the Civil Rights Act, Medicare, the Open Housing Law, the

Education Act, and clean air laws tends to be forgotten. The title of Califano's reminiscences—*The Triumph and Tragedy of Lyndon Johnson*—encapsulates his presidential years.

In his final hours in the White House, Johnson wrote to the general secretary of the National Council of Churches that "[t]hroughout my days in the White House, I have found my strength in the Church."[65] Those close to Johnson agreed that he spent substantial time on religious matters. He steadily corresponded with clergy during his administration. When he received especially complicated letters from clergy, he delegated answering them to the theologically trained Bill Moyers, one of his top aides.

Sometimes, the president corresponded with clergy about the war in Vietnam. "I am comforted by the thought that more things are wrought by prayer than man dreams of," he wrote in 1967 to his pastor at the First Christian Church of Johnson City:

> Our struggle in Vietnam is just, because we believe that man is born to freedom and dignity and that peace is the House of all. Our ultimate purpose in denying aggression is to assure that man will find fulfillment as an instrument of God's will.[66]

To Father Schneider of St. Francis Xavier, he wrote in the same year:

> What a wonderful apostle you are of Pope John's preaching: "Everything can be lost if men do not find some way to work together to save the peace." The day must surely come when God will reward our struggle in Vietnam by bringing all of his flock together in that belief.[67]

Although his communication with clergy and laity could be perfunctory, the sheer number of letters about religion in LBJ's papers displays a concerted effort to engage the religious aspect of American life. Unlike such presidents as Truman and Kennedy, he liked to associate with clergy. "More ministers were in the White House during [LBJ's] administration than during the administration of any other president," Davis said, "of all denominations, of all colors."[68] Billy Graham, who spent extensive time with the president, once noted that Johnson "always liked to have preachers around him."[69] LBJ's chief of staff declared that "Johnson was putty in the hands of preachers. However tough and profane he might be with others, that all disappeared whenever he was in the presence of a religious leader he respected."[70] At the same time, LBJ possessed a large repertory of stories about Texas preachers that he would tell in the most unlikely settings.

Johnson's religious views were broad and generalized. Valenti declared that the president found "rigidly-fixed doctrine as unappetizing in religion as he disavowed it in politics."[71] LBJ was not given to asking deep, probing questions about religion. "I'm not a theologian. I am not a philosopher. I am just a public servant," he once said.[72] Valenti noted that Johnson only smiled in response to unfounded stories that said the president was about to follow his daughter into the Roman Catholic Church. "He was as far from conversion to any certain faith," Valenti wrote, "as he was beyond being tied to predictions about political behavior in his fellow man."[73]

Yet the evangelical roots of Johnson's upbringing in rural Texas remained with him until death. He was raised in the South at the time when it was the most churchgoing area of the United States. He remembered the revivalistic, hellfire atmosphere of Johnson City and the hymns he had learned as a boy. For that reason, Billy Graham—who had essentially been shut out of the Kennedy administration—was able quickly to become LBJ's "unofficial chaplain."[74] George Davis tried hard, but it was Graham who got the headlines.

As late as 1964, Johnson replied to the letters Graham sent him with "Dear Dr. Graham." But the greeting soon changed to "Dear Billy."[75] Graham spent hundreds of hours with Johnson. He stayed at the White House, at Camp David, and at the LBJ Ranch. Although he opposed segregation, he had not directly participated in the civil rights movement of Martin Luther King Jr., choosing to watch the March on Washington on television. But he publicly supported such legislative programs of Johnson as the War on Poverty. In addition, he supported Johnson's continuation of the war in Vietnam.[76]

Graham served as not only a friend but also a religious counselor to Johnson. "They liked each other and used each other," Liz Carpenter declared. "Billy Graham stayed at the White House a lot. LBJ thought it looked good to have a popular religious figure around."[77]

Graham himself asserted that the president was "always a little bit scared of death." Graham remembered an evening spent driving around the LBJ Ranch in Johnson's convertible. When the president pulled over to watch the sun go down, the trailing Secret Service car also pulled over.

In Graham's recollection, Johnson then turned to him and in a serious tone said, "You know, Billy, I know that I've received Christ. I'm not sure in my heart that I'm really going to heaven." Johnson had of course been concerned with hellfire since his childhood in Johnson City. When Graham then asked if the president had ever personally declared Jesus Christ as his savior, LBJ replied, "Well, Billy, I think I have. I did as a boy at a revival meeting. I guess I've done it several times."

"When someone says that, Mr. President," Graham responded, "I don't feel too sure of it. It's a once-for-all transaction. You receive Christ, and he saves you." It was the same classic evangelical interpretation of the New Testament that Graham had explained to Harry Truman in 1950.

When Johnson said little in response, Graham continued by saying, "Why don't you just make this a *definite* moment that you can remember, that you've received Christ?" In Graham's account, Johnson then bowed his head over the steering wheel. With the Secret Service not only watching but probably puzzling in their car behind, the president and the evangelist prayed together. Graham concluded: "And he did [accept Christ]. And I thought that was true—though only the Holy Spirit knows."[78]

On the airplane back to Texas immediately after leaving office, LBJ began to resume the habits that his physicians had told him could cause a second and fatal heart attack. "He drank more freely, smoked two and three packs of cigarettes a day," one of his biographers writes, "ate rich foods . . . and mainly counted work around the ranch as exercise."[79] A biographer of Lady Bird describes the scene:

> The moment Johnson boarded the airplane, he lit up a cigarette and drew several deep breaths into his lungs. Luci begged him to put out the cigarette. His doctors had issued orders that he could not smoke, drink, or eat to excess if he hoped to extend his life. "How could you smoke now?" Luci asked her father. Her son, Lyn, then only eighteen months old, must have been alarmed by his mother's reaction, because Lyn pointed to his grandfather's cigarette and motioned for him to put it out. . . .
>
> "Luci," snapped LBJ, "take that child out of here. . . . Look," exploded Johnson, "for fourteen years I've wanted to smoke when I wanted to smoke and

for fourteen years I had a country to serve, children to raise, and a job to do. Now, the job is done, the children are raised. It's my turn."[80]

"Already," the writer concludes, "LBJ was preoccupied with death."[81] In retirement at the LBJ Ranch, he fell into depression, emerging from it only to concentrate on the affairs of the ranch in an inflated and artificial way. He experienced a major heart attack in June 1972. A prominent visitor to the ranch that summer remarked that Johnson "struck me as a man who really knew he had something terribly wrong with him."[82] In January 1973, LBJ died at the ranch at the age of sixty-four. He died generally unmourned by the electorate who had returned him to office nine years earlier with 486 of 538 electoral votes and 61 percent of the popular vote.

Lyndon Johnson served as president during a period when American culture began to change significantly. Although he has borne the guilt for the Vietnam War, it lasted until 1975. Until 1968, public opinion polls, most members of Congress, and all but one of the national security advisers who had come into his administration from the Kennedy years supported the war.[83] Even in 1972, George McGovern, the Democratic presidential candidate who ran on an anti–Vietnam War platform, won less than 38 percent of the popular vote.

A recent biography may have accurately assessed the principal problems of the war:

> The government of South Vietnam, though often changed, stayed corrupt and inefficient and unable to command the loyalty of its people. This meant that ultimately the South was going to lose and that all Johnson would accomplish by continuing the war was the death of more Americans and Vietnamese. Johnson's failure comes down to the simple fact that he could not bear to lose a war. He was wrong.[84]

But even opponents of the war saw Johnson as right in his many legislative enactments. His continuation of the New Deal and Fair Deal, for right or wrong, immensely expanded the federal role in helping the have-nots in American society. He achieved the passage in Congress of such Kennedy goals as civil rights and Medicare. A principal aide of Kennedy came to view LBJ as "the best legislative mind and operator in the modern era."[85] In the assessment of one biographer, only the thirteen-year presidency of Franklin Delano Roosevelt equals the legislative achievement of LBJ's six years as president.[86]

A man of wide-ranging interests, Lyndon Johnson was a president of many surprises. Writers have often described him as "bigger than life"; he described himself "a cross between a Baptist preacher and a cowboy."[87] Central to his personality was his dislike of being alone, "not for an evening or for an hour. Always there were people, in his office, at his house, in the swimming pool."[88] And church was where people were on Sundays. Thus it is not startling to discover that Johnson was more interested in attending church than most Americans would have guessed.

Lyndon Johnson's background in the Christian Church (DOC) significantly influenced his religious views. As a teenager, he chose a form of Protestant Christianity dedicated to ending denominationalism and uniting all believers in one church. This background, along with a certain amount of broad-mindedness in his personality, caused Johnson to be remarkably tolerant in religious outlook. An aide described him as "the most tolerant man I have ever known about other men's religious beliefs."[89]

Lyndon Johnson "was an ecumenist before the word gained credence," Valenti wrote. "Before and after being president he could attend a Catholic church, a synagogue, or any one of a number of Protestant services with equal passion and participation."[90] Archbishop O'Boyle of Washington once called him "the chief ecumenist in this ecumenical age."[91] A reporter once observed Johnson attending Roman Catholic and Episcopal services back to back during a weekend at the ranch. When he asked the president if he also planned to attend "your own church"—that is, the First Christian Church (DOC) of Johnson City—Johnson replied with a smile, "All of them are mine."[92]

# Richard M. Nixon

*1913–1994* ⟿ PRESIDENT FROM 1969 TO 1974

Richard Milhous Nixon—the middle name came from his mother's German heritage—was born in Yorba Linda, a small town southeast of Los Angeles. He was raised in the evangelical wing of Quakerism. "No one," Nixon wrote, "could have had a more intensely religious upbringing."[1]

The Religious Society of Friends (or Quakers) emerged from the left, or radical, wing of the Puritan movement in England. The Puritans attempted to "purify" the Church of England of what they considered unbiblical beliefs and practices—such as rule by bishops, elaborate liturgy and vestments, and intercessory priests. Puritans of the Puritans, the Quakers went further, eliminating not only formal liturgy but also sermons, clergy, sacraments, and creeds. In their place, the Quakers emphasized the direct revelation of Jesus Christ within each individual. Believing that the Christian churches had become the vassals of secular governments, they also opposed military service, the taking of oaths, and social hierarchies.

Originally, Quaker worship was silent, except when the Spirit prompted members to speak. In the United States, however, some Quaker meetings were influenced by Unitarianism or evangelicalism. Although Friends meetings influenced by these theological currents held to such traditional teachings as nonviolence and plainness, they often had clergy trained in seminaries, programmed services of worship with music, Bible study classes, and Sunday schools. Such Quaker "churches"—a term the evangelicals used instead of the traditional Quaker designation "meeting"—were more prevalent in the western United States.

Like most evangelical Quaker churches at the time, Nixon's church opposed dancing. Unlike silent-meeting congregations, the East Whittier Friends church had a piano. As a boy, Nixon—who had learned from an aunt how to play—sometimes accompanied the church service. As a teenager, he also became president of the church's chapter of Christian Endeavor, a highly evangelical national organization of youth whose membership spanned at least thirty denominations.

The East Whittier Friends Church was sufficiently evangelical that one of Nixon's grade school teachers described it as little different from the rural Methodist churches she knew.[2] Because it served a large area and had to accommodate Protestants of various backgrounds, both the pastor (Harold Walker) who served the church during World War II as well as a childhood friend of Nixon described the church as a "community church." Many young males in the congregation, for example, never really embraced Quaker teachings about nonviolence and later (like Nixon) fought in World War II. Walker, in fact, claimed that he was the church's only conscientious objector during the war.

Born in 1913 to Francis Anthony (Frank) and Hannah Milhous Nixon, Richard was the second of five sons. On his mother's side, Nixon's ancestors had been Friends for over two hundred years. His great-grandmother, Elizabeth Milhous (whom Nixon remembered from his childhood), gained a national reputation as an impassioned preacher. His highly orthodox grandmother, Almira Milhous, used Quaker plain speech at home. In Nixon's words, she "set the standards for the whole family" and taught "honesty, hard work, do your best at all times . . . humanitarian ideals."[3]

Her daughter Hannah, Nixon's mother, continued the highly orthodox Quaker tradition. To the end of her life, she emphasized the importance of finding "peace at the center." She prayed frequently and ensured that the family began each meal with silent grace. Since the Gospel of Matthew (6:6) records Jesus as saying, "But when you pray, go into your room and shut the door and pray to your Father who is in secret," she went to her room to pray when visitors were present.[4]

When Nixon was nine, his father moved the family to Whittier, California. Founded by evangelical Quakers in 1887, the town was named for the Quaker poet John Greenleaf Whittier. By 1901, the town had a Quaker college, Whittier College, which Nixon would enter in 1930. The evangelical Friends ethos so pervaded the town that the Methodist Pat Ryan, who later married Nixon, experienced a certain amount of culture shock when she arrived to teach in the high school in 1937.

Nixon's family was not as poor as he frequently asserted it was. He was raised somewhere between the lower middle and middle class. In Whittier, Nixon's father turned the old Friends church into a grocery store with gas pumps. Raised a Methodist in the emotional "shouting" days of that denomination, he converted to Quakerism upon marriage. He never lost his evangelical approach to Christianity, however, and became an ardent and even flamboyant teacher in the Sunday school of the East Whittier Friends Church.

Politically, Frank Nixon was a populist Republican who sometimes voted for Democratic presidential candidates.[5] He emphasized to his sons that "by self-discipline and application, anyone in the United States could achieve anything."[6] Some writers have taken a negative view of the father, describing him, for example, as "a loud-mouthed and opinionated bully."[7]

Whether accurately or not, Richard Nixon's many psychobiographers have depicted his childhood as troubled. Some have found his mother highly manipulative and his father so overbearing that he kicked his sons when angry. "To understand Nixon," one political insider declared, "you have to understand his relationship to his father, Frank; the dominant factor in his psyche was rejection by his father, and his love-hate relationship with his father was mostly hate with exaggerated exaltation of his mother, Hannah."[8]

Other writers have seen Nixon's flaws in character as stemming from the deaths of two of his brothers, Arthur in 1925 and Harold in 1933. When Harold died, Nixon went into a long period of withdrawal. In Jonathan Aitken's description, he "emerged as a new and much changed eldest son . . . always in the arena, always competing fiercely, always fighting." Rejecting all such hypotheses, Stephen Ambrose wrote that "nothing in his inheritance or in his environment" explained Nixon's inability to trust.[9]

Psychiatrists would remind biographers that psychoanalysis at a distance without a patient present is liable to inaccuracies and distortions. But whether these psychological interpretations of Nixon are valid, he did repeatedly describe his mother as "a saint," even in his resignation speech from the White House. In addition, even though his memoirs portray his father in positive terms, he talked about him in life far less than he did about his mother. At his mother's funeral in 1967, Nixon was so overcome by emotion that he wept upon leaving the East Whittier Church and was comforted by Billy Graham.

Most biographers have assumed that something scarred Richard Nixon during childhood. Whatever it was, it apparently affected the rest of the Nixon children, for most got into ethical or legal scrapes at some point in their lives. These childhood wounds displayed themselves throughout Nixon's life. Psychiatry might have helped. Yet in Nixon's day, the discovery that a politician had visited a psychiatrist essentially could end a political career. During Nixon's career, rumors persisted that he had sought psychiatric help.

For reasons perhaps stemming from his childhood, he adopted an "us" versus "them" mentality. When he entered politics, Nixon tended from the start to see political opponents as "enemies" whom he had to defeat by any means possible. This instinct exhibited itself as early as college. "There was something mean in him, mean in the way he put his questions, argued his points," remembered his college debate coach, years after graduation.[10] Whatever the cause, the majority of Nixon's biographers have viewed his personality as deeply flawed.

Since education, work, and religion were at the center of the Nixon family's life, the school, the store, and the church were the three hangouts of the sons. The Nixons held family prayers and read the Bible together and on some Sundays went to church four times. After his younger son Arthur died of tuberculosis in 1925, Frank began taking the family to revival meetings held by such famous evangelists as Billy Sunday; the Pentecostal Aimee Semple McPherson; and Paul Rader, America's first nationwide radio preacher.

At a revival held in 1926 by Rader, Frank and several of his sons—including thirteen-year-old Richard—walked forward and publicly committed themselves to Jesus Christ and his service.[11] Thus while technically a Quaker, Richard Nixon went through a conversion experience or public commitment to Jesus Christ and was raised in a highly evangelical atmosphere.

Nixon developed tremendous self-discipline because of this family background. Even in his early years, he developed what his father wanted him to display: a strong work ethic and sense of purpose. A voracious reader, he excelled in school. Although he frequently stayed up late to finish homework, he found time for extracurricular activities, playing violin in the school orchestra and participating in school plays. On the debate team, he demonstrated a natural ability.

Yet he was awkward in social situations, a trait that won him few friends. Although he tried to present himself as "a regular guy," his classmates easily dismissed this façade; he was not popular. The girls in Whittier High School, for example, paid him little attention. Despite this lack of popularity, as sometimes happens in high school politics, Nixon was elected president of the senior class.

Although writers often assert that Nixon graduated second or third in his high school class, Whittier High did not maintain class rankings in 1930.[12] But Nixon clearly excelled, for in his senior year he received the Harvard Club Prize for the most "Outstanding All Around Student" in California. The award provided partial expenses for enrollment at Harvard. But what little extra money the Nixon family had in one of the severest years of the Depression went toward medical treatment for his brother Harold. Thus Nixon lacked the financial resources to attend Harvard.

Instead, Nixon entered Whittier College the next fall. Despite a continued lack of popularity, he was president of the freshman class at Whittier and subsequently president of the student body. In addition, he participated in numerous extracurricular activities. Both in high school and college, Nixon played what one sports historian described as "scrub football—the C team." Although he devoted substantial time to practice, he rarely played in games. Nixon's coach at Whittier allowed him to scrimmage with the varsity, but a teammate used the words "cannon fodder" to describe his role. "Small, slow, and awkward," he essentially had only his tenacity to offer the team. At the college's games, he sat on the bench beside the coach (Wallace Newman, whom he greatly admired) and absorbed the cerebral side of football. From Newman, he learned the adage, "Show me a good loser, and I'll show you a loser."

During his political career, Nixon relaxed by watching professional and intercollegiate athletics. Throughout adult life, he loved to discuss sports with others. In 1971, he actually suggested a play by phone to coach George Allen of the Washington Redskins. "[The] macho culture of college football became Nixon's link to a world denied him by his backgrounds and talents," says one historian of American sports:

He was always able to use his losing seasons in football to project his awkward personality to audiences of sports fans and sports celebrities. Nixon's football . . . was a paradigm for the low points in his political career. There was always a new game and a new season.[13]

In his senior year at Whittier, Nixon enrolled for a course taught by Professor J. Herschel Coffin. In that era, Protestant church colleges (whose curriculum required students to take a certain number of courses in religion) invariably had one or more professors in religion or philosophy who taught a class designed to challenge fundamentalist beliefs. Entitled "The Philosophy of Christian Reconstruction," but known among students as "What Can I Believe?," Coffin's highly regarded two-semester course surveyed biblical scholarship, evolution, theology, and philosophy.[14]

Nixon's private papers in the Nixon Library contain the twelve brief essays—or what he called his "intellectual log"—that he wrote for the course. They even include the grades: on the two- and three-page papers, Nixon received one B, one B+, one A-, and nine As.[15] Most presidents of the United States lack such a treasure trove of religious autobiography, but these thirty-two pages of college essays provide one for Richard Nixon. Intelligent and well written, they shed remarkable light on the change that occurred in his fundamentalist religious views by the age of twenty-one.

"My parents, 'fundamental Quakers,'" Nixon writes in his first essay,

had ground into me, with the aid of the church, all the fundamental ideas in their strictest interpretation. The infallibility of the Bible, the miracles, even the whale story, all these I accepted as facts when I entered college four years ago. . . . Many of those childhood ideas have been destroyed but there are some which I cannot bring myself to drop. . . . I still believe that God is the Creator, the first cause of all that exists . . . [but] I am no longer a "seven day-er!"

My education has taught me that the Bible, like all other books, is a work of man and consequently has man-made mistakes. Now I desire to find a suitable explanation of man's and the universe's creation, an explanation that will fit not only with my idea of God but also with what my mind tells me is right.

In another essay entitled "The Symbolic Importance of the Resurrection Story," Nixon reflects on the central teaching of the New Testament—that the Hebrew God raised Jesus of Nazareth, the Messiah, from the grave after his crucifixion. As the word "symbolic" in the essay title indicates, Nixon reaches similarly unorthodox conclusions:

> It is not necessary to show that Jesus rose from the dead on the third day and then lived on earth for 40 days with his disciples before ascending into heaven. The important fact is that Jesus lived and taught a life so perfect that he continued to live and grow after his death in the hearts of men. It may be true that the Resurrection story is a myth, but symbolically it teaches the great lesson that men who achieve the highest values in their lives may gain immortality.

Although that statement placed Nixon in the camp of Unitarianism (or what at the time was also called "modernism"), he still held this interpretation eleven years before his death. In 1983 he told a television interviewer that his "good friend" Billy Graham and other biblical literalists would find his theological views inconsistent with theirs, but that he believed "one can be a good Christian without necessarily believing in the physical resurrection."[16]

At the end of the course, Nixon submitted the required final essay summarizing the change that had occurred in his religious beliefs. "My answer to this question could have been better called 'What shall I do with the religion of Jesus?'" he wrote. "For to me this intellectual log has proved to be a gradual evolution towards an understanding of the religion of Jesus. My greatest desire is that I may now apply this understanding to my life."[17]

Because Coffin was a liberal Protestant, his students conceivably submitted apple-polishing essays that were favorable to their professor's theological views. Few readers, however, would find Nixon's essays other than honest. They reflect what can happen when fundamentalist students are exposed to the scholarly study of religious phenomena. To borrow a term the young Nixon uses in these essays, a student's religious views can be "revolutionized." In Coffin's class, Nixon's views were.

If Nixon's religion changed in college from fundamentalism to modernism, what was the extent of his spirituality in adult life? One biographer declares that "religion was no longer important" to Nixon after the turning point of college, but another biographer may answer more accurately. Nixon, this writer asserts, "subsequently changed course and kept his spiritual beliefs private."[18]

Nixon himself espoused the second view. In later years he described his religious views as "intensely personal, intensely private."[19] Prior to his death, he told a writer: "I read the Bible, but I don't go out there preaching about what I know or think about it. That is mine to hold on to."[20] Thus to view Nixon as an agnostic or a secular humanist after college is inaccurate. But because his Quaker ties became more and more superficial as the years went on, it would be similarly inaccurate to identify him too closely with the Quaker faith.

In 1934 Nixon entered Duke University Law School in Durham, North Carolina. Duke was a new university. It had changed its name from Trinity College ten years earlier and had added a medical school as well as enlarged its law school only in 1930. A prescient letter from Whittier's president supported Nixon's application. "I cannot recommend him too highly," President Walter F. Dexter wrote, "because I believe that Nixon will become one of America's great if not important leaders."[21]

Duke awarded the young Californian a partial scholarship. Since it did not pay for everything, money was again tight for Nixon during his three years at Duke. Despite having one of the best academic records in his law school class and serving as president of the Duke Bar Association, he failed to secure a position upon graduation with the FBI or with any of the leading East Coast law firms to which he applied. In the midst of the Depression, graduates from small law schools could expect some difficulty in finding a job at a federal agency or at a top-tier firm. But coupled with his inability to attend Harvard, these rejections seem to have set the foundation for Nixon's lifelong mistrust of the East Coast establishment.

Reluctantly and with some bitterness, Nixon accepted a position with a law firm in Whittier offered to him by a member of his church. When he found the life of a small-town lawyer unchallenging, he moved shortly after the start of World War II to an administrative job in Washington in the tire-rationing section of the Office of Price Administration.

In the meantime, Nixon had married. One year older than her husband, Thelma Catherine "Pat" Ryan was a teacher at Whittier High School. Learning that she would have the female lead in an upcoming community theater production in Whittier, Nixon auditioned at the first rehearsal and won the role playing opposite her. She was the first woman in whom he had become seriously interested, and he proposed early and often. After two years of dating, the couple married in a Quaker ceremony in 1940.[22]

Religiously, Pat Ryan Nixon came from a mixed marriage. Her Irish American father—who had been a sailor, a gold miner, and a truck farmer—was a lapsed Roman Catholic. Her German-born mother was a Protestant, but when she died she was a Christian Scientist. Pat had paternal aunts who were practicing Roman Catholics, including one who was a nun. Pat herself was raised Methodist.

In later years observers often commented on the lack of affection Nixon displayed toward his wife and described the Nixon family as dysfunctional. But the evidence seems clear that the two spent more time together than often assumed. When Nixon was not on a trip, he and Pat ate dinner together almost every night. They often watched movies together as well. Their two daughters—one of whom married the grandson of President Eisenhower—seem to have been among the happier and better-adjusted White House children.

During World War II, Nixon's government position in Washington automatically qualified him for deferment from military service. Although he never appeared to have embraced the nonviolent teachings of Quakerism, he would have qualified for conscientious objector status. In the context of World War II, however, Nixon believed that nonviolence only aided Germany and Japan. Bored by his bureaucratic job, he accepted a direct commission in the U.S. Navy in 1942. That he was in military uniform saddened his Quaker mother and grandmother, but they did not openly object to his service. During service in the Pacific, Nixon experienced little combat, but he was respected and even admired for the leadership ability he displayed.

When Nixon returned to civilian life in 1946, he quickly entered politics in California. The opinions of his fellow officers during the war differed markedly from those his political campaigns subsequently aroused among Democrats and journalists who covered them. In classic negative campaigns, Nixon defeated a five-term Democratic congressman in 1946 and a respected Democratic senator in 1950. Although at least one biographer denies the accusations, the evidence seems to indicate that Nixon's first campaign for

Congress featured anonymous phone calls informing voters that their five-term Democratic congressman, Jerry Voorhis, was a Communist.

Known as a diligent, churchgoing congressman, Voorhis had been president of the Christian Association while a student at Yale. After graduation, he served as a traveling representative for the YMCA. A Phi Beta Kappa, he had founded a boys' school. Thus his background seemingly provided a weak basis for charges of Communism. Nevertheless, Voorhis had been a Socialist until 1934 and remained a firm supporter of the New Deal. Upon that basis, Richard Nixon successfully attacked him.

In 1950, Nixon ran for the Senate against the Democratic incumbent Helen Gahagan Douglas. A Barnard graduate and former actress who was married to well-known Hollywood actor Melvyn Douglas, she was a liberal Democrat. During the campaign, Nixon called the Roman Catholic Gahagan Douglas not only "a Red sympathizer" but also "a fellow traveler" (or a person who supports the Communist party without being a member). He also referred to her as the "Pink Lady," "pink right down to her underwear."[23] In both elections Nixon's approach worked, and he won handily.

Whether real or feigned, Nixon's concern with the growth of Communist influence and its "appeasement" in the United States extended to his fellow Quakers. Speaking of the American Friends Service Committee, the most prominent cooperative organization of American Quakerism, Nixon declared, "I think many of these Quakers are pink and are getting to be agents or [too] friendly with the Commies."[24] Although known for their pacifism, many of his fellow Quakers refused to accept these attacks peacefully. In 1950, one sent a telegram to Nixon that included the words: "I INTEND TO FIND OUT ABOUT YOU STOP YOUR QUAKERISM IS PUTRID."[25]

This strategy of what historian Gary Wills called the *Denigrative Method* was characteristic of Nixon's campaigning.[26] The most enduring description of Nixon—"Tricky Dick"—emerged during his first senatorial campaign. In all of Nixon's subsequent races, questions about his character and personality tended to overshadow his political platform. Critics used such words as "insincere," "false," "calculating," "duplicitous," "maudlin," "polarizing," and "snarling" to describe him. "Nixon was a compendium of lower-middle-class resentments, which he exploited politically," a liberal columnist wrote. Declaring that he appealed "to the meanness and resentment in others," she maintained that Nixon "made politics in this country much meaner."[27]

As a member of the House Un-American Activities Committee and later as a vocal opponent of Communism in the Senate, Nixon quickly became known as a principal opponent of Harry Truman. He asserted that Truman had coddled Communists and fellow travelers in his administration. Writers and speakers who praise Nixon for reopening American relations with China in 1972 sometimes forget that he was a leading opponent of recognizing "Red China" when the Truman administration considered doing so. "I'm going to campaign up and down in America until we drive the crooks and the Communists and those that defend them out of Washington," Nixon declared in a speech given during the 1952 presidential election.

> Seven years of the Truman ... administration, and what's happened? Six hundred million people lost to the Communists and a war in Korea in which we have lost 117 thousand American casualties. . . . those in the State Department that made the mistakes which caused that war . . . should be kicked out of the State Department.[28]

Republican party leaders selected the young senator as Dwight Eisenhower's vice presidential candidate, partly because he was a well-known anti-Communist, but also because of the electoral importance of his home state of California. Delivered on nationwide TV to answer charges that he had illegally accepted gifts from supporters, Nixon's Checkers Speech of 1952 stands as one of the most memorable speeches in American political history. Although intellectuals and political commentators lampooned it as artificial and melodramatic, the speech convinced the average voter that he should be kept on the Republican ticket.[29]

As vice president from 1953 to 1961, Nixon had an ambiguous relationship with Dwight Eisenhower. The evidence is abundant but ultimately inconclusive that Eisenhower had serious misgivings about Nixon's psychological fitness to succeed him as president. Once Nixon secured the Republican nomination in 1960, few candidates in history worked harder to win the presidency than he did.

During an election brimming with Protestant/Roman Catholic tensions, the apostasy of Pat Nixon from her Roman Catholic heritage was little known and rarely discussed by Democrats. Despite his record of winning elections by portraying Democratic opponents as Communist sympathizers, Nixon did not join supporters such as Billy Graham and Norman Vincent Peale in making an issue of John F. Kennedy's Roman Catholicism. In addition, he did not discuss a potentially devastating topic that he, other politicians, and journalists knew well but that the American public did not: Kennedy's chronic womanizing. Finally, although Nixon and his advisers probably knew of Kennedy's serious physical illnesses, they never made them a part of the campaign. All of these exercises of restraint and discretion seem to redound to Nixon's credit.

The 1960 presidential election was one of the closest in American history. Public revelation of any of these facts about Kennedy's private life would surely have cost him the election. As it was, given the charges of Democratic vote-tampering in Illinois and Texas, Nixon—not Kennedy—may actually have won the election. Approximately two-tenths of 1 percent of the popular votes separated the two candidates. Had Texas and Illinois both ended in the Republican column, Nixon would have won the election by eighteen electoral votes. Despite urgings from his fellow Republicans to challenge the election in the courts, Nixon declined to and was statesmanlike in defeat. "He accepted the results with grace and without rancor," Senator Ted Kennedy, JFK's brother, subsequently declared.[30]

Two years later, Nixon's tendency to see others as enemies reemerged in a press conference after he lost a race for governor of California. "You won't have Nixon to kick around anymore," he famously told the reporters (apparently while battling a fierce hangover from the night before), "because, gentlemen, this is my last press conference."[31] His political obituary seemed to be written. But by dint of the hard work so characteristic of him, Nixon secured the Republican presidential nomination in 1968. By a small margin, he defeated Vice President Hubert H. Humphrey, a former senator from Minnesota highly regarded by fellow senators of both parties.

Nixon inherited a country bitterly divided not only by the Vietnam War but also by the polarizing presidency of Lyndon Johnson. Although he wished to be a peacemaker, he proved to have neither the personality nor the policies to bring the nation together. As the majority of the population wished, he reduced the American military presence in Vietnam, but over 20,000 more

Americans (or more than half those killed during the Johnson years) died in a war that nevertheless ended with a North Vietnamese victory. This figure does not include the more than one million Vietnamese, Cambodian, and Laotian civilian deaths.

These statistics also exclude the tens of thousands of Americans who went missing in action or who were wounded in combat.[32] Few books show the human damage of the war more clearly than a Pulitzer Prize–winning autobiography by Lt. Lewis B. Puller Jr. In *Fortunate Son*, Puller, who later ran for Congress as an antiwar candidate, writes that he left for Vietnam as a lieutenant in the last months of the Johnson administration weighing 160 pounds. After being evacuated from combat to the Philadelphia Naval Hospital, he weighed less than 60 pounds. A Viet Cong booby trap had taken much of his body.

When Gen. Lewis M. Puller, the most decorated marine in the history of the Corps, "surveyed the wreckage of his only son" at the hospital for the first time, he began to weep. Puller's mother could not look at him. His twin sister later confessed that her initial impulse was to pray for his death. Tears streamed down the face of a fraternity brother from the College of William and Mary when he first visited the ward.

"If you were feeling sorry for yourself," Puller remembers, "you could always look around and find someone whose wounds were more grotesque." The Philadelphia hospital was "the last duty station for most marines and sailors ... who had lost limbs in Vietnam," Puller notes, "and in the late 60s, business was booming."[33] But several years later, in 1972, Nixon defeated Democratic peace candidate George McGovern by a margin of 61 percent to 37 percent. The majority of the American people still supported his handling of the war.

As for the role that religion played in Nixon's life, the course he took in Christian reconstruction at Whittier seems to have marked a defining moment in his spiritual life. He entered college an evangelical Quaker. After college, his inner beliefs were essentially those of a Unitarian, though—perhaps for political reasons—he continued to attend churches in the orthodox Christian spectrum.

In the years after college, Nixon's association with Quakerism also steadily declined. He maintained only a minimal contact with his religious heritage. While practicing law in the town of Whittier, he taught Sunday school in the East Whittier Church. Six years after graduation, he married in a Quaker ceremony. During World War II, he read through the Bible several times—something his Quaker upbringing had taught him to do. In 1952 he prayed at a Friends service prior to giving his famous Checkers Speech.

But once Nixon left Whittier for Washington, he was essentially no longer a Quaker. When he did go to church in those post-Whittier years, he and his wife attended mainline Protestant churches. While in law school, he worshipped in the gothic Duke University Chapel. A towering and distinctly un-Quaker-like edifice, the chapel held what could be called high-church Methodist services.

As a congressman and senator in Washington, Nixon along with his wife attended Protestant churches—most frequently Westmoreland Congregational Church in Bethesda and Metropolitan Memorial United Methodist Church located near the border of the District and Maryland. Although Pat Nixon had been raised a Methodist, the Nixons seem to have chosen these churches (only a mile and a half apart) more for proximity to their residence in northwest Washington than for their denominational affiliation. The Florida Avenue Meeting House—which Herbert Hoover (the nation's only other Quaker president) dedicated and regularly attended—was no more than three or four miles from their home, but Nixon seems to have had no association with it.

On election day in 1960, Nixon prayed alone in a Roman Catholic chapel in California. While at his vacation home in Florida, he frequently attended Key Biscayne Presbyterian Church with his friend Bebe Rebozo. Because Nixon was in Florida when the Vietnam War officially ended, his staff arranged for the Key Biscayne church to hold a special service of commemoration.[34]

After losing the presidency to John F. Kennedy and moving to Manhattan to practice law, Nixon worshipped regularly at New York City's Marble Collegiate Church. The church belonged to the Reformed Church in America, popularly known as "Dutch Reformed." He developed a close relationship with its nationally known pastor, Norman Vincent Peale. Author of a bestselling book that Nixon admired, *The Power of Positive Thinking*, Peale exerted considerable influence on Nixon. In 1968, he performed the wedding ceremony when Nixon's daughter, Julie, married Dwight Eisenhower's grandson, David. When Nixon resigned from the presidency six years later,

Peale counseled Nixon. At the 1990 dedication of the Nixon Library and Birthplace Foundation, Peale delivered the dedicatory prayer.

From the 1950s on, Nixon also developed a friendship and spiritual relationship with Billy Graham. The evangelist —who could never quite "bring himself to disagree openly with government policy"—was virtually an overt supporter of Nixon.[35] Graham arranged speaking engagements for Nixon before major Protestant conferences in the 1950s. Prior to the 1960 election, he advised Nixon to attend church regularly in order to increase his appeal to churchgoing voters. In 1960, when Graham wished to endorse Nixon publicly, Nixon advised against it, arguing that an open political endorsement would undercut Graham's effectiveness as an evangelist.[36]

In 1968, Nixon gave principal credit to Graham for persuading him to run for president. Although Graham constantly vowed that he did not endorse political candidates, he informed an interviewer four days before the election that he had voted by absentee ballot for Nixon.[37] On the morning after the election, Graham greeted Nixon's staff with the words "we did it" and then prayed with the family.

During the six years of Nixon's presidency, Graham made many trips to the White House and to Nixon's "Western White House" in San Clemente, California, often staying overnight.[38] He and Graham prayed together, played golf together, and frequently talked in person or by phone. The Nixon White House tapes indicate that the two men's conversations often moved beyond religious topics into politics, social views, and even a surprising amount of anti-Semitism (about which Graham later expressed regret).[39]

In 1970, Nixon spoke at Graham's crusade in Knoxville, Tennessee—the only time, according to Graham, that an American president had ever spoken at an evangelistic meeting. Aside from Bebe Rebozo, Billy Graham became Nixon's best friend. The evangelist grew closer to Nixon—whom he once described as "a splendid churchman"[40]—than he had to any previous president.

Although the spiritual relationship and friendship between Nixon and Graham was well known, Nixon is perhaps best remembered religiously for the services he began in the East Room of the White House. When he became president in 1969, he realized that he had to continue the example of church attendance set for the nation during the previous eight years by Dwight Eisenhower. Thus he and his advisers briefly considered that Nixon should attend Quaker services again. He had never officially left the Quaker tradition, even though he had maintained minimal contact with it.

The nearest Quaker meeting to the White House, however, was the same Florida Avenue Meeting House that Nixon had not attended when he lived in northwest Washington. Located two miles from the White House, the Florida Avenue meeting was an "unprogrammed" (or silent) meeting—the kind of traditional Quakerism with which Nixon had little familiarity. In addition, this District of Columbia congregation had become politicized during the Vietnam War to the point that its spirit-prompted testimonies on Sunday belied the term "silent." Its congregation—committed to nonviolence to begin with—vigorously opposed the Vietnam War.

Nixon's advisers realized that they had no control over what such a Quaker congregation might say into an open microphone when a highly controversial president (with a bevy of journalists in tow) was among them. The advisers envisioned the cartoons and newspaper stories that might appear about the events that had transpired at Sunday's Quaker meeting on Florida Avenue. They feared that voters might look forward to reading every Monday about the latest episode in a new daytime drama entitled "Nixon Faces his Quaker Enemies." In the end, the president and his staff decided to bring services into the White House rather than, like other presidents, going out to them. Such an arrangement, they argued, would put less strain on everybody concerned, including the first family. Moreover, services held within the White House would relieve the Secret Service of many of its worries about presidential safety.

Beginning in the East Room early in Nixon's presidency and continuing until his resignation, the services followed a set routine. Nixon would typically open the service with comments. A specially invited church choir would sing. An invited clergyman, usually Protestant and introduced by Nixon, would preach. Sermons rarely raised searching questions of ethics or belief.

The congregation consisted of members of the White House staff and invited guests. A typical service, in one description, included the presidents or board chairmen of "AT&T, General Electric, General Motors, Chrysler, Goodyear Tire and Rubber, Westinghouse, Pepsico, Bechtel, Boise Cascade, Republic Steel, Federated Department Stores, and Continental Can Corporation."[41] One White House directive limited the number of non-VIP attendees to one quarter of the congregation. "It isn't going to do us one bit of good to have a member of a regulatory agency at the Church Service," Nixon aide H. R. "Bob" Haldeman wrote in a memo. "If they are to be invited, please limit the invitations to . . . an appointee we [are] working on for a specific purpose."[42] The service—with the congregation sitting in chairs—would last for approximately an hour and be followed by a reception.

The invited clergy were almost always ministers, priests, or rabbis viewed as "safe." Prior to issuing an invitation, the administration would perform due diligence to ensure that the political views of the invitees were in line with presidential policies. When the evangelical Quaker theologian Elton Trueblood—known to be "dovish in sentiment and independent in character"—was scheduled to preach, he received two notes from the White House prior to entering the pulpit. Both emphasized that he should not deal with political issues in his sermon.[43] The Nixon White House expected sermons to be as upbeat and as favorable as possible.

Although the Nixon administration was satisfied with the convenience and utility of the East Room services, theologically trained observers criticized them. The disapproval did not spring solely from concerns about the separation of church and state. Above all, they had their basis in the Bible. If Jews and Christians observe the biblical teachings, prophets—one of the offices that shaped the vocation of clergy—should not eat from the table of a king (or president). According to the biblical understanding, no prophetic word will issue from a prophet's lips in such surroundings.

The classic case in the Hebrew Bible (1 Kings 22) tells of four hundred prophets unanimously advising Kings Ahab and Jehoshaphat that their joint armies would secure a sweeping victory if they attacked an enemy the next day. Dubious (perhaps because the prophets spoke like yes-men), Jehoshaphat asks if Ahab has another prophet they can consult. "There is still one other . . . Micaiah . . . but I hate him, for he never prophesies anything favorable about me, but only disaster."

When Micaiah (who neither lives nor dines in Ahab's palace) arrives, the kings hear an accurate prophecy of imminent disaster. In the biblical perspective, Ahab's words, "but I hate him," place Micaiah on the side of God. Thus, in biblical terms, anyone who preaches before a king in his palace or a president in his home stands in danger of becoming a tamed prophet.

And exactly that seems to have happened during the years of Sunday services in the Nixon White House. The carefully screened clergy who accepted invitations to the White House preached tamed sermons, sometimes full of approbation for the president and his administration. For more than five years, the president of the United States heard no new perspectives or ethical challenges during Sunday worship. He heard nothing critical of the deaths or grievous injuries caused by the Vietnam War, and nothing about the immense strain placed on American life by the twenty-five months of the Watergate scandal caused by a president who continued to declare he was uninvolved.

Clergy do not have to preach "political" sermons to place such ethical issues in Jewish or Christian perspective. Many preachers are skilled at using biblical texts to raise moral questions relevant to current controversies without mentioning those controversies. But in the East Room, no modern Nathan (2 Samuel 12:7) said to Nixon, "You are the man!" Unlike Lyndon Johnson at Bruton Parish Church, he encountered no Cotesworth Pinckney Lewis to raise embarrassing questions. Thus, a number of believing Jews and Christians who attended the services thought them inappropriate. Almost immediately after he became president, the Episcopalian Gerald Ford—who viewed Christian worship much differently—ended these services.

The accomplishments of the Nixon administration were wide-ranging. In matters of foreign policy, Nixon achieved major diplomatic breakthroughs with China and the Soviet Union. He fought inflation on the domestic front, expanded the U.S. presence in space, and established the Environmental Protection Agency. A quiet and stable presence behind the scenes, Pat Nixon became the most-traveled first lady in history. Polarizing but still popular, President Nixon was reelected by a landslide over the Democratic peace candidate George McGovern, a minister's son, in 1972.

But then a seemingly minor burglary in Washington's Watergate complex—a group of five buildings consisting of apartments, offices, and a hotel—developed into a national scandal. It included the attorney general, the Nixon reelection committee, the FBI, and several of Nixon's most important aides, and resulted in the firing of the special prosecutor. The Judiciary Committee of the House of Representatives voted twenty-seven to eleven to recommend impeachment to the full House of Representatives. Informed by

Republican congressmen and senators that the votes existed for his impeachment and removal from office, Nixon resigned the presidency on August 9, 1974. Spiro Agnew, his vice president, had resigned ten months earlier after being charged with accepting bribes while holding public office.

In a widely publicized incident on the eve of his resignation, a weeping Nixon asked Secretary of State Henry Kissinger to kneel with him in prayer in the White House. Kissinger was a secular Jew who had been an agnostic since childhood, and kneeling was a Christian, not a Jewish, posture for prayer. "Years later," a biographer notes, "Kissinger still felt uncomfortable discussing the scene, as if it were one last little humiliation inflicted on him."[44]

When the truth about Watergate emerged, the Reverend John Huffman of the Key Biscayne Presbyterian Church was "deeply shocked." Nixon had informed him that he was innocent, and the pastor had defended the president publicly. "I feel he lied to me," Huffman told a reporter. "I feel compassion for him, but God's grace is tempered with God's justice."[45]

But no one was more stunned at Nixon's guilt in the Watergate affair than Billy Graham. Although he initially attributed his friend's disgrace to "demons," the realization that Nixon had lied to him about Watergate caused a chastened Graham to go through a period of serious introspection. "Billy told me he would never make the mistake again of getting that close to someone in office," former White House aide Charles "Chuck" Colson later said.[46] Yet the evangelist's "serious introspection" apparently only went so far. Long after Watergate, an anonymous close associate quoted in the most comprehensive biography of Graham declared, "I honestly believe that after all these years, Billy still has no idea of how badly Nixon snookered him."[47]

In Richard Nixon, the American people elected a man who rejected the hippies, yippies, sexual revolution, drug use, and peace protests of the Lyndon Johnson era. Nixon's political career emerged amid the anti-Communist passions of the post–World War II period. A man of shrewd intelligence, high ambition, and wide-ranging abilities, he played a major role in American politics for almost five decades. He probably exercised more raw power than anyone of Quaker upbringing in history. His party nominated him for president or vice president a record five times.

Nixon's strength lay in foreign policy. He visited Moscow and Beijing and improved relations and reduced tensions with both the USSR and China, and he negotiated a treaty with the Soviet Union to limit strategic nuclear weapons. Even though he allowed the deleterious and enormously expensive Vietnam War—which the United States ultimately lost—to continue for four full years following his election, he ended the draft, which had been an almost continual part of American life since 1940.

Domestically, Nixon accepted the contours of what Republican conservatives called the "Welfare State" begun by Franklin Delano Roosevelt. He also accepted certain economic views generally associated with Democrats. His administration sought to reduce pollution and the reckless use of natural resources. Although the nation struggled with inflation during his administration (and during those of Presidents Ford and Carter), Nixon is credited with achieving the first balanced budget between the Kennedy and Clinton administrations.[48]

In private meetings Nixon almost always impressed leaders of other countries. "Temperamentally incapable of quitting," able to work through physical pain and exhaustion, he was a Darwinian survivor.[49] After 1974, the disgrace of Watergate—the blame for which he largely disavowed—only caused him to redouble his efforts to vindicate his career.[50] In the twenty years following his resignation, he wrote ten books—or one every two years—seeking to justify his presidency or to rehabilitate his reputation.

It is possible to view Richard Nixon as simply a Quaker with a strong work ethic and high ambition. Although he increasingly scuttled his ties with Quakerism after leaving Whittier, Nixon himself believed that his views on such issues as civil rights came from his Quaker upbringing. He did support civil rights, for having experienced the segregated society of prewar North Carolina, he was as much an opponent of Jim Crow laws as many of his Democratic adversaries. In Washington, he and his wife sent their daughters to integrated schools.

But Nixon's career showed that he was more than willing to jettison Quaker principles when they conflicted with his ambitions. In his views of war, in his vindictiveness toward opponents, in his sometimes casual disregard of human life, and in his fairly constant use of profanity, he departed in major ways from his religious heritage. A defiant man, he had more ability than most politicians to infuriate his opponents. Throughout his public life he associated with the affluent, but viewed himself as the underdog.

From youth on, Nixon had difficulty showing any form of emotion. He had trouble looking people in the eye. Because of an apparent inability to trust, he was close to very few people. "His character ... contained a dimension of strangeness," a sympathetic biographer who has interviewed many of Nixon's college classmates writes.

> There was nothing negative to put a finger on. However ... Richard Nixon's human touch was uncertain. ... No one outside his family could really claim to know him. He remained an enigma to his team-mates in debate and football.

When the same biographer interviewed his girlfriend from college, she reported, "most of the time I just couldn't figure him out." His debating partner described Nixon as

> a guy with many sides to him. Insecure in one-on-one conversations but totally sure of himself when debating in front of an audience. Complicated but pretending to be ordinary. I liked him ... but couldn't get to know him. He buried a lot of himself below the surface. It wasn't difficult to see that he had hidden depths.[51]

When Nixon took vacations in the Florida Keys, he was usually alone. He had no real friends, a fact that caused Dwight Eisenhower to marvel that he could not see how any man could live without friends.[52] Senator George Smathers of Florida attempted to give him a friend on the Keys by introducing him to Charles "Bebe" Rebozo, a Cuban American bachelor and businessman. The somewhat superficial friendship lasted for over forty years, although after their first meeting Rebozo complained that Nixon was "a guy who doesn't know how to talk, doesn't drink, doesn't smoke, doesn't chase women, doesn't know how to play golf, doesn't know how to play tennis ... he can't even fish."[53]

Generally insecure and awkward in social situations, Nixon lacked the ability to make small talk even while president. During a major antiwar protest in Washington, he held a clumsy, rambling, and largely irrelevant conversation with opponents of the war. Attempting to make small talk with television interviewer David Frost, he asked him in the presence of his staff if he "had fornicated" the previous weekend. "Always formal, always awkward, even in his farewell wave from the White House helicopter," one Washington correspondent declared, Nixon was "seemingly bereft of spontaneity and charm."[54] Eisenhower's secretary once compared her boss with Nixon in her diary: "The President is a man of integrity and sincere in his every action . . . he radiates this, everybody . . . trusts and loves him," she wrote. "But the Vice President sometimes seems like a man who is acting like a nice man rather than being one."[55]

Haldeman called Nixon "the strangest man I ever met." [56] Substituting another adjective, Kissinger viewed him as "the oddest man he had ever met."[57] Also strange was Nixon's courtship of Pat Ryan. After he proposed to her on their first date and she did not accept, he kept asking. He then sometimes drove her to dates with other men who lacked cars, picked her up afterward, and drove her home.

The death of his wife in 1993 caused Nixon to ponder anew the question of eternity. Although Pat Nixon attended church and White House services faithfully with her husband, her religious views are unclear. She seems to have been less interested in religion than her husband. Significantly, none of the four eulogies given at her funeral at the Nixon Library mention a religious or spiritual dimension to her life. Billy Graham's fifteen-minute funeral sermon neither explicitly identifies Pat as a Christian nor uses the words *religion* or *church.*

The sole mention of faith in Mrs. Nixon's funeral service occurred when Graham quoted daughter Tricia Nixon Cox as saying, "My mother's faith in God sustained her."[58] Nixon's tribute to his wife after the service contains no mention of religion. The statement released upon her death by President Bill Clinton refers to her as "a passionate believer in volunteer service and in Americans helping one another."[59]

During his retirement, Nixon in at least one case significantly helped another person. When a depressed Robert "Bud" McFarlane, Ronald Reagan's former national security adviser, attempted suicide in 1987, Nixon not only flew to his hospital room in suburban Maryland but also counseled and prayed with him. McFarlane described Nixon's visit as a spiritual epiphany.[60]

In retirement, the former president read widely in religious and philosophical writers. During an interview late in his life, he told a biographer that he read the Bible regularly, "not . . . every day which was my custom in my earlier years, but I probably read it more often than many of those who wear their religion on their sleeves."[61] In the year of his wife's death, he told a biographer, "I am a Quaker, and I believe in God, and I believe in turning to Him."[62] Ten years earlier, when an interviewer had asked whether he believed that "there is a God that watches over you," Nixon had replied, "*Oh, yes.*" When the interviewer continued, "[One] who watches the things that you do?" Nixon replied, "Absolutely, absolutely. *Oh, yes.*"[63]

"What shall I do with the religion of Jesus?" the twenty-one-year-old Nixon asked in his final paper written for J. Herschel Coffin's course at Whittier. "My greatest desire is that I may now apply this understanding to my life."[64] In the sixty years that Nixon lived after writing those words, the evidence is clear that he applied the teachings of Jesus to his life only as they suited his political agenda. Those who knew him generally agreed that his life displayed a dark side and a light side. They also agreed that Nixon's dark side came not from religion but from politics. His conversations and writings are rarely free of hostility toward his political opponents. Throughout his career, his political aspirations seemed continually at odds with his Quaker upbringing. In the words of one biographer, the thirty-seventh president "appears to have made the transition from nice Quaker boy to ruthless politician without even noticing."[65]

After leaving Whittier, Nixon maintained a tribal loyalty to the religious tradition in which he was raised, but little more. Neither his pastors, nor the churches he attended, nor his theological beliefs, nor his ethics were those of the Religious Society of Friends. Perpetually concerned with his "enemies," he once declared to an aide, "One day we'll get them—we'll get them on the ground where we want them. And we'll stick our heels in, step on them hard and twist."[66]

As they have gradually been released since 1980, the thousands of hours of conversations recorded on the secret taping system Nixon installed in the White House have increasingly damaged his reputation. At one point in a conversation recorded in 1972, for example, Secretary of State Kissinger explains to the president that American planes had not hit certain supply dumps "because we were afraid to hit the civilian population when we couldn't bomb visually." Nixon responds, "I am not so goddamned concerned about the civilian population. I am not so concerned about it."[67]

Tapes released in 2011 and recorded in the Oval Office in February and March 1973 reveal similar conversations. Recorded sixteen months before Nixon resigned, the latest group of tapes includes his views on the traits of Irish Americans, Italian Americans, African Americans, and Jews. Of the view of a member of his cabinet that African Americans "are coming along and . . . they are going to strengthen our country," Nixon declares that "I think he's right if you're talking in terms of 500 years." Declaring that the Irish and Irish Americans "can't drink" and "get mean" when they do drink, he adds, "it's sort of a natural trait." As for Italian Americans, he remarks, they "just don't have their heads screwed on tight." He leaves his next sentence unfinished: "They are wonderful people, but . . ."

The taped comments that caused the most national and international concern, however, focused on Jews. Earlier tapes from the Nixon White House had displayed his animosity toward Jews, but the 2011 tapes went further. In them, Nixon said that "the Jews are just a very aggressive and abrasive and obnoxious personality." He went on to declare that Jews he knew shared a common trait of needing to compensate for an inferiority complex. "It's the latent insecurity," he concluded. "And that's why they have to prove things." Talking with Chuck Colson, Nixon noted that many of "the deserters" who avoided the draft by going to Canada or Scandinavia during the Vietnam War were Jewish. "I didn't notice many Jewish names coming back from Vietnam on any of those lists [of dead]," he said. "I don't know how the hell they avoid it."

The tapes also include a significant conversation with Kissinger. "The emigration of Jews from the Soviet Union," Kissinger is recorded as telling Nixon, "is not an objective of American foreign policy. And if they put Jews into gas chambers in the Soviet Union, it is not an American concern. Maybe a humanitarian concern." To this surprising comment, Nixon responded: "I know. We can't blow up the world because of it." The 2011 tapes also depict Nixon directing his secretary that no Jew who failed to support his presidential campaign, regardless of office or status, should be invited to a White House dinner. The dinner honored Israeli Prime Minister Golda Meir.

The 265 hours of recordings released in 2011 also show that Nixon spoke less derogatorily of Israeli Jews than of American Jews. Prime Minister Meir was widely quoted as saying that Nixon was "the best friend Israel ever had." But the statements on the tapes shocked and angered Jews across the world. A blogger sardonically noted that, despite their contents, defenders of Nixon could "probably use [the tapes] to say that he was fair, [for] he disparaged (almost) everyone." Summarizing what the newest set of tapes had revealed to him, the blogger wrote: "A bigot? Yes. Complexities in his bigotry? Yes. A friend of Israel? Yes. . . . Has this further soiled his legacy? Yes."[68]

A reader of the transcripts of Nixon's private conversations in the White House may receive a sense of the real man. If so, the real Nixon seems not to be the Nixon of the Quaker meeting or of quiet parenthood or of campaign advertising but rather the Nixon of the Checkers Speech of 1952:

> Now let me say this, I know that this is not the last of the smears. In spite of my explanation tonight, other smears will be made, others have been made in the past. And the purpose of the smears I know is this: to silence me, to make me let up. Well, they just don't know who they're dealing with.[69]

Nixon was vigorously active until his death from a stroke in New York City in 1994. The Air Force One plane used during his administration carried his body to the Nixon Library and Birthplace in Yorba Linda. There his casket lay in state in the library until the funeral on the next afternoon. Thousands viewed the casket or attended the services, including a large representation from Congress and the four living American presidents.

Billy Graham and the chief of chaplains of the U.S. Navy—Nixon's branch of service—presided at the funeral, which was held in the library. "I think he was one of the most misunderstood men," Graham said before the services, "and I think he was one of the greatest men of the century."[70] Former president Ronald Reagan described Nixon as "one of the finest statesmen this world has ever seen."[71]

Richard Milhous Nixon was buried beside the library near the small bungalow in which he was born. Inscribed on his headstone are words from his first inaugural address: "The greatest honor history can bestow is peacemaker."

# Gerald R. Ford

*1913–2006* ∽ PRESIDENT FROM 1974 TO 1977

If history considers Thomas Jefferson as an Episcopalian rather than as a Unitarian, then Gerald Rudolph Ford was the eleventh member of the Episcopal church to serve as president. That he was an active, believing Episcopalian was well known during his presidency.

Raised in Illinois, Ford's mother, Dorothy Gardner, attended finishing school and a year of college. In 1912, after a short relationship, she fell in love with and married her roommate's brother, Leslie Lynch King Sr., the son of an affluent Omaha banker and businessman. The marriage began to disintegrate on the honeymoon when King struck his bride because she had nodded slightly at a man who had taken off his hat as a gesture of respect in a hotel elevator.

Two weeks after their only child, Leslie Lynch King Jr., was born in his paternal grandfather's mansion in 1913, the couple separated with the full support of Leslie King's mother.[1] With her two-week-old infant son, Dorothy went to live with her parents, who had moved from Chicago to the manufacturing city of Grand Rapids, Michigan. She never returned to King and would later rename her son after her second husband, Gerald Rudolph Ford.

As Dorothy's ex-husband would not pay the court-mandated child support, King's father—Ford's grandfather—paid it instead. These payments ended, however, after the grandfather died when Ford was seventeen. Ford met his biological father only once after infancy when King and his second wife surprised the sixteen-year-old in Grand Rapids and took him to lunch. By Ford's report, the conversation was superficial, for father and son were complete strangers.

At that meeting, King gave his biological son $25 (more than $300 in 2010 dollars) and encouraged him to buy something that he could not otherwise afford. Ever the athlete, Ford spent half of the money on an expensive pair of golf knickers.[2] "Nothing could erase the image I gained of my real father that day," Ford later wrote. "A carefree, well-to-do man who didn't really give a damn about the hopes and dreams of his firstborn son. When I went to bed that night, I broke down and cried."[3]

At the time of that meeting, Ford was still legally named after his biological father, but he was known in Grand Rapids as Gerald Rudolph Ford Jr. In 1916 his mother had married Gerald Rudolph Ford Sr., a salesman and businessman whom she had met at a church social at Grace Episcopal Church. Ford later described his stepfather as an emotionally secure parent who was "a marvelous family man."[4] Years later Betty Ford's first impression of her future father-in-law was equally high. "Jerry's stepfather stood as straight as an arrow," she wrote after having dinner at the Ford home for the first time, "and I had the immediate impression that he lived his life that way."[5]

When Ford entered his teens, his mother revealed to him that he, unlike his brothers, was adopted by Gerald Ford Sr. and that his three brothers were therefore only his half-brothers. The information stunned him. He remembered repeating that night a passage from the Book of Proverbs that he had learned in the Sunday school of Grace Church: "Trust in the Lord with all thine heart, and lean not unto thine own understanding. In all thy ways acknowledge Him, and He shall direct thy paths." In later years Ford frequently recited the passage.

Although Ford was of English and Scots-Irish descent, he grew up in the heavily Dutch environment of Grand Rapids. From the 1840s on, the southwestern counties of Michigan adjacent to Lake Michigan had become the focus of immigration for thousands of conservative Dutch Calvinists.

Located 180 miles from Chicago, Grand Rapids became full of Dutch American churches—either Dutch Reformed or the even more conservative Christian Reformed. The area had two of the principal institutions of higher education in Dutch American Protestantism, Calvin College and Hope College; the latter included a theological seminary. Names such as De Jong, De Vries, Huizenga, Vandenberg, Hogeboom, Luedtke, Meijer, Rozema, Vander Vliet, and Schrader filled the phone books. The downtown area contained prominent locally owned department stores with names such as Herpolsheimer's.

Ford described his home town as "a strait-laced, highly conservative town . . . [where] almost everyone attended church and a strict moral code was scrupulously observed."[6] Many Dutch Reformed and Christian Reformed Protestants kept such a strict Lord's Day that they abstained even from reading the newspaper on Sundays. "[On Sundays] I'd just go out and play baseball," Ford later reminisced. "Of course, some of my Dutch friends weren't allowed to do that."[7]

Despite the area's Dutch Calvinist influence, the ties of the Ford family to the Episcopal church were strong. Although his parents were not pietistic in the manner of the Dutch Protestants, they had a high moral code and neither drank nor kept alcohol in the house. Ford's stepfather once grew angry when he found Ford playing poker.[8] Initially the Fords belonged to St. Mark's Episcopal Church in downtown Grand Rapids, but their home parish soon became Grace Episcopal Church in a newer section of town.[9] Gerald Ford Sr. served on the ruling body of laymen, or vestry, at Grace Church, and Ford himself led a Sunday school class there after returning from World War II.

Active in the women's groups of the church, Dorothy Ford not only taught her boys prayers but also insisted that they regularly attend its Sunday school and services of worship. "A handsome woman, with tremendous charisma," Betty Ford described her mother-in-law upon their first meeting: "strong . . . confident and positive."[10] Of his high-energy mother's final years, Ford later wrote that she had expressed a wish "to drop dead with her boots on." Despite massive health problems and two heart attacks, she remained involved in the life of her city and church. "Mercifully," Ford wrote, "she [died] . . . in church one Sunday morning . . . just before the service began. . . . Yet when Betty and I checked her date book, we found that she had scheduled appointments every day for the next month."[11]

In high school, Ford was named to the "All-City" and "All-State" football teams. Ranking in the top 5 percent of his high school class, he was elected to the National Honors Society. In the Boy Scouts he attained the rank of Eagle Scout.

Entering the University of Michigan in Ann Arbor, he graduated in 1935 with a bachelor's degree in economics and political science. Because language was never his strength, his lowest grades were in French and English. He pledged the socially prominent Delta Kappa Epsilon—a fraternity with a somewhat legendary reputation then and later in Ann Arbor. "Academically . . . lousy . . . athletically . . . high, and . . . certainly no slouch as a party house," Ford later described the Deke house.[12] While at Michigan he played on two national championship football teams, was named the university's most valuable player, and competed in the East-West Shrine Game and the College All-Star Game against the Green Bay Packers. As a sports historian writes, these honors were signs that Ford "was one of the best players in the country."[13]

Despite his athletic ability, Ford was often broke in college. Although his stepfather had founded a paint and varnish company, Ford's parents were never financially secure during the Great Depression, especially after losing the mortgage on their first house. Thus Ford held part-time jobs throughout high school and college. In Ann Arbor he regularly donated blood for pay. Harry Kipke, Michigan's football coach, whom Ford idolized, got him a job waiting tables. But at one point he was so close to dropping out of school that he wrote to his real father (now living in Wyoming) and asked for a loan of $600—almost $10,000 in 1933—to pay college expenses. He received no reply.[14]

Upon graduation, Ford was recruited by both the Detroit Lions and the Green Bay Packers. Instead, he desired to enter Yale's prestigious law school. Kipke was influential in getting him a job coaching boxing and assisting with football at Yale. He not only had to convince the law school to admit him but also had to persuade Yale's athletic department to grant him permission to take part-time courses.

Initially failing to receive those permissions, Ford took two summer courses at the University of Michigan Law School and received Bs in both.[15] He was admitted to and entered Yale Law School's class of 1941. Despite continuing to coach while studying law, he graduated in the top third of a class of 125 that included 98 members of Phi Beta Kappa. He returned to Grand Rapids following graduation and opened a law firm downtown with a college fraternity brother, Phil Buchen. Within six months, Japan attacked Pearl Harbor.

Entering the U.S. Navy as an ensign early in 1942, Ford was initially classified as a physical fitness instructor. He served through 1943 at the Naval Academy and then at the Navy preflight school in Chapel Hill, North

Carolina. "But there was a war going on," he declared in his autobiography. "I wanted desperately to be part of it. So I wrote letters to everyone I knew, pleading for a billet on a ship."[16] Finally securing assignment to sea duty in late 1943, Ford experienced extensive combat while serving on aircraft carriers in the Pacific. "The Japanese planes," he remembered, "came after us with a vengeance."[17]

When discharged as a lieutenant commander early in 1946, Ford was thirty-two years old and still unmarried. Because the firm of Ford and Buchen dissolved during the war, he joined his former law partner in an old Grand Rapids firm headed by a highly respected graduate of Harvard Law School. "A superior legal mind," Ford later wrote, despite his Jewish mentor's Democratic politics. "The best I ever knew."[18]

In 1948, Ford ran for the U.S. House of Representatives in his heavily Dutch American district. Challenging a ten-year congressman of Dutch ancestry who had previously enjoyed the support of the Dutch American community, Ford began planning his campaign fifteen months before the Republican primary. The overconfident incumbent opposed not only the Truman administration's Marshall Plan but also almost all forms of foreign aid. Running as both a conservative and an internationalist, Ford unexpectedly gained 62 percent of the vote. In subsequent elections he maintained his congressional seat without difficulty, and generally by larger and larger margins. From 1965 to 1973, he served as House Republican Minority Leader.

Two weeks before he was elected to his inaugural term in Congress, Ford married Elizabeth Anne Bloomer Warren. Born in 1918 to a relatively well-to-do Chicago family, Betty was the daughter of a homemaker and a traveling salesman. The family moved to Grand Rapids soon after her birth. Observing her father's frequent absences from the house, she decided at an early age that she did not want to marry a man who traveled for a living. In this quest Betty proved doubly unsuccessful.

Despite her father's membership in Christian Science, Betty was raised in the Episcopal church, her mother's denomination. When her father died in her sixteenth year, his savings and insurance allowed the family to continue middle-class life. Pretty and popular, Betty was interested in dance from childhood on. She did not continue her education after high school but instead attended the new summer dance program at Bennington College in

Vermont for two summers. There she met the innovative and charismatic Martha Graham and followed her to New York City to study dance at the Martha Graham Studio. While at the studio, Betty supported herself by modeling with the John Robert Powers Agency, perhaps the most famous American modeling agency of the time. Two years later, after being passed over for Martha Graham's permanent troupe, she returned to Grand Rapids to work as a fashion consultant. She formed her own dance group for a time, but ultimately gave up professional dancing.

In 1942, at the age of twenty-four, Betty married a traveling salesman, Bill Warren, whom she had known since grade school. When the rector of St. Mark's Episcopal Church, her home church, refused to marry Betty anywhere but in the church, she found a Presbyterian minister who would perform an Episcopal service in the garden setting she desired. Betty ended the marriage when Warren turned out to be not only a heavy drinker but also a man who preferred the road to the home. The divorce, which took effect in 1947, was remarkably civilized, with Betty accepting a settlement of only one dollar.

After the divorce, she began dating Gerald Ford, then one of the most eligible bachelors in Grand Rapids. Early in 1948, the two became engaged. In October of the same year, after Ford won the Republican nomination for the congressional seat, they married. He was thirty-five; she was thirty. The wedding was delayed precisely because the Dutch Calvinists of the district—most of whom voted Republican—might not have voted in the primary for a candidate married to a divorced woman. Still campaigning against a Democratic opponent until minutes before the ceremony, Ford showed up for the wedding at Grace Episcopal Church with mud on his shoes, which infuriated his mother. After the wedding the wife of one of Ford's brothers cautioned Betty, "Jerry's mistress will not be a woman. It will be his work."[19]

The prophecy proved correct. As he rose higher in the Republican hierarchy, Ford was away from home more evenings than he was present. In 1966, for example, a year in which the GOP won forty-seven House seats, he made two hundred campaign speeches for various congressional candidates. In 1970, he campaigned every week for Republican members of the House in one state or another—some weeks traveling every day to speak. To support his own campaign that year, he spoke forty-six times in the Grand Rapids area.[20]

Ford maintained his membership at Grace Church in Grand Rapids, but he spent most of his time in Washington and attended Episcopal worship regularly there with his family.[21] During most of his congressional career, the Fords lived in Alexandria, Virginia, where their Episcopal parish was Immanuel Church-on-the-Hill. Built on the campus of the Protestant Episcopal Theological Seminary of Virginia and serving both as the seminary's chapel and as a parish church, Immanuel was the closest Episcopal church to the Ford home. Its congregation was filled with political moderates and liberals, many of whom worked on Capitol Hill and some of whom taught at the seminary. Of four children born to Gerald and Betty Ford, the three boys were baptized in Grand Rapids at Grace Church. The youngest, Susan, was baptized in Alexandria at Immanuel Church-on-the-Hill.[22]

Although deeply involved in the work of Congress, Ford volunteered for Immanuel's outreach programs. He not only ushered but also sometimes served as a lay reader at Immanuel's Sunday services.[23] "He served as a member of a parish commission that worked for fair housing in Alexandria," a former rector remembered, "and helped with services to low-income families."[24]

When Ford was nominated in fall 1973 to replace the disgraced Spiro Agnew as vice president, a leading member of the Virginia Seminary faculty who was politically a Democrat was impressed that "after seven hours before the Senate committee testifying for his fitness for the vice presidency, he still came to the All Saints service at the church."[25] From 1967 on, Ford also participated regularly in a Wednesday morning prayer session with several Republican members of the House of Representatives.

Because Ford's presidency is directly tied into the Watergate scandal, a review of the sequence of events is necessary. In June 1972, Washington's metropolitan police arrested five men for breaking into and entering the headquarters of the Democratic National Committee at the Watergate hotel complex. Soon it was revealed that the men were directly or indirectly employees of a fundraising group headed by the U.S. attorney general. Aides to President Nixon denied any connection with their reelection campaign. But by October 1972, FBI agents had determined that the Watergate break-in sprang from an unparalleled campaign of political spying and disruption conducted on behalf of the Nixon reelection effort.

Although Watergate generated an unending stream of negative publicity, the events had little effect on the presidential election. In November 1972, the American public reelected Richard Nixon in a landslide victory over Democratic presidential nominee George McGovern. Beginning in May 1973, however, the Senate Watergate Committee began nationally televised hearings on the break-in. When the committee learned in July that the White House contained a system that automatically recorded all presidential conversations (phone and otherwise) in the Oval Office, they subpoenaed the tapes. Citing executive privilege, President Nixon refused to surrender the recordings.

Nixon nominated Ford for the vice presidency when Spiro Agnew resigned in October 1973 after being charged with accepting bribes. As one historian notes, Ford

> was in many ways the right person in the right place at the right time. . . .
> There were no obvious or discoverable moral blemishes on a long political
> career. . . . He was widely regarded as a good and upright person. . . . His
> background investigation by the FBI . . . was probably the most exhaustive
> ever undertaken in connection with a public figure.[26]

The normally partisan Democratic Speaker of the House, Tip O'Neill, declared "God has been good to America, especially during difficult times. . . . He gave us Gerald Ford—the right man at the right time who was able to put the Nation back together."[27]

Following congressional hearings, Ford was sworn in as vice president on December 6, 1973. Although Richard Nixon seems to have been unconcerned with Ford's religiosity per se, the minority leader's reputation as an upright and honest man clearly contributed to his selection. Nixon and his advisers needed a vice president who could be confirmed without problem. When Nixon resigned on August 9, 1974, Ford was sworn in as America's thirty-eighth president.

Ten months earlier, when sworn in as vice president, Ford's hand had rested on a Jerusalem Bible that his son, Michael, had given him. For his presidential inauguration, Ford used this same Bible.[28] It was open to Proverbs 3:5–6, the passage he had learned as a child and one that he repeated during World War II and nightly in Washington:[29] "Trust wholeheartedly in Yahweh [the Lord], put no faith in your own perception; in every course you take, have him in mind: he will see that your paths are smooth."

When he had spoken to reporters during his vice presidential swearing-in ceremony, Ford had declared that religious faith was "a personal thing" for him. "My religious feeling," he said then, "is a deep personal faith I rely on for guidance from my God." On another occasion he declared that "my religious beliefs give me guidance and strength on a day-to-day basis. My conviction is very personal. I am most reluctant to speak or write about it publicly."[30] Ford's reticence about religion was in keeping with his Episcopal faith. Evangelicals and Pentecostals might "witness" to others, but to Ford and many other Episcopalians, the Christian faith was not "something one shouts from the housetops or wears on his sleeve."[31]

At his presidential swearing-in ceremony, Ford again used distinctly religious language. Because the nation had not elected him president by ballots, he requested that it "confirm me as your President with your prayers. And I hope that such prayers will also be the first of many." During the speech, Ford also asked for prayers "for Richard Nixon and for his family." At the end of the speech, he pledged, as he had at his vice presidential swearing-in ceremony, "to do what is right as God gives me to see the right." He concluded, "God helping me, I will not let you down."[32]

A close friend, a congressman who belonged to Ford's prayer group, declared that the new president's statements at the swearing-in ceremony depicted "the real Jerry Ford." The chairman of the House Prayer Breakfast Committee observed that Ford made "easy references to God. They weren't strained or laborious speech-writers' references."[33]

White House religion changed quickly after the Fords took up residence. The White House services, which had never seemed appropriate to them, ended. Two days after Ford's inauguration, Betty Ford wrote in her diary, "There aren't going to be any more private services in the East Room for a select few."[34]

On his first Sunday as president, the Fords attended their home church, Immanuel Church-on-the-Hill. Arriving just before the beginning of the service, they sat unobtrusively in the church's last pew. During the service they heard prayers for the new president. In his sermon, the Episcopal rector urged the largely Democratic congregation not to "gloat and glower and grimace" over the resignation of Richard Nixon and the installation of a president whose character and ethics they plainly would like better.[35]

On Sunday, September 8, 1974, exactly thirty days after he had assumed the presidency, Ford left the White House. Sitting alone in the presidential pew at the 8:00 a.m. service of adjacent St. John's Episcopal Church, the new president joined fifty other worshippers and received Holy Communion. When he returned to the Oval Office, he completed arrangements to grant Richard Nixon a "full, free, and absolute pardon . . . for all offenses against the United States which he . . . has committed or may have committed or taken part in during the period from January 20, 1969, through August 9, 1974."[36] Ford announced his decision to the nation and world at an eleven o'clock news conference, during which he invoked the name of God five times.[37] All three major networks broke regularly scheduled coverage in order to cover Ford's press conference explaining the pardon.

Subsequently, Ford declared that he had prayed over the question of pardoning Nixon during the previous weeks. He seemed to view the pardon not only in a political but also in a religious light. Politically, he believed the nation could be crippled if it experienced a long-term impeachment of Nixon following twenty-six bitter and divisive months of Watergate. Two decades later, the U.S. Senate would use precisely the same argument when it failed to proceed on the House of Representative's impeachment of Bill Clinton.

Religiously, Ford believed that he and the nation needed to display forgiveness. Theological phrasing ran through his brief address to the nation: "I have promised . . . to do what is right as God gives me to see the right. . . . I am sworn to uphold our laws with the help of God. . . . My conscience tells me clearly and certainly that I cannot prolong the bad dreams that continue." Speaking of the time when he will appear before the bar of God's justice, he asserted: "I . . . will receive justice without mercy if I fail to show mercy."[38]

The national reaction to the pardon was overwhelmingly negative. Many Americans were shocked that Richard Nixon — "Tricky Dick" — had once again eluded justice. Editorial writers tended to be outraged. Some political observers believed that Nixon or his representatives received an agreement, "made a deal" (spoken or unspoken) with Ford before he was chosen as vice president. Overnight Ford's popularity dropped from 71 percent to 49 percent.[39] In press conferences during Ford's first month as president, Jerald F. Ter Horst, his press secretary, had assured reporters that Ford had no intention of pardoning the ex-president. A distinguished Michigan newsman, Ter Horst subsequently disagreed so strongly with Ford's decision that he resigned and resisted Ford's appeal to withdraw his resignation.

Although some commentators explained Ter Horst's resignation as stemming from his knowledge of an agreement between Ford and Nixon, most now believe the press secretary's explanation that he resigned as a matter of conscience. Ter Horst later explained that the pardon, in his view, "set up a double standard of justice."[40] Although Ford fully pardoned Nixon, he refused at the same time to pardon the ex-president's coconspirators. These men with such last names as Haldeman, Erlichman, Mitchell, Ziegler, Mardian, Chapin, Colson, Kalmbach, Buzhardt, Strachan, and Stans faced years of jail sentences and a "wrenching ordeal" that Ford wished to spare Nixon and the nation. He also refused to pardon the many American males who had evaded the draft during the Vietnam War.

Ford subsequently testified before a House subcommittee that "there was no deal, period, under no circumstances."[41] Given Ter Horst's continued explanation of why he resigned and the failure of new evidence to emerge, the number of conspiracy theorists has declined in the more than three decades since the pardon of Nixon.

In the 1976 presidential election, Ford—in the words of Randall Balmer— "faced an electorate that had grown tired of Lyndon Johnson's deceptions in Vietnam, weary of Richard Nixon's endless prevarications, and ready . . . to consider matters of faith and character."[42] To voters Ford seemed free of deception and prevarication, and he possessed the requisite faith and character. But he lost to former governor of Georgia Jimmy Carter by a small margin. Polls taken after the election showed that his pardoning of Richard Nixon represented one of the principal causes of his defeat.

To describe the pardon, a leading journal of Protestant opinion employed the Kierkegaardian terms of "either/or." To an editorial writer, "the sudden and unexpected pardon" of Nixon raised an either-or dilemma:

> *Either* Mr. Ford is telling the truth when he says that he granted the pardon because of compassion—*or* he is lying and the pardon is somehow a part of the overall cover-up.
> *If* Mr. Ford is telling the truth, then he has allowed his sense of compas-

sion to overrule his presidential assignment to govern the nation with an even and reasonable hand.

[But] *if* he is not telling the full story and is trying to end the Watergate "nightmare" before its full significance can be examined, then we are back in the Nixon era of deceit under a president not elected by the people but appointed by the man he now pardons.

The author concluded that Americans might ultimately view the pardon as a "wise and just act." In the meantime, he declared, the nation was "left with a president who has made a decision which we hope represents no more than an unwise judgment—*either* that, *or* the nation is still governed by a man whose highest motivation is self-preservation."[43]

Following on the heels of an unprecedented presidential scandal, Ford's 895 days in office received intense scrutiny. His first lady also gained more attention than many of her predecessors.

Outspoken by nature, Betty Ford often held political positions to the left of her husband. She not only supported *Roe v. Wade*—the landmark Supreme Court decision permitting abortion—but also publicly expressed her understanding of why young people had sexual relationships prior to marriage. In a television interview, she declared that she would have tried marijuana if it had been popular in her generation. But in her book *The Times of My Life*, she indicated that she ideally wanted everyone to "get back in the closet" with their overt expressions of sexuality. She declared: "I do think lesbians are entitled to free speech, the same as anybody else. God put us all here for His own purposes; it's not my business to try to second guess Him."[44]

Although some cultural traditionalists and conservative Christians criticized the first lady's outspokenness and break with traditional teachings, she shared much of her husband's orientation toward religion. Before breakfast Mrs. Ford read the Bible; each night she read a small prayer book.[45] When asked what her favorite biblical passage was, she replied that she did not have one but that 1 Peter 5:7—"Cast all your anxieties on him, for he cares about you"—was good. Queried about her favorite prayer, she answered that she hung the prayer of St. Francis of Assisi in her bathroom so that it would be the first thing she saw in the morning and the last thing she saw at night. Often said in Episcopal churches, that prayer reads in part: "Lord, make me an instrument of Your peace. Where there is hatred, let me sow love; where there is injury, pardon." She read booklets of daily prayers published by her denomination.[46] In the years when her children attended Immanuel Church-on-the-Hill, she taught Sunday school. "I felt I owed it to the church," she wrote. "How could I just drop off my own kids and go blithely on to church without contributing?"

Betty Ford's background in the Episcopal church (where worshippers then knelt for prayer) showed when she and her husband, unlike most Protestants in attendance, knelt to pray over President Kennedy's casket after his assassination. When asked to lead public prayer, she was not at a loss. When the president of the Jewish National Fund experienced a heart attack at a dinner, she instinctively went to the microphone and prayed for the dying rabbi. "We know You can take care of him," she said. "We know You can bring him back to us. We know You are our leader and our strength." After saying these or similar words, she asked everyone at the dinner to pray silently, each in his or her own way.[47]

Mrs. Ford became nationally known for her outspokenness and candor, as well as for her volunteer work for causes such as handicapped children and substance abuse. She played an active role in women's issues, discussed her mastectomy openly, expressed her desire that a woman be appointed to the Supreme Court, and spoke out strongly for the Equal Rights Amendment, the proposed constitutional amendment that banned gender discrimination. Her feeling for the arts paralleled that of Jacqueline Kennedy. Established five years after her husband left the presidency, her Betty Ford Center in Rancho Mirage, California, gained a national reputation for its treatment of drug and alcohol addiction. In her views of the relationship between religious belief and social activism, Betty Ford was much more like Lady Bird Johnson, Hillary Clinton, and Eleanor Roosevelt (whom she had admired as a young girl) than she was like Bess Truman, Mamie Eisenhower, Pat Nixon, or Laura Bush. She died in 2011.

When the Democratic Party nominated the evangelical James Earl "Jimmy" Carter for president in July 1976, many Americans who belonged to evangelical churches expressed their support for the Southern Baptist candidate. In 1976, the evangelical vote amounted to over 30 percent of the electorate and still tended to vote Democratic.[48] Despite being Episcopalian,

Ford did have some evangelical credentials. He belonged to the Capitol Hill prayer group, regularly attended congressional prayer breakfasts, preferred the King James Version of the Bible over the newer translations used by nonevangelical churches, and had a son, Michael, studying for the evangelical ministry. At Gordon-Conwell Theological Seminary in Massachusetts, the students referred to Michael's two omnipresent secret service guards as "Goodness" and "Mercy," in reference to the words of the Twenty-third Psalm: "Surely goodness and mercy will follow me all the days of my life."[49]

The central evangelical figure during Ford's two years in the White House was not Billy Graham, but rather a Grand Rapids evangelist named Billy Zeoli. Zeoli was president of the Michigan-based Gospel Films, one of the largest producers of religious films in the world. Closely associated with the evangelical entrepreneurs of the Amway Corporation of Grand Rapids, he was a pioneer in ministry to professional athletes, an unofficial chaplain to leading figures in sports, and an evangelist to teenagers. Zeoli—known as "Z" to his friends—had a distinctive background.

In Ford's description, Z's father was "a burglar and a drug addict," a fifth-grade dropout raised in South Philadelphia with "street hoodlums" as "teachers." Converting to Christianity in prison, Z's father later pastored a Baptist church in Philadelphia and married a member of its choir.[50] Billy, the couple's only child, graduated in 1955 with a degree in history from Wheaton College, Billy Graham's alma mater.[51]

Described as having "smoldering good looks," Zeoli aroused mixed feelings.[52] Observers criticized his egotism, showmanship, self-promotion, and hip language. Those who found life and religion complex disparaged the simplicity of his theology. "Z [sic] is something of a caricature," a *Sports Illustrated* writer noted. "He wears long adolescent bangs. . . . he dresses in flashy ensembles, the kind that . . . guys in pick-up bars favor . . . [He] has a passion for . . . pop vernacular."[53]

But his admirers, who included Gerald and Betty Ford, found him generous and dedicated. A *Sports Illustrated* writer declared that Zeoli's "self-perspective and good humor are saving graces."[54] Betty Ford was so impressed by Zeoli that she said, "Billy carries his church with him. He doesn't need a building to make you feel close to God."[55] Describing him as "an irrepressible Christian," Ford declared that the evangelist's greatest characteristic was *understanding.* "I am eternally indebted to Billy Zeoli for his understanding," Ford declared.[56]

Zeoli delivered the invocation at the session of the House of Representatives on the day Ford was selected as vice president. He was at the bedside when Mrs. Ford had surgery for cancer. Whenever they were together, in Ford's description, the two men spent their time "talking, reading the Word of God, and praying together." From the time Ford became vice president, Zeoli sent him weekly inspirational messages titled "God's Got a Better Idea." When the evangelist later published these devotions, Ford wrote an introduction to the book that described what they had meant to him in office.[57]

The intriguing dimension in this relationship is that Gerald Ford regularly attended an activist parish of the Episcopal church full of college graduates and noted for its literate preaching. Thus Ford was attending the equivalent of a university church. At the same time, he was taking counsel from a theologically conservative evangelist who held creationist views and who was associated with churches that bore such names as "Independent Presbyterian Church" and "Calvary Undenominational Church." The contrast is striking, but even more striking is the question of how Gerald and Betty Ford could live in these two intellectual and religious worlds.

The Grand Rapids evangelist played little public role in Ford's 1976 presidential campaign. Instead, the Ford campaign made what use it could of Billy Graham. Initially, Graham had felt so stung by the Watergate revelations that he had partially withdrawn from contacts with Washington. To be sure, shortly after Ford's inauguration he had visited the White House to pray and to read the Bible with Ford. He had also invited Ford to attend one of his crusades in Norfolk, Virginia, though Ford had declined.[58] But when Ford invited Graham to the White House in 1975, the evangelist sent his regrets.

Ford's staff was initially concerned that he not grow too closely identified with Graham because of the evangelist's association in the public mind with Richard Nixon. Graham had worked behind the scenes to gain a pardon for Nixon, later claiming that he had talked to Ford before the pardon was issued, while Ford said the conversation came after the pardon. The evangelist was vocal in public support of the controversial pardon, and presidential aides were wary of a close identification of Graham with Ford.

But when the Democrats chose a Southern Baptist evangelical as their presidential candidate, both Graham and the Ford staff changed their outlook. Carter had been involved with Graham's crusades in earlier years. Like Graham, he was also a Southern Baptist. In 1976 Graham told a reporter that he planned to "stay a million miles away from politics this year."[59]

But as early as spring 1976, when Jimmy Carter's chances of winning the Democratic nomination were increasing, a member of Ford's staff asked his colleagues "to be alert for possible events that we could book Billy Graham into with the president." When the health of Graham's wife, Ruth, prevented him from attending the National Prayer Breakfast in Washington in January 1976, both Ford and his staff were concerned about the effect of Graham's absence on Ford's campaign.[60]

Graham had probably voted for every Republican presidential candidate, except, perhaps, Barry Goldwater in 1964.[61] But during the 1976 campaign he maintained more of a stance of political neutrality than was normal for him. Yet he made certain public statements that one author describes as "giving evangelicals permission not to vote" for Carter. He told a leading newspaper, for example, that he would "rather have a man in office who is highly qualified to be president who didn't make much of a religious profession than to have a man who had no qualifications but who made a religious profession." He also equated Ford's evangelicalism with that of Carter. These statements nettled the Carter campaign to the point that one of Carter's sons made a public statement that the doctoral title that Graham used came only from a mail-order degree. Carter himself cautioned about "people like Billy Graham, who go around telling people how to live their lives."[62]

During the presidential campaign, Ford also paid a visit to Graham's alma mater, Wheaton College in Illinois. In order to appeal to born-again Americans, he appeared before the Southern Baptist Convention to remind the "messengers" that his son had attended one of their colleges. He attended the First Baptist Church of Dallas to collect the endorsement of the highly influential Southern Baptist pastor W. A. Criswell; he assured a convention of national religious broadcasters that he was an evangelical; and he also reminded journalists covering the campaign that he prayed and read his Bible daily. But his staff insisted upon most of these events; Ford was always reluctant to advertise his Christian beliefs or to use his faith as a way to get elected. Thus two political writers declared that the 1976 presidential election featured two born-again Christians as candidates, but that "only one was willing to run as one."[63]

By the end of the 1976 presidential campaign, many Americans believed that not simply Jimmy Carter, the lifelong Southern Baptist, but also Gerald Ford the lifelong Episcopalian, could be viewed as evangelicals. Since 1976 only one presidential election—that in 1988—has not witnessed at least one evangelical Christian running as a nominee of the Democratic or Republican parties. In three elections, both candidates have been evangelicals. The correlation with the six-year administration of Richard Nixon and its culmination in the Watergate scandal seems clear. After Nixon's resignation, the majority of voting Americans wanted men of genuine religious values in the White House. Thus the election of 1976 included a distinctly religious dimension. The final year of Gerald Ford's accidental presidency marked the beginning of the surge of evangelical Christianity in White House politics.

A lifelong Episcopalian, Gerald Ford was raised by churchgoing parents who had first met in church. His stepfather served on the vestry, or ruling body, of the family church. His mother not only participated in the women's groups of the church but also died while attending church. He was married in a church to a churchgoing wife. Faithful in his attendance, Ford was as active in his church in suburban Washington as his time permitted. His wife taught Sunday school. He had all of his children baptized and attempted to keep Sunday as a day when the family would attend church together. From the 1960s on, this cradle Episcopalian came under evangelical influence, and by the time he ran for president he had a son studying at an evangelical theological seminary.

Before being succeeded by Jimmy Carter, Ford served 895 days as president. He described himself as "a Ford, not a Lincoln."[64] During his years in the Senate and presidency, Lyndon Johnson had never thought highly of Ford's intelligence. In the expurgated version, lbj famously declared that "Jerry Ford can't walk and chew gum at the same time." While Ford was president, the comedian Chevy Chase jumpstarted his career by depicting the left-handed chief executive as an awkward oaf. Chase's Ford took tumbles, hit spectators with golf balls, mistook water glasses for telephones, and was generally clumsy.

During his two years as president, Ford continued the Nixon administration's commitment to detente in the relations of the United States with the Soviet Union and China. He ordered the removal of all remaining troops from Vietnam. He strongly supported the Equal Rights Amendment (which assured women and men equal rights under the law) and appointed the first woman chair of the Republican National Committee. His most consequential act may have been the Supreme Court appointment of John Paul Stevens, who in his thirty-four years on the bench played an increasingly large role in the Court's decisions. His administration had its critics. Domestically, his years saw problems with the economy as well as rampant inflation. The nation experienced a budget deficit each year of his presidency. Most famously, he refused to bail out New York City when it faced bankruptcy, prompting the well-known *New York Daily News* headline: "FORD TO CITY: DROP DEAD."

Internationally, Ford became involved with the internal politics of both Iraq and Iran and can be viewed as preparing the way for the seizure of the American embassy in Iran during his successor's administration. Some foreign policy commentators viewed him as too soft on the dictator Saddam Hussein, on the unpopular shah of Iran, and on the oppressive administration in Indonesia. His administration also witnessed the heartrending fall of Saigon and the North Vietnamese victory in the Vietnam War.

But at Ford's funeral, television commentator Tom Brokaw praised Ford as "the most underestimated president."[65] Former secretary of state Henry Kissinger described his achievements as president as "sweeping and lasting." Similarly, Jon Meacham has assessed Ford as "in a quiet, unnoticed way, an important figure in America's public religion" because at a critical time in American history, he genuinely believed in the theological imagery he used.[66] When Ford was sworn in, a Democratic senator could declare that he brought to the presidential office "strength of character, belief in God, and a record of family devotion, regular church attendance, and a reliance on our common creator."[67]

Ford died at his home in Rancho Mirage, California, on December 26, 2006. His body lay in state at the church he attended, St. Margaret's Episcopal Church, in nearby Palm Desert, California, then in state at the Capitol Rotunda. In early January, a capacity congregation of 3,700 attended a ninety-minute funeral service at the Washington National Cathedral, conducted according to the Episcopal Book of Common Prayer. Honoring Ford's rank of Eagle Scout, Boy Scouts directed mourners to their seats. The principal mourner was Betty Ford. Describing her as "tiny, stoic, bent, and beautiful," a blogger declared that "she walked down the long aisle on the arm of President Bush, then stood among her children, grand- and great-grandchildren, as Episcopal prayers were recited and hymns were played and sung."[68]

Among the speakers, President George H. W. Bush described Ford as "a Norman Rockwell painting come to life." In the homily, Ford's pastor in Palm Desert, California, remembered that he and Ford had recently discussed the controversy in the Episcopal church over the ordination of openly gay bishops and the blessing of same-sex unions. President Ford, the Reverend Robert G. Certain declared, "said that he did not think they should be divisive for anyone who lives by . . . the great commission to love God and to love neighbor."

Carrying Ford's body to Grand Rapids, Air Force One circled over the University of Michigan football stadium, where the Michigan marching band had assembled in full uniform. An all-night vigil at the Ford Presidential Museum preceded a funeral service in his home Grace Episcopal Church. Following the service attended by four hundred invited guests, including President Jimmy Carter, a motorcade traveled thirteen miles on the streets and avenues of East Grand Rapids and Grand Rapids to the former president's burial site adjacent to his presidential museum downtown. Thousands of men, women, and children lined the streets.

"Gerald Ford brought to the political arena no demons, no political agenda, no hit-list, no acts of vengeance," television correspondent Tom Brokaw said of Ford in his eulogy at the Washington National Cathedral, "[just] Main Street values."[69]

# James Earl Carter Jr.

1924 – ⟋ PRESIDENT FROM 1977 TO 1981

When James Earl ("Jimmy") Carter was elected president, a largely secular press corps spent substantial time pondering the meaning of such terms as "evangelical" and "Southern Baptist." At one of his early press conferences, Carter declared that if reporters wanted to know what a Baptist believed, they needed only to read the New Testament. Being a Southern Baptist was a major part of the thirty-eighth president's identity – so much so that the Secret Service referred to him as "the Deacon" in their communications. But Jimmy Carter was a different kind of Christian and a different kind of Southern Baptist. To a certain extent, the combination made him both a different kind of president and a different kind of former president.

Unlike most of his predecessors in the presidency, Carter did not adhere to a standard, middle-of-the-road form of Protestantism. Instead, he was a Protestant of the evangelical school. Evangelical Christians view the Bible as the supreme authority for faith and conduct, emphasize a born-again conversion experience (and not simply baptism) as the entrance to Christianity, and believe that a personal relationship with Jesus Christ is not only possible for humans but also essential to their salvation.

For Carter, religion was public. Newspaper readers and television watchers knew that he attended church regularly. The American public also knew, and generally viewed as remarkable, that he taught Sunday school both in Plains and when he could in Washington. Carter spoke frankly, frequently, and with little urging about his personal faith.

Born in 1924, Jimmy—the name he preferred and that he insisted appear on ballots—was the oldest of four children of Earl and Lillian Carter. His father, a prosperous peanut farmer and shrewd businessman, owned a peanut-shelling business, a large warehouse for farmers, and hundreds of acres of farmland. The Carter farm is actually in Archery, a tiny town two miles from

Plains. "A deacon and a dependable Sunday school teacher [who] was always present . . . when the church bell rang," Earl was active in the Plains Baptist Church, the largest of the three churches (Baptist, Methodist, and Lutheran) in Plains.[1]

A complex man, Earl was highly disciplined and driven, much as his oldest son became as an adult. Carter describes him as "a stern but fair disciplinarian whose word was absolute law in our house. His two basic requirements were obedience and truthfulness, and any serious violations were punished with a switch on our legs."[2] Approval from Earl Carter often seemed harder to obtain than disapproval. Later in life, Carter wrote a poem that expressed the extent to which he had "despised the discipline" as a child and "hunger[ed] for an outstretched hand . . . just a word of praise."[3]

Yet Carter also describes Earl as "often lively and full of fun with his friends."[4] Although most Southern Baptists frowned upon even social drinking, Carter's father threw parties with alcohol and typically had a drink with dinner. Talented in athletics, he was an excellent tennis player who even built a court on his farm. He was quietly charitable and helped both blacks and poor whites in the area from the Depression years on.

Earl Carter had no known argument with the southern status quo in racial matters. "Certainly by today's standards my father was a segregationist, as were nearly all the white citizens of the area," Carter wrote forty years after Earl's death. "It was a way of life that, in the early 1950s, had rarely been challenged in Georgia."[5] Jimmy Carter's belief in integration and his experience in the integrated U.S. Navy caused him to forget and to ignore racial distinctions. According to his wife Rosalynn, Jimmy and his father "got into real arguments" about integration and segregation during his infrequent leaves home.[6] But Earl Carter was held in high regard by African Americans in the Plains area. Upon his death in 1953, the family was surprised to see the outpouring of grief in the African American community of Plains and to learn the extent of his charity.

Jimmy Carter's mother, Bessie Lillian Gordy Carter, was a southern original who could have emerged from a Flannery O'Connor or Eudora Welty short story. She married Earl Carter shortly after receiving her nursing degree from the Wise Sanitarium in Plains. Raised a Methodist, she became a Baptist following marriage. Although she seemed to believe firmly in the

Christian faith, she attended church only occasionally. "She dressed and acted pretty much as she pleased," one writer says.[7]

Breaking with the southern social conventions of the time, "Miss Lillian" advocated racial equality and entertained blacks in her home. She continued to work as a private nurse or at the Wise Sanitarium not only after marriage but also following the birth of her children. At one point, she was the nurse in charge of the operating room. She provided nursing services to many African Americans in the Plains area, rarely charging for her help.[8]

A strong Democrat in political views, she volunteered to run the Johnson/ Humphrey campaign in Sumter County in 1964, when most southern whites despised President Lyndon Johnson for his stance on civil rights. She would leave work each day amid calls of "nigger lover, nigger lover" to find her car covered with graffiti and sometimes with its radio antenna broken off or tied in a knot. At the age of sixty-eight, following the death of her husband, she joined the Peace Corps. Asking only to be assigned "where it's warm, people have dark skins, and need a nurse's service," she served for almost two years as a nurse in India.[9]

A few biographers have described the Carter family as somewhat dysfunctional. With Lillian frequently unavailable because of work, the four children often saw more of their father than of their mother. According to one biographer, some neighbors and friends of the Carters remember that Earl "was the more nurturing parent—the one who was most interested in his children."[10] According to Carter, as an adult his sister Gloria "would tease Mama by claiming that we always thought the little black table [a place where Lillian left instructions for the children before she went to work] was our real mother."[11] In later years, Jimmy Carter recalled: "The strong memory in my mind is coming home and my mother not being there."[12] Lillian, however, seems to have exerted more influence over the adult character and views of her oldest son.

The Carter children—all of whom except Jimmy died, as did their father, of pancreatic cancer—seemed to go their separate ways. "The diversity among my siblings," Carter has written, "shows how tenuous these kinship ties can be."[13] President Carter also claimed that he and his two younger sisters "led separate lives" and "had little in common during my earlier years."[14]

The older of his two sisters, Gloria, had her first marriage annulled. She encountered lifelong problems with her son, who was in a California prison at the time his uncle became president. A bookkeeper and accountant who worked for the owners of large farms in the Plains area, she became a devoted cross-country motorcyclist with her second husband and served as a kind of den mother to traveling motorcycle clubs. Her funeral included a procession of thirty-seven bikers, and her tombstone reads, "SHE RIDES IN HARLEY HEAVEN."[15]

Ruth Carter Stapleton, the third child, married a veterinarian at age nineteen. Graduating with a degree in English from the University of North Carolina at Chapel Hill, she later took a degree in theology. Despite chronic depression and other emotional problems, she became a well-known southern evangelist whose healing ministry mixed Christian faith with New Age psychology. During Carter's travels, she sometimes served as a pastor to journalists in the back of the plane.

Potbellied William Alton "Billy" Carter III, the youngest child, ran the Plains gas station and later assisted Jimmy in the family business. "Momma often said that Billy was the smartest of her children," Jimmy Carter remembered.[16] While capable of behaving like a clown for journalists, Billy Carter was far better educated and informed than his public image suggested. He not only attended Emory University but also inherited a habit of constant reading from his mother.

Because Jimmy was thirteen years old when Billy was born, the two were not close when Jimmy left for Annapolis. Since his older brother was following a naval career, Billy grew up assuming he would succeed their father in running the family business. When Jimmy left the navy and returned to Plains to take over the business, Billy was stunned and embittered. "Only long afterward did I realize how aversely my decision . . . had affected Billy's plans," Carter later wrote. "The day he finished high school, he joined the U.S. Marines, and he . . . married soon afterward. They left Plains and didn't return after his enlistment expired."[17] Although Billy repeatedly refused invitations from Jimmy to return to Plains and help with the business, in 1963 he finally agreed.

Back in town, Billy became a southern good ole boy and a town character. Gradually developing into an alcoholic, he entered a rehabilitation program late in his brother's presidency. While Jimmy was in the White House, Billy also had a beer—Billy Beer—named after him. When he registered as a foreign agent of dictator Muammar Gaddafi's Libyan government, he became the subject of a full Senate hearing investigating whether he had tried to peddle influence.

Billy once described his family to journalists:

> Look: My mama was a seventy-year-old Peace Corps volunteer in India, one of my sisters goes all over the world as a holy-roller preacher, my oldest sister spends half her time on a Harley-Davidson motorcycle, and my brother thinks he's going to be president of the United States. Which one of our family do you think is normal?[18]

In reality, words other than *dysfunctional* might better characterize the Carter family. In his various autobiographical writings, Carter speaks well of his parents and siblings. He views them as broader in outlook and more intellectually curious than the typical resident of Plains. "I never knew how unusual the members of my family were," Carter has written, "until . . . after we returned from the Navy to live in Plains." Comparing his parents and siblings with those of Rosalynn, his wife, he writes:

> A Sunday dinner at her mother's home always included a long, pleasant, rambling discussion of what appeared to me to be minutiae. The casual conversation of a grandchild with a playmate or the illness of a distant relative would be thoroughly analyzed. . . .
>
> Collectively, they knew almost everything that had happened in our town . . . even when some potentially controversial subject arose . . . there didn't seem to be any rough edges to the discussion. The contrary opinions of everyone around the table were politely respected.
>
> After . . . the meal . . . [we] would sit on the front porch and continue a detailed discussion of the weather, the status of the crops, or interesting news about . . . people. . . . It is surprising how enjoyable it is—and inconceivable to me that the members of my family on either side would do such a thing year after year. [19]

As this description indicates, the Plains in which Jimmy Carter grew up was a traditional southwest Georgia town. Most men were in some way connected to farming. Women had "two garden clubs, a literary club, the

Junior Women's Club, the Red Hat Club, a group of widows who call[ed] themselves PALS, and the most exclusive, Stitch and Chat."[20] Early in the twentieth century, Plains gained some prestige in southern medical circles when three brothers named Wise established its Wise Sanitarium. Known as the "Mayo Clinic of the South," the hospital had a staff of about a dozen physicians. Jimmy Carter was born in the hospital.

Ecumenical associates rather than religious competitors, the Baptist and Methodist churches in Plains sometimes alternated their weekly services for a period so that neither drew from the attendance of the other.[21] Most children devoted Sunday and Wednesday evenings to religious youth programs. The churches even sponsored chaperoned "prom parties" for students. In an era when church and state were loosely separated in much of the South, public school in Plains began each day with "chapel"—a daily assembly that included prayer and even Christmas pageants.[22]

During the summers, both the Baptist and the Methodist churches sponsored weeklong revivals, which often featured well-known evangelists. Although Carter describes the town as not especially revivalistic, most residents went to hear the visiting evangelists. In his eleventh year, Carter had a conversion experience and was baptized at the end of a revival. From that time on, he was officially a Southern Baptist.

It was a distinctive heritage. Like Congregationalists and Presbyterians, Baptists emerged from the Puritan movements in the British Isles and American colonies. But Baptists differ from other Puritans by asserting that the New Testament teaches that only believing adults (or young adults) should be baptized—and then only by immersion. The Baptist tradition also teaches that a Christian must go through an experience of "conversion" or "rebirth" prior to immersion and formal admission to the church. In addition, Baptists have historically advocated the strict separation of church and state. On New Testament grounds, they believe that each Christian congregation is a unitary body capable of making its own decisions without recourse to higher supervision.

Separating in the 1840s from their Northern (or American) Baptist brethren over slavery, the Southern Baptist Convention has become the largest Protestant denomination in the United States. In the words of a leading church historian, the Convention is one of "the last great repositories of the

Puritan tradition in America."[23] More than most Protestant denominations, it has been influenced by revivalism, an organized effort to reawaken Christian faith through emotional conversions (such as the one Carter experienced in his eleventh year). Carter's roots in the Southern Baptist Convention ran deep. When in later years he came to disagree with some aspects of his religious heritage, he still found the Baptist tradition difficult to leave.

In addition to an ingrained religious tradition, Carter's upbringing instilled in him a strong work ethic and sense of determination. From the time he was a child, he had wanted to go the U.S. Naval Academy at Annapolis. Earl Carter had long attempted to persuade his local congressman to secure Jimmy an appointment. In Carter's words, "the Naval Academy became almost an obsession in our family" as he neared high school graduation.[24] But instead of appointing Carter, the congressman suggested he begin college in Georgia and wait for a possible appointment to Annapolis in a future year.

Bitterly disappointed, Carter took a year at Georgia Southwestern College in Americus and another year at Georgia Tech, studying engineering. Although he later wrote that "Tech was the most difficult school I ever attended," he excelled academically, ranking in the top 10 percent of his class.[25] At the end of the year, he received his long-sought-after appointment to the Naval Academy, which he attended from 1943 to 1946. At Annapolis, he continued his record of excellence in both academics and combat training, graduating in the top 8 percent of his 822-member wartime class.[26]

During his academy years, Carter remained introverted and socially distant. Classmates remember him as a loner with few close friends. But they also remember him as pleasant and helpful, with an understanding of the need for community. After the suicide of a senior classmate, Carter petitioned and was granted permission to move the surviving roommate into his dormitory so that "he would not be alone."[27] Carter exhibited a genuine religious devotion while at Annapolis. He attended the academy's Protestant chapel services (which were conducted according to the Episcopal Book of Common Prayer), became well acquainted with the chaplain, and even taught Sunday school to the young daughters of enlisted men. While on active duty in the navy, he sometimes officiated at services of worship aboard ship.[28]

Upon graduation from Annapolis, Carter married Rosalynn Smith of

Plains, who became his lifelong partner and closest friend. Early in their marriage, he worked directly under Admiral Hyman Rickover during the construction of America's second nuclear submarine.[29] But when his father died in 1953, he left his career as a nuclear engineer in the navy to take over the family farm and peanut warehouse. "When her husband announced that he wanted to move . . . back to Plains," a biographer has noted, "Rosalynn was dismayed. She savored independence from family ties and their small town, but then she did what was expected of her"—Sunday school, church, civic activities. Subsequently, she became a quiet but important adviser to her husband in political matters. During his years in the White House, Carter invited her to attend cabinet meetings.[30]

Back in civilian life, Carter followed his father's path in the family's business and in the church. He became first a Sunday school teacher, then a leader of the junior division of the Sunday school, and finally a deacon—the highest lay office in a Baptist congregation. Prior to running for president, he maintained a nearly impeccable record of church attendance.

Carter returned to Plains when segregation ruled the South and white Christians even searched out a biblical basis for their racial practices. Civil rights legislation was still almost a dozen years ahead. Carter was at first a quiet and later an outspoken integrationist in Plains. He was the only white businessman in town, and one of the few in Sumter County, who did not join the White Citizens Council, whose sworn duty was to enlist the aid of every white male in resisting school integration. When members offered to pay his five-dollar dues and reminded him that the decision not to join might hurt his business significantly, Carter responded that he would rather take five dollars "and flush it down the toilet" than join the White Citizens Council. He later wrote that he "was willing to leave Plains, if necessary" rather than support the White Citizens Council.[31]

In the pre–civil rights South, such positions did not go unpunished. While chairman of the Sumter County school board, Carter supported a referendum favoring the consolidation of public schools. Supporters of segregation believed that retaining smaller, often isolated schools would permit the county system to remain largely segregated, whereas consolidation would bring large numbers of black and white children together. When Carter's views on the referendum became known, he was called a "race mixer" and a "nigger lover."[32] Not only was his business briefly subjected to a boycott, but he and Rosalynn were also expelled from the Americus Country Club.

Jimmy Carter believed not only in the integration of schools but also in the integration of Christian churches. When the Plains Baptist Church addressed the issue of accepting African American members in the early 1960s, he and his mother cast two of the three votes supporting integration. "I spoke in favor of welcoming them and any others who came in good faith," Carter later remembered.

> We usually had about fifty members attend our monthly conferences, but on this occasion every pew was filled. When a vote was taken, only one other person voted with our family to admit everyone, while fifty opposed the motion. The significant thing was that almost two hundred others abstained.[33]

In 1962, Carter entered politics. After a stormy campaign and a lawsuit against his opponent's ballot-stuffing political machine, he was elected to the Georgia senate and reelected two years later. In the state legislature he exhibited the same combination of strengths and weaknesses that would later characterize his presidency: keen intelligence, egotism, vindictiveness, hard work, lack of pretension, Christian idealism, micromanagement, and self-righteousness of the kind that some interpreted as arrogance.[34]

During his four years in the legislature, Carter gained the reputation of a "good, hardworking reform legislator" who "did his homework."[35] Devoted to his senatorial position, he even took a speed-reading course so that he could read every bill on which he voted. With some of the reporters who covered the Georgia legislature, however, he gained a reputation for faultfinding, even to the point of criticizing their grammar or punctuation in stories. "You just dreaded to see Carter coming down the hallway in the legislative session," remembered Reg Murphy, the Atlanta reporter who covered the state legislature. In words later echoed by some who had experienced Carter's chilly rectitude in Washington, Murphy concluded: "Jimmy Carter . . . will never be human enough to overlook the faults of anybody else."[36]

Although the opinions of Carter held by his colleagues in the legislature varied, the consensus seemed to place him at least in the top third of all legislators serving at the time. In 1965, the daily newspaper that served Plains, the

*Americus Times-Recorder*, named Carter as one of the eleven most influential legislators in the state.[37]

Four years after entering the legislature, at a time when winning the Georgia Democratic primary was still tantamount to election, Carter ran in the Democratic primary for governor. He received 21 percent of the vote and finished third behind former governor Ellis Arnall and the noted Georgia segregationist Lester Maddox. Known for closing his popular restaurant near Georgia Tech rather than allowing blacks to eat in it, Maddox won the two-candidate runoff and ultimately prevailed in the general election with the help of the legislature.

The loss devastated Carter. The campaign had not only plunged him into serious debt but also caused him to lose twenty-two pounds.[38] He later wrote that he "lost faith in [his] own ability, the political system, and God's will for my life."[39] After losing an election to a candidate whose symbol was "a pickhandle that he used to drive potential black customers from the door of his restaurant in Atlanta," Carter declared:

> I was deeply disillusioned. I could not believe that God, or the Georgia
> voters, would let this person beat me and become the governor of our state.
> Ruth [Carter Stapleton] drove down to see me, quoted a scripture from the
> book of James, and urged me to react to failure and disappointment with joy,
> then patience and wisdom, and finally by striving for a transcendent religious
> experience.[40]

During this time, Carter experienced what he considered a second rebirth.[41] He had felt the pangs of this second spiritual awakening several times—once while walking in the woods with his evangelistic sister, Ruth, and once after hearing a sermon entitled "If You Were Arrested for Being a Christian, Would There Be Any Evidence to Convict You?" Carter now began to read the Bible with a fresh perspective. On the advice of his sister, he left Georgia and immersed himself in missionary work.[42]

Carter became involved with Project 500, an outreach program designed to establish 500 churches and missions. His mission trips took him to Pennsylvania and to Massachusetts, where he worked with the Hispanic residents of Springfield. Carter (who had learned Spanish in the Naval

Academy) "testified" from house to house, typically greeting homeowners with the words: "Hi! I'm Jimmy Carter, a peanut farmer. Do you accept Jesus Christ as your personal savior?"[43] With anyone who was home and interested, he would quote scripture and talk about God and religion. Frequently dropping by local bookstores to replenish his supply of Bibles, he would split the cost with the mission of any Bibles donated to families who had none.[44] Reports indicated that he was directly involved in more than fifty evangelical conversions.[45]

In 1970, Carter returned to politics. Winning both the Democratic primary and the general election, he was elected governor of Georgia. At the time some commentators assessed his campaign as hypocritical, for he seemed to present himself as a political and racial conservative, which he was not. As a means to balance his growing reputation as a closet integrationist, he called for an end to busing, attempted to secure Maddox's endorsement, and scheduled relatively few meetings with African American voters.

All of this led the *Atlanta Constitution* not only to endorse another candidate but also to describe Carter as an "ignorant, racist, backward, ultraconservative, red-necked South Georgia peanut farmer"—an attack that may have actually assisted his campaign.[46] "He wanted to appeal to the large middle class, blue collar type, predominantly white," declared E. Stanly Godbold, "and most of these people are going to be segregationists."[47] Winning the state's rural whites, evangelical Christians, and segregationists, Carter led the Democratic primary with 49 percent of the vote and forced a runoff. He later won the general election with 59 percent.

After his inauguration, however, Carter left little doubt of where his true sympathies lay. His inaugural address to the citizens of Georgia brought him national attention:

> This is a time for truth and frankness. The next four years will not be easy ones. The problems we face will not solve themselves. . . . But this is also a time for greatness. . . . We cannot afford to waste the talents and abilities given by God to one single Georgian. Every adult illiterate, every school dropout, every untrained retarded child is an indictment of us all. . . . It is time to end waste. If Switzerland and Israel and other people can eliminate illiteracy, then so can we. . . .

I say to you quite frankly that the time for racial discrimination is over. Our people have already made this major and difficult decision, but we cannot underestimate the challenge of hundreds of minor decisions yet to be made. . . . No poor, rural, weak, or black person should ever have to bear the additional burden of being deprived of the opportunity of an education, a job or simple justice.[48]

As governor, Carter streamlined Georgia's government. He concerned himself with integration, with improving educational opportunities for the poor, with the environment, and with reforming Georgia's prison system. In later years, Carter remembered that he devoted "more time [to] preserving our natural resources than any other issue."[49] Although Georgia had been known for its chain gangs, the new governor's reorganization allowed a half-dozen prison branches to be eliminated gradually.[50] By 1974, a portrait of the Reverend Martin Luther King Jr. hung in the state capitol.

Starting as an obscure candidate—a self-styled "peanut farmer" from Georgia—Carter won the Democratic nomination for president in 1976 over an impressive collection of leading Democrats. Unpretentious, homespun, rural, a devout Baptist layman, Carter seemed to recall an older, purer America to voters disenchanted by Watergate and Vietnam. During the campaign, he made statements such as

On social justice, human rights, the environment I would be quite liberal. On questions dealing with the management of Government, I would be quite conservative. . . . If I ever lie to you, if I ever betray you, then I want you to leave me.[51]

To all of his qualifications, he added experience as a businessman. In November 1976, he culminated what one religious magazine called his "phenomenal climb" by narrowly defeating incumbent Gerald Ford.[52] If Lyndon Johnson is considered a southwesterner, Carter became the first southern-born president since Woodrow Wilson. He was also the third Baptist (after Warren G. Harding and Harry Truman) to hold the office.

Carter's inaugural day began with a well-attended early morning outdoor People's Prayer Service held on the steps of the Lincoln Memorial. Both his pastor from Plains and his evangelist sister participated. The sermon was preached by Martin Luther King Sr.—"Daddy King"—who had served for four decades as pastor of Ebenezer Baptist Church in Atlanta. After watching the outdoor service on television, Carter attended a private prayer service at the First Baptist Church accompanied by incoming vice president Walter Mondale, cabinet members, and their families. One of the clergy participating was the father of Mondale's wife, Joan Adams Mondale. Mondale himself was the son of a minister.

At the inaugural ceremony itself, a United Methodist bishop, a Jewish cantor, and a Roman Catholic archbishop participated. Carter took the oath of office with his hand on a King James Version of the Bible, which was given to him by his mother. It was open to a passage in the Book of Micah: "He hath shewed thee, O man, what is good; and what doth the Lord require of thee, but to do justly, and to love mercy, and to walk humbly with thy God?"

As that passage indicated, a strong moral tone characterized Carter's address. In its conclusion, Carter expressed his hope that when he left the presidency after four or eight years, people might say that the United States had remembered the words of Micah—that it had torn down the barriers of race, religion, and mistrust; reduced unemployment; strengthened the American family; ensured respect for and equal treatment for all under the law; again become proud of its own government; and built a lasting peace, "not on weapons of war but on international policies which reflect our own most precious values."[53]

Missing from Carter's inauguration was Billy Graham—the first inauguration the evangelist had missed since that of Harry Truman in 1949. His absence was unsurprising. Even though both he and Carter were devout Southern Baptists, they maintained a distant relationship not only in the 1976 election but also essentially throughout their lives.

By all external considerations, the two evangelicals should have been allies. As a young man, Carter had idolized Graham. He had chaired two of Graham's crusades in Georgia and hosted the evangelist overnight when he was governor. In addition, Carter possessed religious qualifications that few other presidents or presidential candidates shared. As late as 2007, Carter singled out Graham, not Reinhold Niebuhr, as the person who had influenced him the most spiritually.[54]

Yet the chemistry was not there. Though he professed political neutrality, Graham was well known in Washington for his Republican sympathies. For six years he had essentially been Richard Nixon's unofficial chaplain and personal confidante. These considerations and others caused Carter to doubt that the two could ever be close. In addition, Graham—burned by his trust in the person and words of Richard Nixon—maintained more than his usual distance from political involvement in the years immediately following Watergate.

During the presidential campaign between Carter and Ford, Graham declared that he was "maintaining a public neutral position—as I always try to do in politics."[55] Yet certain of his statements during the campaign—such as his public reference to Carter as a candidate "who had no qualifications but who made a religious profession"—seemed clearly to support Ford.[56] The Carter campaign fired back. Besides Jimmy Carter's statement that Billy Graham went around "telling people how to live," his campaign aide Gerald Rafshoon (later White House communications director) declared: "Jimmy won't turn the White House into a Billy Graham Bible class."[57]

Carter did turn to Graham for assistance in securing the passage of the Strategic Arms Limitation Treaty (SALT II) with the Soviet Union in 1979. In addition, Graham and his wife stayed in the White House during the Carter administration, and the Grahams and Carters associated at other times. Carter's biographers, however, generally devote little space to his relationship with the evangelist.

Church attendance came to characterize Carter's presidency in a way that distinguished him from most other twentieth-century presidents. In the District of Columbia, he ultimately selected the First Baptist Church (self-described as "the Baptist Church of the Presidents") as his home church.[58] Excluding worship services held at Camp David or at locations other than Carter's home churches, the president's daily diary indicates that he attended First Baptist Church seventy-three times during the four years of his presidency. He taught Sunday school classes there fourteen times.

During the campaign, Carter declared that, if elected, he would attend whatever Baptist church was closest to the White House. Essentially, that decision narrowed his choice to the First Baptist and Calvary Baptist churches. In the end, the Secret Service decided that the larger of the two churches, the First Baptist Church, provided the greater security. A Romanesque Gothic structure dedicated in 1955, it was cruciform in design, and its balconies allowed a clear view of the sanctuary.

Ellen Parkhurst, who was raised in First Baptist Church, found the security arrangements during Carter's presidency relatively unobtrusive. In her words, the Secret Service was "good at blending in." On Sundays when the Carters attended, the agents did some searches and checked for bombs in such locations as flower arrangements and exterior manholes, but they did not obligate worshippers to walk through metal detectors. Because of the additional security provided, the Secret Service relocated the Couples Sunday School cotaught by Carter to the rear balcony, where approximately one hundred persons could sit. Parkhurst remembers ushering in the balcony one Sunday when a Secret Service agent whispered in her ear and asked if a particular person was okay to be in the balcony. By the time Bill Clinton occasionally attended the church as president, the Secret Service had placed sharpshooters on the roof.

The church has saved Harry Truman's pew from its former building, but it is on public display in the second floor lobby. During services, Carter sat in a pew in front of the pulpit, some seven or eight rows back. The president's sons and their wives, Rosalynn's mother, and occasionally other relatives or guests attended with them; their youngest daughter, Amy, attended Sunday school. Also present at each service were members of the press corps, for whom the church reserved a special pew.

At the end of the service, the pastor would ask the congregation to remain seated in their pews. According to Parkhurst's description, he would then escort the Carters to the street, where the Secret Service organized their departure into waiting limousines with "military precision." Close on Carter's heels came the press corps, led by the indefatigable Helen Thomas.

For the First Baptist Church, the Carters' attendance presented a mixture of advantages and disadvantages. The tourists who attended because First Baptist was Carter's church could be somewhat intrusive. But some families who had stopped attending returned, and some remained active after the Carters left. Among the members of the Carter administration who joined the church were Jody Powell, Carter's high-profile press secretary from Georgia, and his wife. Some leading evangelicals, such as the conservative columnist Cal Thomas, temporarily joined. The Carter years, Parkhurst summarized, saw "some rise in membership, definitely an increase in attendance," but also "a blip that was difficult, because a church is accommodating guests but the guests aren't joining the congregation."[59]

In 2008 Cal Thomas reflected on his years at First Baptist Church. "I was fortunate to attend First Baptist Church in Washington when Carter was president," he wrote.

> His regular attendance when he was in town established a type of normalcy that removed what might have been a disruptive experience had he only been an occasional visitor. While a pool of reporters always attended with him (and having reporters in church is a good thing!), they were respectful and did not intrude on the Carters' worship experience....
>
> That all of this seemed normal to Carter made the rest of us treat it as such. Carter even stayed to have coffee with fellow members in the church basement. I once "loaned" him a quarter for coffee because he wasn't carrying any money that particular Sunday.

Two weeks after Carter's inauguration, Charles Trentham, the pastor of First Baptist Church, baptized Amy Carter and another girl during the church's main Sunday service. He administered the baptisms by full immersion in a heated pool located in the chancel. Because Baptists interpret the New Testament as indicating that early Christian churches baptized only converted and believing persons who had received Christ into their lives, Baptists delay the ordinance. When they do administer it, they do so in the biblical manner—by full immersion. They believe children must have reached the stage of life where they can display to the world the credibility of what the pastor described to Amy as "your confession of faith in Christ as your Savior and Lord." Amy had turned nine four months earlier.

Both girls wore white baptismal robes during the baptism. Dressed in fresh clothes with dried hair, the two baptizees later rejoined their families in the pews and took Holy Communion for the first time. Because the Washington media had publicized Amy's impending baptism, the congregation was packed. At the beginning of his subsequent sermon, the pastor said: "I weigh my words when I say more people have thought of baptism this week than probably ever before. You have come, many of you, to see the parting of Baptism waters for the first time."[60]

On the few weekends when he was home, Carter attended the Plains Baptist Church three times in 1977, and once a year from 1978 through 1980. By the late 1970s, he had begun to switch his allegiance to the new and more progressive Maranatha Baptist Church outside Plains. His schedule, however, only allowed him to worship at the new church four times between 1978 and 1980. When he was able to, Carter taught Sunday school while in Plains.[61]

As president, Carter read several chapters of the Bible with Rosalynn every night. He became one of the few chief executives to "witness" about his Christian faith to foreign leaders. Among the heads of state to whom Carter spoke of his relationship with Jesus Christ were the president of South Korea, the first secretary of the Polish Communist government, and Premier Deng Xiaoping of the People's Republic of China. Among other issues, Carter urged Deng to permit Christian worship and to allow the use and printing of Bibles in China.[62] While some commentators and voters disparaged the president's inclusion of his personal faith in political discussions, "witnessing" is a hallmark of evangelicals. At the same time, Carter often "found himself the object of bipartisan accolades" for publicly expressing his Christian beliefs during his presidency.[63]

Carter carried his Baptist aversion to ceremony into his approach to the presidency. Thus he eliminated some of the quasi-royal trappings that accompanied the office. Defying both the Secret Service and tradition, he chose to walk with Rosalynn rather than to ride the one-and-a-half miles to the White House after his swearing-in ceremony. At his direction, "Hail to the Chief" was no longer played, and ruffles and flourishes were omitted during his public appearances. Insisting upon being known as "Jimmy" even while president, he carried his own suit bag when he traveled.[64] He sold the presidential yacht, reduced the use of limousines by the White House staff, and delivered a national address on television wearing a sweater. He and Rosalynn placed their daughter, Amy, in the District of Columbia public school system.

Southerners had long since become accustomed to political leaders who embodied the simple piety of Southern Baptists. But almost thirty years had passed since the unpretentious presidency of Harry Truman. Thus Jimmy Carter presented a different presidential image from such predecessors as Roosevelt, Kennedy, and Nixon.

Although some Americans liked Carter's unpretentiousness, others held that he diminished the respect the presidential office should command. Snatching a bag away from Carter on one occasion, Speaker of the House Tip O'Neill declared: "Bellhops vote too, you know." Carter, however, snatched the bag back. "What Carter failed to understand," O'Neill later wrote, "is that the American people love kings and queens and royal families. They *want* a magisterial air in the White House . . . most people prefer a little pomp in their presidents."[65] After Ronald Reagan defeated Carter and assumed the presidency in 1981, he revived the office's ceremonial trappings. By doing so he seemed to project the image of a stronger leader than Carter had.

In keeping with the Baptist and Protestant doctrine of the priesthood of all believers, Carter saw his presidency as a religious vocation. In a 1979 conversation with Premier Deng Xiaoping of China, he asked the Chinese leader to allow religious freedom, Bibles, and Christian missionaries into his country. "He seemed surprised," Carter noted in his diary, "laughed, and said he would reply the next day." Deng granted Carter's first two requests, but he would not permit missionaries because they "exalted themselves and tried to change the culture of Chinese converts."[66] A later visitor in the same year was newly selected Pope John Paul II. When the two discussed abortion, Carter expressed the difficulty he felt "as a politician sworn to uphold our laws" living with "permissive abortion." Afterward, on the south lawn of the White House, Pope John Paul II spoke to thousands and then blessed the audience. "When he went through the crowd," Carter wrote, "it was amazing to see sophisticated leaders almost collapse, often in tears, when he approached them."[67]

Carter's accomplishments in applying what he considered moral values to foreign policy are many. Principal among them was his negotiation at Camp David (the "Camp David Accords") of a peace treaty between Israel and Egypt. During the twelve days of meetings between the prime minister of Israel and the president of Egypt, Carter quoted the words of Jesus in Matthew 5:9, "Blessed are the peacemakers, for they shall be called the children of God."

Also notable was the administration's human rights legislation that aimed at removing the dictatorial noose, especially in South America but also in Asia. "Everywhere we went," he wrote of his 1979 visit to South Korea, "we pushed human rights."[68] Carter's most controversial decision made on moral grounds involved returning the Panama Canal to Panamanian control. Although a Republican senator from California humorously declared that "we stole [the Panama Canal] fair and square," Carter believed that the existing treaty between the United States and Panama was "profoundly unfair and unjust."[69] Although other presidents had seen the injustice involved, "no president until Carter," one writer declared, "had the courage to risk pushing the treaty through to completion. Carter not only risked it: he brought it off."[70]

In the opinion of Carter's aides, these and other policies stemmed from the president's religious beliefs. In 1979, his Christian faith caused him to give a national address (his infamous "malaise" speech) about a festering spiritual crisis and a need for repentance and sacrifice. Above all, what many critics viewed as his apparent paralysis in dealing with the Iranian hostage crisis of 1979 to 1981 can be seen as stemming from a Christian concern that life should be preserved. If a rescue effort into the heart of Tehran fell short of perfection, the American hostages—initially numbering sixty-six and ultimately fifty-two members of the embassy staff—could be killed, as well as the rescue team, Iranian guards, and—potentially—civilian bystanders.

Thus Carter attempted to use diplomatic channels to secure the release of the hostages. Stalemate and relentless criticism from opponents ensued. "Neville Chamberlain's umbrella-carrying appeasement was grotesquely wrong," the conservative columnist George Will wrote. "[But] Carter's appeasement [of Iran] is even more grotesquely wrong."[71] After five months, Carter yielded to the pressure of his national security adviser and ordered a secret rescue effort. When the helicopters experienced mechanical problems en route and one crashed into a refueling tanker, the mission failed, with the loss of eight American lives.

The central figure of the Iranian Revolution, the Ayatollah Ruhollah Khomeini, attributed the failure of the rescue effort to the intervention of Allah. American liberals and conservatives severely criticized the mission. "I want to express my profound grief at the loss of American lives and my profound shock," a Republican liberal declared. "I'm at a loss of what our government was trying to do."[72] The mission was a "total embarrassment."[73] In an article entitled "The Inexcusable Failure in Iran," a conservative columnist posed a question and then answered it sardonically: "'Why didn't the United States contract with the Israelis . . . to do the job for us? *Answer*: And admit that the Carterized Defense Establishment can't fight its way out of a paper bag?"[74]

To Carter's critics, the seizure of the embassy and the failure of the rescue attempt summed up the decline in American power and influence that characterized his administration. Just as Gerald Ford lost the support of many Americans by pardoning Richard Nixon, so Carter lost a substantial portion of the electorate when he allowed a Middle Eastern country to hold Americans hostage and to toy with the United States. In a final humiliation of Carter, Iran waited until twenty minutes after Ronald Reagan's inauguration to release the hostages. The Middle Eastern theocracy had held them from November 4, 1979, to January 20, 1981—the last 444 days of Jimmy Carter's presidency.

Intensified by daily updates on national television, the seizure of the hostages may have been the principal cause, but it was only one of a number of developments that caused Carter to lose a second term. From August 1979 through the Democratic National Convention the next summer, he experienced a divisive challenge in the Democratic primaries. The candidacy of Senator Ted Kennedy caused bitterness and disaffection among such normally Democratic voters as union members, African Americans, Jews, and residents of the East Coast.

Carter also lost the support of many of his fellow veterans by offering amnesty to men who had fled the country to avoid the Vietnam draft—something that Gerald Ford had refused to do. He lost more supporters because of a perception—one that may have been based more on his campaign statements in 1976 than on his actual expenditures for defense while president—that he had caused the United States to fall behind the Soviet Union in military power. Throughout his presidency, inflation and interest rates increased. In 1979, one year before the election, inflation averaged 11 percent. Finally, only a week before the election, he clearly lost the one televised debate he agreed to have with a man who turned out to be a better orator, Ronald Reagan.

During his one presidential term, American evangelicals especially felt betrayed by Carter. Many abandoned him because of his support of the Equal Rights Amendment (which promised women equal rights under the law) and his interpretation of "family" and "family values." He failed to speak out for prayer in schools. He did not work against the landmark *Roe v. Wade* decision of the Supreme Court. And unlike George W. Bush, he failed to appoint a sizable number of evangelicals to administrative posts. He allowed gays and lesbians to work in the White House, where he also served alcohol. His staff included single parents and same-sex parents in his important 1980 Conference on Families, which sought to define families and family values for the nation.

But the primary cause of the opposition of most evangelicals to Carter seems to have been a ruling of the Internal Revenue Service that removed tax-exempt status from segregated Christian schools. Even though the ruling was issued during the Ford administration a year before Carter assumed office, it was enforced during his presidency. Carter's administration (unlike the subsequent Reagan administration) did not support the Christian schools in court, and Carter received the blame for a decision that—in the words of one evangelical leader—"enraged the Christian community."[75]

The initial source of alienation between Carter and evangelicals was not the question of abortion. Initially, like virtually all mainline Protestant denominations, his own Southern Baptist denomination had approved the right of a woman to an abortion. The woman attorney who filed the initial lawsuit on behalf of the young and unmarried "Jane Roe" was an active member of a Southern Baptist church in Dallas. As early as 1971, the "messengers"—the term used by Baptists to describe representatives from local churches to annual conventions—to the annual meeting of the Southern Baptist Convention (SBC) affirmed their belief that "society has a responsibility to affirm . . . the sanctity of human life, including fetal life." It then adopted overwhelmingly a resolution calling upon Southern Baptists "to work for legislation that will allow the possibility of abortion under such conditions as rape, incest, clear evidence of severe fetal deformity, and carefully ascertained evidence of the likelihood of damage to the emotional, mental, and physical health of the mother."[76]

As Randall Balmer indicates, most Southern Baptists and other evangelicals initially responded to *Roe* not with outrage, but with "silence, even approval." Baptists, he notes, were particularly likely to support the decision because it drew a line between church and state. Balmer further notes that in 1975 an article in a leading Southern Baptist magazine asserted that the Court's decision permitting abortion advanced "religious liberty, human equality and justice."[77]

Many Southern Baptists, in fact, reacted to *Roe* similarly to W. A. Criswell, the immensely influential former president of the SBC and pastor of the First Baptist Church of Dallas, an early megachurch. "I have always felt that it was only after the child was born and had a life separate from its mother," Criswell declared in 1973, "that it became an individual person. And it has always, therefore, seemed to me that what is best for the mother and for the future should be allowed."[78] As early as 1967, while governor of California, Ronald Reagan signed a bill that legalized abortion in his state.

By 1974, however, opposition to abortion was growing in the Southern Baptist ranks. In that year the Convention acknowledged "continuing abortion problems" in American society but nevertheless reaffirmed the 1971 resolution. By 1976, the Convention denounced "the practice of abortion for selfish non-therapeutic reasons" and reaffirmed the "biblical sacredness and dignity of all human life, including fetal life."

By 1977, the messengers began to take an uncompromising position on abortion, calling on "Southern Baptists and all citizens of the nation to work to change those attitudes and conditions which encourage many people to turn to abortion as a means of birth control."[79] By the late 1970s, in the words of one of the Convention's emerging conservative leaders, the SBC was "well on the way to becoming the most pro-life denomination in America."[80] The developments in the SBC mirrored developments in the nation. In 1978, the first incumbent U.S. senator lost his seat to a candidate whose opposition to abortion attracted the votes of pro-life Roman Catholics, evangelicals, and others.[81]

By the late 1970s, some of the same evangelicals who had supported Carter in 1976 were openly campaigning against his reelection. During the same period, theological and political conservatives had begun to dominate Carter's own Southern Baptist Convention. Visiting Carter in the White House in 1979, the newly elected president of the Southern Baptist Convention said, "We are praying, Mr. President, that you will abandon secular humanism as your religion." The statement came as "a shock," Carter later remembered, "I . . . had no idea what he meant."[82]

But as the president and the nation increasingly learned, an activist and highly disciplined "religious right" had begun to coalesce as a force in American politics in the late 1970s. The movement combined religious and social conservatism, Republican politics, patriotism, family values, and traditional views of sexuality. It was led by such evangelical figures as Jerry Falwell and Pat Robertson of Virginia, Hal Lindsey of California, and James Robison of Texas and Colorado Springs. Focused on preserving the Christian heritage in the United States, it supported what it saw as biblical values and advocated pro-life and creationist views.

Though the Religious Right acquired its major influence during the Reagan and two Bush administrations, it steadily grew during the Carter years. Well funded, the movement endorsed and financially supported candidates who agreed with its positions. By rallying religious conservatives behind Ronald Reagan, it substantially contributed to making Carter a one-term president. "I had appointed many women to high positions in government," Carter later declared,

> [and I also] rejected using government funds in religious education, established an independent Department of Education to enhance the public schools, accepted the *Roe v. Wade* abortion decision ... worked with Mormons to resolve some of their problems in foreign countries ... called for a Palestinian homeland ... and was negotiating with the Soviet Union on nuclear arms control and other issues.[83]

All of these actions (including the cooperative attitude toward Mormonism, which many evangelicals viewed as a misguided cult rather than as a legitimate religion) flew in the face of evangelical politics and values.

In 1980, the American people decisively voted Carter out of office in favor of Reagan. Although Carter still had strong support among leaders of the mainline Christian communities, he lost many members of major voting blocs—such as Roman Catholics, evangelicals, blue-collar workers, rural Americans, and some Jews—who had provided the margin for his 1976 victory. To many Americans he had simply proved too liberal and ineffective—"incompetent, weak, and unable to lead," in the words of one writer.[84] The election results display the extent to which he left office politically discredited. He carried only six states and the District of Columbia. On the day before the election, Carter visited his mother, then in the hospital with a broken hip. When he told her his own polls showed he was going to lose the election, Lillian responded:

> It was the day before the election, and all the news was about the anniversary of the hostages being held in Iran, and blaming it on Jimmy. I said, "good!" and I went to sleep. I wanted him out—my whole family had been attacked and split wide open from Jimmy being president.[85]

Just as a distance gradually opened between Carter and the electorate, so Carter and the Southern Baptist Convention gradually grew apart. As the years went on, Carter broadened his interpretation of Christianity. His doctrinal beliefs remained firm, but he was not a dogmatist. On the other hand, the SBC increasingly enforced what it considered biblical dogma and orthodoxy. As conservatives began to take control of the denomination, Carter and Rosalynn felt more and more excluded.[86]

Essentially the Carters and the Southern Baptist Convention disagreed in four areas. Fundamentalism, or the belief in the verbal inerrancy and infallibility of the Bible, was the first point of contention. As highly conservative views of the Bible grew in the Convention, Carter resisted them. Traditionalist in many of his interpretations of the Bible, he nevertheless did not believe—as fundamentalists did—that the Jewish and Christian scriptures were without error. "Today's biblical literalists might believe that the universe was created in 4004 B.C. I don't believe that," Carter said in one interview.[87] Asked whether he was a creationist, he answered:

> I believe there's a supreme being, God, who created the entire universe, yes. And I am a scientist, as a matter of fact. . . . I think we ought to discover everything we can about science. It ought to be accepted as proved unless it's discounted. . . . But, I don't believe you ought to teach creationism in the science classroom.[88]

During the evangelical administration of George W. Bush, Carter became increasingly critical of what he called *fundamentalism*. "Fundamentalism exists . . . overwhelmingly in Washington," he wrote in 2005:

> A fundamentalist believes . . . that I am close to God. Everything that I believe is absolutely right. Anyone who disagrees with me . . . is inher-

ently wrong and therefore inferior. And it violates my basic principles if I negotiate with anyone else or listen to their point of view or modify my own positions at all.[89]

Strictly speaking, some or many of the theological conservatives in the Southern Baptist Convention were not "fundamentalists." A more accurate description might be that Carter came to understand the need for the kind of scholarly examination of the Bible pursued in mainline theological seminaries. Although such teaching and scholarship had once existed in the seminary system of the Southern Baptist Convention, from the late 1970s on it was increasingly repressed.

A second difference between Carter and the developing Southern Baptist norm involved his appreciation of mainline Christian theology. Most Southern Baptists centered their religious reading on the Bible, on biblical commentaries, and on books discussing spirituality. Well before Carter ran for president, however, he was reading such contemporary non-Baptist and nonevangelical theologians as the Lutherans Søren Kierkegaard and Dietrich Bonhoeffer and the Swiss theologians Karl Barth and Hans Küng (one a Calvinist and the other a Roman Catholic). He also read the Jewish philosopher Martin Buber, the German Protestant émigré Paul Tillich, and especially German American historian Reinhold Niebuhr. How extensively Carter read theologians other than Niebuhr remains a question, but he was clearly the most theologically self-educated president since Woodrow Wilson.[90]

Niebuhr taught at New York's Union Theological Seminary from 1928 to 1960. In 1965, when Carter first read *Reinhold Niebuhr on Politics*—a book containing selections from the theologian's writings—he told the friend who gave him the book that it was "the most amazing thing" he had ever read. Later describing Niebuhr's book as his "political Bible," he even wrote to Niebuhr's widow and told her that her husband had "contributed to my private education more than you could know."[91] Although Carter occasionally stressed his appreciation of Tillich's observation that "doubt is an acceptable, even necessary aspect of faith,"[92] no theologian had as great an impact on him as Niebuhr. The theologian's books and articles "seemed to answer the perplexing question of how a deeply committed Christian could conduct himself in politics without compromising his religion."[93]

A third area of disagreement involved the question of whether churches should become involved in politics. As late as the 1970s, most Southern Baptists believed in "the spirituality of the church"—a concept that the church should not sully itself by becoming involved in political activity. Carter sided with the small wing of Southern Baptists who believed that Christian churches had a fundamental obligation to work nationally and internationally on behalf of social justice. The Southern Baptist Convention did get involved with political issues from the Reagan years on, but Carter simply tended to be on the opposite side on most issues.

Sixty-five years after his baptism, Carter decided to leave the Southern Baptists. For some time, he had been uncomfortable with certain public positions taken by the SBC—specifically those that contradicted his sense of social justice. But the issue that ultimately tipped the scales concerned three declarations made by the Convention at its annual meeting in 2000. The first seemed to indicate that the Convention, and not the private judgment of individuals, would now decide the meaning of scripture. The second declared: "A wife is to submit herself graciously to the servant leadership of her husband."[94] The third prohibited women from entering the ministry or important lay positions in Southern Baptist churches.

For Carter, the statement about women was the last straw. "They now have decided that women can't teach men, and that women can't be deacons, and women can't be pastors, and women can't be missionaries, and so forth," he declared.[95] "In my opinion, this is a distortion of the meaning of Scripture," he continued. "I personally feel the Bible says all people are equal in the eyes of God. I personally feel that women should play an absolutely equal role in service of Christ in the church."[96]

"Imprudent and presumptuous . . . pure hubris" was the description Charles Colson gave to these words of the former president. "Carter's denunciation of the plain teachings of the Scripture as 'male interpretation of religious texts,'" the evangelical founder of Prison Fellowship declared,

> transgresses the teachings of the Fathers, the Reformers, and reliable modern interpreters. God's Word doesn't have to conform to the declaration of man or the shifting philosophical sands. . . . I have more confidence in 2,000

years of careful reflection on the ancient texts and the apostolic tradition than I do with the latest fad or somebody's "aha" moment.[97]

Carter's announcement declared that he and Rosalynn had changed their allegiance to the Cooperative Baptist Fellowship. Like the Southern Baptist Convention, this association of some two thousand Baptist churches formed in 1991 espouses the authority and inspiration of the Bible and the priesthood of all believers. Unlike the Southern Baptists, however, the Cooperative Baptists ordain women. They also continue to strongly support the separation of church and state. Granting autonomy to individual congregations, they oppose what a spokesman termed "the smothering hierarchical structure" that developed in the Southern Baptist Convention.[98] As to the inerrancy of the Bible, the Cooperative Baptists take the position that they "dare not claim less for the Bible than the Bible claims for itself. The Bible neither claims nor reveals inerrancy as a Christian teaching. Bible claims must be based on the Bible, not on human interpretations of the Bible."[99]

The Maranatha Baptist Church also joined the Cooperative Baptists. Today the Web page for the Maranatha Baptist Church contains a photograph of Carter. It discusses not only the security precautions the U.S. Secret Service imposes at church services when the Carters are present but also answers questions frequently asked by visitors who wish to attend his Sunday school class. As the Web page indicates, Carter's Sunday school class for adults begins an hour before the main service and meets in the church's three-hundred-seat sanctuary. Visitors beyond that number are seated in the church's fellowship hall, where a large television set allows them to follow the class.

If Carter left the presidency somewhat discredited, his stature steadily grew in the years following 1980. After leaving office, his high-functioning activities and writing may or may not have stemmed from a Nixon-like concern for rehabilitation, but their Christian moorings are clear. His work for world peace, his support for a separate Palestinian state (which has provoked charges of anti-Semitism), his efforts to normalize relations with China, his establishment of a major project to assist Atlanta's poor and homeless, his founding of the Carter Center in Atlanta—all of these efforts and accomplishments have gained him national and international respect.

In its own words, the Carter Center's aims are "Waging peace. Fighting disease. Building Hope."[100] Through the center, Carter has pursued peace and raised hope worldwide through such means as providing leadership in the monitoring of foreign elections; averting a multinational invasion of Haiti; and securing the release of prisoners held by countries such as North Korea. He is also a member of The Elders, a new alliance of senior global leaders formed by Nelson Mandela of South Africa to assist in solving difficult international problems.

In the view of some health experts, the greatest achievement of the Carter Center in fighting disease involves the virtual eradication of the three-foot-long, parasitic Guinea worm that once afflicted fifty million people worldwide and still afflicted more than three million residents of Africa and elsewhere by the time the Carter Center was founded. By 2010, health authorities had discovered less than 1,700 cases worldwide. If fully eliminated in upcoming years, the Guinea worm will represent the first parasitic disease in history to be eradicated. "I'm still determined to outlive the last Guinea worm," Carter told the Associated Press in 2011.[101]

In 2002, these efforts prompted the Nobel selection committee to award Carter the Nobel Peace Prize. "The Nobel Committee has not very often honoured mediators," Gunnar Berge of Norway declared during the presentation:

> But a mediator has rarely played a more important part than [at Camp David in September 1978]. . . . Through thirteen days, and as many nights, Carter showed that a mediator could make a decisive contribution to the creation of peace between Egypt and Israel. But Carter had broader aims . . . he wanted peace in the whole Middle East.[102]

Yet the most striking image of Carter's ex-presidency may not be his work on behalf of peace, but rather his manual labor in building homes for the poor with Habitat for Humanity, whose international headquarters are located ten miles from Plains. Most ex-presidents of recent decades have seemed to play in celebrity golf tournaments or to churn out books in an attempt to give their side of history. Thus the idea of an ex-president, accompanied by his spouse, taking long bus rides and working on houses for a week in places such as the Bronx was novel, arresting, and even biblical to some Americans.

Carter himself gave a high priority to his and Rosalynn's association with Habitat for Humanity. "We have done this for more than twenty years," he wrote in 2005,

> in ghetto areas, rural towns . . . a Native American reservation . . . and also in Mexico, Canada, Korea, the Philippines, Hungary, and South Africa. We work side by side with poor families who will be able to own the houses because Habitat follows the biblical prohibition against charging interest. This has been an enjoyable and heartwarming opportunity for us and many others to put our religious faith into practice."[103]

Jimmy Carter's administration never reached its idealistic goals. "His was . . . a presidency with considerable potential," one biographer has written:

> Jimmy Carter was an exceptionally smart man. He could also be very engaging; few failed to be dazzled by his memorably wide smile. And, at least early on, he sometimes demonstrated a real sense of what many Americans wanted. . . . He was a shrewd political operator who had developed a keen feel for electoral politics.[104]

Carter's intense study of the New Testament, his mother's influence, his views on race, his populist politics, and his reading of theology led him to adopt a large number of the positions he later advocated as governor and president. Although many voters identified with the spirit and programs of Carter's born-again presidency, the majority of the nation did not. The groundswell of national support that had greeted Carter after his inauguration steadily dwindled. From a total of 297 electoral votes in 1976, his total dwindled in 1980 to a mere 49. He won the 1976 election by almost two million popular votes; in 1980 he lost by over seven million. The results represented a devastating repudiation of his programs and vision.

Yet many decades after he assumed the presidency, a reader can still find that same idealistic vision in Carter's acceptance speech at the Nobel Peace Prize ceremony in 2002. Carter's words of acceptance to the Oslo audience differ greatly from those most presidents of the United States would have chosen. They also differ remarkably from those Barack Obama used in 2009 when he accepted the Nobel Prize. In his acceptance speech, Carter said:

I worship Jesus Christ, whom we Christians consider to be the Prince of Peace. As a Jew, he taught us to cross religious boundaries, in service and in love. He repeatedly reached out and embraced Roman conquerors, other Gentiles, and even the more despised Samaritans.

Despite theological differences, all great religions share common commitments that define our ideal secular relationships. I am convinced that Christians, Muslims, Buddhists, Hindus, Jews, and others can embrace each other in a common effort to alleviate human suffering and to espouse peace. . . .

But tragically, in the industrialized world there is a terrible absence of understanding or concern about those who are enduring lives of despair and hopelessness. We have not yet made the commitment to share with others an appreciable part of our excessive wealth. This is a potentially rewarding burden that we should all be willing to assume.

Ladies and gentlemen: War may sometimes be a necessary evil. But no matter how necessary, it is always an evil, never a good. We will not learn how to live together in peace by killing each other's children. . . .

God gives us the capacity for choice. We can choose to alleviate suffering. We can choose to work together for peace. We can make changes—and we must.[105]

# Ronald Wilson Reagan

*1911–2004* ↬ PRESIDENT FROM 1981 TO 1989

"I see two primary threads jumping out of my father's storyline," Ron Reagan wrote in *My Father at 100*: "[a] fierce desire to be recognized as someone noteworthy, even heroic; and his essentially solitary nature."

In his recent biography of his father, President Reagan's youngest son continues:

> In the film unwinding in his mind, Dad was always the loner . . . who rides to the rescue in reel three. . . . [He] was looking to wear an unblemished white hat. . . . He wanted and needed acclaim and recognition. . . . [But] it was crucial to his sense of self that he be seen working on behalf of others, and not for personal gain.

If the first thread Ron Reagan perceives in his "storyline" relates to public life, the second deals with the private life behind it. "Another, quieter Reagan, just as vital," the son writes, "rested invisibly beneath the waves." Calling this second persona "the Private Reagan," the younger Reagan defines its role in his father's life:

> This hermetic self . . . was, in effect, the producer and director for the man on stage. . . . [Inside] the personal drive he publically foreswore burned with a cold but steady flame. This private self . . . formed his core. . . . The Ronald Reagan with whom everyone is familiar could not have existed without the Ronald Reagan he rarely let anyone see.[1]

Shortly before he became governor of California in 1967, Ronald "Dutch" Reagan answered a letter from an inquirer who wished to know his religious faith. "I was raised in the Christian Church," he replied, "which as you know believes in baptism when the individual has made his own decision to accept Jesus. My decision was made in my early teens."[2]

Although many historians of Christianity would not classify the Christian

Church (Disciples of Christ, or DOC) as "evangelical"—it does not, for example, teach the necessity of an emotional conversion experience—Reagan's choice of words in the quotation above describes the kind of decision for Jesus Christ that lies at the heart of evangelical religion. Reagan often used versions of this wording to describe his faith. Answering the central question posed in a letter from an evangelical correspondent in 1976, Reagan declared, "Yes, I do have a close and deeply felt relationship with Christ and believe I have experienced what you refer to as being born again."³

In evangelical Christianity, believers must embrace Jesus to receive salvation. As evangelicals would put it, they must "ask Jesus into their heart" and not merely inherit a religion defined by belief in creeds. A crucial distinction between evangelical and other forms of Christianity involves whether the believer "*knows* Christ" or "knows *about* Christ." When asked about this distinction by the evangelical president of the Southern Baptist Convention in 1980, Reagan answered, "I *know* Him."⁴ The Christian Church that nurtured Reagan valued learning. It taught that a reasoned belief in the New Testament message—rather than a born-again conversion experience—was sufficient for salvation. But the evangelical interpretation Reagan placed upon his decision to be baptized and to join his mother's church was undoubtedly heartfelt.

Reagan's father, John Edward "Jack" Reagan, was born in Fulton, Illinois, in 1883. Both parents had died by the time he was six years old, and an aunt raised him.⁵ His education ended with grade school.⁶ A charming and ingratiating man, Jack was a cutup and a great storyteller. He was also a "footloose shoe salesman" and an alcoholic.⁷ As he went from job to job, his wife and two sons moved from house to house. "Old Jack was not that kind of provider," a neighbor remembered. "And the landlords even in [the] Depression wanted the rent and if you couldn't pay the rent [they would] say 'Go.' . . . Old Jack was all man and a yard wide. . . . He was just thirsty all the time."⁸

Jack Reagan's alcoholism and frequent joblessness caused his family to live in near poverty. "As a family the Reagans had no money," Reagan's older brother John Neil ("Moon") remembered. "We were poor folk." A woman of Republican views who grew up with the Reagans in Dixon once remarked: "I just explode when someone says, 'What does Ronald Reagan know about being poor?' If ever anyone knew what it was like to be poor, it was Dutch."⁹

A first-generation Irish American, Jack Reagan grew up in the Roman

Catholic Church. Officially he remained a Roman Catholic all of his life. But he seems to have taken his religion lightly; he attended Mass sporadically, married a Protestant, and allowed his sons to be baptized in a Protestant church. His oldest son remembered him as "more Elks" than Catholic.[10] When a priest reminded the couple that by church law Neil must be baptized as a Roman Catholic, Jack "snapped his fingers and said, 'Father, I completely forgot!'"[11]

Jack Reagan was a Democrat in a Republican area of Illinois and a Roman Catholic in a Protestant part of the state. He lived in Illinois when many of its citizens were suspicious of Roman Catholicism and when the Ku Klux Klan had a sizable membership. He was no bigot. He did not allow his sons to see the film *Birth of a Nation*. In later years, Ronald Reagan spoke proudly of the time his father chose to spend a winter night in his car rather than check into a small-town hotel where the clerk had told him, "You'll like it here sir, we don't permit Jews."[12]

Reagan's mother, Nelle Clyde Wilson, came from a Scots background on her father's side and an English background on her mother's.[13] The youngest of seven children, she was born in Fulton, Illinois, in 1883. Her father disappeared for several years when she was seven, leaving her mother to raise the children alone until he returned.

Under the care of her mother, Nelle grew up in a devout Methodist home. The Wilsons kept strict Sabbaths, regularly attended church, abstained from alcohol, and read the Bible frequently. According to one biographer, on Sundays the family "would listen to a ninety-minute sermon and then reassemble after brief pleasantries for three more hours of sermon, readings, prayers and hymns."[14]

In 1904, despite her father's objections, Nelle married Jack Reagan in a Roman Catholic ceremony in Fulton's Church of the Immaculate Conception.[15] The priest performed the wedding in his rectory, for Roman Catholic practices at the time normally prohibited mixed-marriages from taking place in the church itself.[16] Two years later, the couple moved to the nearby town of Tampico, where Neil was born. Although a Methodist, Nelle acceded not only to her husband's desire for a Roman Catholic marriage ceremony but also to his wish that their first child be baptized by a Roman Catholic priest. But when her marriage became unstable because of Jack's drinking and his inability to hold a job, she seems to have turned to her Protestant upbringing for support. Ronald Reagan remembered hearing loud arguments about his father's drinking coming from his parents' bedroom as a child.[17] By the time the family came to Tampico, Nelle had become active in the Christian Church (DOC).

In 1920, the family moved to Dixon, Illinois, a county seat with a population of eight thousand. The town's principal business was servicing dairy farmers, but it also included a teacher's college, several large employers, a vaudeville theater, a YMCA, and many churches. After moving there, Nelle joined one of those churches—the local First Christian Church (DOC).

Insisting on raising Neil and Ronald in her own denomination, in 1922 Nelle had both boys baptized by immersion in the First Christian Church. Her sons participated in the full range of the church's activities with her. Neil once outlined the agenda of a typical week: "Sunday school Sunday mornings, church Sunday morning, Christian Endeavor Sunday evening, church after Christian Endeavor and prayer meeting on Wednesdays."[18] His mother also regularly visited patients in mental hospitals and brought baked goods and Bibles to prisoners. Although "demure in appearance," Ron Reagan writes of his grandmother, "she was by nature a dynamo."[19]

For Neil—a teenager and hence more set in his ways at the time his mother required that he change churches—the earnest Protestantism and simple worship of the Christian Church did not take. "As much his father's son as Ronald was his mother's," he returned to Roman Catholicism at age eighteen.[20]

Ron, however, followed Nelle's religious guidance. He regularly accompanied her to services of worship and prayer meetings, performed with her when she visited patients at the state hospital in Dixon, participated in church plays and other performances, cleaned the Dixon church, taught Sunday school from the age of fifteen on, and at the same age led an Easter Sunrise service.[21] Decades later, when he was inaugurated as the president of the United States, he took his oath of office with his hand on his mother's Bible. "Nelle's great sense of religious faith rubbed off on me," he once declared.[22]

An evangelical novel also rubbed off on Reagan's boyhood faith. Young Reagan read Harold Bell Wright's *That Printer of Udell's*, which tells the story of Dick Falkner, a young boy who comes from a broken home. After his parents die, Dick moves to Boyd City, which he vastly improves through his Christian actions. The book ends with Dick's election to Congress and his desire to transform the country. According to Reagan, this novel directly led to his decision to join the Christian Church (DOC).[23]

When he began attending the First Christian Church in Dixon, Reagan met two people who significantly influenced his life. Ben Cleaver, the pastor, became not only his spiritual adviser and mentor but also a kind of substitute father. Cleaver's attractive and intelligent daughter Margaret became his steady companion.

"Well-read and curious, a former student at the University of Chicago who read Hebrew and classical Greek," Ben Cleaver became minister of the First Christian Church in the same year that Reagan was baptized in its new sanctuary.[24] Although some parishioners thought Cleaver too intellectual, he invariably rejuvenated his congregations, increasing membership wherever he served. Reagan hung around his parsonage, where Cleaver frequently discussed intellectual topics with him. The minister even taught Reagan how to drive an automobile. In later years Reagan remembered his boyhood pastor as a "wonderful man" whose influence on his life had been "great."[25]

Reagan dated Margaret Cleaver for eight years and was her constant companion in Dixon. The two performed together in church and school plays and ultimately became engaged. Always the church was at the center of their relationship.[26] Because Margaret chose to attend Eureka College, a college of the Christian Church (DOC) located eighty miles away, Reagan also decided to matriculate there following his high school graduation. Having maintained a close relationship with the pastor and his daughter since age eleven, he entered Eureka "as close to being a 'minister's kid' as one can be without actually moving into the rectory."[27]

In his freshman year at Eureka, Reagan gave a speech to students that influenced them to go on strike until their unpopular college president resigned. During his last two years at the school, he played on the football team as starting guard.[28] His performances in the dramatics club were popular with students. Yet the future president never stood out academically—his grades remained toward the middle of his class.

Margaret Cleaver, however, quickly proved herself an exemplary student. She held high hopes for the future, intending to travel after graduation. Although she became engaged to Reagan in college, the two later began to drift apart. "He was always a leader," Margaret once said. "Still, I didn't think he'd end up accomplishing anything."[29] While spending the year in France with her sister after graduation, she met and fell in love with a young man serving in the American consulate. In 1933—the year after their graduation—she ended her engagement to Reagan, sending him a letter that contained not only his fraternity pin but also their engagement ring.[30] Biographers have not speculated about any relationship between the broken engagement with the minister's daughter and the subsequent decline in his church attendance. Reagan had been almost inseparable from Margaret Cleaver and her father since he was eleven years old. For him, church must have been interwoven with that personal relationship.

After college, Reagan obtained a job as an announcer in Des Moines for a radio station, WHO. By this time, a coworker could describe him as "a deeply religious man [though] not the kind who went to church every Sunday. A man with a strong inner faith. Whatever he accomplished was God's will—God gave it to him and God could take it away."[31]

This description seems to characterize Reagan's religious practices for the rest of his life. After several years working in the radio business, Reagan obtained a job as an actor and moved to California. There he attended church irregularly. In 1940, he married the actress Jane Wyman. The ceremony was performed in the Wee Kirk o' the Heather Church in Glendale, California, one of several nondenominational churches located in Forest Lawn Memorial Park.

In the 1940s, Reagan's mother moved to Los Angeles and soon became active in the Hollywood-Beverly Christian Church (DOC). Reagan then enrolled his children, Maureen and Michael (an adopted son), in the church's Sunday school. Ronald himself began attending church with some regularity, and Jane Wyman not only attended with him but also taught Sunday school. When the marriage began to founder, Michael Reagan reports that his father asked the Christians he knew to "please pray for my marriage."[32] After he and Wyman divorced in 1949, Reagan's attendance declined.

An article for a movie fan magazine indicates Reagan's beliefs in the year after his divorce: "I go to a Protestant church, the Hollywood Beverly Christian Church," he wrote, "though not as regularly as I should."[33] The article, entitled "My Faith," continues:

I wouldn't attempt to describe what God is like, although I place my greatest faith in him. . . . I think the wonderful line in the Bible which says God is love comes as close as words can. . . . I wouldn't attempt to describe what heaven is like. . . . I do think there's something beyond the grave, that we were given souls for a reason, that if we live as the Bible tells us to, a promise will be kept.

I don't believe in hell. I can't believe that an all wise and loving Father would condemn any one of his children to eternal damnation. . . . I believe in prayer.[34]

Wyman's religious development subsequently went in a distinctly different direction. Reagan was her second husband. Following their divorce, she married and divorced twice more. Later, she converted to Roman Catholicism and insisted that Maureen and Michael join her in her new church. Because of her multiple marriages, she needed to receive an indult, or dispensation, from her bishop to receive Holy Communion at Mass. When she died in 2007, she was buried in a nun's habit in Forest Lawn Memorial Park.

Reagan first met Nancy Davis—who had been christened (during her mother's first marriage) Anne Frances but was always addressed as "Nancy" —in 1949, shortly after his divorce.[35] The future first lady was no stranger to divorce herself. Her parents separated and divorced when she was a child. Because her mother was an actress constantly traveling from city to city, she had lived for six years with her aunt and uncle in Maryland. After her mother remarried, Nancy was raised by her mother and stepfather in Chicago.

Her father, Kenneth Robbins, was a Princeton graduate whose fortunes declined to the point that he became a car salesman in New Jersey. Her mother, Edith Luckett, was the youngest of nine children of an old Virginia family. Her father's position with the Railway Express had taken the family to Washington, but Edith's mother returned to Petersburg, Virginia, for the birth of each child so that she would not "give birth to any damn Yankees."[36] As a teenager, Edith dropped out of school and played in various stock companies up and down the East Coast. She came to know many of the rising actors and actresses of her day, including Spencer Tracy, Walter Huston, and Katharine Hepburn.

In 1929, when Nancy was seven years old, Edith married Loyal Davis, a prominent Chicago surgeon. The ceremony took place in the chapel of Chicago's impressive Fourth Presbyterian Church. Raised a Presbyterian, Edith seems to have attended the church occasionally. The Davises occupied the lower ranks of the Chicago social register. Their social circle was generally drawn from Davis's fellow physicians, Republican politics, and Edith's network of friends in show business.

Described by one biographer as perfectionistic, extremely neat, distant, contemptuous of the poor, and bigoted against blacks, but fair, Loyal Davis held extremely conservative political views.[37] Although Reagan once said of him, "He's always been an agnostic," other sources describe him as an outspoken atheist.[38] Nancy's descriptions in her autobiography tend to coincide with these descriptions, though she stresses that Davis was "warm and tenderhearted underneath."[39]

Nancy attended the Girls' Latin School in Chicago, where her principal interest was drama. At age eighteen she had a coming-out party in Chicago. At Smith College, she majored in English and drama. Graduating in 1943, Nancy acted in summer theater, on Broadway, and in Hollywood films. She rarely had major roles. She and Reagan dated for three years before marrying in 1952 in the Little Brown Church. Located in Studio City, California, the church was associated with the Christian Church (DOC), Reagan's denomination.

After marrying Nancy Davis, Reagan changed his church affiliation to the Bel Air Presbyterian Church, a church then popular among Hollywood figures. Located near UCLA and Sunset Boulevard in the highly affluent community of Bel Air, the church belonged to the evangelical wing of mainstream Presbyterianism. Today the Bel Air church's statement of faith describes the Bible as "inspired, the only infallible, authoritative Word of God." Mainstream Presbyterianism would agree that the Bible is both inspired and authoritative, but it would not grant full infallibility to its assertions.

The Reagans attended Bel Air Presbyterian sporadically beginning in 1964. Their affiliation coincided with the arrival of a new pastor, the Reverend Donn Moomaw, a former all-American linebacker at UCLA. Reagan liked Moomaw, his style of preaching, and his use of sports metaphors—such as referring to Jesus as "the quarterback of a person's life."[40] Although he and

Nancy did not formally join the church until after Reagan left the presidency, Reagan regularly tithed to it.

During his eight years (1967–1975) in Sacramento as governor of California, Reagan was not noted for church attendance. "I've never heard it said that Reagan was a church-going guy," declared a former political writer for the *Sacramento Bee* (now an Episcopal priest), "[but] this being California, church attendance is not a political issue."[41]

Reagan's infrequent churchgoing continued during his two terms as president. In Washington the Reagans affiliated with National Presbyterian Church, the same church to which the Eisenhowers had belonged. Because numerous presidents had worshipped at either the National Church or its predecessors, the church followed a set protocol. Whenever a president attended, the pastor saw him into his pew. At the end of the service, the pastor asked the congregation to "please remain seated after the benediction while the pastor escorts the President out."

During Reagan's presidency, the pastor of National Presbyterian was the Reverend Louis Evans. In his own words, Evans spent "quite a bit of time with the Secret Service talking about how we would get the President in and out of the church services." The pastor reported that Reagan "attended several services" in the eleven weeks between the Sunday prior to his inauguration and the attempt on his life at the end of March 1981. Following the failed assassination, Reagan asked Evans to serve him Holy Communion in the hospital.[42] Given their record of church attendance in previous years, "several services" in eleven weeks may indicate that the Reagans planned on attending worship more frequently while in the White House.

After the attempt on his life, however, the Reagans essentially stopped attending church in Washington. Reagan's papers indicate that the Reverend Mr. Moomaw mailed him "tapes of faith" at least once. Both the president and Nancy attributed their absence from church to the new security precautions added by the Secret Service after March 1981. They said they found the extra measures oppressive and disruptive not only to themselves but also to other worshippers.

The Reagans may have been expressing precisely what they felt. Both Billy Graham and Don Moomaw supported the president's decision to forego attending church.[43] "It bothers me not to be in church on Sunday," Reagan wrote in his diary five months after the assassination attempt, "but don't see how I can with the security problem. I'm a hazard to others. I hope God realizes how much I feel that I am in a temple when I'm out in his beautiful forest & countryside as we were this morning."[44]

Some observers, however, saw the Reagans' explanations as lame excuses from a couple disinclined to attend church. "It must be noted," a conservative author wrote, "that such concerns did not stop either ... George Bush or Bill Clinton ... from attending church services outside the White House."[45]

These criticisms have some merit. St. John's Church, adjacent to the White House, was specially outfitted to meet the rigorous security requirements of the Secret Service. In addition to George W. Bush and Bill Clinton, Presidents Eisenhower, Johnson, and Carter regularly attended church while in the Oval Office. Richard Nixon regularly held services in the White House. John F. Kennedy was assassinated not at Mass but in a motorcade. Moreover, the Reagans spent many weekends at Camp David, but they neither arranged for services there nor went to churches in adjoining towns. Although Reagan notes in his autobiography that his biggest disappointment about the weekends he spent at Camp David was that he could not go to church, his statement is not entirely persuasive.[46]

By 1982, Reagan's failure to attend church had become a subject of national conversation. In February of that year, a public affairs officer in Washington wrote to Edwin Meese, counselor to the president. His letter used Reagan's recent attendance at a special service honoring the birthday of George Washington as the springboard for a sweeping proposal that Reagan attend services of worship at a wide spectrum of churches and synagogues:

> As a genuine show of compassion to all mankind and helping to debunk "President of the Rich" accusations—President Reagan might consider attending a "series" of religious services of different denominations creating a new theme—"America Prays Together."
>
> A good beginning was made when the President marked George Washington's birthday by attending services in Alexandria's 209-year-old Christ Church. .... The President's Washington birthday appearance was reportedly only the third time since his inauguration more than 13 months ago that he

attended church. (Nearly every President has gone to church regularly while in the White House.)

It is recognized that President Reagan's infrequent church attendance is attributed to the rigid security measures imposed at public appearances since the assassination attempt. However, since the Secret Service now requires screening of certain crowds—perhaps church-going members would voluntarily permit electronic screening devices in the entrance for any service the President wanted to attend.

President Reagan continues to step up his public appearances with voyages scheduled worldwide. Religious appearances (with no gimmickry) in and out of the East Room would support President Reagan's belief crediting God with having saved his life during the assassination attempt last March 30—plus taking the liberty of worshipping with the minorities and the poor.[47]

The author concluded by listing thirteen examples of services the president could attend on holidays. The list included St. Patrick's Day ("Visit the Irish in New York or Massachusetts—Tip O'Neill and Kennedy country"), Easter Sunday ("A Cathedral"), Father's Day ("Mormon Temple, Salt Lake City or Kensington, Md."), Labor Day ("Detroit"), and Yom Kippur ("Synagogue").

But until after leaving the presidency, Reagan never returned to the regular churchgoing of his youth. Some viewed him as a hypocrite for expressing Christian convictions but staying away from church.[48] The real explanation for this infrequent attendance seems to be that the Reagans did not think regular churchgoing important. Churchgoing is a habit, and Nancy had been raised by an antireligious stepfather and by a mother who may have spent as much time on astrology as on church attendance. While growing up, Nancy had attended church only sporadically.

For his own part, Reagan did not seem to need the spiritual support and fellowship that churchgoing provides. In Hollywood, Sacramento, and Washington, he did not socialize at the end of a day; instead, he smiled, said goodbye, and went home.[49] Nancy Reagan's autobiography stresses that her husband was essentially a loner.[50] Ron Reagan recalls that his father was often "wandering somewhere in his own head," with only "90% or so" of him on public display. "That hidden 10%," he continues, "remains a considerable mystery. His children, if they were being honest, would agree that he was as strange a fellow as any of us had ever met."[51] One biographer seems to capture this individualistic approach to religion when he writes that Reagan's "faith was deep, secure, and part of his daily life rather than a Sunday ritual."[52]

As a result, the president and his wife knew less about Christian worship than might have been expected of a couple who had experienced two decades of campaigns and public service. "The Reagan staff leased a farm in Middleburg, Virginia," White House chief of staff Michael Deaver remembered:

We were there one Saturday when Reagan ambled out of the house and said, "Mike, I'd like to attend church tomorrow. Is there one around here?" I did some quick scouting and found a beautiful Episcopal church. . . . I did not anticipate that the eleven o'clock service would . . . be holy communion.

The Reagans belonged in Los Angeles to Bel Air Presbyterian . . . where trays are passed containing small glasses of grape juice and little squares of bread. The Episcopal service is somewhat more formal, with kneeling and a common chalice and considerably more ritual. . . . Within minutes after we were inside the church they kept sending nervous glances my way. They were turning the pages of the prayer book as fast as they could. . . .

Nancy whispered to me in a mildly frantic voice, "Mike, what are we supposed to do?" I explained the ceremony as quickly and as confidently as I could: how we would walk to the altar and kneel, the minister would pass by with the wine . . . and the wafers. . . . He would bless them and keep moving.

The president, who . . . has a slight hearing problem, leaned toward us but picked up little of what I was saying. We started toward the altar and halfway down the aisle I felt Nancy Reagan clutch my arm. . . . "Mike!" she hissed. "Are those people drinking out of the same cup?"

You have to remember that Nancy is the daughter of a doctor. I said, "It's all right. They'll come by with the wafers first. Then, when the chalice reaches you, dip the bread in the cup. . . . You won't have to put your lips to the cup." The president said, "What? What?" Nancy said, "Ron, just do exactly as I do."

Unknown to me, the church had made its wafers out of unleavened bread. . . . Nancy selected a square of bread, and when the chalice came by she dipped hers—and dropped it. The square sank in the wine. She looked at me with huge eyes.

By then the trays had reached the president. Very calmly, and precisely, he picked up a piece of unleavened bread and dropped it in the wine. I watched the minister move on, shaking his head, staring at these blobs of gunk floating in his wine.

Nancy was relieved to leave the church. The president was chipper as he stepped into the sunlight, satisfied that the service had gone quite well.[53]

From childhood on, Ronald Reagan prayed often—a practice he learned from his mother. While president, he not only spent time in private prayer but also prayed with visitors. His autobiography mentions prayer many times. "I believe in intercessory prayer and know I have benefited from it," he wrote in a letter to a Roman Catholic nun. "I have, of course, added my own prayers to the point that sometimes I wonder if the Lord doesn't say, 'here he comes again.'"[54]

Just as his mother tithed, giving a tenth of her income to her church, so Reagan steadily tithed to the churches to which he belonged throughout life. When he worked in construction between high school and college, he saved everything except for the tithe he gave to the family church. While employed as a radio announcer in Iowa, he gave his tithe to his brother Neil (who followed him to Eureka) to use for college. When his parents moved to California, he resumed not only his church attendance but also his tithing to the church. According to Michael Reagan, his father's donations continued "long after he quit attending."[55] Throughout the two terms of his presidency, Reagan tithed to Bel Air Presbyterian Church. This record is rather remarkable.

Reagan rarely—and perhaps never—took the Lord's name in vain. "In his presence," Ron Reagan wrote, "profanity often felt out of place."[56] He firmly believed that God had a special plan for the United States and for all people. In addition, he believed that God had intervened in the major events of his life—leading him not only into his marriage with Nancy but also into the presidency. He attributed his survival of the assassin's bullet to the will of God. While cognitive, he never asked why God had allowed him to become a victim of Alzheimer's disease.

"I have decided that whatever time I have left is left for Him," Reagan told Roman Catholic archbishop Terence Cardinal Cooke in the hospital following the assassination attempt.[57] Subsequently he believed that God had spared him so that he and Soviet President Mikhail Gorbachev could work together to end the threat of nuclear devastation in the cold war.[58] According to Michael Reagan, his father suspected that Gorbachev was a closet Christian—something that Gorbachev publicly confirmed in 2008.[59] "I find myself believing very deeply that God has a plan for each of us," Reagan declared in a letter.[60]

Almost immediately after arriving at the hospital, Reagan decided that he should forgive his would-be assassin John Hinckley. He later told his Presbyterian pastor: "I was really struggling [for breath], and I didn't know if I would make it. God told me to forgive Hinckley. And I did. I forgave him. And immediately, I began to breathe better."[61]

Theologically, Reagan was not a deep thinker. Unlike Jimmy Carter, he read neither biblical scholarship nor the works of theologians. He was clearly less reflective about his religion than Carter, Harry Truman, Richard Nixon, or Barack Obama. In his appeals for prayer in the public schools and for America to "return God to the classroom," he frequently supported his arguments by quoting founding fathers who held Deistic views. Above all, he quoted Franklin, a prudent Deist who rarely attended church; Jefferson, a Deist best described as a moderate Unitarian; and—remarkably—Tom Paine, the iconic radical Deist who held largely anti-Christian views. "I did not think he was astute in theology," Evans declared, "but he was a believer."[62]

Much of Reagan's theological thought came from his attempts to understand and combat the Soviet Union. While reading about the USSR, he encountered the works of Malcolm Muggeridge, Aleksandr Solzhenitsyn, Wilhelm Roepke, and Frank Meyer. These writers tended to portray Christianity in terms of its opposition to godless Communism, an appealing description of religion for a president in the midst of the cold war.[63]

Especially helpful to Reagan's thinking were the writings of Whittaker Chambers, an author who was a close associate of Richard Nixon. Chambers's autobiographical *Witness* recounts his involvement in and eventual rejection of Communism, which eventually led him to convert to Christianity and to expose the Washington insider Alger Hiss as a Soviet spy. Reagan could quote long passages of *Witness* verbatim, and he often did so in his public speeches.[64]

In addition to these writers, the Christian apologist C. S. Lewis appears to have markedly influenced Reagan. On several occasions, the president cited Lewis in speeches, as he did in his speech to the annual convention of the National Association of Evangelicals in March of 1983. Both in a letter to a minister and in a remark to Evans, Reagan uses Lewis's reasoning to prove the divinity of Christ, claiming that Jesus could only have been a charlatan or the Son of God.[65]

According to Dinesh D'Souza, Reagan believed in original sin.[66] Such a belief would have been normal for a member of a mainstream denomination such as the Christian Church (DOC), though not for many theological liberals. In conversations, Reagan raised the question of Armageddon—the final war between good and evil, described in the Book of Revelation. "I turn back to your ancient prophets in the Old Testament and the signs foretelling Armageddon," he told a lobbyist for Israel in 1983,

> and I find myself wondering if—if we're the generation that's going to see that come about, I don't know if you've noted any of these prophecies lately, but believe me, they certainly describe the times we're going through.[67]

Reagan's concern with Armageddon became a minor issue in the presidential campaign of 1984. Some Democrats questioned the leadership abilities of a president who believed in an imminent nuclear apocalypse that would lead to the end of the world. Denying that he held such views, Reagan said that no one knows whether "Armageddon is a thousand years away or [the] day after tomorrow."[68]

Ronald Reagan first met Billy Graham in June 1952, when both went to a three-day conference in Dallas to discuss the rise of morally questionable content in movies and on television.[69] The two went on to become close friends. While Reagan was president, the evangelist wrote him numerous letters, most of which reflect the concern of "a pastor simply asking God to look out for his friend in the Oval Office."[70] When Graham planned to preach in the Soviet Union, many in America's government opposed his decision. Reagan, however, told him, "Now Billy, don't you worry about this trip. God does work in mysterious ways."[71]

But Reagan's relationship with Graham extended beyond the presidency. After Reagan contracted Alzheimer's disease, Graham was one of the few people always allowed to visit. According to Michael Reagan, "Billy came to pray with my father, sit with my father. Dad always had great respect for him. He knew he was a person he could pray with and ask advice of and do it confident that it would remain in confidence."[72] According to a reliable source, Graham called Reagan "the president he was closest to—and the one he would have liked to have known better."[73]

While in office, much of Reagan's policy reflected his conservative Christian values. As president, he proposed an amendment to the Constitution that would have allowed prayer in schools. He unsuccessfully tried to obtain tax credits for parents who sent their children to religious schools. In 1987, he supported a pro-life bill that defined life as beginning at conception, signing it into law the following year.[74] He markedly increased defense spending.

Yet some influential denominational leaders did not necessarily agree that Reagan based his political views on Judeo-Christian values. As heirs either to the Protestant Social Gospel or to the social teachings of Roman Catholicism and Judaism, many clergy and laypeople believed that government should play a significant role in protecting "the last, the least, and the lost." Despite sharing the president's opposition to big government, even some of Reagan's aides believed that he could do more for the poor. A longtime adviser commented: "He cares about people as individuals. I'm not sure that he ever looks upon the masses and says, 'I must go do something, these are my people.'" A Washington observer described what he termed as "the clash" between Reagan's decent instincts and his conservative, antigovernment ideology. "If you were down on your luck," he wrote,

> and you got past the Secret Service into his office [and said] "Mr. President, I'm down on my luck," he'd give you the shirt off his back. And then, in his undershirt, he'd sit down at his desk and he'd sign legislation . . . throwing kids off the school lunch program, other people off welfare, all in the name of fiscal responsibility, as he sat there shivering because he'd given you his shirt. He had a good heart . . . but when it came to his ideology, his philosophy . . . [was] "off with their heads."[75]

A major critic of Reagan's sense of social justice was Anglican Archbishop Desmond Tutu of South Africa, winner of the Nobel Peace Prize. Reagan's practice of "Constructive Engagement" initially tolerated South Africa's white minority government and its policy of apartheid. This go-slow approach toward apartheid paralleled the gradualist approach to civil rights in the American South denounced by Martin Luther King Jr. in his *Why We Can't Wait.*

With racial violence spreading in South Africa, one angry writer declared that Constructive Engagement gave "the white minority more time to mow down the black majority . . . and keep dreamers of democracy, such as Nelson Mandela, behind bars."[76] Testifying before a congressional subcommittee, Tutu called the policy "immoral, evil, and totally un-Christian." The archbishop declared: "You are either for or against apartheid. . . . You are either in favor of evil or you are in favor of good. You are either on the side of the oppressed or on the side of the oppressor. You can't be neutral."[77]

The Reagan administration viewed these criticisms as overblown. A principal spokesperson argued that Reagan opposed sanctions on South Africa because they would "create economic hardship for the very people in South Africa that the sanctions were ostensibly designed to help."[78] Once Constructive Engagement proved ineffective, Reagan enacted his own set of sanctions against the country, though his approach never satisfied his critics.[79] Largely because of his opposition to the intrusion of government into private lives, he had earlier opposed the Civil Rights Act of 1964, the Voting Rights Act of 1965, and fair housing laws.

Ronald Reagan swept into office in 1980 and 1984 supported by a large number of Roman Catholics and conservative Protestants. He retained fairly close ties to such Christian leaders as the televangelist James Robison; W. A. Criswell, former president of the Southern Baptist Convention; and Pat Robertson, the host of the Christian television program *The 700 Club.* Jerry Falwell, the founder of the Moral Majority and of Liberty University, called Reagan's first election "my finest hour."[80] Prior to the 1980 presidential vote, many ministers in Georgia handed out pamphlets entitled "Ronald Reagan: A Man of Faith" to their church members.[81] By the end of Reagan's second term, religious conservatives composed a sizable percentage of the Republican Party. In 1976, the evangelical vote helped make Jimmy Carter president. In 1980 and 1984, evangelicals voted strongly for Reagan.

Yet Reagan's strong Christian support is not without its ironies, for in at least three areas, he led a life that was contrary to evangelical standards. First, Reagan was a divorced man at a time when the United States had never had a divorced president. His first wife, Jane Wyman, had also been previously married. Second, after his divorce, Reagan dated widely. He was known in worldly Hollywood as a ladies' man. At the time of his second marriage, his bride was pregnant. Third, although Reagan championed family values in his campaign, his four children—with the possible exception of Maureen—went through periods of estrangement from their parents. His daughter Patti posed for *Playboy* magazine. Indeed, writers—and even family members—have described the Reagan family as dysfunctional.[82] "My brother and sisters experienced [our father] as distant and inattentive," Ron Reagan remembers.

> I never felt that he didn't love or care for me, but occasionally he seemed to need reminding about basic aspects of my life.... I could share an hour of warm camaraderie with Dad, then once I'd walked out the door, get the uncanny feeling I'd disappeared into the wings of his mind's stage, like a character no longer necessary to the ongoing story line.[83]

Compared to Reagan, both of his Democratic opponents for the presidency—the evangelical Jimmy Carter and the minister's son Walter Mondale—seemed straight arrows and exemplary role models for the youth and future fathers of America.

Finally, Reagan was superstitious to a surprising degree—he believed, for example, in such things as lucky numbers—and Nancy was more so.[84] Less attached to the Judeo-Christian tradition than her husband, she rarely went to church.[85] In the decades before his election as president, however, Nancy—like her mother—had frequently consulted astrologers.

When her husband was shot on March 30, 1981, Nancy was devastated. Her husband had been closer to death than the public knew. After hearing a San Francisco astrologer, Joan Quigley, claim that she could have prevented the assassination attempt, Nancy turned to her for guidance. "When you're as frightened as I was," she wrote in her memoirs, "you reach out for help and comfort in any direction you can. I prayed what seemed like all the time.... I talked with religious leaders such as Billy Graham and Donn Moomaw."[86]

After the assassination attempt, Quigley gave Nancy guidance (for a fee) on matters ranging from travel to the scheduling of meetings to days when Reagan could safely venture outdoors. Nancy would communicate Quigley's advice—based upon the alignment of stars and planets—to the White House staff. The astrologer's directives often changed White House plans for presidential trips. Calling Nancy's adviser "Madame Zorba," chief of staff Deaver complained, "We couldn't fly at night, we couldn't fly on a Monday."[87] Reagan's later chief of staff, the outspoken Donald Regan, recorded the schedule for daily action that he received from Nancy under the guidance of Quigley:

Late Dec thru March bad

Jan 16–23 very bad

Jan 20 nothing outside WH—possible attempt

Feb 20–26 be careful

March 7–14 bad period

March 10–14 no outside activity!

March 16 very bad

March 21 no

March 27 no

March 12–19 no trips exposure

March 19–25 no public exposure

April 3 careful

April 11 careful

April 17 careful

April 21–28 stay home[88]

Nancy herself claimed that Quigley's advice only affected her husband's travel plans to a slight extent. "Sometimes a small change was made," she wrote. "If a change wasn't possible, I deferred to Mike or Don." Nevertheless, she did acknowledge that Quigley's guidance had played a part in determining Reagan's travel schedule.[89]

Prior to becoming president, Reagan himself had long consulted horoscopes and astrologers. When the press and Washington politicians learned of the influence of astrologers on the Reagans, many expressed concern. The White House, however, vehemently denied that the president based any of his decisions on astrology. "Contrary to press reports," chief of staff Deaver told reporters, "the astrologer had no impact on Reagan's politics or his policies. Zero. Zilch." When interviewed, Ms. Quigley declared that she had only met the president once. "I know his horoscope upside-down," she said, "but I don't know him. I deal with Nancy."[90] Nancy herself declared that "Joan's recommendations had nothing to do with policy or politics—ever."[91] At a photo-taking session, Reagan declared, "No policy or decision in my mind has ever been influenced by astrology."[92]

Despite these denials, astrology clearly carried some weight with Reagan. When elected governor of California, he chose to be inaugurated at the unusual hour of 12:10 a.m. on January 3, 1967. He appears to have chosen this time on advice from an astrologer who told him the hour would let him take advantage of favorable auguries. Both Reagan and his wife denied this story, declaring that he took the oath of office at such an unusual time simply because his predecessor Edmund G. Brown "had been filling up the ranks of appointments and judges" until the final hours of his official term.[93] "Preposterous," declared a sociologist who studied the Reagans' interest in astrology. He noted that Reagan had announced his intention to be sworn in as governor at that odd hour six weeks ahead of inauguration day.[94]

The Hollywood astrologer who took credit for advising governor-elect Reagan about the advantages of a 12:10 a.m. swearing-in was Carroll Righter. Righter, who liked to be called the "gregarious Aquarius," began doing charts for Hollywood stars in the 1930s.[95] His many clients included Marlene Dietrich, Rhonda Fleming (a paramour of John F. Kennedy), and Grace Kelly. His syndicated daily column on astrology reached the hands of many readers. Reagan's autobiography refers to Righter—who decorated his Hollywood office with pictures of the presidential family—as "one of our good friends."[96]

However much astrology mattered to Nancy, it seems to have played a relatively minor role in her husband's adult life. The available evidence seems to indicate that it amounted in the end to little more than an actor's superstition. An old friend of the Reagans declared: "You have to remember where and how that part of their life started. In Hollywood during the thirties and forties, astrologers were social equals and friends—they weren't weirdos."[97]

Ronald Reagan "grew up in Dixon, Illinois, where life was wholesome [and] where people trusted each other," Nancy Reagan writes in her memoirs.

"People in Dixon stuck together and helped each other. To this day, Ronnie thinks that's the way it should be, and it's one reason he bristles at the idea of a large, impersonal government that takes care of the things neighbors once did for each other."[98]

After leaving Illinois, Reagan gradually left behind Democratic politics and a belief in the New Deal. The changes to his religion, however, were not nearly so drastic. Though he transferred denominations, his faith remained at its core the same as when he was a boy. He was a small-town Christian who lived for decades in worldly Hollywood and who married an actress oriented toward the occult.

That Reagan has entered history as a Protestant—and not, like his brother and father, a Roman Catholic—represents a kind of historical fluke. During his youth, most children born to mixed Protestant–Roman Catholic marriages were raised Roman Catholic. Indeed, much in Reagan that appealed to voters—his charm, his humor, his insouciance, his blarney, even some of his oratorical ability—probably came from his Irish heritage. That his best-known movie role was that of "the Gipper" in a film about the University of Notre Dame somehow seems appropriate.

But Reagan was raised by his mother in a particularly earnest form of Protestantism. Despite the influence of the movie industry and of his second wife, he retained both the outlook and many of the values of his childhood religion. If anything, he moved to the right of his denominational heritage as he grew older. When he ran for office, he blended conservative Christian theology with attacks on big government. As an aide remarked, he did not wear "his faith on his sleeve, but it was passionately a part of his governance."[99]

Like all presidents, Reagan was not universally admired. Thomas P. "Tip" O'Neill, the Democratic speaker of the house during both of Reagan's terms, was one such outspoken opponent. Though Reagan was a Protestant and O'Neill a Roman Catholic, both men shared Irish ancestry, a modest background, and a boyhood idolization of Franklin Delano Roosevelt. During 1948, as O'Neill noted, Reagan had campaigned for Harry Truman and Hubert Humphrey. "He attacked reductions in Social Security," the speaker wrote. "He condemned cuts in school lunches. He called for the tough enforcement of civil rights laws, and for low-cost public housing."[100]

But in the speaker's view, Reagan "forgot where he came from and started picking up a different set of values." O'Neill blamed this change on the wealthy friends and executives (largely chosen by Nancy) who surrounded Reagan once he became national spokesman for General Electric in the 1950s. Falling "out of touch with how regular Americans live and the problems they face," O'Neill asserted, caused Reagan to hold "simplistic explanations" of poverty, welfare, economics, and foreign policy.[101] Of the eight presidents under whom he had served since entering Congress in 1953, O'Neill found Reagan the most "distant from the details of public policy and legislation." The president, he reported, preferred to talk about sports and movies.[102]

O'Neill's view was that Reagan was elected in 1980 not because voters desired what the Reagan administration gave them—the greatest increase in defense spending, the greatest cutbacks in domestic programs, and the largest tax cuts in American history. Rather, he was elected because Americans could not wait to get rid of Jimmy Carter.[103] "Ronald Reagan didn't win the 1980 election," O'Neill concluded, "as much as Jimmy Carter lost it."[104]

However unpalatable Reagan's religious and political views were to O'Neill and to many Americans, they represented unchanging American values and beliefs to tens of millions of others. As president, he was immensely popular. Most of the reporters who covered the White House liked him, even though they may not have voted for him. But the votes Reagan did receive for president—nearly 44 million in 1980, and over 54 million in 1984—bear formidable testimony to his popularity. With many in the nation, including a substantial number of nominal Democrats, he maintained a virtually indestructible rapport. O'Neill found that voters in his district believed that any Reagan programs they disagreed with had been initiated not by the president but by "people around him." They would not believe that Ronald Reagan "would do anything to hurt them."[105]

Despite a widespread belief that Reagan not only restored American pride but also ended the cold war, his presidency has acquired a substantial number of critics. During his eight years, for example, the income gap between the rich and poor in the United States widened significantly. Although income for the top 40 percent of the populace often grew substantially, income for the remaining 60 percent stagnated. After decades of decline, the poverty rate rose in the 1980s by as much as 15 percent.[106]

Reagan also sharply reduced the taxes paid by corporations and by wealthy individuals—a reduction that critics believe negatively affected American life.[107] In what came to be called "the savings and loan crisis," his deregulation of America's savings and loan banks and subsequent looseness of supervision of bank practices eventually caused the failure of more than seven hundred banks. In some estimates the subsequent cost to the nation exceeded $500 billion.[108]

Simultaneously, the Reagan administration spent massively on defense. The expenditures created a quasi-wartime economy not experienced in the nation since the conflicts in Vietnam and Korea. This increase in military readiness accelerated the end of the cold war. But coupled with the tax cuts, it also caused the national debt to soar. Reagan's economic legacy is debated, with leading economists taking positions on both sides. Some hold that Reagan's policies led to the largest peacetime economic boom in American history.[109] Whatever the true figures, the economy did not grow sufficiently in the 1980s to close the gap from a $980 billion federal debt when Reagan entered office to a $2.6 trillion debt when he left office.[110]

Critics also maintain that Reagan's cutting of the budgets of programs aimed at social ills caused a marked rise in homelessness, teen pregnancy, and drug abuse.[111] Similarly, his administration initially failed to devote needed funding to combating AIDS, which medical science recognized as a disease early in the 1980s. In 1986, Reagan supported a cut of 11 percent in the small federal budget devoted to the disease. "On the exact night that [Reagan said] the word 'AIDS' for the first time in public," the *San Francisco Examiner* later noted, "21,000 Americans had already died from the disease."[112]

For some critics, the defining episode of the Reagan years was the Iran-Contra Affair, during which some members of his administration illegally sold arms to Iran to fund counterrevolutionary rebels in Nicaragua. But the many who consider Reagan one of America's great presidents defend such measures as necessary to the conduct of the cold war. For them, Reagan wore the unblemished white hat. Morris speaks of Reagan entering the Oval Office "with his usual fluid grace, tall, beaming, apple-cheeked, amethyst-eyed, tailored, giving off waves of benign power."[113] Ron Reagan speaks of "the trademark wink and nod, the thick, seemingly invincible head of hair, the soft burr of his voice."[114]

Ronald Reagan died at his home in California on June 5, 2004. He had suffered from Alzheimer's disease at least since 1994.[115] During an elaborate state funeral and service in the Washington National Cathedral, former President George H. W. Bush gave the eulogy. "I learned more from Ronald Reagan than from anyone I encountered in all my years of public life," Bush declared. "I learned kindness; we all did. I also learned courage; the nation did."[116] As a lone bagpipe played "Amazing Grace," the man who had long viewed himself as an exemplar of the American Dream was buried in the grounds of his presidential library in California.

Ronald Reagan's political career spanned more than twenty years. During those decades not only his opponents but also journalists continually underestimated his political appeal. It seems clear that many Americans also underestimated the genuineness of his Christian convictions. America's fortieth president possessed the earnest faith of his mother, but the attendance record of his father. "One thing I do know," he wrote in 1973 to the pastor who nurtured him, Ben Cleaver, "all the hours in the old church in Dixon (which I didn't appreciate at the time) and all of Nelle's faith, have come together in a kind of inheritance without which I'd be lost and helpless."[117]

# George Herbert Walker Bush

*1924–* ⌐ PRESIDENT FROM 1989 TO 1993

The old house in Beijing that served as a makeshift church was unremarkable, ill-kept, and for the American envoy and his wife, a far cry from the traditional Episcopal sanctuaries of home. The services were in Chinese. The ministers were Anglican, Methodist, and Presbyterian. The Sunday congregation—about a dozen in all, typical for this house-church—included a mix of African, European, and Asian Protestants whose native tongues made an enthusiastic cacophony of familiar hymns.

But for the American envoy (or unofficial ambassador) to China, George Herbert Walker Bush, the odd setting became a treasured church home, offering "unbelievable" and "most moving" services that (as he wrote in his diary) "we wouldn't miss."[1] On a typical Sunday, Bush wrote: "Sunday, our little church service. Head count—two African ladies, one African man, three Canadians, two Bushes, four Chinese in the audience, and one preacher. They sing the most wonderful hymns. 'Nearer My God to Thee,' 'Holy, Holy, Holy.' All the old favorites. It is a nice touch."[2]

No service in that unlikely sanctuary may have been more important to the future president and his wife, Barbara, than the one that took place on June 29, 1975, at the Chongwenmen Church. Bush was serving as U.S. envoy to China during a time when that country's Communist government severely restricted the practice of Christianity. Yet he had managed not only to convince the Chinese to permit the baptism of his youngest child on that day; he had also managed to gather three of her four far-flung brothers (including the eldest, George W.) for the event. It was, as Bush wrote, "A very special day, an occasion."

Dorothy, or "Doro" as she was called, was fifteen years old, the youngest of five children, and the only daughter. She was the girl Bush had prayed for after the loss of the couple's second child, Robin, who died of leukemia in 1959, just weeks before her fourth birthday.

Doro's baptism had been deferred several times because of what Barbara Bush described as "deaths, politics, long distances, and floods."[3] But now, in the unlikely location of post–Cultural Revolutionary China, that day had finally come. George Bush's diary entry for June 29 reads: "The big thing that day—Doro was baptized at our little Chinese church. The ministers were extremely happy and smiling—pleasant, wonderful."[4]

While the ecumenical Chinese ministers presided at the baptism, suspicious government representatives photographed and tape-recorded the strange ceremony. As far as the Bushes knew, Doro was the first American citizen publicly baptized in China since the Communists assumed power in 1949.[5]

"Arranging for a baptism in a communist country is no small feat," Doro later wrote. Able at fifteen to pick her own godfather, she sent a telegram to "one of Dad's funniest and most handsome friends" in Maine, inviting him to come immediately to China for the service. The telegram arrived in Chinese.[6]

It was a memorable event in a lifetime of religious practice that holds little mystery. George Herbert Walker Bush was an aristocratic Episcopalian in the tradition not only of Franklin Delano Roosevelt and the founding fathers but also of his own father. He grew up in a home where the Book of Common Prayer of the Episcopal Church guided daily family devotionals. He was sworn into office on the same Bible—a 1767 King James Version initially provided by a New York Masonic lodge—used at George Washington's inauguration in 1789.[7]

Bush's two middle names came from the well-to-do Walker family of St. Louis. Although the Walkers were Roman Catholic, Bush's maternal grandfather, George Herbert Walker, adopted the Presbyterian affiliation of his wife, Lucretia Wear. An investment banker, Walker became president of a leading Wall Street firm. He was also president of the United States Golf Association when it initiated the biennial transatlantic tournament that now bears his name, the Walker Cup Match.

On his father's side, Bush was descended from influential Congregationalist, Presbyterian, and Episcopal families—three churches of the early American establishment—in colonial and early national New England and New York. His paternal great-grandfather, James Bush, was an Episcopal minister. In an 1886 speech before the Concord Lyceum, the Reverend Mr. Bush described how he put out a fire on board a ship en route to South

America. "Is it not by the courage always to do the right thing that the fires of hell shall be put out?" the minister asked the lyceum. His words—"Do the right thing"—became the Bush family motto.[8] James's son and Bush's paternal grandfather, Samuel Prescott Bush of Columbus, Ohio, was a leading industrialist who served as the first president of the National Association of Manufacturers and as a charter member of the U.S. Chamber of Commerce.

Prescott Sheldon Bush, Bush's father, graduated from St. George's School, a prestigious Episcopal preparatory school in Rhode Island. At Yale, he sang with the noted a cappella group the Whiffenpoofs and was tapped for Skull and Bones, perhaps the most renowned secret society in American colleges. After graduation, Bush served in France in World War I, married Dorothy Walker of St. Louis, and ultimately became a partner in the leading Wall Street investment firm of Brown Brothers Harriman. A millionaire and a Republican, he won a special election for the U.S. Senate in 1952 and served until ill health compelled his retirement in 1962. Politically part of the "Republican Eastern Establishment," a group largely distrusted by the party's conservatives, he supported civil rights legislation and opposed Senator Joseph McCarthy of Wisconsin.

Gentlemanly, authoritarian, formidable, and Episcopalian, "six feet four inches of commanding presence," Prescott Bush was an almost regal figure who looked (as a colleague observed) like a Roman senator.[9] Associate after associate confessed that they felt him too imposing to approach comfortably. Raising his family in a large Victorian home in the moneyed suburb of Greenwich, Connecticut, he required his children to wear coats and ties or dresses at the dinner table. The family had a cook, handyman-chauffeur, and maids. Following his election to the U.S. Senate in 1952, Bush instructed his children to address him as "Senator."[10]

The formality of the Bushes' home life extended to religious practice. Each morning the children would gather around the table. Prescott, and sometimes Dorothy, would then preside over readings from the Episcopal church's Book of Common Prayer. This family worship occurred whether the Bushes were in Connecticut or in their seaside home in Kennebunkport, Maine (an eight-bedroom summer residence whose function as a familial gathering place rivaled that of the Kennedys' compound at Hyannis Port).

"Open my lips, O Lord, and my mouth shall proclaim your praise; Create in me a clean heart, O God, and renew a right spirit within me." These words of Psalm 51 would have been part of a familiar morning ritual for the Bush family. The reading from the Book of Common Prayer would often end with the words: "Lord God, almighty and everlasting Father, you have brought us in safety to this new day: Preserve us with your mighty power, that we may not fall into sin, nor be overcome by adversity . . . through Jesus Christ our Lord."

The family also read from *A Diary of Private Prayer*, a noted devotional book by the Scots Presbyterian theologian John Baillie. The Bush children were expected to learn the lengthy catechism of the Episcopal Church, and the family maintained a strict observance of a quiet Sabbath. In Greenwich they attended Christ Church, the town's large Episcopal church. In Maine, the family attended historic St. Ann's by the Sea Episcopal Church during the summer. When it was closed during spring and fall, they attended the First Congregational Church in Kennebunkport. A one-minute drive down the beach road from their summer home, St. Ann's (consecrated in 1892) was the scene of many weddings for the Walker and Bush families.

Into this world of polo, preparatory schools, debutante cotillions, country clubs, Republican politics, private hunting lodges, relatives in high positions, and easy social skills, George H. W. Bush was born in 1924, the second of five children. It was the heyday of the old-boy network.

After attending private school in Greenwich (to which he was driven by a chauffeur), Bush graduated in 1942 from Phillips Andover Academy in Massachusetts. Founded during the American Revolution, the academy has a seal designed by Paul Revere. As the academy's yearbook for 1942 indicates, Bush's list of offices and accomplishments dwarfed those of most of the other members of his class. The yearbook—the *Pot Pourri*—lists Bush as "George Walker Bush," adding the nickname of "Pop" or "Poppy." His offices and memberships include president of the senior class, president of two student societies, secretary and treasurer of the student council, and captain of the soccer and baseball teams. In addition, he was a member and manager of the basketball team, a member of the boards of the newspaper and of the yearbook, and a member of the four-person advisory board for the senior prom. His membership in one of the academy's secret societies,

A.U.V., which stood for *Auctoritas, Unitas, Veritas* (Authority, Unity, Truth), is placed at the top of his list of achievements.

In addition, the *Pot Pourri* customarily polled members of each graduating class to name the top four seniors in twenty-seven areas. In five of those categories, Bush ranked among the top four students in his class. In the category of most "faculty drag" ("drag" refers to clout or influence), his classmates voted Poppy Bush second. In the categories of most popular, most respected, best athlete, best all-around fellow, and handsomest, he ranked third. This level of peer approval was remarkable. Only a few other members of the class placed in five or more of the categories.

Active in sports at Phillips-Andover throughout the academic year, Bush went from soccer in the fall to basketball in the winter to baseball in the spring. He was far more active in committees and clubs than most of his classmates. His teachers, however, did not view him as especially scholarly. In later years he confessed to a writer that "I don't read that much"—something that could also have been said by his oldest son, George W. Bush. A master at the academy who taught Bush English described him as a mannerly and pleasant student whose papers "showed no imagination or originality."[11]

While at Andover, Bush remained involved in religious activities. He chaired the board of student deacons for the academy's chapel.[12] Above all, Bush served as chairman of the Society of Inquiry, "the representative religious organization of the students of Phillips Academy."[13] Founded at the academy in the 1830s, the society originally supported overseas missions, but by Bush's time it had become affiliated with the Young Men's Christian Association. During Bush's chairmanship, the society raised money for a medical mission in Labrador.[14]

The United States entered World War II during Bush's senior year at Phillips Andover. Immediately after graduating, he enlisted in the U.S. Naval Reserve on his eighteenth birthday. After flight training, he was commissioned an ensign in June 1943, several days before his nineteenth birthday. He was the youngest pilot in the U.S. Navy. A letter written to his mother in 1943 from the U.S. Naval Air Station in Corpus Christi, Texas, indicates his concern with attending church while in the service.[15]

In 1944, Bush's plane was hit while attacking a Japanese installation on a

Pacific island. Reaching his target and releasing his bombs even while the plane's engine was on fire, Bush then bailed out. Of the three crew members, he alone survived. After spending four hours on an inflatable raft, he was rescued by a U.S. submarine. He spent the next month on the submarine while it continued on patrol. By the time he was discharged in 1945, Bush not only had flown fifty-eight combat missions but also had received the Distinguished Flying Cross and three Air Medals.[16] He became a genuine war hero.

For Bush, that month on the submarine brought into stark relief the fear and wonder of those times. He found something special about standing watch in the predawn hours aboard a surfacing sub. Many years later he would remember those watches as a time when faith was a comfort and prayer came naturally. Hours before Bush accepted his party's nomination for a second term as president, he told an audience at a prayer breakfast in Houston:

> For me, prayer has always been important but quite personal. . . . It has sustained me at every point of my life: as a boy . . . as a teenager . . . or . . . 48 years ago, aboard the submarine *Finback* after being shot down in the war.
>
> I went up topside one night on the deck . . . and stood watch and looked out at the dark. The sky was clear. The stars were brilliant, like a blizzard of fireflies in the night. There was a calm inner peace. Halfway around the world in the war zone, there was a calm inner peace: God's therapy.[17]

Even before his enlistment, young Bush knew whom he was going to marry. He had met Barbara Pierce, the New York daughter of the president of the McCall Corporation, at a dance when he was sixteen years old. The two were engaged before he shipped out, and Bush had "Barbara" emblazoned on three of the planes he flew into combat. Just two weeks after his return from the Pacific, the couple was married at the First Presbyterian Church of Rye, New York, before "aunts and uncles and cousins by the dozens."[18]

Bush's final assignment was to a naval squadron stationed in Tidewater, Virginia. When the Japanese surrendered in August 1945 and the four years of war were finally over, members of the squadron rented a cottage on Virginia Beach—where they intended to "have the celebration of our lives." Barbara Bush had joined her husband in Virginia by that time, but the

Bushes arrived at the party late. As a member of the squadron later told an interviewer, "I asked where they had been. 'We went to church to say thanks to God for His blessing,' said George. Of all the people in the squadron," Bush's fellow pilot declared, "they were the only ones who went to church. That kind of maturity and character impressed me more about George than almost anything else."[19]

Released later that year from active service, Bush attended Yale and was initiated into Skull and Bones. He was not only on Yale's baseball team but also became its captain in his senior year. In addition, he became a member of the Torch Honor Society and won the Gordon Brown Prize (awarded for "all-around student leadership"). Exhibiting a different attitude toward study than he had demonstrated in prep school, he was elected to Phi Beta Kappa. By all reports he was attentive to religious services while a student. By the time Bush graduated in 1948, he was the father of a son, George Walker Bush, later the forty-third president of the United States.

After graduation, Bush moved to west Texas, joining the rush to tap oil reserves in the rich Permian Basin. In 1950, he and Barbara and four-year-old George W. settled in Midland, Texas. "A virtual Athens on the prairie," one writer has noted:

> Midland boasted about its art collections, book and music shops, commu-
> nity theater, and symphony orchestra. Once the gathering place of cowboys
> and itinerant oilmen, [the town] had become more notable for the incongru-
> ous skyline created by the office towers of banks and . . . petroleum corpora-
> tions. . . . Before the 1950s were over, Midland had over 500 business firms
> and a population that had tripled to 70,000.[20]

In their new home, the Bushes joined the First Presbyterian Church, the denomination in which Barbara had been raised. The church was a center for young professionals—oil executives, lawyers, physicians, and business people of all kinds. Both of the Bushes taught in the church's Sunday school. In addition, the congregation elected George Bush an elder in 1957. Lay elders work in tandem with the minister and govern Presbyterian churches.[21]

The family grew, and by 1953 George Bush had a three-year-old daughter, Pauline Robinson ("Robin"), and a newborn son, John Ellis ("Jeb"), later governor of Florida. But in the spring of that year, Robin became seriously ill with what physicians diagnosed as advanced leukemia. The Bushes consulted specialists. They hospitalized Robin at the Sloan-Kettering Institute in New York. It was a sign of the influence of the extended Bush family that George H. W.'s uncle, John Mercer Walker, was president of Sloan-Kettering. Despite innovative treatments, Robin died seven months after the diagnosis. "There is about our house a need," Bush subsequently wrote to his mother:

> We need a girl.
>
> We had one once—she'd fight and cry and play and make her way just like the rest. But there was about her a certain softness.
>
> She'd stand beside our bed till I felt her there. Silently and comfortable [sic], she'd put those precious, fragrant locks against my chest and fall asleep.
>
> Her peace made me feel strong, and so very important. . . .
>
> But she is still with us. We need her and yet we have her. We can't touch her, and yet we can feel her.
>
> We hope she'll stay in our house for a long, long time.[22]

During the time of Robin's illness, Bush later remembered, "I really learned to pray."[23] The First Presbyterian Church opened its doors for Bible classes every morning at 6:15, and Bush was in the sanctuary every morning at 6:30. "I would ask God why? Why this little innocent girl?"[24] When the church custodian noticed the young father coming daily, he informed the pastor, the Reverend Matthew Lynn. "The minister then came every day," Barbara Bush reported. "He didn't say anything. But he was there."[25]

If the events at First Presbyterian Church say something about Bush's suffering as well as about his faith, they also say much about the Reverend Dr. Lynn, subsequently a revered figure in Southern Presbyterianism. Barbara later said: "I know there's a God, and secondly, I know Robin left. . . . We combed her hair and she wasn't there."[26] In 1999, Bush told a TV interviewer, "we [still] hurt."[27]

In 1959, the Bushes moved from Midland to Houston, where they affiliated with St. Martin's Episcopal Church. Founded only seven years earlier, the church had attracted 125 people to its first service of worship. By the end of the decade, it had added a new sanctuary, offices, and Sunday school classrooms and grown to include more than 2,700 baptized members. Full of young families and business people, it had become home to one of Houston's wealthiest congregations.

At St. Martin's, the Bushes continued to teach Sunday school, and Bush was elected to the church's vestry, the equivalent in an Episcopal church to the board of elders in a Presbyterian congregation. In an address at the church, he later recalled the many Sundays spent in "the sixth or seventh pew from the back [and] how it wiggled and shook" as his five children "got the giggles or got mad or couldn't see during the Christmas pageant."[28]

From 1966 on, when Bush held such offices as congressman, chairman of the Republican National Committee, or director of the Central Intelligence Agency, the family's life shifted to Washington. They maintained their regular membership at St. Martin's Church in Houston. But both before and after his election as vice president and president, they attended Episcopal churches in the District—first St. Columba's Church in northwest Washington and then St. John's Church, Lafayette Square, adjacent to the White House. During his frequent travels, Bush often went to church on Sunday. "I am trying very hard as President to go to Church every Sunday," he wrote to an Episcopal priest in 1990.[29] During a television interview with David Frost, he declared that he and Barbara said prayers every night before going to bed.[30]

Like the Eisenhowers and Nixons, the Bushes had a close relationship with Billy Graham and his wife, Ruth. Long before Graham had his well-known conversation about conversion with their son, George W., in the 1970s, the evangelist had played golf with Prescott Bush and addressed Dorothy Bush's Bible study group. But by the 1980s, the Grahams and the George H. W. Bushes were vacationing together. Graham and his wife became familiar presences during August vacations in Kennebunkport when all the Bush children gathered. The two men often attended church together, fished, and rode bicycles. Their wives—from different social backgrounds, but sharing many values—maintained a sustained correspondence over many years.

By the mid-1980s, Graham had become the unofficial pastor of the Bush family. He was one of the few clergy with whom Bush would discuss his spiritual life. During several Kennebunkport summers, Bush asked Graham to speak with his children about personal faith and to answer their questions. The sessions made an impression on Doro, then in her twenties. They also impressed her elder brother, George W., who recalled that Graham talked about "the real meaning of life, and about Jesus. And heaven and sin. And wonder."[31]

When the courtship of evangelical voters became an important part of his presidential campaign in the later 1980s, then vice president Bush was urged by aides—led by born-again Christian motivational speaker Doug Wead—to publicize his ties to Graham. Evangelical Christianity has a special language of its own, and that language is not regularly used in conversations by mainline Protestants, Roman Catholics, or Eastern Orthodox Christians. Words and phrases such as "born-again," "become a Christian," "accept Jesus Christ," "in Christ," "under the blood," "a baby in Christ"—these and other words the Episcopalian Bush had to learn in order to display evangelical inclinations. Wead essentially taught Bush the language of evangelicalism. While president, Bush supported evangelical priorities such as pro-life legislation and a constitutional amendment to allow prayer in public schools.

Although the vice president rejected the idea of exploiting his relationship with Graham for political gain, at the same time he was willing to greet the crowd at the evangelist's 1986 Washington crusade. At that crusade, he repeated a theme central to his views: "In this nation, we do believe in separation of church and state." But he added: "We also believe that when all is said and done, we are indeed one nation under God."[32] Later that year he canceled plans to visit Graham in North Carolina, saying, "I did not want to appear to be 'using' him in any way."[33]

Graham, however, was not always averse to speaking about their relationship. In an interview with *Time* magazine that appeared in the second year of Bush's presidency, Graham said the president "is easy to talk to about spiritual things . . . he says straight out that he has received Christ as his savior, that he is a born-again believer, and that he reads the Bible daily, and so forth."[34]

In 1990 and 1991, while deciding whether to invade Iraq and start the Gulf War, Bush encountered vocal opposition from mainline Protestant leaders, including the presiding bishop of his own Episcopal church. But Graham, who could usually be counted on to support an American war and who had supported all American wars fought during his lifetime, came to his defense. On January 6, 1991, the evangelist phoned Bush and offered him a quotation from James Russell Lowell: "Once to every man and nation comes a time to decide"—a line Bush undoubtedly knew, for it was the title of a frequently sung hymn in the Episcopal hymnal.

Apparently Graham was unaware that Lowell wrote "The Present Crisis"—the poem from which the hymn was taken—in 1845 to *oppose* the American invasion of Mexico and the Mexican-American war. The second line of the hymn Graham cites reads, "In the strife of truth with falsehood, for the good or evil side." In the context of the hymn, the "evil" side equates with invasion and the "good" side with refraining from invasion. Whatever the merits of the Gulf War, the hymn Graham sent to Bush argues against invading another nation. In his diary Bush noted that Graham "offers his help . . . talks about Saddam Hussein being the anti-Christ [*sic*] himself . . . [and] wants to speak out in any way he can."[35]

Bush spent much of early January 1991 talking to foreign leaders and clergy. The clergy included Graham, Pope John Paul II, Bernard Cardinal Law of Boston, and Edmond Browning, the presiding bishop of the Episcopal Church. Bush and Graham prayed together three times before the president spoke to the nation in the evening and informed them of his decision to attack Iraq. The following day, Graham came to the White House, and he and the Bushes watched CNN as the bombs dropped.

That night Bush "didn't sleep very well," a biographer noted; "he got up three times, visited the medical unit in the wee hours, hoping to shake off tightness in his shoulders. At five in the morning, unable to get back to sleep, he walked into the Situation Room."[36] The next day, Graham joined Bush at a military prayer service, where he delivered a message on peace. "There come times," he said, "when we have to fight for peace."[37]

Bush's geniality and manners, plus his reputation as a kind and decent man, masked his high ambition. His ambition, however, seems to have differed from that of many politicians; he "will not advance himself if it means hurting someone else," an associate once wrote.[38] But like many Washington figures, Bush wished to be president. After Carter defeated Ford, he hoped to remain in Washington as director of the CIA—a position and organization he liked—but he was not kept on.[39]

He spent the next few years in Texas involved in various business enterprises. In 1979, viewing himself as the most qualified Republican candidate, he announced his bid for the presidency. Most of the positions he had held to this point had been appointive, not elected. In the words of one observer, he had lost two Senate races, "had never defeated an incumbent office holder—and had beaten only one opponent of any kind, in 1966."[40]

But the posts to which Bush had been appointed were significant. In addition to heading the CIA, he had served two years at the United Nations and one year as envoy (or unofficial ambassador) from the United States to China. He also accepted Nixon's invitation to spend 1973 and 1974 as chairman of the Republican National Committee. Because those were the years of the Watergate scandal, Bush spent most of his time traveling back and forth across the country defending Nixon. His counterpart on the Democratic National Committee, like Bush a Texan, commiserated. Bush's job, he said, reminded him of "making love to a gorilla"—because a person cannot stop until the gorilla wants to.[41]

Although some of his opponents in the Republican primaries derided him as having "a resume, not a record," in reality Bush had gained a wide variety of global experience and knew many international leaders.[42] An inveterate writer of ingratiating notes of thanks and friendship, he had also developed a broad network of support among Republican leaders.

After initially leading in the polls, Bush lost the Republican nomination to Ronald Reagan in 1980. During the primaries, his use of the term "voodoo economics" to describe Reagan's proposal of cutting taxes but increasing military spending angered Reagan and almost caused Bush to be dropped from the vice presidential list. Ultimately, because his moderate reputation would balance Reagan's conservatism and because Bush possessed the foreign policy experience that Reagan lacked, Reagan chose Bush as his running mate. Bush was also selected because he lived in a state rich in electoral votes.

Reagan and Bush never became warm friends during the eight years of their administration, but—perhaps a surprise to both—they came to like each other. At Reagan's request, they dined together alone every Thursday and had frank, unrecorded discussions of policy. Not superior to the average politician in being willing to sacrifice ideals for victory, Bush became increasingly conservative after being selected for vice president. In Randall Balmer's words, he was "listing right," as was the nation.[43] Most notably, he reversed his position on abortion and became pro-life (though his wife did not change her position).[44]

In 1988, as heir to the Reagan legacy, Bush won the Republican primaries against candidates who included the televangelist Pat Robertson and Senate Minority Leader Robert Dole. Though known in Washington as a considerate and sympathetic man, Bush allowed his staff to conduct one of the most slashing and misleading campaigns in presidential history against his opponent, Governor Michael Dukakis of Massachusetts. The campaign, "generally regarded as one of the nastiest in history," was an anomaly in Bush's political life.[45] Having begun the campaign significantly behind in the polls, Bush ended by carrying forty states and winning the popular vote by eight percentage points.

Accompanied by his family and two hundred guests, Bush attended a 9:00 a.m. service at adjacent St. John's Church, Lafayette Square, on inauguration day, 1989. The scripture readings in the service came from Isaiah, chapter 26, verses 1–8, and from the apostle Paul's letter to the Romans, chapter 13, verses 1–10. In the words of one writer, the passages "reflected the self-effacement and the dedication to public service that are a bedrock of Bush's belief system."[46] Perhaps unknown to Bush, the reading from Romans included one of the most controversial passages in the history of Christianity. Over the centuries some major Christian figures have interpreted Paul's words to mean that all governments should be honored and obeyed. Even if unjust and corrupt, civil authorities have been put in power by God.[47]

Bush's inaugural address in January 1989 contained religious themes. In it Bush spoke about attracting community organizations and volunteers to fight such urban ills as drug abuse and homelessness. Calling for "1,000 points of light, of all the community organizations that are spread like stars throughout the nation doing good," he emphasized the volunteerism of individuals over the assistance of government agencies. "We all have something to give," he declared in his 1991 State of the Union Address:

> So, if you know how to read, find someone who can't. If you've got a hammer, find a nail. If you're not hungry, not lonely, not in trouble, seek out someone who is. Join the community of conscience. Do the hard work of freedom.[48]

In Bush's eyes, government still had a role to play. When he accepted the Republican nomination, Bush told the delegates that he was "going to do whatever it takes to make sure the disabled are included in the mainstream." During his administration a major achievement, and one with religious overtones, was the passage of the Americans with Disabilities Act of 1990. The new law prohibited discrimination against disabled Americans in transportation, public accommodations, and employment. But in Bush's administration, "the private sphere [was] the preferred sphere."[49]

Throughout his four years in office, Bush stressed the importance of family and religion. "Family and faith represent the moral compass of the Nation," he told a joint session of Congress in his first year as president.[50] In an Independence Day speech in 1992, he declared that "America is special because of fidelity to God. We have not forgotten that we are one Nation under God, and that's an important thing to point out on July 4th."[51]

References to religion and the phrase "one Nation under God" recurred in Bush's speeches. But as one author perceptively notes, Bush appeared ecumenical when he referred to religious faith as a principal strength of the American people. In reality, the writer points out, he was "only ecumenical as that term is understood by the mainstream American religious traditions. . . . Practitioners of faiths derived from other traditions — Buddhists, Muslims, Native Americans, for example — were at least potentially excluded."[52] All American presidents have inevitably tended to use Judeo-Christian rhetoric in their speeches. As multiculturalism has increased in the years since the Bush administration, the explicit Judeo-Christian content of presidential addresses has declined. The administration of Bush's evangelical son, George W. Bush, represents an exception to this trend.

Bush's time in office witnessed the fall of the Berlin Wall and the dissolution of the Soviet empire. But it also saw the killing of several thousand protesters in Beijing's Tiananmen Square and the questionably legal invasion of Panama. Throughout Bush's years as president, satellite states of the former Soviet Union became independent. Robert Gates, who was appointed director of the CIA during the Bush administration, described Bush's handling of the Soviet Union's problems. "He did not gloat," Gates wrote:

He did not make grandiose pronouncements. . . . He did not declare victory. He did not try to accelerate events. . . . He did not threaten. . . .

There is much an American president could have done to derail or at least complicate those revolutions. . . . Bush played it just right, as virtually all of the leaders of the new democracies in Eastern Europe would later attest.[53]

Bush viewed the 1991 Gulf War as one of the most successful accomplishments of his four years as president. In the previous summer, Saddam Hussein's Iraq forcibly annexed the adjoining country of Kuwait and seemed to threaten the major American ally Saudi Arabia. When Saddam refused to withdraw his troops, Bush prepared for war. He won the support of the Senate for the war only by a five-vote margin, but he gained broad support from other nations.

Unlike the later invasion of Iraq during his son's administration, George H. W. Bush's coalition consisted of thirty-four countries, including France, Italy, Poland, Pakistan, Egypt, Greece, Belgium, Argentina, the Netherlands, Mexico, many Arab nations, the United Kingdom and former Commonwealth countries, several African nations, and two Scandinavian countries. Other major powers—such as Germany—gave financial aid.

Even with this international support, the invasion of an Islamic country presented unforeseen religious problems. Saudi Arabia, an important supplier of money and bases for the war, demanded that no officers or enlisted men who were Jews be allowed on its territory. In addition, it initially prohibited Bibles, crucifixes, or Jewish services of worship inside its borders.

The Gulf War began in mid-January 1991 with one of the most enormous air attacks in history. Its successful conclusion forty-two days later caused Bush's popularity to rise significantly. Though the war had its critics, its outcome was generally seen as a triumph for Bush.

One year prior to the 1992 election, the president's public approval rating was 60 percent. Not only his staff but also many other observers assumed that no Democrat could beat a president who had served as commander-in-chief during such a resounding victory. Leading Democrats such as Governor Mario Cuomo of New York, Governor Bruce Babbitt of Arizona, and Senator Paul Simon of Illinois declined to run. Ultimately, a governor from one of the poorest southern states, Bill Clinton of Arkansas, secured the nomination.

Clinton and his running mate, Senator Al Gore of Tennessee, won the election for many reasons. The American economy had been moving toward recession since 1990, unemployment was climbing, and a sense had grown among the electorate that it was "time for a change." Bush had never been able to shake the image of a privileged prep school graduate and Ivy Leaguer who failed to understand the needs of the average American. Ward Just's description of Adlai Stevenson applies equally to George H. W. Bush: "Not a man of the common experience, a stranger to ordinary American life."[54] Thus in his twelve years as vice president and president, he had attracted less of the reservoir of confidence and goodwill than many of his predecessors. In addition, Clinton—a far better campaigner than Bush—won most of the debates against an opponent who sometimes gave stumbling answers.

But the principal reason Bush lost was probably the existence of an independent candidate, the nominal Republican Ross Perot, who received 19 percent of the vote. The founder of several computer and communication systems that major corporations subsequently purchased for billions of dollars, Perot ran a campaign out of Dallas. Most of his support apparently came from independents or Republicans who otherwise would have voted for Bush. With Clinton receiving 43 percent of the popular vote, Bush 37.5, and Perot 19, the consensus was that Bush would have pulled out a victory had Perot not entered the race. The election results annulled the highly conservative Pat Buchanan's prophecy at the Republican National Convention. The forthcoming presidential election, Buchanan told the delegates in his speech,

> is about what we believe. It is about what we stand for as Americans. There is a religious war going on in our country for the soul of America . . . and in that struggle for the soul of America, Clinton & Clinton [Gore?] are on the other side, and George Bush is on our side.[55]

Eight years after George H. W. Bush left the presidency, his oldest son entered it. The careers of the two Bushes differed significantly. Whereas George H. W. projected the "genial and preppy ethos" of a patrician Episcopalian, George W. embodied a Texas outlook and value system, even embracing the state's dominant evangelicalism.[56] Father and son attended the same elite prep school and university, and both became members of the same premier society at the university. Both served as military pilots, one immediately following prep school and the other immediately following college.

But while George H. W. Bush enlisted and became a war hero, George W.'s commission into the Air National Guard over a long waiting list raised serious questions of entitlement. Following military service, both worked in the oil business in Texas, although George H. W. Bush succeeded far more than his son. Neither were readers. Whereas the younger Bush entered the presidency after five years of experience in political office, the elder Bush held a variety of high-level appointments, served two terms as vice president, and then became president. Both invaded the Middle East dictatorship of Iraq, though with widely divergent levels of support and success.

Yet George W., unlike his father, was elected to a second term, whereas his father became one of only four presidents in the twentieth century to run for a second term and suffer defeat. In 2004, an experienced reporter who had covered both Bush administrations declared that he and other Washington correspondents "have been able to see for ourselves the plain fact that the father was then a more relaxed, approachable, and less driven, perhaps single-minded, man than his son is now."[57]

George H. W. Bush was raised in a churchgoing family. Since he never had a serious quarrel with the interpretation of Christianity in which he was raised, he remained an Episcopalian. Throughout its postrevolutionary history, the Episcopal Church has tended to attract Americans who are educated, economically comfortable, and inclined toward culture and aesthetics. Thus in his religious affiliation, Bush was more in the tradition of such founding fathers as Washington, Jefferson, Mason, Henry, Madison, Jay, and Monroe than of such presidents as Truman, Eisenhower, Nixon, Carter, and Reagan. He was more distinctly from the Episcopal ethos than Gerald Ford, who could essentially be described as a working-class Episcopalian.

But the Episcopal Church, like any religious group or political party, has parties or wings. During most of Bush's lifetime (and that of his father), the major tensions in the church stemmed from the Reformation debate over whether the Anglican tradition was a form of Catholicism or Protestantism. Bush was "low church" (or Protestant-inclined). He attended churches of other denominations, never insisted that his wife leave her Presbyterian faith, served as a Presbyterian elder, and had a Southern Baptist as a spiritual adviser. He was willing not only to allow Doro's baptism to take place in a foreign land with interdenominational ministers but also to let it be delayed until she was sixteen years old. In fact, for many years the Bushes planned on being buried in the historic churchyard of the First Congregational Church in Kennebunkport.[58]

Prescott Bush, the father of George H. W. Bush, was also a low-church Episcopalian, but less ecumenical. Except on spring and fall weekends in Maine, he rarely attended other than Episcopal services on Sundays. President Bush's oldest son, George W. Bush, converted in his forties to an interpretation of Christianity sufficiently evangelical that at one point he believed that non-Christians would not go to heaven. John Ellis "Jeb" Bush married a Roman Catholic and converted to her faith. In contrast, George H. W. Bush was raised and has remained throughout life a middle-of-the-road Episcopalian and a religious moderate.

In 1989, when he was president, Bush went back to the church in Beijing, now fully sanctioned by the government and housed in a new building. "We were startled not only by the size of the congregation . . . but also by the tremendous . . . overflow," Barbara Bush remembered. "The congregation was Chinese, with a smattering of westerners."[59] During the service the ministers asked the congregation to "remember their sister, Dorothy, a member of the church."[60]

When Bush addressed the worshippers, he recalled that the church had served the family as a "home away from home."[61] Again noting in his diary that the service was "very moving," Bush wrote: "I felt a tear well up when the choir began singing."[62]

Throughout life, George H. W. Bush followed the forms of his faith, from attending church regularly, to serving communion as a student deacon at Andover, to teaching Sunday school in Texas, to saying his prayers before bedtime, to serving on the governing bodies of congregations. But his strongest religious expressions were associated with moments of intensely personal feelings: the awe-filled starlit nights on his rescue vessel in the Pacific; the anguished early mornings in a Texas sanctuary praying for his dying daughter; and the weekly cacophony of familiar hymns sung in strange languages in that old house in Beijing.

# William Jefferson Clinton

1946–  ⌒ PRESIDENT FROM 1993 TO 2001

William Jefferson Clinton was born into a southern family descended from a long line of struggling farmers named for founding fathers. On his mother's side, he was of Irish and Cherokee heritage. His biological father's lineage is difficult to determine, but the family name is Scots. His maternal grandmother, Edith Grisham Cassidy, grew up a Methodist. His grandfather, James (or "Eldridge") Cassidy, was raised Baptist. Neither his mother, father, nor stepfather attended church regularly.

In 1940, six years before Clinton's birth, Arkansas's population of nearly two million was roughly three-quarters white and one-quarter black. Clinton later described his home state, one of the most impoverished in the nation, as "composed mostly of white Southern Baptists and blacks."[1] Of the total number of Baptists, African Americans accounted for approximately 40 percent. Evangelicalism permeated the state's rural and small-town culture, and white and black children received substantial instruction in religious matters outside the home. Thus Clinton was brought up as and has remained a Southern Baptist.

In 1923, Clinton's maternal grandfather, James Eldridge Cassidy—Clinton later described him as "an uneducated rural southerner without a racist bone in his body"[2]—left his small farm at his wife's insistence and moved to the market and railroad town of Hope. Located in southwest Arkansas not far from the Texas border, Hope had a population of roughly five thousand.[3] Following a series of other jobs, Cassidy eventually operated a grocery store and sold bootleg liquor. Clinton's grandmother, a stern but compassionate woman who was frustrated by the difficulties life had dealt her, worked as a registered nurse.

The Cassidys' daughter, Virginia Dell—Clinton's mother—was intelligent, ambitious, and passionate. While a student at Hope High School, she served as secretary of her class, belonged to numerous clubs, and was elected to the

National Honor Society. Yet she also began "a lifelong affair with provocative clothing and megamakeup" in her teens.[4] In time, judgmental citizens in Hope looked down upon Virginia for "loose morals, inattentive mothering, love of money [and] costume jewelry, excessive make-up, tawdry bright colored clothes, glitter, partying, [and] drinking."[5]

Later, in Hot Springs, townspeople were more tolerant. "Oh, she gambled and all that kind of stuff," a childhood friend of Bill Clinton's noted, "but she was a lady of very high standards in terms of helping other people and making a difference in this life."[6] Unable to afford college but wishing to get away from home, Virginia chose the best alternative available. She took a two-year course in nursing at Tri-State Hospital in Shreveport, Louisiana. There she continued the active social life she had begun in Hope.

In 1943, in the midst of World War II, Virginia fell "crazy in love," as she later described it, with William Jefferson Blythe Jr.[7] A traveling auto equipment salesman who had a hardscrabble upbringing in Texas, Blythe had dropped out of school after the eighth grade. At the age of fifteen he had become his family's provider when his father died.[8] Genial, eager to please, and possessed of an easy intelligence and wit, he was also, as Virginia eventually learned, "contradictory and mysterious . . . constantly reinventing himself . . . surviving off charm and affability."[9]

After a two-month wartime romance, the pair married shortly before Blythe left for military duty in Europe. Unknown to Virginia, he was still married to his third wife at the time. He secretly divorced her seven months later. Discharged from the army at the end of 1945, Blythe died in a freak car accident a few months before Bill Clinton's birth in August 1946. Virginia was left to raise their son, Billy, with the assistance of her parents.

After four years as a young widow, Virginia married the divorced Roger Clinton in a Baptist parsonage in Hot Springs, Arkansas. Her parents opposed the marriage. A gambler, alcoholic, and notorious womanizer, "Dude," as he was known, was an abusive husband prone to jealous rages. "He and Virginia didn't seem to match," a friend from Hot Springs declared, "her being the loud and him being the quiet, and her being a medical professional and him being an advanced mechanic."[10] During this marriage, Virginia endured a dozen years of violence and heartache. She divorced Clinton in 1962, but remarried him after only three months.

Around the time of the divorce, young Bill went to the Garland County Courthouse. With the permission of his mother, he legally changed his name to William Jefferson Clinton—the name he already used in school. Although Roger never officially adopted his stepson, Bill wanted the same surname as his half-brother, Roger Clinton Jr. (born in 1956). The change may also have been a symbolic way to show his underlying affection for the man whom he always called "Daddy," even in the face of all the pain his stepfather caused the family.

In 1967, Roger Sr. died, but Virginia soon married again. Ultimately, she was widowed three times before her death in 1994. While known during her son's presidency as Virginia Kelley—the name of her last husband—upon her death she was buried beside her first husband in Hope.

Young Clinton's first exposure to church came during the two years he lived with his grandparents in Hope while Virginia furthered her education by studying anesthesiology in New Orleans. His grandmother regularly took him to the preschool Sunbeams program at First Baptist Church, where three- and four-year-olds learned about Jesus and Baptist missionary work. Virginia subsequently enrolled him in Sunday school, and on his summer vacations he attended Bible school. She herself usually went to church only on Christmas and Easter. When Billy was six years old, Roger Clinton relocated the family to his hometown of Hot Springs, where he worked in a Buick dealership run by his more successful brother, Raymond Clinton.

For a poor, rural state like Arkansas, cosmopolitan Hot Springs was a remarkable anomaly. It was also a notoriously corrupt city—"wide open," in the words of Clinton's cousin.[11] A southern parallel to Las Vegas, it had a postwar population of about 35,000, although up to 100,000 visitors came each year to enjoy its baths, gambling, horseracing, and other legal and illegal activities. A thriving tourist economy made the city remarkably diverse for a mostly homogeneous state.

Hot Springs included not only Baptist and other Protestant churches but also two synagogues, two Roman Catholic churches, and a Greek Orthodox church. The Roman Catholic presence stemmed in part from supposedly retired Mafia leaders who sought refuge in Hot Springs. Among them was the feared Irish gangster Owney Madden, who settled into life in the town in 1935 and lived there as its "illegal gambling monarch" for thirty years.[12]

"Hot Springs is like a big old Catholic church," a cousin of Clinton once said. "There is somebody from every place in the world, from Estonia to Albania to Malaysia to whatever."[13]

In addition to a substantial number of Irish and Italian families, Hot Springs included a large number of African Americans, as well as a small but visible population of Jews. Clinton grew up with Arab American neighbors, a Japanese American friend, and a Czech schoolmate. Paul David Leopoulos, one of his best friends, was part of the town's sizable Greek community. This exposure to ethnic diversity in Hot Springs helped advance Clinton's commitment to tolerance and civil rights at an early age. "That I had friends and acquaintances from such a diverse group of people when I was young may seem normal today," Clinton wrote in his autobiography, "but in 1950s Arkansas, it could have happened only in Hot Springs."[14]

On most Sundays young Clinton would dress himself in his best suit, pick up his Bible, and walk three blocks to attend Sunday school at Park Place Baptist Church, followed by the adult church service. An impressive brick edifice built in 1902 and subsequently expanded, Park Place was one of the largest churches in Hot Springs. Although his mother urged him to attend, Clinton went of his own accord, saying he felt it was important to go to church every Sunday to "try to be a good person."[15] Park Place's pastor, the Reverend James Fitzgerald, recalled that the eager boy seemed to be at the church "every time the door opened."[16]

Toward the end of their Sunday worship services, Southern Baptist churches often have an invitation, or "altar call." Worshippers who wish to commit their lives to Jesus Christ and be baptized, as well as baptized persons who wish to rededicate their lives or simply join the congregation, are invited to come forward. Pastors and counselors then often take those who have come down the aisle to a side room for counseling.

At the age of nine, Clinton walked forward at Park Place Church and made that commitment. "Rev. Fitzgerald convinced me that I needed to acknowledge that I was a sinner and that I needed to accept Christ in my heart, and I did," he later remembered. "I have a very vivid memory of exactly what he looked like and the way he talked, and he touched my heart."[17] On another occasion, Clinton recalled, "I came down the aisle at the end of the Sunday service, professed my faith in Christ, and asked to be baptized."[18]

The Reverend Mr. Fitzgerald later came to the Clinton home to discuss the meaning of baptism with both Billy and his mother. During a Sunday service in the fall of 1956, he baptized Clinton and others by immersion in a baptismal pool located prominently at the front of the church. Clinton later described the decision to be baptized as his "first serious religious experience."[19]

From his gambling, fun-loving parents, Clinton undoubtedly received little instruction in religion or morality. At the time of his baptism, the principal religious influence in his life was the family housekeeper, Cora Walters. A devout Christian who took care of Billy because his parents worked, she served as his nanny for eleven years. "Maybe the most Christian person I've ever known," Virginia Kelley wrote in her autobiography, she was "the kind who *lived* her Christianity. . . . Mrs. Walters taught Bill the Golden Rule and other lessons about how to live and get along and how to treat people in this world."[20] Virginia herself kept her spirituality low-key but says that she prayed frequently. In her autobiography, she writes that her religious philosophy was simple: "if you just leave God alone and don't nose around too much, He'll take care of things."[21]

Always fiercely protective of and devoted to her son, Virginia was worried about the quality of the small rural public school near the family's rented home just outside Hot Springs. Training and working as a nurse and nurse anesthetist, she had learned firsthand that a good education can open doors. Thus Bill attended the second and third grades at St. John's Catholic School, a highly regarded parochial school run by the Sisters of Mercy in downtown Hot Springs.

At St. John's, Clinton recollects that he routinely tried to absent himself during the daily recitation of the rosary. But he was "fascinated by the Catholic Church, its rituals and the devotion of the nuns."[22] When his second-grade teacher gave him a C in conduct for not allowing other children to answer a question before he blurted out the response, Billy immediately changed his behavior. He excelled in school. According to a story, a nun subsequently told Virginia that her son could be president some day.

The challenges of growing up in an unstable home caused Clinton serious emotional distress. He was viewed as the star in the family, and his mother even let him sleep in the master bedroom. But as his stepfather became increasingly violent toward his mother, Clinton grew frustrated by his continued inability to protect her. By age thirteen, his responsibility as the man of the house placed an enormous strain on him. He experienced what he called a "major spiritual crisis."

Clinton kept his troubles to himself, not even telling his pastor. "My faith was too weak to sustain a certain belief in God in the face of what I was witnessing and going through," he later reflected. "I now know this struggle is, at least partially, the result of growing up in an alcoholic home and the mechanisms I developed to cope with it."[23]

Although he was questioning his faith, he continued to rely on worship to help overcome religious doubts and family anxieties. The pews at Park Place became a sanctuary, a place of peace from the tensions and conflicts of his home. As is the case with many people, he would continue this pattern of turning to God during the darkest moments of his life. When chaos threatened to engulf him, church was a place that young Clinton could depend upon for normalcy, routine, and spiritual guidance. His religion seemed the strongest, or at least the most visible, when he was lowest.

In 1959, Little Rock hosted a revival held by Billy Graham that helped Clinton work through the crisis. His Sunday school teacher took his class to the crusade. Although Little Rock officials and the White Citizens Council had strongly suggested that Graham segregate the crusade, the evangelist refused. Clinton remembered his awe at seeing "blacks and whites coming down the aisle together at the football stadium—it was an amazing, amazing thing." At "that age where kids question everything," he recalled, "all of a sudden I said, 'This guy has got to be real, because he did this when he didn't have to.'" The experience impressed Clinton so much that for months afterward he donated part of his weekly allowance to Graham's ministry. "I was just a little boy," he said. "I never forgot it, and I've loved him ever since."[24] Clinton later recalled the Graham revival as the "beginning of the end of the Old South in my home state," as over the next decade the civil rights movement ushered in a new era of southern history.[25]

Only with some exaggeration was an early biography of Clinton titled *First in His Class.* An extrovert, invariably eager to please, he always ranked academically at or near the top of his classes. At Hot Springs High School, then one of the premier public schools of Arkansas, he benefited from a cadre of dedicated teachers who challenged and inspired him. High school classmates later described young Clinton as "an attentive listener" who "knew everything about this . . . everything about that." They remembered him as "an excellent student" who "read all the time" and "was interested in almost everything." A classmate who lived next door to Clinton and was the daughter of a Baptist minister recalled that "he wasn't in the geek crowd, but he competed academically at a geek level."[26]

Clinton's principal, Johnnie Mae Mackey, acknowledged and cultivated his early political talent, even allowing him to miss classes in order to speak to local organizations about his Boys Nation experience or her own favorite theme, the importance of civic engagement. His world history teacher encouraged his love of analysis and debate, while his Latin teacher was "exacting and inspirational." After learning and practicing rhetoric and persuasion in the Latin class, Clinton decided to become a lawyer. He was selected not only for Boys State in Arkansas but also for Boys Nation in Washington, D.C.[27]

Although he was elected president of the junior class in high school, Clinton was not senior class president. Citing his numerous other extracurricular commitments — "All-State Band, Student Council, Key Club, Mu Alpha Theta, Beta Club, Junior Classical League, Band Key Club, Trojan Pep Band, Starlight Dance Band, Trojan Marching Band, Junior Class President, Boys State, and Boys Nation," according to one list[28] — his principal refused to let him run.[29] Thus for an Arkansan student of the times, Clinton had no shortage of intellectual stimulation, leadership experiences, and competition — all of which augmented his lifelong drive to impress, to win, and to engage in serious issues.

Graduating fourth in a class of 327 students and winning designation as a National Merit semifinalist, Clinton gave the benediction, or prayer, at his high school's graduation ceremony. In it he implored God to help the graduates as they strove to improve the world and to fulfill their God-given purpose. Years later, during his 1992 presidential campaign, he echoed these statements when he declared, "My faith has taught me to see [public service] as a ministry. I think everybody has work to do, and you're supposed to do the best you can. . . . Every person has a calling in life . . . and can fulfill the intention of God for human life by giving dignity to whatever work they do."[30]

Because he wished to study in its prestigious School of Foreign Service, Clinton continued his education on a scholarship at the Jesuit-run

Georgetown University. Despite being on scholarship, he was not an impoverished student; by at least his senior year, he owned a white Buick convertible.[31] Clinton arrived at Georgetown in the fall of 1964, before the widespread effects of the Second Vatican Council (1962–1965) had reduced the influence of Roman Catholicism on its campus. Then 96 percent Roman Catholic in enrollment, the all-male College of Arts and Sciences employed mostly Jesuit priests or lay Roman Catholics on its faculty. Although the more diverse School of Foreign Service included several hundred Protestant and approximately forty Jewish students, it was still overwhelmingly Roman Catholic, white, and male.[32]

Most of Clinton's classmates hailed from upper-middle-class, traditional Roman Catholic families. So infused was the atmosphere of Georgetown with the teachings of Roman Catholicism that one Presbyterian mother sent her son a book titled *What Presbyterians Believe*. Clinton was the first Southern Baptist his roommate, an Irish American from Long Island, had met.[33] When Kit Ashby, a friend from Texas, "joked that he and Clinton were 'about the only Southern Protestants at Georgetown that fall,'" the statement was not all that far from the truth.[34]

During his four years at Georgetown, Clinton went to church irregularly. When he did go, he attended Protestant services with other Protestants and Mass at the university chapel with Roman Catholic friends. Because Kit Ashby claimed that "there were no 'good' Baptist churches" close to campus, Clinton and Ashby sometimes went to a nearby Presbyterian church.[35] During his junior year, Clinton wrote to his stepfather, Roger Clinton, then dying of throat cancer, to urge him to attend church more frequently. "Good always outweighs bad," the letter declared, "and even death doesn't end a man's life."[36]

At Georgetown, Clinton continued his interest in holding class office. A classic student politician who ambitiously sought votes as he honed what would become his trademark campaign style, he was elected president of the freshman and then of the sophomore class. During his senior year, he lost the election for student council president because his classmates, who by then had begun to rebel against authority at the school, viewed him as one of the favored boys of Georgetown's establishment.

Although not at the top of his class, he graduated cum laude and thoroughly enjoyed his courses. One classmate remembered Clinton as "a taster of ideas . . . a skillful user, but not a lover [of ideas] for their own sake."[37] But in a class on introductory philosophy, Clinton performed so well that the Jesuit scholastic who taught the course, Otto Hentz, invited him to dinner and suggested that Clinton consider becoming a Jesuit. The young instructor was stunned when Clinton replied that he was Southern Baptist. "I saw all the Jesuit traits in him," Hentz later said, "serious, political, empathetic. I just assumed he was Catholic."[38]

From another class at Georgetown, Clinton developed an interest in world religions. In place of the course in theology required of Roman Catholic students, Father Joseph Stebes taught a course required of non-Catholics entitled "Comparative Cultures" and known among students as "Buddhism for Baptists." Stebes's class inspired what Clinton later called a "feel . . . for what I believe is the innate religious nature of human beings." All cultures, "no matter how different they were," he later declared, "had a hunger to find some meaning in their lives beyond the temporal things that consume most of us through most of our days."[39]

Beginning with his two years in parochial school, Clinton may have had more exposure to Roman Catholicism than any president other than John F. Kennedy. Unlike many of his southern Protestant classmates at Georgetown, he remained unconcerned that most of his professors were practicing Roman Catholics. Although Clinton did not leave his Protestant faith at Georgetown, "he absorbed the perspective of many of the school's father-professors, which turned out to be more catholic than Catholic."[40] Yet the rituals of his alma mater—its Masses, its rosaries, and its doctrinal aspects—seem to have left no permanent mark on him. Likewise, he appears to have remained unchanged by the Church of England to the extent that he was exposed to it during two years at Oxford as a Rhodes Scholar following graduation from Georgetown in 1968.

A fellow Rhodes Scholar sums up Clinton's two years at Oxford: "Rhodes Scholars don't have to do much academically if they don't want to," Robert Reich observed. "Some of us took our studies more seriously than others. Bill did not take them terribly seriously." Reich (who later served as secretary of labor in the Clinton administration) sees the value of the Oxford years in the opportunity they gave Clinton for travel. "We all spent our holidays travelling," Reich remembered. "He was enormously excited by the world that he was seeing. Bill had a ravenous appetite for facts, ideas, new perspectives, new points of view."[41]

Clinton's graduation from Georgetown in 1968 was accompanied by his reclassification as 1-A, or eligible to be drafted immediately, by his Hot Springs draft board. Although the Johnson administration had canceled deferments for graduate students in February of that year, Clinton's draft board—in the words of its executive secretary—"leaned over backwards" to allow him to continue study at Oxford as a Rhodes Scholar.[42] While at Oxford in the spring of 1969, Clinton received a draft notice. When he left for Arkansas in the summer of 1969, his classmates did not expect him to return.

Although Clinton opposed the war on moral grounds, he realized that he would not assist his political career by fleeing the draft. With the help of the office of Senator William Fulbright of Arkansas (for whom he had worked part-time while at Georgetown), Clinton reached an agreement with his draft board and with Colonel Eugene Holmes, a survivor of the Bataan Death March who directed the ROTC program at the University of Arkansas. In return for his local board's withdrawing his draft notice, Clinton agreed to enroll in the fall of 1969 in both the university's law school and its ROTC program. As a result, he was reclassified 1-D (a classification given to members of the Reserves or National Guard and to students enrolled in ROTC).

That fall, however, Clinton returned to Oxford for a second year. When he returned to the United States at the end of that second year, he enrolled not at Arkansas but at Yale. As 1969 went on, reductions in the number of young men drafted monthly reduced the chances of Clinton's being drafted. Late in 1969, when the Nixon administration instituted a lottery for the draft, Clinton received a number "too high to put him at risk."[43] Although the draft continued into 1973, Clinton studied at Yale Law School with little fear of being drafted.

Clinton's deferment became highly controversial during the presidential campaign of 1992. Two months before the election, Colonel Holmes submitted an affidavit, or written declaration under oath. Expressing his concern about "the imminent danger to our country of a draft dodger becoming Commander-in-Chief of the Armed Forces," Colonel Holmes related the story of Clinton's deferment and then declared:

In retrospect I see that Mr. Clinton had no intention of following through with his agreement to join the Army ROTC program at the University of Arkansas or to attend the University of Arkansas. . . . I believe that he purposefully deceived me, using the possibility of joining the ROTC as a ploy to work with the draft board to delay his induction and get a new draft classification.[44]

At Yale Law School, Clinton's extracurricular activities centered on politics and efforts to end the Vietnam War, and not on Yale's Battell Chapel, then the center of antiwar protests. Although the chapel was only two blocks from the law school, Clinton's autobiography mentions neither churchgoing in New Haven nor Yale's front-page chaplain, the Reverend William Sloane Coffin. In part, the omission may stem from the fact that Yale's and Coffin's days of activism had reached their pinnacle in the academic year of 1967–1968, some time prior to Clinton's enrollment.

Clinton returned to Arkansas to teach law from 1973 to 1976. In a state that then limited its elected offices to two-year terms, he served from 1976 to 1978 as attorney general. In 1978, he became the second-youngest governor in the history of Arkansas. As attorney general and governor he had attended church sporadically, but he began regularly attending again in 1980 after he lost his bid for reelection. The man who defeated him, Frank D. White—a Republican and fundamentalist Baptist—proceeded to provoke statewide controversy during his two-year term. He not only outlawed the use of alcohol at gatherings on any state property but also signed a law—subsequently struck down as unconstitutional—that directed the public schools in Arkansas to teach both "creation science" and "evolution science." When Clinton ran against White again in 1982, he won.[45]

During his two years out of office, Clinton began attending Immanuel Baptist Church. The largest church in Arkansas, its lofty complex of buildings loomed over the capitol. Many of its four thousand members belonged to Little Rock's business and social elite, and its Sunday services were televised throughout the state.

Clinton's churchgoing helped his political career in Arkansas. When he ran for attorney general of Arkansas in 1976, members of evangelical churches would ask on the campaign trail if he was a Christian, and then, when he said yes, whether he was born-again. Clinton answered the last question as most Southern Baptists would: he always said yes.[46] At one point he asked Dale Bumpers, the popular governor-turned-senator and a "good liberal Methodist" from Arkansas, for advice on handling such questions. Bumpers responded that when voters asked if he was a Christian, he always said, "'I sure hope so, and I've always tried to be. But I think that's a question only God can judge.' That usually shuts them up."[47]

Although Clinton used Bumper's answer for the rest of his campaign (which he won unopposed), his relationship with the group called the Moral Majority after he became governor of Arkansas was more complicated. Founded by the Virginia evangelist Jerry Falwell in 1979, the Moral Majority existed to influence government policies by electing candidates, usually Republican, who shared the organization's conservative religious and political views. As a relatively liberal Democrat who lacked a strong base of evangelical supporters, Clinton did not fit the mold of the typical Moral Majority candidate.

Falwell's organization officially dissolved in 1989. But its numerous splinter organizations—such as the Christian Coalition, Focus on the Family, and Operation Rescue—have continued to support candidates who espouse their values into the twenty-first century. Despite his Southern Baptist and evangelical affiliations, Bill Clinton was no favorite of religious conservatives. Following the Monica Lewinsky scandal, Paul Weyrich, cofounder of the Moral Majority, wrote, "If there really were a moral majority out there, Bill Clinton would have been driven out of office months ago."[48]

Throughout his life, Clinton occasionally attended Pentecostal revival meetings, at which he sometimes even played saxophone. "It changed my life," he once remarked of the first Pentecostal meeting he attended, "and has never failed to be a blessing to me."[49] His autobiography declares that a gospel hymn sung at a Pentecostal meeting caused him to break into tears.[50] No president has been more influenced by Pentecostalism than Bill Clinton.

When Clinton returned to church, his critics in Arkansas viewed his attendance as a form of calculated political rehabilitation. They noted, for example, that his membership in the Immanuel choir allowed him to sit behind the pulpit directly in view of the television camera. But while the accusations were frequent and often harsh, Clinton's overall statewide image benefited from his churchgoing. "When he moved to Little Rock and began making decisions that affected millions of lives," a biographer who interviewed Clinton later wrote, "his need to return to church was as strong as the impulse that moved him to church as a boy."[51] Since 1980, Clinton has rarely shied from emphasizing his religious side.

Clinton joined Immanuel Church in part because of its pastor, the Reverend Worley Oscar Vaught. Telephone calls and talks with the scholarly and theologically conservative Vaught became a regular part of Clinton's workweek following his 1980 defeat. "I admired W. O. Vaught," Clinton declares in his autobiography, "because he had forsaken the hellfire-and-brimstone preaching of his early ministry in favor of carefully teaching the Bible to his congregation. . . . Jesus never had a more faithful follower. And I never had a more faithful pastor."[52] In 1980 Clinton and his wife Hillary went on a pilgrimage to the Holy Land led by the pastor. When Vaught was dying of bone cancer in 1989, Clinton visited him weekly, took Billy Graham to see him, and served as a pallbearer at his funeral.

Vaught's view of Clinton and the spiritual advice he gave Clinton have been the subject of controversy. According to Clinton's autobiography, Vaught advised him that the words "thou shalt not kill"—a commandment that relates directly to a governor's responsibility of confirming death sentences—did not prohibit capital punishment (an interpretation with which few biblical scholars will argue). According to Clinton, Vaught himself opposed most abortions, but he advised Clinton that the Bible neither condemned abortion nor declared explicitly that life began at conception. When Clinton then asked about the meaning of the influential passage in Psalm 139 (which declares that God "knit me together in my mother's womb"), Vaught replied "that the verse simply refers to God being omniscient, and that it might as well have said God knew us even before we were in our mother's womb, even before anyone in our direct line was born." Finally, in Clinton's account, Vaught said that he thought Clinton would be president some day and that God would never forgive him if he failed to stand by Israel.[53]

Few Southern Baptist ministers today take a pro-choice position on abortion. Ever since *Roe v. Wade*—the Supreme Court decision of 1973 that affirmed a woman's right to an abortion—became a national issue, most Southern Baptist clergy have adamantly opposed abortion. Along with Roman Catholics and evangelicals in general, they have believed that life begins with conception and have viewed the abortion of a fetus as murder.

Thus some of Vaught's ministerial colleagues have denied that the Little Rock minister held the views Clinton attributed to him. "It is quite rare to find a Southern Baptist pastor embracing such a position," one colleague has asserted.[54] "Vaught," the editor of a leading Southern Baptist publication has written, "was as conservative as they come."[55] Wiley Drake, a highly partisan and conservative Baptist pastor who claims to have discussed abortion with Vaught, has denied that Clinton's pastor believed that life began at birth rather than at conception. According to Drake, Vaught held serious reservations about Clinton. Vaught once warned him, Drake has declared, that Clinton was "not the person he made himself out to be."[56]

On the other hand, as this book discusses in its chapter on Jimmy Carter, leading clergy in the Southern Baptist Convention initially supported *Roe v. Wade.* In the early 1970s, many Southern Baptist pastors accepted what came to be known as pro-choice positions. Their numbers included the Reverend W. A. Criswell, pastor of the First Baptist Church of Dallas, a church whose membership exceeded 25,000 and whose downtown campus comprised one million square feet. "I have always felt," declared Criswell in 1973, "that it was only after a child was born and had a life separate from its mother that it became an individual person."[57]

Criswell had served a term as president of the Southern Baptist Convention only three years before the Supreme Court decision. Although most Southern Baptist pastors subsequently changed their views in the later 1970s, Vaught may have continued to accept abortion on biblical grounds. In addition, Vaught's son Carl has supported Clinton's statements. He has said that his father told Clinton that the Hebrew word for "life" is "breath," so that life in the biblical view begins at birth when a baby takes its first real breath. Under this definition, abortion—while still not right—could not be classified as murder.[58] Vaught may have given precisely that advice to Clinton.

Finally, the relentless criticism by Drake may be unreliable. If Clinton is controversial, so is Drake. Some in the Southern Baptist Convention view him as a poor source. The Internal Revenue Service has investigated him for using church letterhead and church radio broadcasts to support a presidential candidate.

Drake has also gained notoriety for calling upon parishioners to pray—not for, but rather against—the leaders of the Americans United for Separation of Church and State, the organization that prompted the IRS investigation. "Persecute them. . . . Let them be put to shame and perish" and "Let his children be fatherless, and his wife a widow" are examples of the imprecatory prayers Drake recommended to his congregation.[59] During the presidential election of 2008, Drake publicly stated that "according to my Bible and in my opinion, there is no way in the world a Christian can vote for Barack Hussein Obama."[60]

Both Clinton's and Drake's descriptions of how Vaught viewed abortion stem from private conversations between two people—one of whom (Vaught) is dead. Thus the result seems an impasse. Readers should also realize that the decentralized system of Baptist leadership leaves each minister responsible for advising parishioners on issues according to his own interpretation of the Bible. Pastors such as Vaught have no higher authority than the Bible and their conscience.

Clinton attributes his return to regular churchgoing in Little Rock to his wife, Hillary Rodham Clinton. Raised in the upper-middle-class Chicago suburb of Park Ridge, Hillary possessed many of the same traits as her husband. An academic standout in grade school and a class leader in high school, she received so many awards at her high school graduation that her family was embarrassed. Her father, Hugh Rodham, a Chicago manufacturer, was a conservative Republican in politics; her mother, Dorothy Howell Rodham, was concerned about matters of social justice.

In Park Ridge, the Rodham family belonged to the First United Methodist Church, a church noted for its large Sunday school program. When Hillary was confirmed at age eleven, the church's youth minister confirmed more than one hundred other young people on the same occasion.

By the time Hillary reached her teens, the Reverend Don Jones, a navy veteran and recent seminary graduate, had become the youth minister. Jones's effect on Hillary's social consciousness cannot be overestimated. He was an avid reader of the World War II martyr Dietrich Bonhoeffer and of such leading Protestant theologians as Reinhold Niebuhr and Paul Tillich. He introduced Hillary to their teachings about human nature, social justice, and the moral responsibility of a Christian to enact change and to fight discrimination and poverty. "Jones stressed that a Christian life was 'faith in action,'" she later recalled. "I had never met anyone like him."[61]

In emphasizing the Christian's obligation to work for a just society, Jones built upon a long tradition in Methodism. The practice began with the denomination's founder, John Wesley. An Anglican priest in England who emphasized the obligation of his church to take the Christian faith to the industrial poor, Wesley taught that Christians should "do all the good you can, by all the means you can, in all the ways you can, in all the places you can, to all the people you can, as long as ever you can."[62] Hillary has often used this quotation in speeches, her favorite of Wesley's, to express her commitment to charity and to social justice. In fact, according to family tradition, the Rodhams became Methodist in England because Wesley had included their small coal-mining village in his preaching mission.

Describing himself as "neo-orthodox, guided by the belief that social change should come about slowly and without radical action," Jones brought his interpretation of the Protestant Social Gospel to Hillary's high-school youth group.[63] Through a program he called "the University of Life," he exposed his students to literature, theology, and art they had not yet discovered.

In addition, the young minister organized exchanges with black and Hispanic youth at community centers and churches in inner-city Chicago. His class went into the city to hear Martin Luther King Jr. speak about the failure of Americans to recognize and embrace the social revolution that was happening around them. Through Jones, Hillary first learned that life consisted of more than the comfortable existence and manicured lawns of Park Ridge. "Curious . . . just insatiable," was how the youth pastor described her eager responses to both intellectual questions and issues of social justice.[64] In Hillary's words, she came home from the University of Life on Thursday nights "bursting with excitement."[65]

When she left suburban Chicago to study at Wellesley College in 1965, Hillary was still a Republican. In the previous fall's presidential election, she had supported Barry Goldwater. Within two years, however, she changed her views. At Wellesley she joined many Democratic students and faculty in opposing the Vietnam War. She apparently retained her religious convictions, joining the interdenominational Chapel Society. As the first student commencement speaker in Wellesley's history, Hillary made national headlines after a stirring and provocative speech that pleased students but annoyed many parents.

The first encounter of Hillary Rodham and Bill Clinton is well known. After graduating from Wellesley, she entered Yale University Law School. Both studied in Yale's law library every night, looking at each other across the shelves, until Hillary, always outspoken and sure of herself, walked up to Bill and announced, "If we're going to keep staring at each other like this, we ought to at least know each other's names."[66] Hillary later wrote, "He wasn't afraid of me." The "sunny southerner with Elvis sideburns," as someone described Clinton during this period, "could just look at her and tell she was interesting and deep."[67] In 1975 their wedding occurred not in a church but in the living room of their newly bought house in Fayetteville, Arkansas, with a Methodist minister conducting a simple service. "Probably more has been written or said about our marriage than about any other in America," Clinton later wrote in his autobiography.[68]

One writer has described Hillary as a "deeply religious" Methodist.[69] Yet her autobiography makes no mention of church attendance at Wellesley or at Yale, which may help explain the secular setting of her marriage. Upon moving to Little Rock, however, Hillary resumed active churchgoing at the First United Methodist Church, located in downtown Little Rock. During the years Bill Clinton was governor, the church—politically liberal for Arkansas—had a "wealthy congregation filled with young professionals, many of them upper class, with a special attraction to attorneys—seventy-six of its members were lawyers."[70] First United also had a tradition of progressive civil rights and social activism, which suited Hillary's ideology. She taught Sunday school and supported the church's creation of the Child Development Center in downtown Little Rock. The Clintons' daughter and only child, Chelsea, was baptized in First United.[71]

Both Bill and Hillary Clinton had established themselves as regular churchgoers by the time Bill was elected president in 1992. When the Clintons moved from Arkansas to the White House, they ensured that religious symbolism played a prominent role in their introduction as the new first family. On their way to Washington, they chose to worship at Culpeper Baptist Church in Virginia, following the observance with a late-night prayer service at the First Baptist Church in Washington.

The family's choice of Baptist churches showed its commitment to Bill's home denomination in the days surrounding his inauguration. On the morning of the inauguration, Clinton requested that the traditional service of worship be held at Washington's Metropolitan African Methodist Episcopal Church, "the Cathedral of African Methodism." This service marked the first use of an African American church for the service of worship customarily held before the swearing in of a new president. In a testament to his years of spiritual relationships with the chief executive, Billy Graham delivered the inauguration's benediction.

Prior to his presidency, Clinton had attended two crusades led by Graham in Arkansas, and he spoke at the second crusade. Two writers see Graham as offering Clinton a positive male role model, one who treated him differently and who often talked with him about personal issues.[72]

Over the years, Graham developed a close personal relationship with the Clintons. After giving the benediction at the inauguration, the evangelist and his wife spent the night at the White House. He remained close to both Bill and Hillary during the difficult months following revelations of the affair with Monica Lewinsky. Hillary remembers Graham as "incredibly supportive to me personally" throughout the trial process.[73]

Graham himself would publicly forgive Clinton for his indiscretions shortly after the news of the affair broke. "If he is guilty," Graham told an interviewer in early March 1998, "I would forgive him and love him just the same because he's a remarkable man. . . . And he's had a lot of temptations thrown his way and a lot of pressure on him."[74]

Many Americans believed Graham's offer of forgiveness premature. At the time of the evangelist's interview, the president had declared to reporters and in a deposition under oath that he "never had sexual relations with that woman."[75] Critics questioned whether Graham's "forgiveness" was a blanket offer, extended to cover the alleged adultery, perjury, and any other sins the president may have committed.[76]

Other critics took issue with Graham's excuses for Clinton's adultery. "He has such a tremendous personality," Graham told one interviewer, "that I think the ladies just go wild over him."[77] This almost dismissive attitude toward the president's behavior aroused some anger. One newspaper headline of the following day read sarcastically: "GRAHAM TO CLINTON: GO AND SIN SOME MORE."[78]

For the Clintons, however, Graham's forgiveness provided comfort and strength. Hillary especially appreciated the evangelist's support of her own forgiveness of Bill. "The entire world was judging my decisions and my actions," she later told an interviewer, "and there weren't very many people who, frankly, were understanding, and he was."[79]

While the United Methodist and Baptist churches differ not only in their views of church government but also on the question of whether the New Testament teaches the baptism of children, the difference between their beliefs and styles of worship is relatively small. In Little Rock, the Clintons often attended the same services. In Washington, after visiting a number of Protestant churches, they settled on Foundry United Methodist Church, located one mile from the White House.

That Foundry Church "included people of various races, cultures, incomes, and political affiliations, and openly welcomed gays" pleased the Clintons, who supported diversity and inclusiveness.[80] According to the pastor, J. Philip Wogaman, the Clintons became remarkably consistent churchgoers while in Washington, attending Foundry nearly every Sunday they were in town. Paul Kengor, the conservative author of *God and Hillary Clinton*, notes that not only did the liberal Wogaman hold pro-life views but also his sermons focused on social justice rather than on "inconvenient matters like the sanctity and dignity of human life."[81] Thus the Clintons could attend Wogaman's church without worrying that statements from the pulpit would embarrass them. According to one biographer, the Clintons "found that religion eased the burden of their high-profile personae, sometimes offering solace and escape from the contentious world of politics, other times providing theological support for their personal actions and political choices."[82]

When spending weekends at Camp David, Clinton attended its Evergreen Chapel, where he sang in the small choir. The chapel's organist and choir director would supply sheet music for the anthem ahead of time, and Clinton would practice it on his own.[83] In addition to attending church, Bill Clinton regularly participated in national and local interfaith prayer breakfasts throughout his presidency. He set up recurring breakfast sessions with various clergy and lay religious leaders to address contemporary moral and social issues. During a visit to China, he worshipped and briefly spoke to a packed congregation in Chongwenmen Church, the same Protestant church the Bushes had attended and in which Doro Bush had been baptized. Many Chinese Christians fervently hoped that Clinton's presence would help advance Christianity in China, but the state-controlled press hardly mentioned his visit.

At home, Clinton kept contacts open with the United States Conference of Catholic Bishops, with rabbinical associations, with African American clergy, with televangelists, and with evangelicals such as Bill Hybels of Willow Creek Community Church, the best-known megachurch in America. Ignored by the Reagan and Bush administrations, the mainline National Council of Churches—representing forty-five million American Protestant and Eastern Orthodox Christians—again received invitations to White House conferences during Clinton's presidency. "Clinton was open to many different ministers and meetings throughout the years," declared Rex Horne, Clinton's pastor at Immanuel Church during his last term as governor and throughout his presidency.[84]

Although his administration broadened the religious spectrum recognized in the White House, Clinton tended to disregard his own Southern Baptist Convention, which had become increasingly conservative and removed its moderate leadership.[85] During his eight years in office, numerous state Baptist conventions passed resolutions denouncing Clinton's views on abortion and homosexuality. The president claimed "the Southern Baptist label," a denominational editor declared, but did not "behave the way they want or expect a Southern Baptist to behave."[86]

Eventually, Clinton left the Southern Baptist Convention. While living in Chappaqua in suburban Westchester County, New York, he and his wife have often attended Methodist churches—most frequently Park Avenue United Methodist Church in New York, but also Methodist and other churches in the county. Along with a rabbi, their former pastor at the Park Avenue church performed the wedding ceremony of Chelsea Clinton in 2010. Clinton also reportedly attends a Baptist church in Chappaqua. In the past decade he has joined Jimmy Carter in rallying Southern and other Baptists into the acceptance of a broadly inclusive "New Baptist Covenant."[87]

Seeing Clinton "not just as a political enemy but also as a wayward relative" guilty of misrepresenting the Southern Baptist faith and many of its tenets, the Southern Baptist Convention took action against both him and his home church.[88] In September 1998, the president of the Convention asserted that Clinton could be "instrumental in corrupting all our young people" and called on him to resign.[89] In its national meeting, the Convention ultimately rejected a resolution to disfellowship Clinton's home church in Little Rock for refusing to publicly reprimand his actions. The vote, however, was close: 1,005 for to 1,071 against.

Because the Baptist Church is organized according to a highly democratic structure, individual churches exercise substantial autonomy. They alone possess the power to discipline members. Thus the annual convention of the Southern Baptists could apply pressure only on Immanuel Church regarding its reluctance to disfellowship Clinton—it had no say over Clinton's individual church membership. Furthermore, the convention constitutionally cannot disfellowship individual members.

In late summer 1998, the embattled president issued to the nation a televised "apology," written by an adviser but heavily revised by Clinton. Opinion polls seemed to indicate that the American public accepted the apology, if somewhat grudgingly. Yet not only editorial boards of major newspapers but also Clinton's ecclesiastical opponents sharply criticized the speech because of its apparent lack of sincerity and admission of guilt. "I don't believe what I saw on television was anything even closely approaching . . . an apology," Wiley Drake declared.

> And even if he were to apologize, I don't believe that is a biblical term. . . .
> 1 John 1:9 . . . says, "If we confess our sins, he is faithful and just to forgive
> us our sins, and to cleanse us from all unrighteousness." I did not hear him
> confess. I heard him say "I lied." I heard him say "I deceived." But I did not
> hear what I believe to be a biblical confession or a biblical repentance.[90]

Several weeks later in a series of meditative remarks at the National Prayer Breakfast in Washington, Clinton himself agreed with the critics who thought he was "not contrite enough." He spoke of his "broken spirit" as well as of his "willingness to give the very forgiveness I seek." He told the nation that the sorrow he felt was "genuine" and that he asked forgiveness of all the people he hurt. "I have repented," he asserted.[91] Almost a year later, in an interview with Hybels, Clinton described his admission at the prayer breakfast as "clear, unambiguous, brutally frank, and . . . personally painful." He told the megachurch pastor that he finally realized that "it would never be all right unless I stood up there and said what I did and said it was wrong and apologized for it."[92]

In the aftermath of the Lewinsky scandal, Clinton asked three ministers to counsel him on a regular basis. One was his Washington pastor, Philip Wogaman. Another was the progressive evangelical author and professor Tony Campolo. The third—and perhaps the most interesting choice—was Gordon MacDonald, a major figure in evangelical circles who had lost his own pastorate and reputation for a time because of an adulterous affair.[93] Although Clinton's opponents viewed his sessions of spiritual counseling as yet another political trick, the three clergy defended Clinton's penitence as genuine. Campolo, for example, declared that Clinton "holds to an evangelical theology, affirms the doctrines of the Apostles' Creed, and 'believes the Bible to be an infallible message from God.'" Wogaman described Clinton as "a deeply connected spiritual person" who prayed and read the Bible regularly.[94] As in his youth, Clinton again seems to have turned to spiritual guidance during a difficult moment in his life.

Clearly Clinton's childhood is the key to the man. His grandmother was strict; his mother highly competent but brassy, fun-loving, somewhat wayward, and highly ambitious for her son; his stepfather abusive. From this dysfunctional background emerged a man with a need to please, a driving political ambition, a flexibility bordering on temporizing, a selective memory, a willingness to shave the truth, a cavalier attitude toward marital fidelity, a need for praise, and an almost pathological inability "to admit wrongdoing or even his own mistakes."[95] Much like his biological father, William Blythe, Clinton developed an extreme desire to perform, to be the most popular and likable person in the room. This insatiable need got him into trouble as an adult.

But dealing with a turbulent home life also made Clinton resilient and able to bounce back from defeat. In addition, the abilities he later demonstrated as a mediator and peacemaker began during his childhood. Just as he tried to negotiate at home to keep his aggressive stepfather at bay, so he sought to reconcile his classmates on the playground. From an early age, he learned to lie if necessary, to say what he thought others wanted to hear, and to separate his public and private lives. Years later, he could remember the phone number of a high school classmate but had blocked out entire violent episodes at the hands of Roger Clinton.[96]

Clinton's concern with reconciliation helped give rise to his close association with African Americans. Although he grew up in the pre–civil rights South, he seems to have held integrationist views from his early years. When he listened to Martin Luther King's "I Have a Dream" speech in Hot Springs in 1963, he has declared, "I just wept like a baby all the way through it."[97] In 1968, King's assassination "had as profound an effect on Bill as anything else that had happened in his life," his Georgetown roommate declared. "He was more in tune with what King meant to black people than the rest of us were."[98] A friend from Hot Springs who visited him at Georgetown at the time of King's assassination recalls above all his "pale face."[99]

As president, Clinton frequently consulted religious leaders of the African American community. In his first year, he spoke to black ministers in the Memphis church where King delivered his last sermon urging them to uphold his legacy and to work toward ensuring freedom from violence. During the Monica Lewinsky ordeal, he invited the Reverend Jesse L. Jackson (whose presence in the White House had not always been welcome) to pray with and to counsel his family. In 2007, he attended the Southern Christian Leadership Conference in Atlanta, marking the fiftieth anniversary of its founding by King and others. Clinton's subsequent ability to connect with African American issues and voters has caused him to be called the "first black president."

As a boy, Clinton discovered that churches—places pervaded with goodwill and idealism—offered a refuge from the war continually going on at home.[100] Despite his marriage to a Methodist, he seems to have remained a Southern Baptist because it is the folk religion of the South and he has remained a southerner at heart. Clinton tapped into the stream in the Baptist tradition that has confronted such "social sins" as prejudice, segregation, and corporate greed. He inherited the same Baptist beliefs as not only King and Jimmy Carter, but also Walter Rauschenbusch, the Baptist pastor in the Hell's Kitchen area of Manhattan who is known as the father of the Social Gospel.

To be sure, Clinton has exploited religion for political purposes. Like some other presidents, he had adulterous sexual affairs. He lied about them under oath, to his wife, to his staff, and to national television audiences. He entered the presidency under attack from religious conservatives for his moral delinquency and womanizing. His affair with a White House intern hurt his standing with members of all faiths. "There is always the sex," an author remarks about the challenge that confronts a biographer of Clinton.[101] It should be noted, however, that Clinton has been the only president to have his extramarital affairs examined so publicly and at such length. Kennedy and Johnson, among others before him, had numerous extramarital affairs, and a president who served not long before Clinton had a long-term affair. But none faced the scrutiny and interrogation Clinton endured, during the process of which he lied under oath and was eventually impeached.

Clinton has shrugged off recurring accusations that his churchgoing is an act. "I don't do it for anybody else," he said, "I do it for me. . . . I'm sitting there in church, just like everybody else, except needing it maybe more, and it's one of the best hours of the week for me. I just let everything else go, take my Bible, read, listen, sing. . . . It's a way of not only validating my faith but deepening it and basically replenishing it."[102] A pastoral adviser who was once close to Clinton declared that he sometimes saw "a spiritual side to Bill Clinton . . . a vast and somewhat mystical spirituality that has a great deal to do with what he does and how he thinks."[103] Clinton himself told Russian President Boris Yeltsin that "my faith is probably the most important thing in my life."[104]

One biographer of William Jefferson Clinton titles his book *A Complicated Man*. Another describes the president as "always a man of contrasts and contradictions," adding that "no single world could keep him content for long."[105] A third writer calls him "one of the most fascinating and complex figures of 20th-century American politics: endlessly reinventing himself, dazzlingly talented and deeply flawed."[106] A longtime journalist in Arkansas declares:

> Politicians like Bill Clinton don't come along very often. I can't think of a person who's met him, even those who don't like him— and there are a lot of people who don't like him—who immediately and instinctively doesn't recognize a towering political force.[107]

Unsurprisingly, when a television network presented a one-hour program on Clinton in 2011, it titled its documentary *President of the World: The Bill Clinton Phenomenon*.[108]

No president owes more to the influence of African American Christianity than the forty-second holder of that office. Although the United States has had twenty presidents since the Pentecostal movement emerged in 1901, only Bill Clinton has attended Pentecostal services. One thing is clear: the American people may not soon again elect a president whose autobiography recommends: "If you ever get a chance to go to a Pentecostal service, don't miss it."[109]

Two images may help to explain Clinton religiously. The first is that of Hot Springs, the town in which he grew up. There, church spires coexisted with gambling and prostitution, and "ancient corruption [mingled] with purely American idealism."[110] This first image is important, for when Clinton ran for president he was not only the "Man from Hope"—the title of the seductive campaign biography portraying his small-town origins that the Democratic National Committee showed extensively across the country in 1992. He was also the young man from Hot Springs, a city where religion and immoral behavior not only existed side by side in his youth but were often manifested in the same people. "A known haven for mobsters, gambling, philandering and any other sort of debauchery that people could find while vacationing," a film commentator described the Hot Springs of the 1950s and 1960s. "Clinton was exposed to a much more sordid life than the idyllic life [depicted] in *The Man from Hope*."[111]

The second image is a striking perception by a longtime political associate that two William Jefferson Clintons actually exist:

> The Sunday-morning President Clinton is . . . pious, optimistic, brilliant, principled, sincere, good-willed, empathetic, intellectual, learned, and caring. . . .
>
> But the Saturday-night Bill who cohabits within him is . . . willful, demanding, hedonistic, risk-taking, sybaritic, headstrong, unfeeling, callous, unprincipled, and undisciplined. . . . Each side of Clinton seems unaware of the other. This division of Clinton's personality makes him hard to comprehend.[112]

# George W. Bush

George W. Bush represents the one president since World War II who converted to evangelicalism from a background in mainline Protestant Christianity. His conversion, which occurred in the mid-1980s, became central not only to his life but also to his political outlook. Not since the year 1900 had Christianity played such a role in a presidential campaign as it did in 2000. In 1900, William McKinley—a Methodist of strong beliefs who espoused the duty of the United States to spread Christianity (which he interpreted as Protestantism) to other nations—ran against the leading fundamentalist spokesman and orator, William Jennings Bryan. In 2000, the presidential campaign featured two evangelicals, George W. Bush and Albert Gore Jr.

George Walker Bush was born on July 6, 1946, in New Haven, Connecticut, where his father, George Herbert Walker Bush, was completing his bachelor's degree at Yale. The younger Bush was raised in Midland and Houston, Texas.

Despite his Connecticut birth, George W.—the name the Bushes used to distinguish him from his father—became viewed in his family as the child most closely attuned to Texas and its values. "His homage to his parents, his respect for his elders, his respect for tradition, his belief in religion, his opposition to abortion," Midland resident Joe O'Neill mused, "that's the philosophy he grew up with here."[1] If people "want to understand me," Bush declared during his first presidential campaign, "[they] need to understand Midland and the attitude of Midland."[2]

Dusty and segregated, Midland in the postwar years was an oil boomtown characterized by many churches and unlocked doors. In later years Bush and many of his classmates looked back on the town as an idyllic place in which to spend a childhood. Although George H. W. and Barbara Pierce Bush came from East Coast upper-class society, their eldest son was raised more in the upper middle class. In his 2010 autobiography, George W. remembers Midland as a place where he "rode bikes with pals, went on Cub Scout trips . . . sold Life Savers door-to-door for charity . . . and . . . play[ed] baseball for hours."[3] These experiences gave Bush the "common touch" that became so apparent in his presidential debates with Al Gore. That common touch fostered not only much of his later political success but also his move to the evangelical form of Christianity. "He understands Bubba because there is more Bubba in him," his chief political adviser, Karl Rove, once said.[4]

Bush had a close relationship with his parents. Although George H. W. Bush's frequent business trips required that Barbara essentially raise the children herself, young George W. idolized his father. "What makes him tick?" asked an old friend of the Bush family about the son. "It's daddy."[5] In *Decision Points*, Bush notes speculation about a negative relationship with his father, but he writes: "The simple truth is that I adore him. Throughout my life I have respected him, admired him, and been grateful for his love."[6]

Slurs against African Americans were common in segregated Midland, but Bush's parents refused to tolerate such language from their children. On one occasion Barbara washed George W.'s mouth with soap when he came home from school and said a prohibited word. "His family was probably the only one around that didn't use racial slurs," a childhood friend commented.[7]

The major trauma of Bush's childhood was the death of his sister, Robin, after a seven-month battle with leukemia. Having been told only that she was sick and undergoing treatment in New York, the seven-year-old George W. rushed out when he saw the family car arrive at his elementary school one weekday in October 1953. Although he was certain that Robin was home for a visit to Midland, he was told in the car that she had died.

On the short ride home, Bush saw his parents cry for the first time.[8] Following Robin's death, a pall hung over the Bush home for many years. George W. had nightmares about her death. In a sense, Robin's death caused him to become an only child, because his other four siblings—Jeb, Neil, Marvin, and Dorothy—were considerably younger. Their presence turned the household, in Bush's later description, into a "happy chaos."[9]

During her illness, Bush's father had prayed for Robin every morning in the First Presbyterian Church of Midland. Then a thriving congregation of young couples, First Presbyterian was the family church. Although writers have assumed that the parents selected the church because Barbara Bush (unlike her husband) had been raised Presbyterian, the reason probably stemmed from the composition of the congregation and the high reputation of its pastor. George H. W. Bush taught in the church's Sunday school. Like most Texas cities, Midland contained a large number of evangelical churches, but there is no indication that George W. was attracted as a boy to evangelicalism.

After graduating from public elementary school in Midland, Bush began attending public junior high school in the city in his twelfth year. When the family moved to Houston in 1959, they enrolled him in the private and exclusive Kinkaid School. The Bushes also joined St. Martin's Episcopal Church, where Bush became an altar boy. "I served communion at the 8 a.m. service at St. Martin's," he wrote in his first campaign autobiography. "I loved the formality, the ritual, the candles, and there I felt the first stirrings of a faith that would be years in the shaping."[10]

When Houston's prestigious St. John's School rejected George W., his parents—whose educations came entirely from private schools—decided to send him to Phillips Academy in Andover, Massachusetts. Although the historic academy turned away more than three-quarters of applicants at the time, children of alumni stood a better chance of admission than children of nonalumni. Both Bush's father and his grandfather had been leaders of their classes at the academy. Bush was accepted and entered Andover in the fall of 1961.

In later years, Bush viewed Andover—which he called "a serious academic challenge"—as "the hardest thing I did until I ran for president almost forty years later."[11] In his four years there, Bush was noted for his sunny disposition and for what one classmate called his "wise-cracking showmanship."[12] He played junior varsity football and varsity basketball and baseball, but he was especially known for being head cheerleader. A classmate remembered the one year he roomed with Bush as "probably the funniest year of my life."[13] At Andover, Bush began his lifelong practice of nicknaming associates. Then and throughout his later life, he displayed a remarkable memory for people's names.

At the academy, George W.'s friends came from the jock set and not from its scholarly circle. As in grade school, he displayed little interest in reading outside of class. From Andover on, he tended to mock students he thought overly serious about their studies. Other classmates later recalled that he paid scant attention to the civil rights movement or to other burning issues of the early 1960s.

Founded as a Congregationalist academy in 1778 when Congregationalism was the state church of Massachusetts, Andover required its students to attend chapel on all days except Wednesday and Saturday. Many of its weekday services focused on such matters as public affairs, but others—and all of its Sunday services—were Christian. Bush would have heard good preaching in the chapel. Because Congregationalism and Presbyterianism are sister Calvinist denominations united in England and elsewhere, the worship would have differed little from what Bush had become accustomed to in Midland. Bush became a lay deacon in the chapel, a position that by the 1960s became largely supervisory and honorific.

When George W. graduated in 1964, he was one of the best-known members of his class. Although he failed to win any of the major awards annually conferred upon seniors by Andover classmates—such as handsomest or most likely to succeed—he finished second in the voting for big man on campus. The academy had no class rankings, but Bush clearly did not earn high grades, for—unlike 110 members of his class—he never made the honor roll during any of his eight semesters.

After Andover George W. had planned to go to Yale, as his father and grandfather had done. But when Andover's dean reviewed his test scores and transcript, the dean "tactfully suggested," in Bush's words, "[that] I might think of other universities as well."[14] From that point on, classmates remember him speaking enthusiastically about attending the University of Texas.[15]

But to his surprise, Bush was admitted to Yale. The academic transcripts and scores for freshmen admitted to the university's class of 1968 were significantly higher than his. The class's median score on the SATs, for example, was 180 points higher. But Yale gave special consideration to children of alumni. When George W. filled out the part of Yale's application that asked for a list of relatives who were alumni, he listed not only "my grandfather and my dad . . . all his brothers . . . and my first cousins" but also noted he had to write the names of his second cousins on the back of the card.[16] His grandfather, Senator Prescott Bush, was also both a trustee of Yale and a former member of the Yale Corporation.

George W. Bush was a C student at Yale in an era prior to grade inflation. Yet during the 2000 presidential election, a Democratic classmate who served as special counsel to President Clinton and supported Gore for president used the term "very smart" to describe the Bush he knew at Yale. "There are times when George coasted through Yale courses or through exams or seemed overly facetious," he said in an interview, "but don't mistake that for not being intellectually acute."[17] Bush's director of Catholic outreach classified all claims that Bush lacked intelligence as being "very unfair and stupid. . . . I have known many successful businessmen," he said, "and Bush has the cagey intelligence of a successful businessman."[18]

Long a bastion of WASPs and Republicans, Yale was gradually becoming more diverse in the 1960s. But in his four years in New Haven, Bush remained more of a traditional Yalie than many of his classmates. He drank, smoked heavily, played pranks, and maintained a jokey social style. Dating widely at women's colleges, he was viewed by classmates as a "good-time guy." He aimed for, and received, mostly Cs in classes, and chafed at the views of liberal intellectuals. Although he majored in history, the instructor of a fifteen-member history seminar later had no memory of him. In the one year for which academic rankings exist for his class, Bush ranked in the twenty-first percentile, with 79 percent of his class placing above him.

As at Andover, however, Bush became one of the best-known students on Yale's campus. After studying class rolls, he was able to memorize the names of some 25 percent of Yale's undergraduates. He joined Delta Kappa Epsilon ("Deke") fraternity, viewed by many as the most prestigious and the hardest-drinking fraternity at Yale. When elected Deke's president, he joined a series of predecessors who later rose to high positions in American business. Like his father, he was tapped in his senior year for membership in Yale's premier secret society, Skull and Bones.

The family connection with Skull and Bones caused Bush some minor distress in his freshman year. The Reverend William Sloane Coffin Jr., the chaplain of Yale and a partisan, liberal Democrat, was also a member of Skull and Bones. When George H. W. Bush urged his freshman son to introduce himself to Coffin, Bush went over to the chaplain's office at Battell Chapel expecting a warm welcome. But after a brief conversation, Coffin apparently spoke of the elder Bush's recent defeat in the Texas senate race by incumbent Democrat Ralph Yarborough: "Frankly," Bush remembered Coffin saying, "your father was beaten by a better man."[19] Most biographies of George W. Bush include this episode, as does Bush's autobiography. Although Coffin later said that he retained no memory of the episode, he wrote to apologize in 1998 when he learned that Bush remembered their conversation with resentment. "I have a hard time imagining my saying to you—and with the utmost seriousness—'your father was beaten by a better man,'" he declared. "But if you say I said so, I believe you. It was a thoughtless remark and for it I wish to offer you my apology. I hope you will be able to forgive what you cannot condone."[20]

The remark was indeed thoughtless. Bush remembers that the chaplain's "words were a harsh blow for an eighteen-year-old kid."[21] Yet the odds are in favor that Coffin made the comment. In later years the minister frequently spoke of George H. W. Bush in such terms as a "perfect example of skim milk rising to the top."[22] George W. replied to Coffin from the governor's mansion in Austin: "I am honored by your letter. I believe my recollection is correct. But, I also know time passes, and I bear no ill will. I hope all is well with you. Warm regards."[23]

The conversation with Coffin clearly had repercussions. While George W. attended church at Andover (where it was mandatory) and attended more or less voluntarily when home, he never attended Battell Chapel in his four years at Yale. Despite Bush's note in response to Coffin's apology, one biographer may be accurate when he states that "George W. never forgave it. . . . [Coffin's insult] came to represent for George W. the presumptuousness of the liberal elite."[24]

When Yale's chaplain emerged as the central figure in the antiwar protests and draft-card burnings at Yale, Bush was not among his supporters. The conversation at Yale clearly influenced Bush's subsequent distaste for politically liberal clergy. Coffin's "self-righteous attitude," Bush writes in *Decision Points*, "was a foretaste of the vitriol that would emanate from many college professors during my presidency."

Although Yale's campus seethed with antiwar protests, lectures, and teach-ins during his junior and senior years, George W. avoided them. In fact, in

2000 he said that he did not recall antiwar protests occurring at Yale during his undergraduate years.[25] Bush was also uninvolved in any of the campus protests and marches in support of Martin Luther King Jr. and the civil rights movement. He found the typical attitude of Yale professors and students toward the Vietnam War "sanctimonious and condescending."[26] He was arrested while a student not for protesting but rather for disorderly conduct and overconsumption of alcohol.

Besides Bush's apparent lack of interest in world affairs and his focus on the social side of college, the reasons for his detachment seem clear. He grew up in a traditional family and in a state known for its patriotism. His father had almost died in World War II. While serving as a congressman from 1967 to 1971, the senior Bush supported the Vietnam War. As a result, as Nicholas Kristof notes, George W. "never wore his hair long, agonized over Vietnam, wrestled with existentialism, or cranked up Rolling Stones songs."[27] In later years, Bush came to believe that Americans had to display more self-discipline and to abandon the permissiveness and liberalism that characterized the late sixties and early seventies.

The evidence indicates that Yale University, despite George W.'s good times there and the many friends he made, was not a good fit. His autobiography devotes some paragraphs to discussing his enjoyment of classes in history. Otherwise, however, his disaffection was clear.[28] He disliked what he called Yale's "intellectual snobbery."[29] After graduation, he did not maintain his connections with Skull and Bones. Prior to assuming the presidency, he never attended a reunion of his Yale class. When solicited for a contribution to commemorate his class's twenty-fifth reunion, he initially declined to contribute.

Bush returned to Texas from New Haven without clear professional goals. "My nomadic years" is the way he has described the years from 1968 through 1977, the year he married. While running for president, he told a reporter, "There are some people who, the minute they get out of college, know exactly what they want to do. I did not. And it didn't bother me. That's just the way it was."[30]

During these years Bush's jobs included employment by one of his father's friends in an agricultural conglomerate as well as work on the campaign staffs of Republican senate candidates in Florida and Alabama. In addition, he worked in several of his father's campaigns and assisted in the administration of an inner-city mentoring program in Houston. In 1970, the University of Texas Law School declined to accept him, but two years later Harvard Business School did. He spent 1973 through 1975 at Harvard earning an MBA.

He emerged from the two years in Cambridge more ambitious and focused. In Texas he entered the oil industry. At first a freelancer, he subsequently formed a gas and oil exploration company during the tumult of a volatile 1980s oil market. Despite a consensus that his work in the rags-or-riches business was only average, Bush left the industry in 1986 a wealthy man. He seems to have been better at raising money for investments than at returning profits to his investors.

During these "nomadic years," Bush was often between jobs or unemployed. A laundry-challenged bachelor, he lived in Massachusetts, Georgia, and Alabama, but he spent most of the period in and around Houston, a boom city then alive with wildcat oil drillers and speculators. His various accommodations included "the loud side" of an exclusive apartment complex, a bachelor officer's quarters, and a small, cluttered, roach-infested apartment.[31]

Almost everyone who knew Bush at this time seemed to like him, although a few acquaintances—especially older people—found him cocky and immature. Enthusiastic, impulsive, cheery, uncomplicated, he was "funny and fun to be around."[32] When the New York Times interviewed dozens of his friends from this period for a series of articles in 2000, almost no one—even when quoted anonymously—had anything negative to say about Bush.[33] As one Times writer noted, his many ex-girlfriends not only spoke fondly of him but also seemed to hold him in higher regard than women typically do their husbands.[34]

Bush was popular even at Harvard Business School. He spent far more time there on his studies than at Yale. Still, he dressed scruffily, listened to country music, sat in the back of classes, and chewed and spat tobacco during lectures. The young Austin-based political strategist Karl Rove, who first met Bush around this time, declared that his first impression of Bush was "huge amounts of charisma, swagger, cowboy boots, flight jacket, wonderful smile, just charisma—you know, wow."[35]

Part of this role-playing in graduate school may have stemmed from Bush's opposition to the vehement anti-Republicanism then prevalent among students and many faculty at Harvard. At the time, his father was chair of the Republican National Committee. In previous years Bush Sr. had been an ambassador to the United Nations and a member of Congress. Whatever these connections meant to his fellow students, they clearly did not hurt George W.'s application to Harvard.

Although he projected himself in Cambridge as a Texas antielitist, he remained at heart a conventional young man. His friends saw him as essentially conservative. "He was the straightest guy I knew," one girlfriend noted. Another remembered: "He could be wild and go to a party and drink a lot, but he was . . . very conventional. . . . He could have been a college guy from the early '60s."[36] Although the counterculture flourished in the late 1960s and 1970s, George W. did not embrace it. In 1969—the year of Woodstock, when young people were rebelling across the nation—he sent his parents a note indicating that he and his siblings had been "lucky" to be raised in a home where they were "surrounded by love."[37] Whenever Bush was home during this period, he attended church with his parents.

Meanwhile, Bush continued his college habits of drinking excessively. In 1976, he was arrested in Maine for driving under the influence of alcohol while vacationing at the family compound in Kennebunkport. The arrest occurred on a night in which an Australian tennis star taught him how to drink beer with no hands—a tradition he brought to America from his homeland. Pleading guilty, Bush not only had his license to drive in Maine suspended for two years but was also fined $150. Had the voting public known of this conviction for drunk driving earlier—it was not reported until the week before the 2000 election—Al Gore might have won.

In the presidential election, Democratic opponents and investigative journalists also raised questions about whether he used other drugs during this postcollege period. If his opponents could have shown that he definitely did, Bush might have lost a significant number of votes. He diffused the controversy by simply saying that in 1989 his father's administration had asked White House staffers to swear that they had not used illegal drugs for at least fifteen years. He would have passed that test, Bush declared.

More important was the controversy that emerged over Bush's military service. In May 1968, two weeks before he graduated from Yale and thus lost his student deferment from the draft, Bush was sworn into the Texas Air National Guard. Because 1968 was a peak year in the Vietnam War, the National Guard unit—which flew jets that were probably too old to be called up for duty in Vietnam—had a lengthy waiting list. Bush, however, was not only admitted to the Guard immediately upon application but also specially photographed with the unit's commanding officer.

Investigation later showed that George W. had been jumped to the front of the waiting line because his father was then a congressman from Texas. In addition, Ben Barnes, the influential speaker of Texas's House of Representatives, had intervened on his behalf. Although Bush reportedly proved to be an excellent pilot, he never left the United States during his full-time (which seems to have lasted only fifty-five weeks) and part-time service with the Guard.[38] Because his privileged leap to the top of the waiting list inevitably meant that one less applicant got into the Guard and may instead have gone to Vietnam, the issue was controversial. Supporters of Bush have held that he was trying to compromise between his father's support of the war and his generation's opposition to it. "He didn't dodge the military," one of his old friends declared. "But he didn't volunteer to go to Vietnam and get killed, either."[39]

Although investigation of Bush's military service continued into his second term, the results remained inconclusive. In 2004 inaccurate assertions made in a CBS program on the controversy ultimately caused the firing of some of its staff. Of the twelve presidential and vice presidential candidates of the Republican and Democratic parties from 1992 to 2000, two (George H. W. Bush and Robert Dole) served in World War II, two (George W. Bush and Dan Quayle) served in the National Guard, and four (Bill Clinton, Jack Kemp, Joseph Lieberman, and Dick Cheney) avoided all military duty. Only one candidate (Al Gore) served in the regular army in Vietnam.

In the meantime, Bush had married. His old friends Joe and Jan O'Neill introduced him in 1977 to Laura Welch, a native of Midland who had become an elementary school librarian in Austin. The two were very different in many areas—Laura was, for example, not only a lover of books and reading but also a Democrat and reportedly (like her future mother-in-law) pro-choice on abortion. But they shared similar roots as well as many of the same friends; they had even been in the same seventh-grade class in

Midland. "I never would have thought of it," one of their mutual friends said. "Then, when I thought about it, it made sense."[40]

Three months after meeting—"the courtship moved fast," Bush writes in his autobiography—Bush and Laura married.[41] Both were thirty-one years old. The wedding occurred in the First United Methodist Church of Midland, Laura's family's church. Making their home in Midland, the couple initially alternated between attending First Methodist and First Presbyterian, whose Sunday school Bush had attended as a child and in which he was now teaching.

When the couple's twin daughters, Barbara and Jenna, were born in 1982 and baptized in the Methodist church, Bush officially became a member of that congregation. In 2010 he reflected on the view he held of religion up to that point:

> I went to church at Andover because it was mandatory. I never went at Yale. I did go when I visited my parents, but my primary mission was to avoid irritating Mother.
>
> Laura and I . . . started going regularly after the girls were born, because we felt a responsibility to expose them to faith. I liked spending time with friends in the congregation. I enjoyed the opportunity for reflection. Once in a while, I heard a sermon that inspired me. I read the Bible occasionally and saw it as a kind of self-improvement course.
>
> I knew I could use some self-improvement. But for the most part, religion was more of a tradition than a spiritual experience. I was listening but not hearing.

In the meantime, Bush had decided to follow his father's and grandfather's steps in politics. In 1978 he won the Republican primary in the sprawling nineteenth congressional district of Texas against an opponent backed by Ronald Reagan. Depicted by his Democratic opponent in the general election as an arrogant and spoiled rich kid, he learned important lessons from his loss in November. "He wasn't going to be out-Christianed or out-good-old-boyed again," his opponent—who subsequently became a Republican and Bush supporter—declared years later. "He's going to be the good old boy next door."[42]

In the mid-1980s, Bush experienced a classic evangelical conversion—one that developed in at least three stages. In 1984, he met with Arthur Blessitt, an evangelist who by that year had carried a heavy twelve-foot cross to over sixty countries. Blessitt was holding a six-day "Jesus meeting" in a large auditorium in Midland. After listening to Blessitt's radio broadcasts, Bush asked an evangelical friend from the oil industry to arrange a meeting.[43]

At the meeting, according to Blessitt's Web site, Bush declared that he wanted to talk with the evangelist about how to know and to follow Jesus Christ. A series of questions from Blessitt then followed about whether Bush had a "relationship with Jesus," about whether he was assured that he would go to heaven if he died that day, and about whether he would rather live with Jesus in eternity or live without Jesus. To these queries, Bush replied, "I'm not sure," "No," and "With Jesus."[44]

Using biblical passages to explain how George W. and others could follow Jesus, Blessitt remembered praying the Sinner's Prayer one sentence at a time and having Bush repeat it. Well known in evangelical circles, this prayer confesses the penitent's need for salvation through Christ. It gives and requests forgiveness, recognizes the need to love others, and accepts Christ as a personal savior.

> Dear God, I believe in you and I need you in my life. Have mercy on me a sinner. Lord Jesus as best as I know how, I want to follow you. Cleanse me from my sins and come into my life as my Savior and Lord....
>
> I forgive everyone and ask You to ... give me love for all people. Lead me to care for the needs of others.... I accept the Lord Jesus Christ as my Savior.

Following the prayer, Blessitt said that he informed Bush that he was now "saved." The submission of the avowed sinner to Christ, the acceptance of Jesus as divine Lord and Savior, and the subsequent assurance of salvation represent the classic evangelical form of conversion.

On his Web site, Blessitt called this moment "awesome and glorious." He remembers that he wrote Bush and spoke with him on the phone several times during the next two years, but Bush for some reason omits Blessitt's influence both from his brief campaign memoir, *A Charge to Keep*, and from his autobiographical *Decision Points*. Although Bush focuses the narrative of his conversion on a subsequent meeting with Billy Graham and omits

Blessitt entirely from his autobiography, writers have generally acknowledged that Blessitt played a significant role in it. Some observers have declared that Graham's influence on Bush's conversion has been exaggerated and Blessitt's minimized because of Graham's national status and Blessitt's far more eccentric career.[45] For George W. Bush, one writer insists, "The real, honest-to-God conversion experience took place in a Holiday Inn coffee shop on April 3, 1984, when the itinerant preacher Arthur Blessitt brought his salvation show to Midland, Texas."[46]

Although Blessitt played a significant role in Bush's conversion, all of George W.'s close friends agree that a meeting with Billy Graham was decisive.[47] Bush's autobiography praises Graham.[48] Prior to this 1985 meeting, Bush had attended some of Graham's crusades but had never answered the call to come forward and make a decision for Jesus Christ. But on that summer weekend, Graham, then sixty-six years old, preached at the Bush family's summer Episcopal church, St. Ann's by the Sea, in Kennebunkport, Maine.

In a subsequent conversation about religion at the Bush summer home, Graham's venerability, demeanor, and words "sparked," in George W.'s memory, "a change in my heart. . . . A seed that grew. . . . He led me to the path. . . . And it was the beginning of a change in my life. . . . The beginning of a new walk where I would recommit my heart to Jesus Christ."[49] In the description of one writer, the meeting was not a lightning bolt but rather a catalyzing force that moved Bush further toward a renewal of his inherited Christian faith. "As a result of our conversations and [Graham's] inspiration," Bush declared, "I searched my heart and recommitted my life to Jesus Christ."[50]

The effect of this meeting on Bush's Christian faith and practice was almost immediate. In Midland, for example, he joined a large men's community Bible study. Yet Bush's conversion was still incomplete in 1985, for he continued heavy social drinking. He was more of a binge fraternity drinker than an alcoholic. But drinking could make him belligerent and unpleasant, and at parties it led to obnoxious and inappropriate behavior. To some observers, even though he was almost forty years old, George W.'s approach to alcohol still seemed to be that of an immature college undergraduate.

Urged by Laura, who not only saw his drinking as affecting their marriage and family life, but who may also have delivered an ultimatum about it, Bush began to realize that alcohol was costing him focus and energy as well as respect. In July 1986, the Bushes traveled with two other couples from Midland to Colorado Springs to celebrate what Bush called "the big 4-0," his fortieth birthday.[51] At the lavish party at the Broadmoor, an elegant seven-hundred-room resort hotel, Bush consumed an excessive amount of wine.

The next morning, during which the group had planned to attend services at the nearby Air Force Academy chapel, Bush awoke with a painful hangover. Nevertheless, he ran his usual three miles. Back in the hotel room, he became sufficiently sick to resolve to quit drinking. He was not the only member of the group of old friends to think "never again" that morning and to skip services at the chapel. But in Bush's case, he not only gave up alcohol on that day in 1986 but also, as far as any reliable report indicates, has not touched it since. "Anyone who becomes sober after a lifetime of alcoholism," an evangelical author writes,

> will recognize the almost spiritual sense of change that sobriety brings. . . . George W. had . . . arrived at a powerful understanding of what the Christian faith really means. . . . His mind and spirit had been absorbing Christian truths from the Bible. But now, unencumbered by old, strong, alcohol-induced habits, he was free to live out those truths.[52]

Even after giving up alcohol, Bush remained lighthearted and somewhat immature for some years. Biographer David Aikman notes that as late as the early 1990s, the leading evangelist James Robison was not entirely convinced that Bush was a fundamentally spiritual person.[53] But in those years after 1986, many of Bush's friends and associates saw a transformation. "I could tell that he had changed in some significant ways," a business associate wrote:

> He was more caring; he appeared to have genuine interest in other people. He had given up drinking. He appeared more devoted to his family. He had started studying the Bible . . . his whole personality had been transformed.[53]

By the early 1990s, Bush had given up smoking—one of the few remaining vestiges of his former lifestyle. He led an increasingly active prayer life. He frequently talked to others about his faith. His reading of evangelical devotional material increased. Works that became his favorites were *The One Year Bible*, which separates the Bible into 365 passages to allow its completion in one year; Oswald Chambers's *My Utmost for His Highest*; and works by such Baptist writers as Charles Spurgeon and Charles Stanley. In 1987, when he worked in his father's vice presidential campaign as a liaison to evangelical groups, he spent many hours with the evangelical author and political strategist Doug Wead. In later years, Wead would work closely with Bush in his presidential campaigns and in the White House.

In 1989, George W. used the several hundred thousand dollars he had gained from the sale of his oil company to join a group of investors who purchased the Texas Rangers baseball team. For the next nine years, he was the team's managing general partner or co-owner. Although he owned only a small part of the Rangers, he served as their public face. When the team built its new stadium outside Dallas–Ft. Worth, he became highly visible.

While Bush's earlier jobs had been makeshift, short-lived, or only partially rewarding, he succeeded in professional baseball. He was proud of the accomplishment, which fulfilled one of his boyhood dreams. The sale of his shares in the team in 1998, when he was governor of Texas, not only made him a multimillionaire but also gave him the money and freedom to run for high office.

In 1993, though he had not yet held elective office, George W. decided to run for governor of Texas. The Democratic incumbent was the plain-spoken and humorous Ann Richards, a throwback to the progressive strain of Texas politics and a champion of minority rights and feminism. However popular she was in Texas, she was not popular in the Bush family, for they had not forgotten her lampooning of George H. W. Bush when he was a presidential candidate. "Poor George," she had declared during a keynote address at the Democratic Convention of 1988, "he can't help it. He was born with a silver foot in his mouth." In the gubernatorial campaign, Richards similarly belittled George W., referring to him as "Shrub," criticizing his inexperience, and declaring that "he was born on third base and thought he hit a triple." [54]

Bush, however, refrained from personal attacks during the campaign. Instead, he depicted Richards as a liberal Democrat out of step in an increasingly conservative state. He especially tied her to President Bill Clinton, then so unpopular that the Democrats lost both houses of Congress in the same year. Richards's negative campaigning backfired, for voters found Bush more likable. In addition, Texas—like Bush—was extremely religious; surveys have long shown a majority of Texans believed that the Bible was the word of God and that its prophecies were true.

Finally, Bush was well known not only as a Christian believer but also as the son of a former president. Carrying almost every county, he won a stunning victory. Rove was instrumental in his victory, for he correctly anticipated two developments: first, an upsurge of conservative Democrats who would align with Republicanism in Texas and, second, Bush's attractiveness to the state's evangelical voters.

Billy Graham gave the invocation at the inauguration ceremony. Not only standard Republican policies—such as limited government, major tax cuts, and sweeping reforms of welfare, education, and torts—but also evangelical religion characterized Bush's six years as governor. In his first year, he signed a proclamation naming June 10 as Jesus Day. As governor, he filed a brief before the Supreme Court supporting the right of high schools to allow voluntary school prayer at football games. He regularly held brown-bag Bible study luncheons in the governor's mansion. Occasionally he spoke about his faith at churches in Texas. In an inaugural address, he said: "We're all made in the image of God. We're all equal in God's eyes."[55]

Above all, Governor Bush advocated what he called "compassionate conservatism"—an approach to government that "confronts human suffering and helps the disadvantaged."[56] Although he believed that God's grace can change people, he disagreed with the kind of government programs that caused unproductive citizens to feel entitled. Such programs, he thought, enabled recipients to continue lives of dependency. To assist in achieving his reforms, he enlisted the aid of the private sector, especially religious groups.

To Bush and to his advisers, Charles "Chuck" Colson's Prison Fellowship and similar groups seemed to do a better job than government agencies, not only because they were smaller but also because people who felt called to serve others administered them. In speeches, Bush occasionally quoted the pastor of a Texas megachurch: "On every street corner there are places that know how to deliver help to people in the neighborhood, where you can turn for help. They're called churches."[57] Subsidized by the Texas government, these "faith-based groups" became the prototypes for the later "faith-based initiatives" that characterized Bush's presidency.

Inevitably, Bush's governorship reaped criticisms from Texas Democrats and others. Three of the most frequent reproaches involved Bush's inflated statistics of success for faith-based groups, the use of taxpayer money to support them, and his record of approving more executions—including those of mentally retarded inmates—than the number approved by any recent U.S. governor.

But Bush had strong bipartisan support. When he ran for president, a vast majority of Texans rated his governorship as good or excellent. Returning to office in 1998 with almost 70 percent of the vote, he became the first elected Texas governor in history to serve back-to-back terms. He possessed a wide appeal.

From the governorship to the presidency, Bush viewed himself as a Christian leader. First in the governor's office and later in the Oval Office, he hung an oil painting titled *A Charge to Keep*, given to him by his old friends the O'Neills. Based upon a hymn by Charles Wesley, it depicted, in Bush's words, "a horseman determinedly charging up what appears to be a steep and rough trail."[58] Bush viewed the painting as "epitomizing our mission" to "serve One greater than ourselves."[59] In part, the hymn reads:

A charge to keep I have
A God to glorify . . .
To serve the present age
My calling to fulfill
O may it all my powers engage
To do my Master's will![60]

One year after publishing an autobiography with the same title as Wesley's hymn, Bush announced his candidacy for president. In George W.'s words, the "defining moment" in his decision occurred during a sermon by his Austin minister. Preaching on a biblical passage about Moses, the Reverend Mark Craig stressed that the nation needed leaders of moral courage who did good for the right reasons. "The sermon spoke directly to my heart and my life," Bush declares in his autobiography. Subsequently, Barbara Bush, who had been in the congregation, told her oldest son: "He was talking to you."

After Bush decided to seek the presidency, he talked with the evangelist James Robison. "I want to be remembered as the man who walked in Wal-Mart to buy fishing lures, who used to be governor," Robison remembers him saying. "[But,]" Bush continued, "I honestly believe that I am supposed to run for president. . . . I believe it's something God wants me to do. . . . I can't explain it, but I believe my country's going to need me at this time."[61]

Defeating five opponents, including Senator John McCain, in the Republican primaries, Bush became the Republican nominee. When asked in a debate to name his favorite philosopher, he gained special attention when he answered without hesitation, "Christ, because he changed my heart."

His Democratic opponent was Albert Gore Jr., a three-term senator from Tennessee. Gore's father, who had served seven terms in the House of Representatives and three terms in the U.S. Senate, had always hoped to be president. But his southern identity hampered him at a time when the nation was turning away from segregation. Because the Gores' hopes had devolved upon their son, Al Gore came across in the campaign as a far more driven candidate than the more relaxed Bush. "I served with Gore . . . and I like him," declared Kent Hance, the Democrat (later a Republican) to whom Bush had lost in 1978. "But I'd hate to ride from Lubbock to Los Angeles with him."[62]

A Southern Baptist who called himself "born again," and a reader who seemed to know the Bible better than Bush did, Gore had graduated from an Episcopal preparatory school. Although conservative religious voters viewed him as essentially secular in outlook, those close to him knew that he was a religious person. He had even spent a year after Vietnam in divinity school. The race also featured a third major candidate, the Green Party's Ralph Nader, who ultimately played a decisive role in its outcome.

Bush ran an organized and disciplined campaign shaped by Karl Rove. As in his gubernatorial races, he clearly enjoyed campaigning and interacting with voters. Like Sarah Palin in 2008, he was sometimes mocked by Democrats for his lack of knowledge of domestic and foreign policy. But he continually stressed his record in Texas—a state that, if ranked as a nation, had at the time the eleventh largest economy in the world.

Emphasizing the Republican approach to limited government, he highlighted the ability of faith-based programs to solve America's social problems. He also emphasized the need for educational reform and the importance of faith and moral values. Although he remained steadfastly opposed to abortion, he otherwise tended to talk about broad ethical themes. Traditional and evangelical religion permeated his public policies and speeches, and he became one of the only presidents to telephone pastors during a campaign to talk and pray. His staff used evangelical church membership lists for campaign coordination and fundraising. Bush tapped a rich vein; in 1997 a poll of the Barna Research Group had indicated that more than 40 percent of Americans viewed themselves as born-again Christians.

Bush's candidacy benefited from difficulties within the Gore campaign. The dalliances of President Clinton with Monica Lewinsky caused many Americans to lose confidence in the Democrats as a party of moral values. The backlash severely handicapped the Gore candidacy. Essentially Gore lost the election in the first debate when—as Nixon did in his first debate with Kennedy—he came across as more experienced and knowledgeable, but clearly less likable. As the debates progressed, polls showed that voters harbored serious doubts both about Bush's grasp of national and international issues and about Gore's personality and stability. Full of Bush's malapropisms, the debates occasionally displayed him looking like a deer caught in the headlights when answering certain questions. But from the first appearance of the candidates together onstage, Bush came across as more of a regular guy than Gore.

In November, Bush won the electoral vote 271 to 266 but lost the popular vote by over a half million votes. Maps printed after the election showed that Bush won the American churchgoing heartland, whereas Gore won the urban areas and "postmodern" coasts. Some 60 percent of Bush's votes came from evangelicals, Mormons, and Roman Catholic and Protestant traditionalists. The vast majority of Gore's votes came from secular voters, members of mainline denominations, theological liberals, and Jewish and African American voters.[63]

The evidence of whether Gore really won an election where he was ultimately declared the loser by 537 votes—the margin in Florida—remains inconclusive. A survey of discounted ballots by the *Palm Beach Post* in 2001 found that Gore lost 6,607 votes because voters marked more than one name on that county's new and confusing "butterfly ballot." The major problem with the butterfly ballot was that although Florida law required Gore and Bush to be listed as the first two choices, Buchanan was listed opposite and between them. The *Post* found that almost half of the Gore-Buchanan overvotes came from precincts where voters typically voted Democratic.[64]

Bush also benefited from Ralph Nader's candidacy. Over 97,000 Floridians and 22,000 residents of New Hampshire voted for Nader. In New Hampshire Bush's margin of victory was 7,211 votes; a Gore victory in that state would have won him the presidency. Postelection polls showed that the majority of Nader voters would have chosen Gore over Bush. One of the most thorough studies of the election concedes that more Floridians probably awoke on election day intending to vote for Gore than for Bush, but that their votes went astray. Yet the subsequent Supreme Court decision in Bush's favor, the study's author asserted, was nevertheless "a rather good" decision because it averted an impending and perilous national crisis.[65]

Bush's first inauguration included a private service at St. John's Episcopal Church, Lafayette Square, with Mark Craig preaching. The new president's inaugural address included ten religious references in fifteen minutes and a call for a national day of prayer and thanksgiving. On the next day, the ceremonies included a large service held in Washington National Cathedral with a sermon by the Reverend Franklin Graham, son of Billy Graham.

Four days of celebration, including a "Black Tie and Boots Ball," accompanied Bush's second inauguration. It culminated with a National Prayer Service in the Washington National Cathedral led by Christian and Jewish clergy. The one Muslim expected to take part was absent. Billy Graham, now eighty-six years old, led one prayer.

During his two terms, Bush frequently stated that he sought guidance from God. Even when compared with the Carter years, his administration must be viewed as the most openly religious in recent memory. A conservative rabbi saw the Bush years as a reversal of the "aggressive fundamental secular liberalism" that had characterized both terms of the Clinton administration.[66]

Although Bush's staff was advised to limit its use of words such as "born again" and "saved" because voters connected the terms with the Religious Right, prayer characterized his presidency. One writer estimates that seven separate prayer fellowships or Bible study groups met weekly in the White House or its adjoining buildings, with some two hundred of Bush's staff participating.[67] According to observers, Bush began every day by reading the Bible and by kneeling in prayer. Meetings began with prayer, meals with grace, and the president often led both. He prayed with prime ministers who visited Washington. Reports circulated of him being found flat on the floor of the Oval Office in prayer.

Unlike those of some previous presidents, most of the principal members of the Bush White House staff regularly went to church or synagogue. Among the devout evangelicals in this coalition of religious conservatives were Attorney General John Ashcroft, National Security Advisor Condoleezza Rice, chief speech writer Mike Gerson, and Bush intimate Don Evans, who became secretary of commerce. Among Bush's leading evangelical advisers in the White House were Ralph Reed, first executive director of the Christian Coalition (whom Bush placed in charge of evangelical outreach), and his father's evangelical adviser, Doug Wead, who is credited with coining the term "compassionate conservative."

Evangelical ministers who advised Bush included the highly influential Southern Baptist Richard Lamb, leading African American pastors Tony Evans and Kirbyjon Caldwell (both Democrats), and James Dobson, head of the vast Colorado Springs–based ministry called Focus on the Family. In 2004, Dobson told the seven million Americans who listened to his daily radio program that not casting a presidential vote would be a sin. One of the White House's Roman Catholic advisers complimented the high quality of the evangelicals on its staff: "There can be a lot of odd people in the religion business. There weren't any in the Bush White House. You didn't meet moralizers. They weren't quoting scripture."[68]

The Bush White House also reflected the alliance between conservative evangelicals and traditionalist Roman Catholics formed during the Reagan years. Both groups tended to oppose many of the changes in American life that had occurred during the Vietnam era, including abortion, euthanasia, homosexuality, same-sex marriage, and women clergy. At least one writer has termed Bush "the first Catholic president" because of the degree to which Roman Catholic social doctrines in general and the advice of Father Richard Neuhaus in particular influenced Bush's policies.[69] A convert from Lutheranism, Neuhaus was a prominent Catholic editor as well as Bush's unofficial adviser on such bioethical issues as stem-cell research. Along with other Roman Catholics, he had a significant influence on Bush's thinking. But so did the larger body of evangelical advisers in the White House.

Thus the identification of Bush as the "first Catholic president" seems dubious.[70] To be a Roman Catholic, a Christian must believe in the magisterium—or the teaching office of the pope, bishops, and priests that supplements scripture and interprets and decrees church policy. To be sure, John F. Kennedy did not follow the magisterium—and on that basis traditional Roman Catholics and other observers might challenge his status as the nation's first Roman Catholic president. But Bush does not accept the magisterium either. In the words of Deal Hudson, the White House's director of Catholic outreach, Bush holds to the classic evangelical doctrine that "says the scriptures guide you and you submit your will to God."[71]

Hudson, who served from 2000 to 2004, was among the unusually high number of Roman Catholics appointed by the Bush administration. A Texan who attended a Protestant theological seminary, took a PhD in philosophy, and converted from the Southern Baptist Convention to Roman Catholicism, he conceived a strategy to attract Republican votes from Catholics who tended to vote Democratic. In both elections, he focused on Roman Catholics who attended Mass regularly rather than on nonpracticing ethnic voters of Catholic background.

In the 2004 election, his strategy involved spending extra campaign time and money on the conservative Roman Catholic vote in two states—Florida and Ohio. His ideas about attracting more Roman Catholic voters to Bush went so far as to include a visit by the president to the Shrine of Our Lady of Guadalupe near Mexico City. In Hudson's words, such a devotional act would have been "most riveting for Hispanic American Catholics." The idea progressed to the point that both the president of Mexico and the archbishop of Mexico City invited the Bushes to visit Guadalupe. In the end, the president declined the opportunity because he did not wish to use a shrine for politics.[72]

Other leading Roman Catholics in the Bush White House included John J. Dilulio Jr., a professor who served as the first director of the Office of Faith-Based and Community Initiatives, and his successor, Jim Towey, a former aide to Mother Teresa. But the principal appointments of Roman Catholics during the Bush years were to the Supreme Court.

Following the death of William Rehnquist in 2004, Bush appointed John Roberts, a practicing Roman Catholic, to succeed him as chief justice. When Justice Sandra Day O'Connor—an Episcopalian—resigned in 2005, Bush's first choice to replace her was a fellow Texan, Harriet Miers. Some conservatives and White House staff initially supported the nomination of Miers, a longtime political confidante and legal adviser to Bush. In one observer's words, she was "a very serious Christian."[73] Raised Roman Catholic, Miers had become an evangelical, and the Supreme Court had no evangelical justices.

But when opposition gradually arose to Miers, Bush nominated in her place appeals court judge Samuel Alito, a conservative Roman Catholic. The appointments of Roberts and Alito were unsurprising, for Bush's favorite Supreme Court justices were Antonin Scalia and Clarence Thomas, also conservative Roman Catholics. Like Scalia and Thomas, Roberts and Alito were resolutely pro-life. Following their appointments, members of pro-life organizations wore pins containing photographs of the two new justices and bearing the words "Thank You, W."[74] The Supreme Court—long dominated by Protestants, and especially by Episcopalians—now had a Roman Catholic majority for the first time in history, although neither Justice Kennedy nor the later Obama appointee, Sonia Sotomayor, practiced their inherited Catholic faith.

At least a half-dozen leading members of the White House staff were Jewish, and at least two others were of Jewish descent.[75] During the Bush administration, Jewish staffers heard many prayers ending with an ascription to Jesus Christ. At White House meals, the president asked observant Jews who were present to say grace in their own way.[76] This coalition of religious conservatives did contain such mainline Protestants as Dick Cheney, Karl Rove, and Donald Rumsfeld, but the three were known more for political experience than for piety.

The moral teachings of contemporary evangelicalism characterized many of Bush's major policies while in office. On domestic matters, he opposed abortion and euthanasia, tied the funding of sex education strictly to abstinence programs, and banned the use of taxpayer funds to support abortions, not only in the United States but also abroad. He signed the Partial Birth Abortion Ban Act and on the basis of her "right to life" intervened in the case of Terry Schiavo, a Florida woman declared by many specialists (correctly, as autopsies subsequently showed) as brain-dead. He severely limited stem-cell research, though his fellow conservative Nancy Reagan complained it could have benefited her husband. He left unchanged President Clinton's "Don't Ask, Don't Tell" policy about homosexuality in the armed forces, however, and was the first Republican president to appoint an openly gay man to a high position.[77] As governor of Texas, he had opposed the repeal of a criminal prohibition on "homosexual conduct." As president, he supported legislation that banned gay and lesbian marriage.

On environmental matters, Bush —like a number of evangelicals—questioned whether humans really caused global climate change. At his direction, the United States became one of the few nations to refuse to sign the Kyoto Protocol on climate change. He proposed drilling for oil in the nineteen-million-acre Arctic National Wildlife Refuge. In educational matters, he advocated the teaching of evolution and intelligent design side-by-side in schools.

Perhaps the programs most influenced by evangelicalism in the Bush administration were a federal version of the faith-based groups begun in Texas. The Bush administration supported at least nine major faith-based programs, some of which received substantially more federal support than others. Leading examples included Catholic Charities, a global network that seeks to eliminate poverty and is the second-largest provider of social services in the nation; Access to Recovery, which assists drug addicts to secure treatment; the President's Emergency Plan for AIDS Relief, which gives life-sustaining drugs to perhaps two million Africans; and the President's Malaria Initiative, which initially planned to spend $1.2 billion by 2010 to fight malaria. Hudson summed up the rationale of such programs: "Social services are more effective when they're handled by people of faith in the private sector because they're doing it out of a private, inner drive. The programs are less expensive because they're driven by volunteers and because they're animated by caring."[78]

Inevitably these faith-based programs aroused opposition. Opponents included advocates of the strict separation of church and state, leaders of religious groups who feared the effect of federal aid on denominations, and Democrats who worried that the programs might cause major cuts in established federal programs for the poor. Other detractors noted that the administration's guidelines did not fully require organizations to report how they spent the money.

Much of the Bush administration's work during its first year concerned faith-based programs. But after September 11, 2001, the administration expended most of its energies on the war against terrorism, the invasion of Iraq, Hurricane Katrina, and the collapsing national economy. Today, America's forty-third president is known far better for the war on terrorism and for the Iraq War than he is for what he intended to be an extensive network of faith-based programs that would fulfill the biblical mandate to lift up the poor.

Although some writers have emphasized an apparent competition with his father, George W. Bush seemed far freer from psychological conflicts and neuroses than some of his predecessors. Those who knew him emphasized his honesty, integrity, and straightforwardness. Attentive to the small people in his life, he also exhibited a strong sense of loyalty to associates. Although his staff feared his temper to the point that they hesitated to give him bad news on Iraq or Katrina, he was generally likable up close—a regular guy.

After a somewhat raffish youth, Bush gradually developed into a disciplined and focused adult. His hard work in his congressional campaign, his overcoming of his drinking problem, his punctuality, and his daily runs were signs of that discipline. Even as president, he continued to go to bed and to rise early. His fellow evangelicals viewed him as possessing a high sense of ethics. Few genuine scandals emerged from his administration—something that seems to have sprung from his evangelical faith and concern for discipline.

Malapropisms, mispronunciations, and an awkward speaking style initially leapt out to the public as flaws of Bush. As his presidency went on, other shortcomings became apparent—impatience, shortness of temper, glibness, dogmatism, and overly conventional patterns of thought. Although his speechwriter David Frum declared that Bush's virtues substantially outweighed his faults, he also described Bush as "dogmatic, often uncurious, and as a result ill-informed."[79] His staff knew that he sometimes boasted that he did not read newspapers.

Political writers and opponents added other flaws: a dismissing of critics and a confidence that bordered on cockiness and arrogance. Throughout his career, one writer declared, Bush "has resolutely cultivated an anti-intellectualism and chafed at what he describes as the arrogance of liberal intellectual elitists."[80] Some critics also viewed Bush's conversion and his almost literalist view of the Bible as demonstrative of a man who fails to ask critical questions.

Many of these criticisms seemed to converge in late summer of 2005, when Hurricane Katrina flattened the Gulf Coast and flooded New Orleans. The hurricane overwhelmed state and local governments. The one federal agency formed to handle national disasters—the Federal Emergency Management Agency (FEMA)—quickly and disastrously proved that it was not up to the job. Although Bush knew the storm was severe, he took many days to comprehend its magnitude and the resulting anarchy. In a book that marked his break with the administration in which he had served, former Bush press secretary Scott McClellan declared that

> one of the worst disasters in our nation's history became one of the biggest disasters in Bush's presidency. Katrina and the botched federal response to it would largely come to define Bush's second term. And the perception of the catastrophe was made worse by previous decisions President Bush had made, including, first and foremost, the failure to be open and forthright on Iraq and rushing to war with inadequate planning and preparation for its aftermath.[81]

Even though the disaster had broad ethical and religious dimensions, one Bush aide described the atmosphere of the White House two weeks after the hurricane as "strangely surreal and almost detached."[82]

Three years earlier, Bush's decision to invade Iraq had aroused widespread and continuing protests across the world. Politically, he and his advisers based the decision to invade principally on two grounds: first, that Iraq had aided the terrorist attacks of September 11, 2001; and second, that dictator Saddam Hussein possessed secret weapons of mass destruction (WMDs). Religiously, the administration argued that the invasion met the criteria for the Christian (and especially the Roman Catholic) theory of a "just war."[83]

After thorough examination, Hudson's group of Roman Catholic advisers decided that the invasion qualified as a just war, especially on the basis of the "imminent threat" posed by the WMDs repeatedly cited by intelligence. Christian opinion, however, was divided about the morality of the war. Even before the invasion, Pope John Paul II delivered more than fifty public addresses condemning possible military action. He also sent a special emissary to Washington to express the Vatican's opposition.

In addition, most heads of Protestant denominations in the United States condemned the invasion as unwarranted and unjust. They included the president of the Council of United Methodist Bishops, Bush's own denomination. When it was discovered that the UN inspectors had been correct in their reports that Iraq had no WMDs, the war fell outside of the definition of a just war. "The collapse of the administration's rationales for war . . . became apparent months after our invasion," McClellan wrote.[84] "Founding a democracy is not a justification for war," Hudson declared in an interview. "And I don't think anybody in the White House was originally for that."[85] Many supporters of the administration, however, continued to argue that the war was necessary for compelling military reasons.

In his autobiography, Bush admits that he made a mistake in not sending or keeping a sufficient military force in Iraq. He declares that "the growing number of deaths" associated with the war "filled me with anguish." He also confesses to experiencing "a sickening feeling" whenever he thinks about the failure to find weapons of mass destruction in post-Saddam Iraq. He regrets the sense he gave in 2003 of a "mission accomplished" when the struggle actually continued for many more years. Nevertheless, Bush continues to believe that what he said about the war in the "mission accomplished" speech remains true: "The transition from dictatorship to democracy will take time, but it is worth every effort. . . . we will leave behind a free Iraq."[86]

Future generations will decide whether the invasion and occupation of Iraq was worth the casualties, expenditures, and international ramifications the United States caused or encountered. Estimates inevitably vary and change monthly, but the deaths that occurred by the end of 2010 seemed to number some 5,000 American and multinational troops and at least 90,000 Iraqi military, police, and civilians. In addition, more than 150,000 Iraqis and over 30,000 Americans were wounded in the same period. Although generally unpublicized, the injuries to American troops inevitably included thousands who were paraplegics, multiple amputees, brain injured, and blinded. Both

Iraqi and American military hospitals were flooded with seemingly endless cases of wartime injuries. In war, deaths and serious injuries to combatants and civilians alike devastate families.

"History appears poised to confirm what most Americans today have decided," McClellan wrote in 2008,

> that the decision to invade Iraq was a serious strategic blunder. No one . . . can know with absolute certainty how the war will be viewed decades from now when we can more fully understand its impact. What I do know is that war should only be waged when necessary, and the Iraq War was not. Waging an unnecessary war is a grave mistake.[87]

Bush left office with a popularity rating that approximated 22 percent, some 10 percent below that of Harry Truman when he left office. In the last months of his administration, former Secretary of State Condoleezza Rice declared, "I believe President Bush will be vindicated." Bush told the same interviewer, "History will eventually see . . . that not only was it necessary to take the steps I took, but [they] led to a better world."[88] At approximately the same time, a national commentator declared, "If Iraq became the model democracy or even just a democracy, and in doing so changed the whole complexion of the Middle East, then obviously that would be the legacy that would justify what Bush did and what our troops did."[89]

Bush's upbringing, his marriage to Laura Welch, and the environment of Texas contributed in crucial ways to his life. But his evangelical conversion became the main influence on his career and perspective. Following it, he often cast himself as the prodigal son who had returned to God after years of worldliness and superficialities. In David W. Balsiger's documentary *George W. Bush: Faith in the White House*, a Democrat asks whether W.'s religion is genuine and answers the question negatively.[90] The evidence, however, strongly argues that the answer is in error.

To be sure, Bush's form of evangelicalism varied from that of many religious conservatives. Attending an Episcopal church in Washington and a Methodist church in Texas, he occupied "a niche between the mainstream and the evangelical right."[91] Bush was not known for his knowledge of the Bible. He did not become a theologian or someone who read widely in the field of religion. But evangelicals quickly recognized him as one of their own, for he spoke the language of conservative religion better than any president since Jimmy Carter. "He's so unhesitatingly unembarrassed by his faith," one evangelical religious broadcaster declared. "He works it into his verbiage, his public policy, his comportment. . . . His faith so totally defines him."[92]

With a converted evangelical as its head, the Bush administration became one of the most openly religious administrations in American history. During its eight years, in the words of one writer, "secularism became almost a sin."[93] With the election of 2000, Bush essentially replaced the evangelist Pat Robertson as the leader of America's religious right—a distinction that even Ronald Reagan never received. Infusing religion into public policy, he identified America's commitment to advancing "freedom" and "liberty" as a call from God. He was careful about identifying his words with those of the God he worshipped, and he did not view his administration as a theocracy. But he once told a rally of supporters, "I trust God speaks through me. Without that, I couldn't do my job."[94] On another occasion, he cited the number of times as president that he had requested, prayed for, and benefited from "guidance from God in prayer."[95]

Supporters of Bush asserted that he and his administration possessed a sense of mission and a moral clarity far superior to the "relativist world view" held by many American liberals and by contemporary European leaders.[96] For many religious Americans, the two words *principle* and *resolve* summed up Bush's presidency. "I think President Bush is God's man at this hour," one of Bush's aides told an evangelical magazine.[97] Many of the fifty million Americans who voted for Bush in 2000 and the sixty-two million who voted for him in 2004 clearly felt the same way.

During George W. Bush's first presidential campaign, a journalist wrote these words:

> Looking at the careers of President Clinton or Vice President Al Gore, one gets the sense of a man running a marathon, resolutely pushing on with thoughts of glory at the finish tape. Mr. Bush's career, in contrast, brings to mind a cheerful hitchhiker who has the incredible good fortune to be picked up by a series of limousines.[98]

The limousines of privilege did pick up Bush at crucial points in his life. They carried him from Houston to Phillips Andover Academy, from prep school to Yale, from Yale to the top of the waiting list for the Texas Air National Guard, and from an officer's life in the Air National Guard into a series of business ventures in which family connections played a pivotal role. Not a limousine but hard work, ability, and evangelical appeal carried him into the Texas governor's mansion. Although he lost the popular vote in the United States by over a half-million votes on Election Day 2000 and won the Electoral College only by five votes, he was carried past a recount in Florida into the White House. But in this case, five justices of the Supreme Court were behind the wheel.

In social activities, in fraternity affairs, in matters dealing with people, in sincere expressions of his Christian faith, and in his home state of Texas, George W. Bush was largely successful. In intellectual matters, in academic contexts, in Washington, and in places outside of Texas, he often seemed over his head.

As of 2011, Bush's vision of the Iraq War seems to many to be as discredited as Lyndon Baines Johnson's futile support of the Vietnam War. In addition to over a half-dozen years of death and havoc in Iraq, the invasion created a knee-jerk rejection of the United States by a chilling portion of the Middle Eastern and Muslim worlds. With costs of at least $689 billion by late 2009, the war's ultimate costs promised to exceed $1 trillion and, by some estimates, to reach $3 trillion. If these current negative assessments of his administration persist, those limousines of privilege may have carried George W. Bush too far.

# Barack Hussein Obama

*1961–* ⌇ PRESIDENT FROM 2009

During Barack Obama's presidential campaign, voters asked whether a Protestant Christian with two Muslim grandparents, a Muslim father, a Muslim stepfather, and a first name that means "blessed" in Swahili and Arabic had ever been a Muslim himself. In 2007 a rumor circulated that Obama had attended a radical Muslim school in Indonesia as a child. In Florida, Jewish voters received e-mail messages declaring that Obama supported radical Islam over Israel.[1]

Five months before the election in 2008, a national survey showed that 10 percent of Americans viewed Obama as a Muslim and that only 53 percent knew his true religion.[2] Obama's headquarters received so many questions about his purported Muslim affiliation that it established a page on his campaign Web site dealing with the issue.[3] More than two years after the election, at least one Web site still asserted that Obama's "background, education, and outlook are Muslim."[4] As late as March 2011, a former Republican presidential candidate discussed Obama in a radio interview in the context of a spurious African childhood. "I would love to know more," he answered when the show's host questioned the lack of what he considered a true Hawaiian birth certificate for Obama:

> What I know is troubling enough. And one thing that I do know is his having grown up in Kenya, his view of the Brits, for example, [is] very different than the average American. . . . But then, if you think about it, his perspective as growing up in Kenya with a Kenyan father and grandfather, their view of the Mau Mau Revolution in Kenya is very different than ours because he probably grew up hearing that the British were a bunch of imperialists who persecuted his grandfather.[5]

The birth certificate the host and candidate discussed — and the one Obama had released during the 2008 presidential campaign — was the short-form certificate normally issued by the Health Department of the State of Hawaii. That Obama did not also produce the more complete long-form birth certificate led some opponents to believe that he had been born in Africa and hence was ineligible for the presidency.[6] Although two Honolulu newspapers had reported his birth in August 1961, theorists believed that Obama's mother (as her biographer sardonically declared) had "duped the state of Hawaii into issuing a birth certificate for her Kenyan-born baby, on the off chance that he might want to be president someday."[7]

In April 2011, Obama held a press conference in the White House and released the long-form birth certificate. Titled "Certificate of Live Birth," it certified his birth in Honolulu on August 4, 1961, as well as a number of other details. After releasing the document, Obama stated, "We do not have time for this kind of silliness."[8] While the full birth certificate reduced the number of ardent theorists, a small minority of opponents continued to express doubts, calling into question the authenticity of the second certificate.[9]

As for the charges that Obama's rearing and outlook were Muslim, he spent several years of his childhood in a Muslim country—but the country was Indonesia, not Kenya. In primary school in Indonesia, he received only one year of instruction in the Islamic faith—compared to three years of Roman Catholic catechism. Obama's father, whom he saw only once after the age of two, had left Islam for atheism prior to meeting Obama's mother. Obama's stepfather, who sometimes took Barack to a mosque for prayers on Fridays, attended worship infrequently enough that one observer described his visits as "rare."[10] In Obama's words, his mother was "a lonely witness for secular humanism."[11] His half-sister, who grew up in Indonesia, describes herself as a Buddhist. She describes Barack, however, as a Christian. The label of Muslim, she told a reporter in 2008, "has been erroneously attached to my brother."[12]

Barack Hussein Obama was born on August 4, 1961, in Honolulu, Hawaii. His mother was Stanley Ann Dunham. In *Dreams from My Father*, Obama explains that she was named for her father, Stanley Dunham, because he had wanted a boy. While in school, in fact, Obama's mother used to introduce herself with the words, "I'm Stanley. My father wanted a son, but he got me."[13] But Obama's half-sister, Maya, doubts that explanation, as do relatives.[14]

Obama's grandparents, Stanley Armour Dunham and Madelyn Payne

Dunham, grew up in adjacent towns in Kansas. In Obama's words, Madelyn's middle-class parents practiced "a straight-backed form of Methodism that valued reason over passion and temperance over both."[15] Stanley Armour's family, however, was blue-collar and dysfunctional. His mother committed suicide, and his father left the family. Once both parents were gone, Stanley went to live with his devout Baptist grandparents.

Obama's campaign autobiography, *The Audacity of Hope*, states that his "grandmother's flinty rationalism [and his] grandfather's joviality and incapacity to judge others or himself too strictly" led his grandparents to turn away from their strict childhood religions.[16] Although Madelyn was a gifted student, she secretly married Stanley in 1940, a few weeks before graduating from high school. While Stanley was serving in the U.S. Army during World War II and Madelyn was working at a Boeing bomber plant in Wichita, Obama's mother was born.

Following the war, Stanley moved his wife and daughter to California. He enrolled under the GI Bill at the University of California at Berkeley, where his brother was also a graduate student.[17] After one or two years at the university, he began managing furniture stores. Perpetually in search of new business opportunities, he moved his wife and daughter to five states. When he relocated his family to Washington State in 1955, he continued selling furniture while Madelyn worked in a Seattle bank. The Dunhams lived on Mercer Island, a rural island separated from Seattle by Lake Washington. Now one of the wealthiest areas in the state, the island then contained a small conservative white population.

When interviewed, classmates and friends at Mercer Island High School remembered Ann as sarcastic yet amusing, unconcerned with looks, and uninterested in such common concerns as dating, marriage, or motherhood. They used such descriptions as "intense, hardheaded, humorous, idealistic, informal, [and] exacting."[18] One classmate later described Ann as "not a gum-chewing, blinky-eyed bimbo."[19] Another described her as "not a standard-issue girl of her times . . . [not] part of the matched-sweater-set crowd."[20]

Ann often frequented Seattle's coffeehouses, talking with classmates for hours about her ideas. Her worldview, a classmate remembered, "was embracing the different rather than . . . shunning the different."[21] In the words of another classmate, Ann was "intellectually way more mature than we were and a little bit ahead of her time in an off-center way." If she had a boyfriend, no one knew about him.[22]

After moving to Mercer Island, the Dunhams and their daughter began to attend Sunday services at East Shore Unitarian Church. Although her principal biographer describes the religion to which the teenage Stanley Ann was exposed as "Christian and liberal," that description is misleading. American Unitarianism contains subgroups, and the East Shore church clearly belonged to the nontheistic humanist and syncretistic wings of the Unitarian movement. Located on the mainland, it was known not only for its religious skepticism but also for its political liberalism. The church's current minister described its 1950s congregation as "religious humanists." Their faith, he told a writer, was

> rooted more in "lived experience" than in supernatural and revealed truth.
> They had a sense of awe and wonder, an appreciation of . . . nonrational
> experience—idealism, the mystery of love, the moving power of music—
> without attributing it to a traditional god.

At Christmas, the minister said, the children of the church "reenacted the birth of Jesus Christ, Confucius and the Buddha."[23]

The East Shore congregation supported community service, tolerance, social justice, nuclear disarmament, and fair-housing legislation. A woman who attended its youth groups in the 1950s told a writer that her exposure to religion at the church made her "a lifelong seeker." She became, she said, "aware of the spirituality around her, but not committed to an organized religion." As the writer noted, the religion of the adult Stanley Ann Dunham could be described in the same words.[24] Obama recollects that his grandfather "liked the idea that Unitarians drew on the scriptures of all the great religions."[25] In time, however, when Madelyn Dunham lost interest in the church, the family's attendance dropped.

By some point in high school, Ann Dunham ceased even to be a Unitarian. "For my mother," Obama later wrote, "organized religion too often dressed up closed-mindedness in the garb of piety" and "cruelty and oppression in the cloak of righteousness."[26] Elsewhere, he said his mother believed that "rational, thoughtful people could shape their own destiny."[27]

In 1960, again pursuing a business opportunity, Stanley moved the family to Hawaii. Although Ann strongly wished to remain in Seattle, her father only allowed her to finish high school on Mercer Island. At age eighteen, she entered the University of Hawaii at Manoa in Honolulu.

Either at the university library or in a Russian-language class during her first semester, Ann met Barack Obama. Then twenty-four, he was the first African student in the history of the university. Raised in a mixed family of Muslims and Christians in Kenya, Obama Sr. had already abandoned Islam and become an atheist by the time he met Ann.

A product of British schooling in Kenya, Obama Sr. spoke English with an accent that "suggested Oxbridge." Tall, well-built, and darker in color than any student, he became an immediate and striking presence on campus. He had a booming and mellow baritone voice. "No matter what you were doing in the room," one classmate later commented, "if you heard this voice, you would turn around."[28]

Obama Sr.'s teachers and fellow students in the newly established East-West Center Program also found that he possessed an excellent mind—"a very quick mind," in the words of a later associate, "a good numerical mind." A classmate remembered that the professor of their economic development course "fell uncharacteristically silent and respectful when Obama spoke in class." Ann Dunham was enthralled by him. "Every time she described him," a friend later said, "she talked about his brilliance."[29]

Both Obama's mother and his paternal grandmother subsequently told him of the circumstances surrounding his mother's marriage. When he visited Kenya prior to entering law school, his African grandmother said: "After less than two years, we received a letter from Barack [Sr.] saying that he had met this American girl, Ann, and . . . would like to marry her." As Obama recalled his grandmother's words in *Dreams from My Father*, she continued:

Now, Barry, you have heard that your grandfather [Onyango] disapproved of this marriage. This is true; Onyango did not believe your father was behaving responsibly. He wrote back to Barack [Sr.], saying:

"How can you marry this white woman when you have responsibilities at home? Will this woman return with you and live as a Luo woman? Will she accept that you already have a wife and children?

"I have not heard of white people understanding such things. . . . But if I am wrong . . . let the girl's father come to my hut and discuss the situation properly. For this is the affairs of elders, not children."

"He also wrote to your grandfather Stanley and said many of these same things," she told Obama:

As you know, your father went ahead with the marriage. . . . But your grandfather was very angry at the time, and threatened to have Barack's visa revoked. And because he had lived with white people, perhaps Onyango did understand the white people's customs better than Barack [Sr.] did. For when Barack finally returned to Kenya, we discovered that you and your mother had stayed behind, just as Onyango had warned.

In *Dreams*, Obama also includes the similar account his mother gave him of her marriage. In it, she calls the letter that his African grandfather sent to Stanley "long" and "nasty." She tells him, "He didn't approve of the marriage. He didn't want the Obama blood sullied by a white woman. Well, you can imagine how Gramps reacted to that."[30]

In February 1961—a time when almost half of the American states prohibited marriage between races— Ann married Obama Sr. in Hawaii. In August 1961, their son Barack was born. For some years Ann did not know that her husband was already married and had left children behind in Kenya.

Graduating with Phi Beta Kappa honors in 1962, Obama Sr. left Hawaii unaccompanied a few months later for graduate study in economics at Harvard University. Asking Ann, "How can I refuse the best education?" he passed up a full scholarship to a less prestigious university that would have allowed the family to accompany him. "I think he didn't want the impediment of being responsible for a family," a mutual acquaintance later told a reporter. "He expected great things of himself, and he was going off to achieve them."[31] After trying various living arrangements, Ann soon moved back to Hawaii. In 1964, when young Barack was three years old, she and Obama Sr. were divorced.

Although young Barack and his father corresponded, they remained apart until Obama Sr. visited Honolulu for a month when his son was ten—a visit Ann arranged as a Christmas gift. After completing a master's degree in economics at Harvard in 1965, the older Obama had returned to Kenya with the intention of gaining a high position in its newly independent government. In Cambridge, he had married for a third time (again to an American) and fathered three more children but again had divorced. Seemingly unembittered about her divorce, Ann made certain over the years that Obama Sr. knew of his son's development. She also made sure Barack knew of his father's intellectual achievements and of the government positions he held in postcolonial Kenya.[32]

When two former graduate students from Hawaii later visited Obama Sr. in Africa, they found him bitter, frustrated, and drinking excessively. He never asked his visitors about his ex-wife or about his son in Hawaii.[33] By the time Barack Sr. died in Kenya in an automobile accident in 1982, he had fathered at least eight children by four women.[34] Essentially the only influence he left on his American son was genetic.

Although Ann had been divorced from him for eighteen years, she cried out upon learning of his death over the phone. The next day she broke down and wept in her office in Indonesia after telling a coworker of her ex-husband's death. He had been not only her first husband but also her first boyfriend.[35]

Reenrolling at the University of Hawaii after her divorce, Ann became especially attracted to its East-West Center, which appealed to fellows from across the Pacific. One such fellow was Lolo Soetoro, a twenty-six-year-old graduate student whom the Indonesian government had sent to the center in 1962 to obtain a master's degree in geography. In *Dreams*, Obama describes Soetoro as "handsome" and possessing "the good manners and easy grace of his people. . . . His tennis game was good, his smile uncommonly even, and his temperament imperturbable."[36] Calm, amiable, considerate, stable, and sweet-tempered (though he displayed a stern side in Indonesia following marriage), Soetoro was in many ways the opposite of Barack Obama Sr. "That was part of his appeal to Ann," Janny Scott comments, after her "gale-force encounter with Obama [Sr.]."[37]

Following her formal divorce from Obama Sr., Ann married Soetoro in 1964. He remained at the university until 1966, when the Indonesian government of President Sukarno—threatened by a coup—recalled its students studying abroad for military service. After Soetoro fulfilled his obligation, Ann and Barack followed him to Indonesia.

The three of them lived in a rented house in a middle-class area of central Jakarta—staffed, like many other Indonesian households, by low-paid servants. In *Dreams from My Father*, Obama recalls his mother's practice of rising before dawn, waking him, and teaching him English lessons from a correspondence course. When he would complain, he remembers that she would respond: "This is no picnic for me either, buster." That her long-time houseboy no longer remembered Ann doing so may or may not be significant.[38]

Following his discharge, Soetoro worked for the Union Oil Company of California and became increasingly westernized. Part of his job involved socializing with American oil company executives and their wives, much of it at the Indonesia Petroleum Club, the country club the oil companies had established in Jakarta. Although Soetoro hung prayer beads over his bed and attended a mosque infrequently, he was the kind of Muslim Harry Truman might have called "Lightfoot." He enjoyed alcohol, extramarital affairs, and bacon—all of which the Koran forbids. A photograph taken during his years at the University of Hawaii shows him drinking beer with Ann's father.[39] "Yeah," a classmate at the university said in an interview, "he loved to party."[40] A Muslim nephew once described him as "the naughtiest one in the family."[41]

During his presidential campaign, Obama told an interviewer that he laughed whenever he heard stories that his stepfather had embraced radical Islam. "I mean, you know, his big thing was Johnny Walker Black and Andy Williams records," Obama said. "I still remember [the recording of] 'Moon River.' He'd be playing it, sipping, and playing tennis at the country club. That was his whole thing."[42] When Soetoro died, the cause was liver problems.

In 1970 in Jakarta, Barack's mother and Soetoro had a daughter, Maya Kassandra Soetoro. Ann increasingly came to love Indonesia, wore Indonesian garb (unlike most American women who lived there), and wanted to be a working mother. Lolo Soetoro, however, desired more children and became more and more westernized. He wished to move to the United States, where he saw greater economic opportunity. Two years after Maya's birth, Ann left him and returned to graduate study in Hawaii.

Returning to Indonesia in 1975 to conduct research for her dissertation, Ann lived there again until 1995. When completed in 1992, her dissertation exceeded one thousand pages. "She was the most hard-working person I maybe ever have met," her mentor Professor Alice Dewey said of her.[43] Beginning with tensions stemming from her unwillingness to socialize with other oil company wives at the Petroleum Club and continuing with disagreements over Lolo's acceptance of corruption in his business dealings, the marriage of Ann and Lolo gradually deteriorated. Questions of lifestyle were crucial. "She didn't know," a Dutch anthropologist and friend from Jakarta said in an interview

> how. . . .Indonesian men like women to be easy and open abroad, but when you get to Indonesia . . . you have to be the little wife. . . . You [are] not sup-posed to make yourself visible besides being beautiful. . . . [Ann] didn't care about getting dressed [up], wearing jewelry, the way Indonesian women do. . . . He expected her to do it. . . . She absolutely refused to.[44]

Lolo Soetoro also seems to have changed during the marriage, in part because of the horrors of the civil war that brought him back to Indonesia from Hawaii. After leaving Hawaii, Obama writes, Lolo seems to have "pulled into some dark hidden place, out of reach, taking with him the brightest part of himself."[45] In 1980, the Soetoros divorced. Modernizing her husband's name, Ann now referred to herself as Ann Dunham Sutoro.[46]

Remaining in Indonesia, Ann followed a career that focused both on the country's poor and on the status of its women. Known for her drive and de-termination, she became fluent in Indonesian. In her more than two decades in the country, she developed a broad acquaintance among its populace. She served as a consultant for many groups, advised women's rights, and taught classes. She worked for the U.S. embassy, for Indonesia's leading bank, for the Ford Foundation, and for similar groups. Organizations such as the U.S. Agency for International Development and the World Bank funded her work. She traveled frequently. She regularly associated not only with residents of numerous rural villages but also with artists, craftsmen, academics, writers, journalists, foundation officials, diplomats, and American, British, and Dutch expatriates.

Diagnosed with uterine cancer, she spent her last months in Hawaii with her mother. She died in 1995 at age fifty-two at a time when her Chicago-based son had not yet held public office. When friends gathered in remem-brance of her in Jakarta and at the East-West Center in Honolulu, the gath-erings were essentially without religious rites.[47]

While living with Ann in Jakarta, Obama attended the first through fourth grades. For his first three years, he attended the Roman Catholic St. Francis Assisi Foundation School.[48] There he received religious instruction in Christianity and prayed four times a day. The Foundation School's records, which are full of errors, incorrectly list his nationality as Indonesian and his religion as Muslim. In addition, they misidentify his previous school.

In late 1970, when Soetoro moved his family to another neighborhood in Jakarta, Obama began attending Public Elementary School Number 1. A former Dutch boarding school, it was considered one of the best public schools in Jakarta. During that one year, probably because of the wishes of Lolo Soetoro, Obama attended classes on Islam.

The students and staff of the school were predominantly Muslim, but persons of a wide variety of religious backgrounds were present as well. The school celebrated both the Islamic holiday of Eid al-Adha and the Christian holiday of Christmas—the latter with a tree and carols. It offered religious instruction in many different traditions. So different was Public School Number 1 from a traditional Islamic school that some of its women teachers taught in miniskirts or sleeveless dresses. The only member of the faculty to wear a Muslim headscarf was the woman who handled the classes in Islam. "When I taught sports," the Protestant headmistress told a reporter, "I wore shorts."[49]

As Obama recalled, he annoyed the teacher at the Muslim school by making faces during studies of the Koran. During prayers in the Roman Catholic school, he remembered that he would pretend to pray but in reality looked around the classroom. "Nothing happened," he later remembered, "no angels descended. Just a parched old nun and thirty brown children, muttering words."[50]

Although Obama's mother "viewed religion through the eyes of [an] anthropologist," she did provide him with religious instruction beyond that given in school. She would "drag" him to church on Easter Sunday or Christmas, just as she "dragged" him to Buddhist, Shinto, and other religious sites. But she told him that these "religious samplings" did not require him to consider membership in any religion. His mother's "fundamental faith," he wrote, lay "in the goodness of people and in the ultimate value of this brief life we've each been given." Organized religion, she would explain to him, was "an expression of human culture . . . not its wellspring, just one of the many ways—and not necessarily the best way—that man attempted to control the unknowable and understand the deeper truths about our lives."[51]

In 1971, Ann sent Barack back to live with his grandparents in Hawaii because she wanted him to attend an American school. "She had always encouraged my rapid acculturation in Indonesia," Obama writes:

> She had taught me to disdain the blend of ignorance and arrogance that too often characterized Americans abroad. But she now had learned, just as Lolo had learned, the chasm that separated the life chances of an American with those of an Indonesian. She knew which side of the divide she wanted her child to be on. I was an American, she decided, and my true life lay else-where.[52]

In 1972, Ann herself returned to Hawaii, enrolled for graduate study at the university, and lived with her two children in a small apartment in Honolulu. Initially she still considered herself married to Lolo, but living apart until she completed a PhD. But when Ann returned to Indonesia for fieldwork several years later, she and Lolo rarely spent time together. In 1979 they agreed to divorce. "She left him," a Dutch friend of Ann's said, "on the pretext that she had to work. . . . The real reason was that it was hopeless. He couldn't accept the way she was, and she couldn't accept the kinds of things he expected."[53]

Obama, then a student at Honolulu's elite Punahou School, asked to remain in Oahu and to live with his grandparents while completing high school. Ann approved his request, for the education he was receiving at Punahou far surpassed what he would receive back in Jakarta. But the decision was extremely difficult. Maya later told an interviewer that "leaving Barry behind was the single hardest thing" her mother "had ever done."[54]

The Dunhams lived in a small high-rise apartment in the Makiki area of Honolulu, near Punahou. Stanley Dunham, who died in 1992 from prostate cancer, lived out his years on the islands surrounded by what one writer called "a cast of marginalized older men and poets."[55] He did daily crossword puzzles, watched television game shows, and started projects that often went unfinished.[56] Madelyn Dunham, however, secured a position at the Bank of Hawaii and rose within ten years to become one of the first female vice presidents in Hawaiian banking circles.

In autobiographical statements, Obama has invariably credited the women in his life with the transmission of values. He remembers his grandmother as "a very tough, sensible, no-nonsense person."[57] Speaking of his grandfather, father, and stepfather, Obama once told an interviewer, "The truth is that none of the men in my life were that successful or that stable. They made an awful lot of mistakes."[58] Madelyn Dunham continued to live in the same Honolulu apartment until she died two days before her grandson's election as president. After settling in Chicago, Obama usually visited her annually.

Scholarships and his grandmother's salary helped to pay Barack's tuition and expenses at Punahou. One of the largest private academies in the United States, the school was established in 1841 by the Congregationalist missionaries who carried Christianity to the Hawaiian Islands. A classmate who was one year ahead of Obama described Punahou as having "superb academic and athletic programs."[59] For generations, he reported, "the school's students and parents have dominated the island's and state's sports, economic, and political life." When he and Obama attended Punahou, the classmate said, so did the children of the governor, a U.S. senator, the publisher of a daily newspaper, and the owners of leading businesses, hotels, and restaurants.

By the time Obama enrolled in the fifth grade in 1972, Punahou's curriculum emphasized the multiculturalism that had long been part of its heritage. During his eight years at the school, Obama was popular among other students. He never stood out in the classroom. His teachers viewed him as academically unexceptional—but "in that environment," the classmate notes, "it took a great deal to be considered exceptional."

The teenaged Obama—now known as Barry—was far more complex than he appeared. With his father and stepfather gone and his mother and half-sister living on a distant island, the young Barry felt somewhat abandoned. He was one of only a handful of African Americans among over one thousand Punahou students. "I was more likely to meet a dark-skinned Melanesian than an African American," the classmate remembered. "And if I had to guess about Obama's racial background, Melanesian would have been my first guess." He added, "Our island culture did not comprehend African American identity in any current or meaningful way." Among affluent classmates who lived in large houses with swimming pools, Obama remembered that he felt isolated. A white student once asked him if his Kenyan father "ate people."[60]

"A fitful interior struggle" is the way Obama described his adolescence.[61] "I was living out a caricature of black male adolescence," he remembered, "itself a caricature of swaggering American manhood."[62] Inwardly, Obama harbored a sense of being a misfit. "I kept finding the same anguish, the same doubt," he wrote, "a self-contempt that neither irony nor intellect seemed able to deflect."[63] He coped with these feelings through drugs, alcohol, and working hard on basketball.[64]

When it came to representing himself to peers, Obama chose to be photographed for the Punahou senior yearbook wearing a leisure suit. His page also contains pictures of a beer bottle and a pack of rolling papers used for marijuana. That he often associated with the few black residents of Oahu island and read many African American authors were things his classmates and teachers did not know. "He never let on," a teacher who had him in class for four years told an interviewer.[65]

In 1979 Obama left Hawaii. He was barely eighteen when he enrolled at Occidental College in Los Angeles on a scholarship. Occidental had historically attracted Punahou students, as Congregationalist missionaries had established both institutions. Obama described his two years at Occidental as filled with alcohol, drugs, and parties. He played basketball only for one year. Although he knew some campus activists and contributed two poems to the student literary magazine, he apparently did not have a high profile on campus. His name appears neither in the yearbook, for example, nor in the student newspaper.[66] When interviewed by journalists decades later, however, his classmates described him with such terms as "very popular," "effortless charm," and "suave demeanor."[67]

But they also recalled another dimension. One Occidental alumnus remembers the clarity of Obama's thought. Another recollects lengthy discussions with Obama about the Soviet invasion of Afghanistan and similar political matters. A third remembers attending a political rally with him.[68] His sophomore roommate describes him as "a bookworm" who "quit basketball to concentrate on his schoolwork."[69] For whatever reason, Obama stopped calling himself by the name of Barry at Occidental. Instead, he began to use the name of his father, Barack.[70]

At the start of his junior year, Obama transferred to Columbia University. Because he was concerned that he was not taking courses seriously enough at Occidental, he took advantage of a transfer program the college had with Columbia. As he writes in *Dreams*, he felt "unanchored" in Los Angeles, whereas at Columbia he would be "in the heart of a true city, with black neighborhoods in close proximity."[71] The difference in the schools' student bodies, however, may have provided another motivation for the move—Occidental was largely Caucasian and Asian, whereas Columbia sat above Harlem.

Because Obama has given few details about his two years at Columbia, the information that exists largely comes from faculty or other students. Majoring in political science and international relations, he lived off campus and moved from one makeshift apartment to another during his two years there. In the seminar required for his senior thesis on Soviet nuclear disarmament, the professor gave him a grade of A for the course. Viewing him as one of four outstanding seniors in the seminar, he recommended Obama for Harvard Law School.

"Very smart . . . a very, very active participant," a member of the seminar described Obama.[72] "I think he was truly distinctive from the other people in that class. He stood out."[73] Unlike Occidental, where Obama told an interviewer that he spent "a lot of time having fun," Obama described his two years in Morningside Heights as "an intense period of study."[74] He ran three miles a day.[75] He told a Columbia college publication, "I didn't socialize that much. I was like a monk."[76]

During his time at Columbia, Obama read not only in the areas of his majors but also in philosophy and theology. He read writers varying from the church father Augustine to the twentieth-century Roman Catholic novelist Graham Greene. He also read widely in the writings of the American Protestant theologian Reinhold Niebuhr, who spent much of his life teaching at the adjacent Union Theological Seminary. On "rare" Sunday mornings, he writes in *Dreams*, he sat "in the back pews of [Harlem's] Abyssinian Baptist Church, lifted by the gospel choir's sweet, sorrowful song." There, he was able to "catch a fleeting glimpse of that thing which I sought."[77]

Obama graduated from Columbia in 1983. To repay his student loans, he remained in New York to work as a research assistant for the Business International Corporation. A Manhattan firm with several hundred employees, the corporation assisted companies in making foreign investments. Obama remembers his experiences in the firm differently from some who worked there. In order "to make it a good story," a coworker told a reporter, Obama's account seems to follow the writer's prerogative of leaving in what he wants and omitting what he wants.[78]

Bored and restless, Obama resigned from the consulting firm, took a series of unsuccessful short-term jobs, and began to read classified advertisements. He increasingly saw community organizing as fulfilling the values his mother had communicated to him.[79] By his own account, he was reading a "newsletter for do-gooder jobs" when he saw an advertisement placed by the Calumet Community Religious Conference (CCRC).[80] The CCRC was located on the South Side of Chicago and extended into the city's working-class suburbs, where many laid-off factory workers lived. It consisted of twenty-eight churches, mostly Roman Catholic, many of which were located in formerly ethnic neighborhoods. Although still headed by white pastors, most were surrounded by blacks whose religious heritage was Protestant. As a result, the churches had tiny, struggling congregations. The CCRC was advertising for an African American who could bring African American churches and their members into the conference's collective effort to improve living and economic conditions for the area's residents.

"What is this guy, Obama, is that [name] Japanese?" Jerry Kellman—the chief organizer of the CCRC—asked his Japanese American wife. "Actually, it could be," she answered.[81] In his late thirties, Jewish, and a native of New York City, Kellman—or "Marty Kaufman," as Obama refers to him in *Dreams* to protect his privacy—had begun organizing in the 1960s. After the Vietnam protests had ended, he continued organizing—"farmers in Nebraska, blacks in Philadelphia, Mexicans in Chicago."[82] When he learned that Obama was African American rather than Japanese, Kellman arranged an interview. "Most of our work is with churches," he remembers telling Obama when they met in New York:

> If poor and working-class people want to build real power, they have to have some sort of institutional base. With the unions in the shape they're in, the churches are the only game in town. That's where the people . . . and . . . the values are, even if they've been buried under a lot of bullshit.[83]

Churches would not work with community organizers "just out of the goodness of their hearts," Kellman explained. They might smile approvingly, devote a sermon to an organization's work, and perhaps take a special offering. "But if push comes to shove," he concluded, "they won't really move unless you can show them how it'll help them pay their heating bill."[84] Explaining that he was "trying to pull urban blacks and suburban whites together around a plan to save manufacturing jobs in metropolitan Chicago," the organizer told Obama that his being white presented an obstacle in an area that was almost one hundred percent black.[85] Hence he needed an African American to work with him.[86]

During the interview, Kellman found Obama "very bright, very articulate, very personable, and very idealistic."[87] He was also pleased to learn that the young Columbia graduate found Martin Luther King Jr.'s philosophy of nonviolence inspirational. Selecting him on the spot, Kellman subsequently sold Obama to his board.

Consisting of all of Chicago south of the downtown Loop, the South Side had originally included an industrial center and many ethnic neighborhoods. Following World War II, African Americans gradually became the South Side's largest single body of residents. After factory closings severely damaged its economic base, the South Side continued to exhibit a diversity of income levels, but a large portion—much of which lay within the territory of the CCRC—grew impoverished. This area included Altgeld Gardens, a housing project of some fifteen hundred row houses situated near landfills, waste dumps, sewage plants, and polluted waterways.

In July of 1985, Obama drove from New York to Chicago in an old Honda. For the next three years, he lived sparingly in Hyde Park, a middle-class island in the South Side. He worked out of a small, shared office at Holy Rosary Church in Roseland, a formerly Irish neighborhood in the far South Side near the Indiana border. Shortly after he arrived, the CCRC spun off its work in Chicago into a new organization, the Developing Communities Project (DCP), of which Obama became the principal organizer.

When Obama wrote *Dreams*, he described his three years as a community organizer as the hardest work of his life.[88] Defined by one writer as "a combination of educator, confessor-priest, social activist, motivational expert, mediator, and campaign leader," a community organizer motivates a community to take collective action and to bring pressure upon local, state, or federal offices to fix the problems besetting their area.[89] Obama soon found in himself "the same vision that drove Kellman," a vision that included "his confidence in the populist impulse and working-class solidarity; his faith that if you could just clear away the politicians and media and bureaucrats and give everybody a seat at the table, then ordinary people could find common ground."[90]

Obama's internal toughness and the intensity of his commitment quickly impressed his fellow workers. He became known for deliberateness, for meticulous planning, for sensitivity, and for resisting the tactics of confrontation that many community activists employed. Many in the organization came to revere him, despite his youth.

Obama confronted major problems of racial antagonism among Chicago residents. "Listen . . . what's your name again?," a Baptist minister said at a meeting of South Side black pastors whom the young community organizer was trying to attract to the CCRC. The minister continued:

> You may mean well. . . . But the last thing we need is to join up with . . .
> white money and Catholic churches and Jewish organizers to solve our
> problems. . . . The archdiocese in this city is run by stone-cold racists.
> Always has been. White folks come in here . . . hiring a buncha high-talking
> college-educated brothers like yourself who don't know no better. . . . It's all a
> political thing, and that's not what this group here is about.[91]

When the meeting ended, Obama noted that none of the pastors there took the flyers he had prepared for them.

Other problems also confronted Obama during his time with the CCRC. He had no practical political experience. He had grown up partially in Indonesia and largely in Hawaii—islands far removed from the difficulties of Chicago. At twenty-four, he was sometimes half the age of the residents he advised. In addition, he was still earnestly seeking his own identity as a black male. Finally, he was working with churches, and he was not a Christian.

When Obama left Chicago in 1988, however, he was close to becoming a Christian. At least six considerations seem to have influenced him to make a Christian commitment.

First, despite her lack of formal affiliation with any religion and her declared secularism, Ann Sutoro appears to have been a highly spiritual person.

A close friend in Indonesia remembered that she and Ann rarely talked about religious belief. "I would not say Ann was a Christian or a Hindu or a Buddhist," she told an interviewer. "But she had a general interest. And I think she probably had more spiritual stuff in her than most people who profess to be religious and faithful. She never once used words in my presence about being atheist or agnostic."[92]

In *Audacity*, Obama himself describes his mother as "in many ways the most spiritually awakened person" he has ever known. He depicts her as having "an abiding sense of wonder, a reverence for life and its precious, transitory nature that could properly be described as devotional." Without citing biblical passages or any claims of divine revelation made by Christianity, he writes, "she worked mightily to instill in me the values that many Americans learn in Sunday school."[93] When Ann was dying, her maternal uncle—an Episcopalian—asked that she be included in his congregation's prayers. As far as he could tell, he said, she "had been doing what Christians always said saints did—helping people."[94]

Second, Obama had entered Chicago intensely committed to improving the way things were. Intellectually, he knew of the crucial role Christian teachings had played in the civil rights movement. And on the South Side he saw the churches' work firsthand. "I was drawn to the power of the African-American religious tradition to spur social change," Obama wrote in *Audacity*.[95] "What moved me," he explained to one writer, "was the role all the congregations I worked with played in the life of the people I was working with."[96] The black clergy of the South Side especially impressed him. "As a group," he wrote, "they turned out to be thoughtful, hard working men, with a confidence, a certainty of purpose.... They were generous with their time, interested in the issues, surprisingly ... open."[97]

Third, Obama came to Chicago already somewhat attracted to Christianity. At Columbia he had not only read widely in theology and philosophy but also attended church in Harlem. In fact, Kellman remembers that the prospect of working with churches proved decisive in persuading Obama to accept the community-organizing position.[98]

Fourth, the fellowship of the African American churches of the South Side attracted him. As a single biracial male, geographically separated from his family, Obama "had no community or shared traditions in which to ground my most deeply held beliefs."[99] In the churches of Chicago's South Side, he began to find the fellowship he had longed for since adolescence. In Trinity Church he saw "a powerful program, [a] cultural community, one more pliant than simple nationalism, more sustaining than my own brand of organizing."[100]

Fifth, Obama realized that he would enjoy more success working with black churches if he were attending church regularly himself. The black pastors whom he sought to attract to the DCP repeatedly told him he would be more credible if he belonged to a church. "Had I heard the Good News? some of them would ask me," he wrote in *Dreams*, "Do you know where it is that your faith is coming from?"[101] He remembered that he reflected on the suggestions and finally decided in 1988, "Well, I guess that makes sense."[102]

In the midst of community organizing, Obama pondered the role of religious faith. "To be right with yourself, to do right by others, to lend meaning to a community's suffering and take part in its healing—that required . . . faith. . . . I had faith in myself. But faith in one's self was never enough."[103] In an address to the national meeting of his denomination, Obama told the rest of the story. "So one Sunday," he told the delegates,

> I put on one of the few clean jackets I had, and went over to Trinity United
> Church of Christ on 95th Street. . . . And I heard Rev. Jeremiah A. Wright
> deliver a sermon called "The Audacity of Hope." And during the course of
> that sermon, he introduced me to someone named Jesus Christ.
>
> I learned that my sins could be redeemed. I learned that those things
> I was too weak to accomplish myself, He would accomplish with me if I
> placed my trust in Him. And in time, I came to see faith as more than just
> a comfort to the weary or a hedge against death, but rather as an active,
> palpable agent in the world and in my own life.[104]

Wright's sermon also provided Obama with a religious context for the work he was doing on the South Side. "At the foot of that cross, inside the thousands of churches across the city," he wrote, "I imagined the stories of ordinary Black people merging with the stories of David and Goliath, Moses and Pharaoh, the Christians in the lion's den, Ezekiel's field of dry bones. Those stories—of survival and freedom, and hope—became our story, my story."[105] In another passage in *Dreams*, Obama speaks of "a forceful wind carrying the Reverend's voice up into the rafters." Obama declares that he "felt for the first time how that spirit carried within it, nascent, incomplete, the possibility of moving beyond our narrow dreams."[106]

Obama also credits the African American church community of the South Side for his conversion. "And something else happened during the time I spent in those neighborhoods," he later told a university audience:

> Perhaps because the church folks I worked with were so welcoming and understanding, perhaps because they invited me to their services and sang with me from their hymnals, perhaps because I witnessed all of the good works their faith inspired them to perform, I found myself drawn—not just to work with the church, but to be in the church. It was through this service that I was brought to Christ.[107]

The catalyst, however, was Wright's preaching. The sermon at Trinity Church on that particular Sunday reduced Obama to tears. It affected him so much that he used the sermon title—*The Audacity of Hope*—as the title for his second book. Wright's words transformed him from being an outsider to becoming a fellow traveler of the Trinity community, although he was not baptized until he returned from Harvard Law School. After his marriage to Michelle the next year, he officially became a member of Trinity Church. Thus the preaching and charisma of Jeremiah Wright provides the sixth influence that caused Obama to become a Christian.

Jeremiah Wright was born in 1941 in Philadelphia into a church family. His mother was a vice principal in the city's school system. His father, the son of a Baptist minister, was the longtime pastor of a Baptist church in Philadelphia. Following high school, Wright attended Virginia Union University in downtown Richmond. The university has an attached theological seminary, attended not only by Wright but also by his father and grandfather.

Dropping out of Virginia Union in 1961, Wright spent six years in military service. After his discharge in 1967, he received bachelor's and master's degrees in English from Howard University. Following Howard he went to the University of Chicago Divinity School, where he concentrated on Islam and earned a second master's degree in the history of religions. In 1990, after he entered the parish ministry, Wright completed a doctor of ministry degree (intended for parish clergy) at the United Theological Seminary in Dayton, Ohio.[108]

Originally Wright had intended to complete a PhD and teach in a theological seminary. But in the early 1970s he entered the ministry partially out of a concern that African Americans were becoming unchurched—either that, or they were leaving Christianity for such alternatives as the Nation of Islam and the Black Hebrew Israelites. Believing that these departures stemmed from an ignorance of the many positive relationships that had existed between African American history and the Christian faith, Wright became intent on proving that Christianity is neither a white nor a racist religion. With the organizing center of the Nation of Islam located in Chicago, he tried to show that Islam and other religions had condoned slavery equally as much as Christianity. During his years at the University of Chicago, he also became increasingly militant about the African aspects of his religious heritage.

No Baptist church called Wright to its pulpit when he graduated from divinity school.[109] He then accepted the pastorate of the small Trinity United Church of Christ on the South Side. A 1957 merger of four mainline Protestant denominations, the United Church of Christ (UCC) melds European and American Protestant traditions, with the New England Congregationalist (or Puritan) element the most dominant.

In 1961, this largely white denomination founded Trinity Church to attract middle-class and upper-middle-class whites and blacks in the changing South Side. The earliest members of the congregation were "teachers, people with middle-class jobs, resistant to doing anything radical in terms of justice."[110] The UCC expected the Trinity congregation to worship without the displays of emotion common to African American churches. Wright dates the end of this middle-class vision to the assassination of Martin Luther King Jr. In 1968, as one writer declares, the congregation began to believe that it "couldn't continue to do Christ's work and not speak out against racism and injustice."[111]

When Wright assumed the pastorate, his congregation numbered only eighty-seven members.[112] He soon asked his parishioners to decide whether Trinity should be "a black church in the black community" or "a white church in blackface."[113] When the congregation selected the first option, he identified Trinity Church with African American culture.

Gradually Wright introduced altar calls, baptism by immersion, revival hymns, and gospel music to the church—practices uncommon to United Church of Christ worship. As in black Baptist and Methodist congregations, emotion, hand waving, and shouted affirmations came to characterize a Sunday in Trinity's sanctuary.[114] Under Wright, services at Trinity also became "a weekly master class in how to move an audience."[115] He regularly held the attention of his congregation in sermons that could last for fifty minutes.

During the thirty-six years of Wright's pastorate, Trinity Church grew immensely. It established more than seventy ministries and support groups, created dozens of musical groups, and planted more than fifteen new congregations. In one five-year period, its collection plates and gifts funded almost four million dollars in missionary work for the UCC. Because the church paid tuition for any member who attended a theological seminary, more than forty of its members were attending seminaries in 2008.[116] A University of Chicago professor declared that Trinity Church's scholarships and preparatory classes for the SAT examinations placed "more African-American students in college than any other organization in Chicago."[117]

Steadily increasing in size and membership under Wright's leadership, Trinity Church built a new sanctuary seating nine hundred worshippers in 1978. Sixteen years later, it constructed the large complex of buildings it currently occupies, with seating for 2,500 worshippers. Trinity became a megachurch, occupying most of a city block and holding three services of worship each Sunday. At the height of Wright's pastorate, the church's membership exceeded 8,500.

Ultimately, the formerly small, middle-class, integrated Trinity Church became the largest congregation in the United Church of Christ and one of the leading African American churches in Chicago. Both black and white pastors throughout Chicago admired Wright's preaching ability. "When the preachers of the land decide whose sermons and lectures or preaching they want to hear," a leading white Presbyterian minister in Chicago told his congregation, "Jeremiah Wright's are near the top of the list."[118]

Why Obama chose Trinity over other African American churches in Chicago seems clear. Although other reasons contributed—for example, Trinity's congregation was diverse, including "celebrities and welfare recipients, PhDs and GEDs"—Jeremiah Wright was undoubtedly the primary reason for his joining.[119] Obama admired not only the pastor's erudition but also the political dimensions he gave to the mission of Trinity. And above all, Wright had been instrumental in Obama's conversion.

At Trinity, Obama found a distinctly African American version of Christianity. Cultural adaptations have been a part of Christianity since the earliest years of the religion. As belief in Jesus of Nazareth spread, Eastern or Byzantine churches presented Christianity differently from Western or Latin churches. Russian Orthodoxy diverged from Greek Orthodoxy; Irish Roman Catholicism differed from Italian Roman Catholicism; and Polish American Catholic parishes (some of which in time offered polka Masses) diverged from Mexican American Roman Catholic parishes that emphasized devotion to Our Lady of Guadalupe. Similarly, German Lutheran parishes in the United States worshipped somewhat differently from Lutheran parishes founded by Swedish immigrants.

Many of these Christian ethnic parishes kept ties—liturgical, geographical, and linguistic—to their homeland. Even in the United States, for example, they celebrated holidays of their native countries. The ornamentation of their churches and the garb of their clergy employed symbols from their homelands. Similarly, in a process that began in the colonial period and that has continued into the twenty-first century, African Americans established distinct forms of Christian worship.

In Chicago, Wright saw Afrocentrism (or "Africentrism") as critical to the growth of the Christian faith. He also saw it as vital to the survival of Trinity Church in a neighborhood where the Nation of Islam evangelized children and adults on the street. Defined as the effort to "remove Europe as the center of black sacred life and replace it with Africa," Afrocentrism emphasizes Africa and African heritage.[120] "Churches that are, say, Lutheran first but then just happen to be black secondarily, don't grow," Wright's successor as pastor at Trinity Church has said.[121] The Afrocentric emphases Trinity Church adopted under Wright placed the church outside the mainstream of the UCC but within the mainstream of African American Christianity.[122]

In 1988, Obama resigned his position with the Developing Communities Project to enter Harvard Law School. Though he attended Trinity Church, he had not yet been baptized. He left Chicago without securing either the economic revitalization of the South Side or the return of lost jobs that he and the DCP sought. But members of his community organization credited him with several significant achievements. "There was no campaign without Barack," Kellman asserts. "He was there to get people to organize when they wouldn't organize at all."[123]

At Harvard, Obama was elected the first African American president of the law review. In his description, he spent "most of three years in poorly lit libraries poring through cases and statutes." He devotes several pages of *Dreams* to his reflections about the disappointments and the accomplishments of the American legal system.[124] No information seems to exist about his church attendance in Cambridge, but he apparently listened to tapes of sermons sent to him by Wright. During the summers, he interned in Chicago law firms. When he attended church, he went to Trinity.

After graduating in 1991, Obama returned to Chicago. There, he worked out of the DCP office to lead a voter registration drive, joined a prestigious firm as a civil rights attorney, and became a popular lecturer in constitutional history at the University of Chicago Law School. In 1996, he was elected to the Illinois State Senate, and in 2004 to the U.S. Senate. In his Senate office he hung paintings of Abraham Lincoln, Mohandas Gandhi, and Martin Luther King Jr., men whom he calls his heroes.

In October 1992, Obama married Michelle Robinson at Trinity Church in a service performed by Jeremiah Wright. The two had met while Obama was working as a summer intern in the Chicago law firm Sidley Austin, where Michelle was an associate. She later recalled that she viewed his name as "strange" and thought to herself that "any black guy who spent his formative years on an island had to be a little nerdy, a little strange."

The product of a close-knit African American family whose identity was rooted in the South Side of Chicago, Michelle's lineage went back to antebellum South Carolina and Alabama. "I am married to a black American," Obama once declared in a speech, "who carries within her the blood of slaves and slave owners."[125] Since Michelle's ancestors also include Native Americans, one writer has declared that her background models the African American experience as much as that of Alex Haley, the author of *Roots*.[126] When Obama first met her family, he saw in it the stability he had always wanted but never had attained.[127]

Michelle and her older brother, Craig, grew up in a cramped one-bedroom apartment on the second floor of a bungalow owned by their aunt. Her father, who suffered from multiple sclerosis from the age of thirty, worked daily as a pump operator in the Chicago water department. Stressing the importance of education, her mother permitted the two children to watch only one hour of TV a night. Valuing open-mindedness and intellectual autonomy, the Robinsons attended church infrequently.[128]

While her brother attended a nearby parochial school, Michelle attended a magnet school in another part of the city. Subsequently, both Robinson children graduated from Princeton, after which Michelle graduated from Harvard Law School.[129] Craig went on to work as a bond trader, subsequently leaving for what he saw as the less materialistic career of coaching basketball at Brown and Oregon State universities.

When Obama announced his intention to run for the presidency, Michelle was a vice president at the University of Chicago Medical Center. Her coworkers described her as "a problem solver" and "totally unflappable."[130] During the campaign, when opponents attacked her for supposed racism and lack of patriotism, Michelle avoided becoming a controversial figure by explaining her comments and by emphasizing her blue-collar background.[131]

In 1998, Michelle gave birth to Malia Obama, and in 2001 to her and Barack's second daughter, Sasha. Jeremiah Wright baptized both, just as he had baptized Obama in the early 1990s. Obama "kept coming back to talk and started worshipping with us and then he joined," Wright told a reporter.[132] The Obamas' attendance at Trinity, never perhaps regular, declined after the births of their children. Michelle once remarked to friends that she had difficulty conceiving of any mother of young children going to church every week—a comment that does not seem to take into account the extensive childcare programs of Trinity and other churches.[133] Obama himself explained that it was "not easy" to take "young, squirming children to church. Trinity was always packed and so you had to get there early. . . . It was just difficult." His comment seems to exclude Sunday school instruction for the children.[134]

As the children grew, the Obamas began to attend Trinity more often. But they came less frequently during Obama's political campaigns. The evidence seems clear that their churchgoing was irregular. "When it comes to absolute doctrinal adherence," Michelle Obama has said (in words that many members of churches, synagogues, and mosques could also say), "I don't know that there would be a church in this country that I would be involved in."[135] Asked at the National Press Club about how frequently Obama attended Trinity, Jeremiah Wright—who by that time had become somewhat estranged from the campaign—told the journalists that Obama "goes to church about as much as you do."[136]

During his years in the legislature, the future presidential candidate often listened to tapes of Trinity services while driving between Chicago and Springfield. During his 2004 senate race, Obama—like many candidates—was often in church on Sunday. The churches he attended while campaigning, however, were not necessarily his own. "We might not have gone to Trinity for two, three months at a time," he told reporters.[137]

In February 2007, Obama announced his presidential candidacy from the steps of the Old State Capitol building in Springfield, Illinois—the city of Abraham Lincoln. He began his announcement with the words that often precede a sermon in African American Christianity: "Giving all praise and honor to God." Obama defeated his principal Democratic opponent, Senator Hillary Clinton, in the primaries. He and his running mate, Senator Joseph Biden, then faced the Republican ticket of Senator John McCain and Governor Sarah Palin.[138]

In a 2006 speech repeated in *Audacity*, Obama said, "I think we make a mistake when we fail to acknowledge the power of faith in the lives of the American people." He warned that

> the discomfort of some progressives with any hint of religiosity has often inhibited us from effectively addressing issues in moral terms. . . . Scrub language of all religious content and we forfeit the imagery and terminology through which millions of Americans understand both their personal morality and social justice.[139]

Thus Obama emphasized faith and gave it a more prominent place in his campaign than any Democratic presidential candidate since Jimmy Carter. Prayers frequently opened Obama rallies, and invocations often closed them. Attempting to bridge the gap between religious conservatives and secular liberals, Obama admonished his fellow Democrats to cease permitting the

Republican Party to depict itself as the party of religion. "We need to take faith seriously," he wrote in *Audacity*, "not simply to block the religious right but to engage all persons of faith in . . . American renewal."[140]

Throughout his campaign, Obama repeatedly referred to religion as an enormous influence on American life. "To say that men and women should not inject their 'personal morality' into public-policy debates," he wrote in *Audacity*, "is a practical absurdity. Our law is by definition a codification of morality, much of it grounded in the Judeo-Christian tradition."[141] He laced his speeches with biblical allusions. Citing the biblical mandate that Jews and Christians be their "brother's keeper," he underscored the role it played in the abolitionist and civil rights movements.

Following Clinton's example, Obama formed a faith advisory committee of five influential evangelical pastors. He met in Chicago with Franklin Graham, the son of Billy Graham, as well as with several dozen other evangelical leaders. The evangelicals who assisted with Obama's campaign shared his conviction that religious faith provides a critical base for the struggle against injustice and inequality.[142] "He has seized the religious discursive ground," a divinity school professor declared over a year before the election. "No Democratic candidate since Jimmy Carter has been able to do that."[143]

Most Americans viewed Obama's faith as genuine. Voters and journalists found him more willing to speak about the relationship between religion and democracy than even Senator McCain, an Episcopalian who for some years had attended a Southern Baptist megachurch. Obama spoke as comfortably about his beliefs as George W. Bush did. Asked about the role that Jesus and his teachings played in his life, Obama answered: "I am a Christian. What that means for me is that I believe Jesus Christ died for my sins, and . . . [that through] his grace and his mercy and his power . . . I can achieve everlasting life."[144]

Obama's approach proved effective. During the campaign, he retained what had been the Democratic base since the 1970s: secular voters, Jews, African Americans, mainline Protestants, moderate Roman Catholics, and many Hispanics. While Obama made no great inroads in white evangelical support, more regular churchgoers supported him than had voted for Democratic candidate John Kerry four years earlier.[145]

Yet for a time, the campaign seemed poised to lose many of these religious supporters. In the final months of the primaries, television networks and Obama's opponents distributed a series of excerpts from sermons preached by Jeremiah Wright over the past few decades. First released by ABC News in March 2008, the sound bites included vehement assertions by Wright about American racism. They also included his definition of Zionism as "white racism," a charge that the government attempted to annihilate African Americans through drugs and diseases such as AIDS, and a reference to the United States as "the US of KKKA"—meaning "the U.S. of Ku Klux Klan America."[146] In another clip, Wright continued the allusion to the KKK by declaring, "I can worship God on Sunday morning wearing a black clergy robe and kill others on Sunday evening wearing a white Klan robe."[147] Television news played these videos repeatedly, and the clips found wide circulation on the Internet.

As the days went by, more controversial information about Wright became public. Voters learned that Wright had praised Muammar al-Gaddafi of Libya, befriended Nation of Islam leader Louis Farrakhan, and traveled to Fidel Castro's Cuba. Especially infuriating was Wright's assertion that the government had brought the September 11 attacks of 2001 upon itself. "America's chickens are coming home to roost," he pronounced in one sermon, alluding to what he considered American acts of terrorism abroad.[148] But the video played the most on both TV and the Internet portrayed Wright uttering these words from his Chicago pulpit:

> The government gives citizens of African descent the drugs, builds bigger prisons, passes a three-strike law and then wants us to sing "God Bless America." No, no, no, not "God Bless America." God damn America—that's in the Bible—for killing innocent people. God damn America, for treating our citizens as less than human.[149]

To many Americans, it now appeared that Obama maintained a pastoral relationship with a militant crackpot. Wright's image changed from "the pastor who once preached a sermon that gave Obama the uplifting title for *The Audacity of Hope* ... [to] someone who sounded rabid, crackpot, appalling."[150] The excerpts caused Obama's opponents to question not only his choice of associates but also his Christian faith. Any other candidate, they implied, would have left a church with such a pastor. As the Democratic nominee's relationship with Wright began to jeopardize his campaign, opponents began to see Wright as their WMD.

As the controversy developed, Obama tried to find a middle path. In interviews, he described Wright as "a child of the sixties [who] . . . often expresses himself in that language."[151] He also characterized Wright as "an old uncle who sometimes will say things I don't agree with."[152]

Nevertheless, the firestorm continued. In response, Obama delivered a nationally televised speech in mid-March. Agreeing with critics that the excerpts displayed Wright using "incendiary language to express views that . . . rightly offend white and black alike,"[153] he said:

> Did I know him to be an occasionally fierce critic of American domestic and foreign policy? Of course. Did I ever hear him make remarks that could be considered controversial while I sat in church? Yes. Did I strongly disagree with many of his political views? Absolutely.[154]

Explaining that he had not been in church on the Sundays when Wright made these statements, Obama used such words as "wrong," "divisive," and "racially charged" to describe the comments.[155] But Obama expressed concern that the media had taken sentences from Wright's sermons out of context. Urging his television audience not to categorize his pastor as "a crank or demagogue,"[156] he declared:

> The profound mistake of Rev. Wright's sermons is not that he spoke about racism in our society. It's that he spoke as if our society was static; as if no progress had been made; as if this country—a country that has made it possible for one of his own members to run for the highest office in the land and build a [diverse] coalition . . . is still irrevocably bound to a tragic past.[157]

For Wright's generation, he added, "the memories of humiliation and doubt and fear have not gone away nor has the anger and bitterness of those years."[158] Yet he explained that he could not disown Wright. "As imperfect as he may be, he has been like family," Obama declared.[159] "He strengthened my faith, officiated at my wedding, and baptized my children . . . I can no more disown him than I can disown the black community [or] . . . my white grandmother. These people are a part of me."[160]

Continuing into spring 2008, additional controversial excerpts from Wright's sermons and statements became public. Ultimately, the national furor climaxed in late April, when Washington's National Press Club invited Wright to be their weekly speaker. In the previous week, Bill Moyers had interviewed him on PBS, and the NAACP had featured him as its speaker in Detroit. Now Wright was scheduled to face the Washington press corps—a meeting that one African American journalist described as "a recipe for disaster."[161]

Organized by Washington journalists in 1908, the National Press Club describes itself as the "sanctum sanctorum of American journalists." American presidents and leading statesmen have spoken at its weekly breakfasts. Instrumental in organizing the breakfast in April and inviting Wright was Dr. Barbara Reynolds, a theologically trained journalist and syndicated religion columnist. As an African American minister, Dr. Reynolds knew that the Samuel DeWitt Proctor Conference, a black organization that focuses on issues of social justice and community and economic development, was meeting for two days in Washington in late April. She arranged for Wright (a member of the conference) to speak at the press club. "Jeremiah Wright had preached probably five thousand sermons," she said in an interview, "but the press had taken thirty-second excerpts from a few of them and played them over and over. I thought that as soon as he gave a talk to the National Press Club, that would be cleared up. But he was too truthful."[162]

On that Monday morning, television networks covered Wright's address. The front rows of the first floor consisted of members of the Proctor Conference, other supporters Wright had invited to the talk, and some press. Most members of the press club sat in the balcony. The shout of "We love you, Reverend Wright" that greeted Wright as he walked to the podium indicated that this would not be a normal breakfast of the Washington press.

Wright delivered an articulate speech that displayed his scholarly background. He traced the African American religious experience and stressed the prophetic basis of black preaching, which Wright declared motivated black clergy to criticize society:

The prophetic theology of the black church has always seen . . . all God's children as sisters and brothers . . . equals who need reconciliation, who need to be reconciled as equals, in order for us to walk together into the future which God has prepared for us.

Wright continued to speak in a calm, measured tone:

We root out any teaching of superiority . . . hatred or prejudice. And we recognize . . . that the other who stands before us with a different color of skin . . . different music, different preaching styles and different dance moves . . . is one of God's children just as we are, no better, no worse, prone to error and in need of forgiveness just as we are.

Wright claimed that the media had misunderstood the black church and misrepresented his words. "Black preaching is different from European and European-American preaching," he stated. "It is not *deficient*; it is just different."[163] The message of black church pastors, he asserted, is one of liberation, transformation, and reconciliation. Rarely, if ever, he declared, had critics who condemned excerpts from one of his sermons heard that sermon in its entirety. The media firestorm, he argued, was "not an attack on Jeremiah Wright [but] an attack on the black church." He asserted that his critics were people who "know nothing about the African-American religious tradition." This charge of lack of familiarity and information was central to his argument.[164]

Normally, an audience at the National Press Club would remain silent until the question and answer period. But Wright's audience included a substantial number of supporters, seated together in front of him, who were accustomed to the call-and-response preaching of African American Christianity. Thus more than a dozen instances of laughter, applause, boos, cheers, and outcries of "yes" and "that's right" punctuated Wright's speech. During the question and answer period, when Wright answered written questions journalists submitted to the moderator, similar cries of support came from the black members of his audience. This outpouring of vocal encouragement seems to have caused Wright to become increasingly confident and emphatic as he talked.

Some of Wright's answers were highly positive. He declared, for example, that God loves all people, regardless of color, and he praised the work of many white Christians with African Americans.[165] But in other answers

Wright seemed belligerent. Dr. Reynolds said that she "became more and more concerned as the question and answer period went on."[166] In the words of one black journalist, the Chicago minister "let loose" in his answers. In a hostile atmosphere, but with supporters present and directly in his line of vision, he became increasingly comfortable. He even flashed the membership sign (known as "Throwing Up the Hooks") of Omega Psi Phi, his African American fraternity. The conservative *New York Post* subsequently ran a cover picture of him flashing his fraternity sign accompanied by the headline "Pastor Disaster."

For the Obama campaign, the question and answer period threatened disaster. In one answer, for example, Wright described the controversial Louis Farrakhan as "one of the most important voices in the twentieth and twenty-first centuries."[167] Defending his patriotism, he cited his six years of military service and asked how many years then vice president Dick Cheney had served. Asked to defend his statement that the "chickens had come home to roost in the September 11 attacks," Wright responded, "Have you heard the whole sermon? No, you haven't heard the whole sermon. That nullifies the question." In the same tone, he asserted that his preaching had a background in "Biblical history, which many of the working press are unfamiliar with."[168]

Wright also refused to back away from his insinuations that the U.S. government created AIDS to kill people of color. Citing two books, he told the press, "Based on the Tuskegee experiments . . . and based on what has happened to Africans in this country, I believe our government is capable of doing anything." Clarence Page, a leading African American journalist, subsequently commented about the Tuskegee experiments: "There hasn't been evidence of similar atrocities since then, except in fringe literature that Wright unfortunately appears to believe."[169]

Inevitably a journalist asked about Wright's most controversial statement, "not God bless America [but] God damn America." Obama's pastor replied that television networks had misrepresented the quotation by cutting words from it. As Wright explained it, he had originally said, "God damn America for treating our citizens as less than human." Hence this less controversial statement had concerned American "policy, not the American people." And Wright told his audience that his assertion, no matter how controversial, was true to the Bible. "God doesn't bless everything," he declared, "God con-

demns something—and d-e-m-n, 'demn,' is where we get the word 'damn.'
God damns some practices."[170]

The video of Wright's "God damn America" sermon supports his explanation. The ABC News story of March 13, 2008, that started the national
firestorm over Obama and Wright's association begins with these words:
"Sen. Barack Obama's pastor says blacks should not sing 'God Bless America'
but 'God damn America.'" Not until six paragraphs later does Wright's full
sentence—"God damn America for treating our citizens as less than human"—appear.

Written by Brian Ross and Rehab El-Buri, the ABC News article contains numerous inflammatory quotations from more than three decades of
Wright's sermons. Its eighteen paragraphs rarely say a positive word about
Wright or his ministry. Nowhere do they quote from a sermon that speaks
about the love of God, the Beatitudes, the Golden Rule, the ethical demands
of Christian discipleship, or the need for brotherhood and the call to Christian service—all characteristic of Wright's preaching.

The article does indicate that Wright "declined to be interviewed by ABC
News." The pastor's refusal was unfortunate, because a face-to-face conversation would surely have improved the piece's tone and content. As it was,
Ross and El-Buri's overwhelmingly negative article, which prompted a flood
of similarly negative exposés, caused Wright to enter the National Press
Club in a hostile and defiant mood. In his mind, the national media was attacking him personally. The story by ABC News does not seem to represent
responsible journalism.

Most African Americans reacted in one of two ways to Wright's appearance at the press club. Many black clergy appreciated Wright's presentation,
especially his charge that attacks on him were really attacks on the black
church. Wright "acquitted himself well," a professor at the Methodist Garrett
Theological Seminary in Illinois declared. The former dean of the chapel
at Howard University described Wright's speech as controversial "only to
those who don't understand or don't want to understand what he is saying."
Although some African American clergy believed that Wright had gone
too far, most saw the pastor as simply preaching the Christian Gospel and
speaking—as he had done for years in Chicago—truth to power.[171]

Similarly, some African American journalists supported Wright's statements. When he spoke about the inequities and injustices of American life, "we knew where he was coming from," Zenitha Prince of the *Baltimore Afro-American* said.[172] Those who firmly supported Wright not only asserted that the mainstream media depicted his views in a "distorted and dysfunctional" context but also deplored the reporting as "savage, unjustified, [and] taken out of context."[173] But other black journalists left the press club with mixed feelings. "Wright's Wrong, but White's Right?" was the title the writer for the *Washington Informer* gave his story.[174]

Many journalists for African American papers believed that Wright's newest statements resembled "a bad penny" that would "revisit Obama over and over again."[175] One commentator wrote that the pastor's negative statements about America would give voters a "permission slip" to vote against the Democratic candidate. "Why," another rhetorically asked, "would he—literally, and in God's name—choose this moment to lose his mind?"[176]

The journalists also deplored Wright's timing. After agreeing with Ecclesiastes that "there is a time to keep silent and a time to speak," a writer for the African American *Miami Times* declared that the minister "played his way right into the hands of a hostile media that will consider a black man as president, but . . . does not want a black president."[177] Another black writer declared that Wright's "timing was way, way off. . . . Even truth, when spoken out of season, does not bear fruit."[178]

Ad hominem arguments abounded. Attributing Wright's words and actions to "envy, self-service . . . egomania," one journalist depicted him as "a loose cannon of a preacher strutting around on stage . . . silly, old, self-serving."[179] Another declared that the nationwide attention "fed Wright's ego, raised his national profile, and brought him in speaking fees."[180] Suggesting that Wright wished the outcome of the election to show that the United States had made no significant racial progress since the nineteenth century, former Republican presidential candidate Mike Huckabee asserted that "Jeremiah Wright needs for Obama to lose so he can justify . . . his hostile bitterness against the [nation]."[181] Clarence Page summed up the views of many African American colleagues: "Wright may have single-handedly done enough damage to make sure Obama never gets to the Oval Office," he wrote. "If so, Wright probably will blame the white man for the defeat, but the rest of us will know who helped."[182]

"I saw the National Press Club broadcast," a white member of Trinity Church said, "and I was despondent about it."[183] He continued:

> How can we explain what happened? It's pure conjecture, but I have to think that Jeremiah is human and that there must have been a large sense of anger over the way he had been portrayed. . . . I'd accept ego as contributing, too. . . .
>
> And I think he responded very much to the supporters who were in the audience. In some ways, the atmosphere must have appeared to him to be more like Trinity Church than like the National Press Club.[184]

The white parishioner, who married a member of Trinity Church and had attended for many years, continued:

> Even his mannerisms were off the path a little bit. . . . Mannerisms that are a part of preaching in a black church you wouldn't bring to the podium at the NPC. His mannerisms were provocative. Whatever it was, it made him take down his guard.[185]

Whatever caused Wright's words and attitude in Washington, the results were serious. One of his longtime clerical colleagues attributed his speech and answers to defensiveness. "I know ya'll ticked off at him," a Dallas protégé of Wright told his congregation on the Sunday after the press breakfast, "but he was a cornered lion. And when a lion's got cornered and they're already wounded, *they don't back down*."[186] Almost all of Wright's defenders acknowledged that he undoubtedly remained bitter for being asked to withdraw in 2007 from the ceremony at which Obama announced his candidacy.

The day after Wright's appearance in Washington, Obama broke with him. In a speech delivered in Winston-Salem, he called his minister's "rants" not only inexcusable and "appalling," but also a "show of disrespect to me."[187] The "divisive" and "destructive" statements by the pastor, Obama asserted, "offend me, they rightly offend all Americans, and they should be denounced. And that's what I'm doing very clearly and unequivocally here today."[188]

Obama stated that he wanted to make it "absolutely clear" that his relationship with Wright had changed. He declared that Wright no longer represented him, his politics, his presidential campaign, or "the perspective of the black church."[189] The next day, an editorial in the *New York Times* described Obama's words as "the most forthright repudiation of an out-of-control supporter that we can remember."[190]

Before Obama announced for the presidency, Wright had known that his past statements and associations might cause the candidate "to publicly distance himself" from his pastor.[191] But when Obama finally broke with him, Wright criticized his former parishioner for choosing electability over loyalty. As late as Obama's inauguration, he still seemed angry, especially at what he called "arrogant, evil, and devious" journalists and at ABC News in general.[192] Some of his statements about Obama verged on personal attacks.

Following the rupture, Wright tended to stop commenting on Obama publicly. Once Obama was elected, he spoke more freely, and his public remarks became more supportive. "He was in my ministry for twenty years," Wright told interviewers prior to the inauguration. "We're the only . . . black church in the nation to produce a president. We're all proud."[193]

But the pastor who had converted, baptized, and married Barack Obama neither participated in nor attended the inauguration. He seems to have had no influence in his former parishioner's administration. As late as 2010, when an African American organization asked him for his aid in securing government assistance, he replied that "no one in the Obama administration will respond to me, listen to me, talk to me or read anything that I write to them. I am 'toxic.' . . . When Obama threw me under the bus, he threw me under the bus literally."[194] As of the writing of this book, the two men no longer associate.

Barack Obama is more intellectual and reticent than many of his predecessors. Thus his inner religious life requires more inference and reconstruction from outside sources. Excerpts from the sermons Wright preached at Trinity Church almost lost Obama the presidential election. How should American voters and the press have reacted to Wright's sermons? What do they say about the interpretation of Christianity that Obama accepted in his twenty-seventh year?

Anyone seeking impartiality needs to see the Chicago minister's preaching in a historical context. Wright's sermons emerge from a long tradition of Christian preaching that "mixes social commentary, scriptural citations, and political activism."[195] Today, mainstream Protestant and Roman Catholic clergy as well as pastors in megachurches embody this tradition.

In part, Wright's sermons borrow from the preaching patterns of other Protestant traditions. Delivered during the colonial period by Puritan clergy and magistrates, jeremiads voiced anguished concern that New England had fallen into moral apostasy. In these sermons, preachers claimed that God had sent epidemics, natural disasters, and devastating warfare with Indians as a punishment—in other words, God had damned America. In a typical jeremiad, the Puritan General Synod of Massachusetts declared in 1679 that the colony's "visible, manifest Evils" had provoked God to cause "War to be in the Gates, and cityes to be burnt up."[196]

Jeremiads were a ritual—a rhetorical experience intended to reinforce the values of the American Puritan community. It was something that the Puritans went through together and that reinforced their ideals and past history. In colonial New England, Puritan congregations did not necessarily receive such words as "God has damned New England" at face value.[197]

In modern Chicago, Wright's form of jeremiad was especially shaped by slavery. When separate black churches formed in the new republic, their ministers frequently warned that God would punish—that is, damn—the nation for supporting slavery. "Consider how hateful slavery is in the sight of that God, who hath destroyed kings and princes for their oppression of poor slaves," the founder of the African Methodist Episcopal Church declared in a jeremiad in 1794. "[God is] the protector and avenger of slaves."[198] In his Chicago church, Wright invoked God as the avenger of social injustice.

In addition, the sermons of the Chicago pastor also reflect Afrocentrism, the worldview that emphasizes the importance of Africa and African people in the development of civilization. Black clergy have long attempted to instill pride in parishioners about their ancestry and race—just as militants did in the "Black is Beautiful" movement of the 1960s. As early as the nineteenth century, black preachers forbade their congregations from singing hymns such as "Wash Me and I Shall Be Whiter Than Snow." "Quit singing that song and quit trying to be white," an African Methodist Episcopal bishop once told a conference. "The time has come when we must be proud that we are black."[199]

In Barack Obama's Chicago, nationalism and cultural pride characterize far more than just African American churches. Perhaps the most significant of the American immigration centers, Chicago once contained white

Roman Catholic, Eastern Orthodox, Lutheran, and other ethnic congregations within its bounds. At the corner of Halsted Street and Roosevelt Road, for example, Chicago residents could see ethnic churches of Bohemian, German, Irish, and Italian heritages. These and other ethnic Roman Catholic churches observed certain feast days celebrated in their homeland but unknown to Roman Catholics from other nations. They also adored specific national saints—Our Lady of Guadalupe, the Miraculous Virgin of Czestochowa, or the Infant of Prague—that parishes with other national ties did not. Christmas celebrations in Polish parishes, for example, differed markedly from Christmas celebrations in Italian American parishes.

Lutheran churches in Chicago displayed similar diversity. When German, Swedish, Norwegian, Danish, Finnish, Baltic, Hungarian, Slovakian, and other Lutheran congregations held services, each did its own nationalistic thing. They held services in the languages of their homelands well into the twentieth century. In keeping with native traditions, some Lutheran churches in Chicago had statues, ornate interiors, and ritualistic and formal worship. Others had brought across the Atlantic a simple revivalist tradition that emphasized a conversion experience.

Depending on ethnic background, some Lutheran pastors wore black preaching gowns; others wore white priestly gowns; a few wore elaborate vestments similar to those of a priest celebrating High Mass. Chicago's Latvian Lutheran pastors wore the ruff—a round, starched collar protruding some inches from the neck. Roman Catholics as well as Lutherans from ethnic neighborhoods who ventured into churches in another neighborhood often found the worship or practices strange, even eccentric. For these European immigrants, as for African American Christians, the use of a distinct language and heritage of worship preserved them from less desirable parts of American society.

Thus critics of Jeremiah Wright should take into account his sermons' roots in African American Christianity. He directed his homilies not to YouTube audiences but to black congregations.[200] During the controversy, at least one white journalist saw Wright's sermons in context. "The typical black church service," the editor of the New Republic wrote, "is not a Unitarian prayer meeting or Catholic devotions. It is something 'other' that many of us have not experienced and do not know. It is not ours but theirs."[201]

Many white clergy who admired Wright also saw his statements in context. "I'm distressed by white people, out of a very different religious, cultural, racial, theological/ecclesiastical experience presuming to judge African-American faith practices," the Reverend John Buchanan, pastor of Chicago's landmark Fourth Presbyterian Church, told his congregation following Wright's appearance before the press club. "Senator Obama's critics wonder," his sermon continued,

> how the senator could have remained in Wright's congregation and under his leadership for twenty years. The answer is that Wright didn't say "God Damn America" every Sunday. In fact, Wright's sermons were biblically based, relevant, literate, and eloquent, week after week.[202]

During the national controversy, the white president of Wright's denomination lamented the "caricature of a congregation that has been such a great blessing." He described Trinity Church as a place where "the worship is always inspiring, the welcome extravagant, and the preaching Biblically based and prophetically challenging."[203] Another white UCC pastor described Jeremiah Wright as "a man of gracious hospitality, humor, generosity, who paid attention to detail but also a man who does not call attention to himself," and he called Wright's church "everything a Christian community is supposed to be."[204]

But for many Americans, Jeremiah Wright appeared not only outspoken but also too identifiably African American for a postracial society. Like some nineteenth-century Irish American sermons that included denunciations of England, the excerpts from some of Wright's sermons were polarizing when removed from their parish setting. Even if their comments betrayed their unfamiliarity with African American preaching, his critics correctly deplored the excessive nature and sweeping inaccuracy of some of his statements.

To say, correctly, that the U.S. Public Health Service recruited four hundred syphilitic black sharecroppers from 1932 to 1972 and withheld penicillin from some as a means of proving that the drug cured the disease is one thing. To say, as Wright did, that the U.S. government placed AIDS (first identified in the early 1980s) in the African American community as a means of genocide is something else entirely. Similarly, to say (correctly) that Eurocentric historians have underestimated Africa's role in the spread of world civilization is one thing. But to say, as Wright has, that Egypt was the bedrock of Western civilization and that both the ancient Israelites and the inhabitants of kingdoms surrounding them descended from Africans is stunningly inaccurate. In its most exaggerated form, Afrocentrism represents an effort to restore—in the words of one scholar—"a past that never was."[205] Wright's assertions about African history have sometimes fallen into that category. Two of his biographers have lamented that his work and reputation have "been sullied by his dissemination of Afrocentrism and by his political demonization in the white media."[206]

"Passion born of difficulty does not always manifest itself in the kind of words with which we are most comfortable," says the white business executive who belongs to Trinity Church and was interviewed for this chapter.[207] In an op-ed, he asserted that he had heard his pastor preach about racial inequalities "many times, in unvarnished and passionate terms."[208] In an interview, he pointed out that "a sermon from a fiery African-American minister is a symphony of sorts—it has various movements."[209] He called it "very troubling that we have distilled Wright's thirty-five-year ministry to a few phrases, [with] no context whatsoever."[210] Americans, he asserted, should recognize "that the basic goodness of people like Jeremiah Wright is not always packaged conventionally."[211]

The most accurate assessment of Jeremiah Wright's downward spiral may come from Martin Marty of the University of Chicago. A leading American religious historian, Marty taught Wright at the University of Chicago. He not only knew Wright and his reputation among Chicago clergy but also had worshipped several times at Trinity Church. In an interview, he extolled Wright not only as a minister but also as a presence in the South Side. He then added, "But when the national spotlight fell on him, he began to lose it. And when he spoke before the National Press Club, he lost it, *big time*."[212]

Though Jeremiah Wright announced his retirement in February 2008, he continued to speak publicly. In retrospect, Barack Obama's longtime pastor was of course free to voice any opinion that reflected sentiments common in the black community. That they might differ from white perspectives was a nonissue. But his doing so—especially at the National Press Club—at the expense of a historic candidacy embraced by the same community was problematic and probably unwarranted. In this case, discretion for the sake of Obama's campaign probably should have trumped freedom of expression.

The 1960 presidential campaign, in which religion was also a volatile issue, offers a parallel. The controversy then centered on John F. Kennedy's Roman Catholicism. One slur during that campaign about Protestant "heretics," one bash at Martin Luther, or one Roman Catholic priest or bishop asserting that his church was the only true one could have tipped the election to Richard Nixon. But while the Roman Catholic clergy of the time took great care about what they said, Wright did not. His words before the National Press Club seemingly validated the brief sound bytes taken from his complex and lengthy forty- to sixty-minute sermons. "Just a guess," a columnist for an African American newspaper correctly noted after Wright's appearance, "but I am betting he did himself no favors."[213]

Because of the ruptured relationship with Wright, Obama entered the White House without a home church or pastor. Between the election and inauguration, his staff and friends unobtrusively visited churches in the Washington, D.C., area to find a new church for the Obama family. Reports soon circulated that his representatives had visited three Baptist churches and three Methodist churches.[214]

Obama's decision was complicated. His politics and his refusal to stress race during the campaign made an integrated church highly appropriate. Yet he had converted to Christianity in an African American church and found in such a church the community he long sought. Finally, his family might also desire to remain in an African American church.

Whatever church the Obamas selected needed to meet certain criteria. It had to satisfy the security requirements of the Secret Service. The church also needed to be accessible from the White House and to offer a Sunday school or youth ministry for Sasha and Malia. In addition, it needed adequate space to accommodate regular members, hosts of tourists, and a Secret Service detail—all of whom would be present whenever the Obamas attended church. Following his election, Obama repeatedly expressed his concern that members of any church the family joined would inevitably compete with visitors for seats in the pews.

Yet Obama's election to the presidency meant that he needed a less controversial minister than Jeremiah Wright. The national fervor over Wright's sermons taught Obama and his wife that "the church we attend can end up being interpreted as speaking for us at all times."[215] Finally, given his belief that the Judeo-Christian tradition requires a concern for poverty as well as his background in community organizing, the church Obama selected in Washington probably needed an outreach to the poor.

Throughout Obama's campaign for the presidency, religion, in the words of one writer, represented "a key part of his pitch"—something that set him apart from more secular Democrats.[216] Many of his campaign appearances began with prayer. He frequently cited Biblical phrases (especially Genesis 4:9, "I am my brother's keeper"). He often spoke in churches. During the Democratic primary in South Carolina, Obama's workers flooded churches with campaign literature headed by the phrase "COMMITTED CHRISTIAN." The literature included images of Obama at prayer. One Obama flier used during the primary declared that he had "accepted Jesus Christ into his life."[217] As a result of Obama's faith-based campaigning, the Democratic presidential campaign of 2008 was more reminiscent of those of William Jennings Bryan than of the campaigns of such recent party nominees as Michael Dukakis or John Kerry.

During the first month of Obama's presidency, most observers assumed that his family would join a historically black congregation in the District. But as the months passed, the president did not commit to a specific church. "How we handle church when we're here in D.C. is something we're still figuring out," he told an interviewer in July 2009, six months after entering the White House.[218]

The family did try out certain churches. Two days before inauguration day, the Obamas attended Nineteenth Street Baptist Church, the oldest African American church in the District. On the morning of the inauguration, the family attended a private service at St. John's Lafayette Square, the Episcopal church adjacent to the White House. Almost twelve weeks later, they again attended St. John's church, this time for Easter services.

On the weekends the president spent at Camp David, the Obama family attended Protestant services at Evergreen Chapel. When a national magazine announced in June 2009 that the Obamas had decided to make Evergreen Chapel their "church home—away from home," a White House spokesperson denied the story almost immediately.[219] But in a television interview in March 2010, Obama described the Camp David chapel as "probably our favorite place to worship because it's just family . . . [with] a wonderful chaplain."[220]

His preference for Camp David prompted a sardonic comment from a critical blogger: "Obama, like George W. Bush has . . . said he enjoys attending services at the chapel at Camp David. But, unlike Bush, he hasn't spent much time at Camp David since taking office."[221]

During his early months in office, Obama began to express a desire "to worship privately."[222] He participated in a regular prayer circle with pastors from across the nation. He received daily devotionals on his BlackBerry from the head of the White House's Office of Faith-Based and Neighborhood Partnerships. At various prayer breakfasts and in certain speeches, he spoke of his Christian faith. In his address to the graduating class at the University of Notre Dame in May 2009, for example, he spoke of "God's creation" and discussed the "spiritual dimensions" of the debate over abortion. He referred to the good works and worship of Christian churches, through which "I was brought to Christ."

Toward the end of the address, he told the graduates that "it is beyond our capacity as human beings to know with certainty what God has planned for us or what He asks of us, and those of us who believe must trust that His wisdom is greater than our own." Above all, he spoke in South Bend of the

> law that we can be most certain of . . . that . . . exists in Christianity and Judaism, in Islam and Hinduism, in Buddhism and humanism, it is, of course, the Golden Rule—the call to treat one another as we wish to be treated.
> The call to love, to serve, to do what we can to make a difference.[223]

The commencement speech ended with a peroration that invoked God and contained sermonic overtones.

Obama did not attend services of worship during the Christmas holidays of 2009. But in mid-January 2010, on the Sunday prior to Martin Luther King Day, the family worshipped at Vermont Avenue Baptist Church, a congregation formed in 1866 by freedmen. Like King, Obama spoke from the church's pulpit. Three months later, on Easter Sunday 2010, the Obama family attended Allen Chapel African Methodist Episcopal Church in southeast Washington.

By June 2011, Obama had attended church in the District of Columbia slightly more than a half-dozen times. In August 2010, the Pew Research

Center released the results of a national survey about Obama's religious faith. Eighteen percent of the poll's respondents—a number almost double the number who held those views when he became president—believed that Obama was a Muslim. Forty-three percent of those surveyed did not know what Obama's religion was. Only 34 percent said that he was a Christian.

The Pew survey found that beliefs about Obama's religion corresponded closely to the views respondents held of his presidency. Americans who disapproved of his job performance were far more likely to view him as a Muslim. Yet many of the doubts about the president's Christian allegiance seemed to have stemmed not from his politics but from his failure to attend Christian churches.[224] "The president is, obviously, Christian," a White House press secretary responded to the Pew survey. "He prays every day. His faith is very important to him, but it's not something that's a topic of conversation every single day."[225] Still, the survey concerned Obama's staff. It also seems to have caused a temporary increase in Obama's church attendance and a clear rise in the references to Christianity embedded in his speeches.

In September 2010, one month after the poll became front-page news, the Obamas again attended St. John's Episcopal Church. On the last Sunday in December while visiting Hawaii, the president took his family to Christmas services in a Marine Corps chapel. Two days later, a journalist who had traveled with the presidential party to Hawaii wrote of the "steady rebirth . . . over the past three months in public expressions" of Obama's Christian faith. Although the president had gone to church only twice in the months since the poll was released, she noted, he had "publicly mentioned his faith more often" during those months "than he did throughout the past year." The writer also cited the increase in Obama's use in speeches of biblical passages.[226]

By the time this book went to press in 2011, the Obamas had still not joined a church. The principal reason the president has given for his lack of church attendance has been the disruption that a presidential visit causes at services of worship. "We've decided for now not to join a single church," he told an interviewer in 2010. "Michelle and I have realized we are very disruptive to services."[227]

Eight postwar presidents attended District of Columbia churches with some regularity while living in the White House.[228] All of these churches were largely white in membership. Both their congregations and the presidents adapted to the new conditions of worship. "I attended Foundry Methodist church in the last months of President Clinton's attendance there," a Washington journalist declared:

> Because of his presence, there were Secret Service agents, metal detectors, police on the streets, snipers on neighboring buildings. Sometimes even a helicopter would be circling above.
>
> But after the first couple of times, it all became very routine. You forgot that the president was there until you saw him walk out with the pastor. You'd look up at some point and see him and think, 'Oh, there's the President.' It was not a spectacle. . . . The president can go for a hamburger any time he wants, so it's not out of line to expect that he could go to church any time he wants.[229]

Obama's concerns about causing a spectacle should not be quickly dismissed. As the nation's first black president, he tends to attract even more attention than his white predecessors. The atmosphere he has experienced while attending services of worship would daunt most people. Even at sedate St. John's Church, where the historic Episcopal liturgy in no way focuses on him, not only visitors—but also regular parishioners—have taken photos of the Obama family on their cell phones or digital cameras as they passed the presidential pew on their way to communion. Most worshipers would find such an experience unsettling.

A description of the presidential family's visit to Allen Chapel African Methodist Episcopal Church on April 4, 2010, gives a sense of what Obama means when he speaks of being "disruptive":

> A crowd began to form . . . just before 3:30 A.M. . . . First came the men wearing suits and the women in high heels, followed a few hours later by 30 police officers who barricaded nearby roads. Then came the Secret Service, the news helicopters, the city politicians and the bomb-sniffing dogs. . . . Hundreds of onlookers lined the streets. . . .
>
> As Obama worshipped with 700 others for two hours, the parishioners and preachers made him a focal point of the service. . . . Allen Chapel seemed temporarily transformed. . . . Two metal detectors guarded the

entrance . . . a tent had been erected behind the building. . . . Parishioners entered the service an hour early. Then a fire marshal blocked the entrance, leaving several hundred people lingering outside. . . .

Few who sat behind Obama looked. . . . relaxed. Two Secret Service officers occupied the pew behind the first family and acted as a moving shield, standing when they stood, swaying when the Obamas swayed, sitting when they sat. . . . Secret Service agents . . . kept lookout from the church balcony. Some parishioners held cellphone cameras above their heads . . . .

Most speakers . . . focused . . . on Obama's attendance. [Michael E.] Bell, the pastor, called him "the most intelligent, most anointed, most charismatic president this country has ever seen. . . ." But Obama never responded to the attention. . . . His first significant movement came at the end of the service, when he walked to the [Communion rail] to kneel and take Communion with his family. . . .

"Mr. President, we know you are going to do great for this country," said Bishop Adam J. Richardson. . . . Obama nodded and walked out. . . . A few minutes later, the congregation filtered out. . . . The tent . . . had been disassembled. The Secret Service had left. Police had taken down barricades and reopened the streets. . . . Several dozen parishioners lingered outside, sharing their hazy digital photos of Obama and talking about what his visit had meant.[230]

The Obamas had a similar experience when they attended Metropolitan African Methodist Episcopal Church with their daughters in January 2011. Located a few blocks from the White House, the historic church calls itself "The National Cathedral of African Methodism." Both in 1993 and 1997, President Clinton held inaugural prayer services in the church.

During this service on Martin Luther King Jr. Sunday, the associate pastor spoke to Michelle Obama directly and invited her and the president to join the church. Because the first lady was turning forty-seven the next day, the congregation sang "Happy Birthday." As a gift, they gave Michelle a CD of church hymns. Preaching from his historic pulpit, the pastor compared Martin Luther King Jr., Rosa Parks, and Obama. "You will get weak and tired at times," he said directly to Obama, "but God has singled you out."

Two reporters who attended the service wrote that "the Metropolitan congregation clearly tried to make the Obamas feel at home." Their words may have been unintentionally ironic, in that virtually without exception presidents have not wanted churches to take notice of their attendance or to change their services because they were present.[231]

Church attendance confronts Barack Obama with a dilemma. During the presidential campaign, he did not hide his Christian beliefs. Faith played a prominent role. He has said that he turns to his Christian faith for guidance as president. Thus the nation seems to have expected him to attend church while in office. Yet more than two years after he was inaugurated, it has become something close to national news when the president of the United States goes to church.

Initially, Obama seems to have intended to join an African American church in the District. After his inauguration, all of the first services he attended, except for nearby St. John's Episcopal Church, occurred in African American churches. But in such churches—some of which are located in neighborhoods where the unemployment rate exceeds 25 percent—the presence of a black president is a cause for celebration. As a result, these churches have welcomed Obama and focused their already exuberant services on him to such a degree that his concerns about being "disruptive" have proved true. White House insiders have indicated that Obama, like Truman before him, has been displeased with the circus-like atmosphere and the personal adulation his presence in a congregation has caused.

In the future, Obama may continue to feel a duty to affiliate with a largely black congregation. Obviously Evergreen Chapel is an attractive solution, but the Obamas spend relatively few weekends at Camp David.

If Obama increased his churchgoing and rotated his attendance among area churches, he might satisfy both himself and his critics. Based on his experiences at Trinity Church in Chicago, he knows the value of belonging to a specific congregation. In an interview six months after taking office, he declared that rotating attendance among churches "takes away somewhat from the church experience of being part of a community and participating in the life of the church." But, he continued, he and Michelle "are resigned now to the fact that we change the atmospherics wherever we go, and it may be more sensible for us to get in and out on any given Sunday and not try to create blockades around places where we attend."[233]

In the period since that interview, Obama seems not to have changed his view. Should he continue to attend church infrequently during the rest of his term and to reject church membership, he will do little to decrease the number of Americans who remain confused about his religion. "Part of the president's church-going problem," the editor-in-chief of Religion News Service comments, "is that people never see him going to church. They know he likes basketball because they see him playing basketball, and they know he likes taking the first lady on dates because they see him doing that, too. They don't know he goes to church because they never see him going to church."[234] If the American public continues to "never see him going to church," the identical questions that opponents raised in 2008 about Obama's true faith will therefore recur to some extent in the presidential campaign of 2012. Inevitably, they will not only cost him some votes but also will play into the hands of any opponent who may happen to be a practicing Jew or Christian.

In the more than two decades since Obama became a Christian, he has rarely been a regular church attender. Churchgoing is a habit, and Obama seems never quite to have acquired it. To be sure, as a candidate he took no oath to frequent weekly services of worship. "Theologically," a writer for the *Washington Monthly* correctly notes, "a person can be devout without regularly visiting houses of worship." Thus Obama's refusal to change his pattern of church attendance may signal a certain integrity and a concern about converting Christian worship into a circus. Yet in purely political terms, he should probably do more to show that he is a Christian.[235]

Barack Obama's life is a story of a journey. Until the age of forty-seven, he traveled much of the world, moving from Hawaii to Indonesia to Hawaii to California, then to New York, Chicago, and Washington. He left Occidental College for Columbia University, Harlem for Chicago's South Side, and the Illinois legislature for the U.S. Senate. More swiftly than expected, he left the U.S. Senate for the presidency. Although his early moves were imposed upon him, those during and after college sprang from his own choice.

This restlessness mirrors the restlessness of his maternal grandfather, who imposed move after move upon his family. Although Obama's maternal grandparents and especially his highly capable grandmother helped to shape him, his mother provided the principal influence on his life. A white anthropologist who moved from state to state as a child, she subsequently married in Hawaii. As an adult, she relocated from Hawaii to Indonesia and then to Honolulu before settling in Jakarta and dying in Hawaii. Her daughter has described her as "always a wanderer."

But that description fails to convey the depth and professional achievements of Ann Dunham Obama Sutoro.[236] Respected by anthropologists, government officials, and rural villagers alike, she acquired insights into Indonesian society possessed by few other Westerners in her time. Person after person who knew her confessed their indebtedness. A journalist of Hindu background, for example, declared that she taught him open-mindedness and the existence of shades of gray in life.[237] "She was cheerful, down to earth," Professor Dewey declared. "She absolutely was the kind of person you wanted on your side in any situation, from a bar room brawl to an academic argument, and she was always there for the little guy, particularly the little woman."[238]

As "the single constant" in their lives, she profoundly influenced her two biracial children. "We were not permitted to be rude, . . . to be mean, . . . to be arrogant," Maya told a writer. "[She was] sort of compelling us ever towards empathy and . . . not allowing us to be selfish. That was constant, steady, daily."[239]

Wishing her son to possess a sense of obligation to give something back to society, Ann worked hard to inculcate a belief in public service in him. Obama once humorously declared that she wanted him to be a combination of Einstein, Gandhi, and Harry Belafonte. "She lived by strong values, which she passed on to her children," her principal biographer writes. "She believed that people's lives could be made better, and that it was important to try. Directly or indirectly, she accomplished more toward that end than most of us will."[240]

In addition to being the story of a journey, Obama's life is also the story of a conversion. As a child, he rarely thought about religious matters. His family's deep distrust of organized religion bordered on the outright denial of any religious truth. If his story were a novel, it would speak of a young man who grows up in a secular skeptical family, experiences some spiritual diversity, reads the works of leading Christian theologians in college, and visits churches awash with faith in Harlem and in Chicago. He then hears a transforming sermon, discovers the power of faith in Jesus Christ, embraces Christianity as a significant force for political change, and finds in a Chicago church the community he has long been seeking. Thus Chicago—not Jakarta or Honolulu—is the city from which his spiritual roots ultimately derive.

If, as one of his close friends said, John F. Kennedy "traveled in that speculative area where doubt lives," so has Barack Obama.[241] The questioning background in which his mother reared him, coupled with his intellectual orientation, has caused doubt to play a role in his beliefs even after his conversion. His decision to become a Christian "came about as a choice and not an epiphany," he writes in *Audacity*. "The questions I had did not magically disappear."[242]

As president, Obama has displayed little of the churchgoing impulse typical of an African American Christian. But Americans would be wise not to question his Christian orientation. He has walked down the aisle of a church to commit his life to Jesus, he has been baptized, and he has publicly expressed his belief in God and in Jesus Christ as Lord and Savior. He has declared that "the gospel of Jesus [is] a gospel on which I base my life."[243] He has also joined a church and maintained a close relationship with its pastor. He has read the Bible regularly. He has expressed a belief in the Kingdom of God and in the second coming of Jesus.[244] Obama, one of his religious advisers declares, takes seriously the biblical passages that deal with the obligation of Jews and Christians to alleviate poverty. The president believes, the adviser asserts, in "taking God's words and extending them beyond the four walls of the church."[245]

Asked during the campaign if he prayed, Obama answered: "Yes, I do. Yeah, every day." Declaring that he prayed before making important decisions, he said he prayed above all for

> forgiveness for my sins and flaws, which are many, the protection of my
> family, and that I am carrying out God's will, . . . not in a grandiose way,
> but simply that . . . an alignment [exists] between my actions and what He
> would want. And then I find myself sometimes praying for people who
> need a lift, need a hand.[246]

The historian Ira Berlin views African American history as a story of four journeys: from the west coast of Africa to the East Coast of America, from the southeastern coast to the Deep South, from the rural south to the industrialized northern cities, and, most recently, from the black-majority nations of the world to the United States.[247] During the first two journeys, African Americans embraced the Christian faith.

On his father's side, Barack Obama springs from the fourth migration. When he entered politics, some black opponents challenged both his Christian and his African American credentials. But the flood of support Obama received as a presidential candidate showed that most African Americans had no such qualms. On election night, on the Sunday following the election and on inauguration day, black churches across the nation held special services and sermons. African American neighborhoods, that is, celebrated. "Black history was being made," as one writer put it, "and they knew it."[248]

Some Americans still believe Obama holds his father's and stepfather's ancestral faith; others suspect he maintains his mother's and grandparents' skepticism. But those close to the president disagree. "The man has been a Christian for twenty years," his sister asserts.[249] "Obama genuinely comes out of the social justice wing of the church," says a black pastor who has followed Obama's career closely. "That's real. The community organizing stuff is real."[250] The University of Chicago church historian Martin Marty, who has observed Obama's career from its start, simply says, "He is unassailably Christian."

The twelve post–World War II presidents fall into four distinct patterns in their church attendance. Throughout their lives, six—Truman, Ford, Carter, the two Bushes, and Clinton—went to church frequently. Three—Eisenhower, Johnson, and Reagan—attended church regularly for one part of their lives and rarely attended during other times. Two more—Kennedy and Nixon—seem to have been inwardly skeptical of central Christian teachings but nevertheless maintained a fairly regular church attendance for political reasons. The sole recent president who was raised under secular humanist influences and came to Christianity as a grown man, Barack Obama, seems so far to be the most like his fellow Illinoisan, Abraham Lincoln, in his view of church attendance.

# NOTES

## Harry S. Truman

1. Since Protestant denominations often experienced divisions among themselves, the survey included several kinds of Baptists, Methodists, Presbyterians, and other denominations. The Mormons, for example, had three separate groups in Independence. The Independence-based Reorganized Church (which followed the leadership of Joseph Smith's son) reported 1,008 members, whereas one of its schisms (the "Hedrickites") counted only 15 members. In 1907 only eight members of the dominant Utah branch of Mormonism (the "Brighamites") lived in Independence.

2. Harry S. Truman, *Mr. Citizen* (New York: Bernard Geis, 1960), 128.

3. "Our History," www.fbcgrandview.org, accessed 20 May 2008.

4. Robert H. Ferrell, ed., *The Autobiography of Harry S. Truman* (Boulder: Colorado Associated University Press, 1980), 33.

5. Truman, *Mr. Citizen*, 128.

6. Meyer Berger, "Mother Truman: Portrait of a Rebel," *New York Times Sunday Magazine*, 23 June 1946, 54.

7. Ferrell, *Autobiography of Harry S. Truman*, 127.

8. Doug Weaver, "Baptists and Presidential Elections: Harry Truman," *Baptist Studies Bulletin* 7, no. 2 (February 2008). Available from http://www.centerforbaptiststudies .org/bulletin/2008/february.htm, accessed 21 May 2008.

9. Mary Ethyl Noland, interview by James R. Fuchs, 16 September 1965, Independence, Missouri, Harry S. Truman Library and Museum. Available from http://www .trumanlibrary.org/oralhist/noland3.htm, accessed 21 May 2008.

10. Alonzo L. Hamby, "The Mind and Character of Harry S. Truman," in *The Truman Presidency*, ed. Michael J. Lacey (Cambridge: Cambridge University Press and Woodrow Wilson International Center for Scholars, 1989), 21–22.

11. Harry S. Truman, *Memoirs*, vol. 1, *Year of Decisions* (Garden City, N.Y.: Doubleday, 1955), 116.

12. Harry Truman to Bess Wallace Truman, 22 June 1936, in Robert H. Ferrell, ed., *Dear Bess: The Letters from Harry to Bess Truman, 1910–1959* (New York: W. W. Norton, 1983), 268.

13. William Hillman, *Mr. President* (New York: Farrar, Straus and Young, 1952), 190, 217.

14. Ibid., 84–85.

15. William E. Pemberton, *Harry S. Truman: Fair Dealer and Cold Warrior* (Boston: Twayne, 1989), 11–12.

16. Alan Axelrod, *When the Buck Stops with You: Harry S. Truman on Leadership* (New York: Portfolio, 2004), 266.

17. "Here's Why," *Time*, 26 November 1945. Available from http://www.time.com /time/magazine/article/0,9171,776390,00.html, accessed 10 May 2008.

18. Harry S. Truman to Edward H. Pruden, 26 November 1950, Truman Library. Pruden was the minister of the First Baptist Church of Washington, D.C.

19. Welbern Bowman, interview by Niel Johnson, 4 February 1981, Grandview, Missouri. Available from http://www.trumanlibrary.org/oralhist/bowmanw.htm, accessed 10 May 2008.

20. Harry Truman to his mother and sister, 21 October 1945, in Monte M. Poen, ed., *Letters Home* (New York: Putnam, 1984), 200.

21. Richard S. Kirkendall, "Faith and Foreign Policy: An Exploration into the Mind of Harry Truman," *Missouri Historical Review* 102, no. 4 (July 2008): 218.

22. Harry S. Truman and Robert H. Ferrell, *Off The Record: The Private Papers of Harry S. Truman* (New York: Harper & Row, 1980), 123.

23. A good study of Truman's relationship with Graham appears in the early pages of Nancy Gibbs and Michael Duffy, *The Preacher and the Presidents* (New York: Center Street, 2007).

24. From Truman's diary, 8 February 1948, as quoted in Hillman, *Mr. President*, 134.

25. Transcript, Edward H. Pruden Oral History Interview, 17 February 1971, 3, Truman Library.

26. Edward H. Pruden, *A Window on Washington* (New York: Vantage Press, 1976), 48–50.

27. Kirkendall, "Faith and Foreign Policy," 219.

28. Welbern Bowman, interview by Niel Johnson, 4 February 1981, Grandview, Missouri. Available from http://www.trumanlibrary.org/oralhist/bowmanw.htm, accessed 10 May 2008.

29. Telephone interview of Faye Wood by author, 21 May 2008.

30. Margaret Truman, *Bess W. Truman* (New York: Macmillan, 1986), 5.

31. Margot Ford McMillan and Heather Roberson, *Into the Spotlight: Four Missouri Women* (Columbia: University of Missouri Press, 1994), 98.

32. Truman, *Bess W. Truman*, 5.

33. Ibid., 163.

34. Ibid.

35. Ibid.

36. Patric Hutton, interview by Andrew Dunar, 31 August 1989, Kansas City, Missouri, Oral History #1989–12, Harry S. Truman National Historic Site, Independence, Missouri.

37. Alice Gross, interview by Jim Williams, 16 August 1991, Independence, Missouri, Oral History #1991–21, Harry S. Truman National Historic Site, Independence, Missouri.

38. Kirkendall, "Faith and Foreign Policy," 216.

39. Robert H. Ferrell, *Truman and Pendergast* (Columbia: University of Missouri Press, 1999), 7.

40. Donald R. McCoy, *The Presidency of Harry S. Truman* (Lawrence: University Press of Kansas, 1984), 4.

41. Harry L. Abbott, interview by Niel M. Johnson, 4 April 1990, Independence, Missouri, Harry S. Truman Library and Museum. Available from http://www.trumanlibrary .org/oralhist/abbott.htm, accessed 20 May 2008.

42. Alistair Cooke, "Harry S. Truman—A Study in Failure," *The Guardian*, 1 November 1948.

43. Ibid.

44. Henry P. Chiles, interview by J. R. Fuchs, 14 August 1962, Independence, Missouri, Harry S. Truman Library and Museum. Available from http://www.trumanlibrary.org /oralhist/chilesh.htm, accessed 20 May 2008.

45. David McCullough, *Truman* (New York: Simon & Schuster, 1992), 336.

46. Kirkendall, "Faith and Foreign Policy," 217.

47. Harry S. Truman to Bess Wallace, 31 July 1918, in Ferrell, *Dear Bess*, 268.

48. McCullough, *Truman*, 108, 436.

49. Kirkendall, "Faith and Foreign Policy," 223.

50. Harry S. Truman to Art Ulseth, 26 October 1960, Religion Folder, Truman Library Vertical Files, Harry S. Truman Library and Museum, Independence, Missouri.

51. Harry Truman to Bess Wallace Truman, October 16, 1939, in Ferrell, *Dear Bess*, 425.

52. Harry S. Truman to Margaret Truman, 12 June 1951, Harry S. Truman Library and Museum, Independence, Missouri.

53. Ralph E. Weber, ed., *Talking with Harry: Candid Conversations with President Harry S. Truman* (Wilmington, Del.: Scholarly Resources, 2001), 153–54.

54. Truman, *Mr. Citizen*, 128.

55. Robert H. Ferrell, ed., *Off the Record: The Private Writings of Harry S. Truman* (Columbia: University of Missouri Press, 1997), 40–41.

56. Winston S. Churchill, *The Second World War: Triumph and Tragedy* (New York: Bantam Books, 1962), 546.

57. Samuel McCrea Cavert to Harry S. Truman, 9 August 1945, and Harry S. Truman to Samuel McCrea Cavert, 11 August 1945, Miscellaneous (April–October 1945) folder, Box 1527, Collection WHCF: OF 692-A, Truman Library and Museum, Independence, Missouri.

58. Michael Beschloss, *Presidential Courage: Brave Leaders and How They Changed America, 1789–1989* (New York: Simon & Schuster, 2007), 198–99.

59. Ibid., 286–87.

60. Alfred Steinberg, *The Man from Missouri: The Life and Times of Harry S. Truman* (New York: Putnam, 1962), 308.

61. Quoted in Beschloss, *Presidential Courage*, 200.

62. Michael T. Benson, *Harry S. Truman and the Founding of Israel* (Westport, Conn.: Praeger, 1997).

63. Harry S. Truman diary, 1 June 1945, Truman Library. Other sources list the statement as appearing in a private memorandum or a letter written by Truman on the same date.

64. John Morton Blum, ed., *The Price of Vision: The Diary of Henry A. Wallace, 1942–1946* (Boston: Houghton-Mifflin, 1973), 607.

65. Harry S. Truman to Congressman Arthur G. Klein, 5 May 1948, Truman Library.

66. Harry S. Truman diary, 21 July 1947, Truman Library.

67. All quotations from Monty Noam Penkower, "The Venting of Presidential Spleen: Harry S. Truman's Jewish Problem," *Jewish Quarterly Review* 94, no. 4 (Fall 2004): 615–24.

68. Benson, *Harry S. Truman and the Founding of Israel*, 9.

69. McCullough, *Truman*, 597.

70. Public Papers of the President, 241. Address to the Washington Pilgrimage of American Churchmen, Truman Library.

71. "Army Lays Intricate Plans for a Presidential Funeral," *New York Times*, 28 December 1972.

72. "Truman's Body Lies in State in His Library," *New York Times*, 28 December 1972.

73. "The World of Harry Truman," *Time*, 8 January 1973.

74. "Truman Buried in Presidential Library Courtyard," *New York Times*, 29 December 1972.

75. Truman statement, 15 August 1950, found on Truman Library Web site, as introduction to his daily prayer. Available from http://www.trumanlibrary.org/kids/prayer .htm, accessed 18 January 2011.

76. Quoted in Martin Marty, *Modern American Religion* (Chicago: University of Chicago Press, 1996), 181.

77. Quoted in Hillman, *Mr. President*, 11.

78. Truman, *Memoirs*, 19.

79. Harry S. Truman, First Speech to Congress, 16 April 1945. Available from http://millercenter.org/scripps/archive/speeches/detail/3339, accessed 10 November 2009.

80. Harry S. Truman to Bess Wallace, 7 February 1911, in Ferrell, *Dear Bess*, 22.

81. Harry S. Truman to Bess Wallace, 19 March 1911, in Ferrell, *Dear Bess*, 24–25.

82. Harry S. Truman to Bess Wallace, 19 March 1911, "Correspondence from Harry S. Truman to Bess Wallace Truman, 1910–1959," Collection HST-FBP: Harry S. Truman

Papers Pertaining to Family, Business and Personal Affairs, 1876–1959, Harry S. Truman Library and Museum, Independence, Missouri.

83. Truman, *Memoirs*, 128.

84. Cooke, "Harry S. Truman."

85. James Reston, "President and Dewey Spar with Well-Padded Cliches," *New York Times*, 19 October 1948.

86. Harry S. Truman, Special Message to the Congress on Greece and Turkey: The Truman Doctrine, 12 March 1947. Available from http://www.trumanlibrary.org/publicpapers/index.php?pid=2189&st=&st1=, accessed 21 January 2011.

87. D. Clayton James, *The Years of MacArthur: Triumph and Disaster, 1945–1964* (Boston: Houghton Mifflin, 1985), 590.

88. Harry S. Truman, Navy Day Address, 27 October 1945. Available from http://millercenter.org/scripps/archive/speeches/detail/3342, accessed 21 January 2011.

89. Kirkendall, "Faith and Foreign Policy," 221.

90. Charles McMoran and Wilson Moran, *Churchill: The Struggle for Survival, 1940–1965* (Boston: Houghton Mifflin, 1966), 303.

91. McCullough, *Truman*, 1042.

92. Ibid., 992.

## Dwight D. Eisenhower

1. Gerald Bergman, "The Influence of Religion on President Eisenhower's Upbringing," *Journal of American and Comparative Cultures* 23, no. 4 (Winter 2000): 95–96. Bergman's article contains an abundance of information about Eisenhower's family and religious belief. At times, however, it is marred by questions of accuracy and documentation.

2. The name was anglicized from Eisenhauer in the eighteenth century.

3. Geoffrey Perret, *Eisenhower* (New York: Random House, 1999), 9.

4. Robert F. Burk, *Dwight D. Eisenhower: Hero and Politician* (Boston: Twayne, 1986), 7.

5. Quoted in Stephen E. Ambrose, *Eisenhower* (New York: Simon & Schuster, 1983), 21. Original source in Bela Kornitzer, *The Great American Heritage* (New York: Farrar, Straus, and Cudahy, 1955), 32.

6. Perret, *Eisenhower*, 11.

7. Matthew F. Holland, *Eisenhower between the Wars: The Making of a General and Statesman* (Westport, Conn.: Praeger, 2001), 29.

8. Stephen E. Ambrose and Richard H. Immerman, *Milton S. Eisenhower* (Baltimore: Johns Hopkins University Press, 1983), 11.

9. Carlos D'Este, *Eisenhower: A Soldier's Life* (New York: Henry Holt, 2002), 47.

10. Earl Eisenhower, "Dwight Finds His Future," *Sydney Morning Herald*, 22 July 1954; news release, "Front Porch Chat with Earl Eisenhower Jr.," Dwight D. Eisenhower

Library Archives, 23 August 2005. Available from http://eisenhower.archives.gov, accessed 3 June 2009.

11. Jerry Bergman, "Why President Eisenhower Hid His Jehovah's Witness Upbringing." Available from http://www.seanet.com/~raines/eisenhower.html, accessed 3 June 2009.

12. Bela Kornitzer, *The Great American Heritage*, 15–16.

13. Ibid., 16.

14. Bergman, "Why President Eisenhower Hid His Jehovah's Witness Upbringing."

15. Ibid.

16. Dwight Eisenhower's grandson, David Eisenhower, discusses the career of Abraham Eisenhower in *Eisenhower at War, 1943–1945* (New York: Random House, 1986), 201–2.

17. Dwight D. Eisenhower, *At Ease: Stories I Tell to Friends* (Garden City, N.Y.: Doubleday, 1967), 305.

18. Kornitzer, *The Great American Heritage*, 20.

19. Merle Miller, *Ike the Soldier: As They Knew Him* (New York: Putnam's Sons, 1987), 79.

20. Craig Allen, "Peace, Prosperity and Prime Time TV: Eisenhower, Stevenson and the Television Politics of 1956," PhD diss., Ohio University, 1989, 236.

21. Eisenhower, *At Ease: Stories I Tell to Friends*, 305.

22. David Lester, *Ike and Mamie: The Story of the General and His Lady* (New York: Putnam, 1981), 251.

23. Ambrose and Immerman, *Milton S. Eisenhower*, 13.

24. James Golden, email message to author, 30 December 2009.

25. Quoted in Susan Eisenhower, *Mrs. Ike* (New York: Farrar, Straus, and Giroux, 1996), 10.

26. Marilyn Irvin Holt, *Mamie Doud Eisenhower: The General's First Lady* (Lawrence: University Press of Kansas, 2007), 116.

27. Eisenhower, *Mrs. Ike*, 4.

28. Holland, *Eisenhower between the Wars*, 28.

29. Gibbs and Duffy, *The Preacher and the Presidents*, 35.

30. Ira Chernus, *General Eisenhower: Ideology and Discourse* (East Lansing: Michigan State University Press, 2002), 331n19.

31. Allen, "Peace, Prosperity and Prime Time TV," 235.

32. Gary Scott Smith, *Faith and the Presidency* (New York: Oxford University Press, 2006), 223.

33. The quotation comes from an oral history of Clare Boothe Luce, quoted in Smith, *Faith and the Presidency*, 227.

34. Ibid.

35. "National Affairs: Homecoming," *Time*, 16 June 1952. Available from http://www .time.com/time/magazine/article/0,9171,859682-2,00.html, accessed 31 December 2009.

36. Martin Gilbert, *Winston S. Churchill*, vol. 8 (London: Heinemann, 1988), 1161.

37. "Heroes: MacArthur," *Time*, 10 April 1964.

38. General Dwight D. Eisenhower, "D-Day Message," June 6, 1944.

39. Allen, "Peace, Prosperity and Prime Time TV," 240.

40. Churchill, *My Early Life* (London: Thornton Butterworth, 1930), 127–28.

41. Peter G. Boyle, *Eisenhower* (New York: Pearson/Longman, 2005), 20. According to Susan Eisenhower, Mamie Eisenhower noted that Ike had returned from World War II "more serious, and though not a church-goer, much more spiritually inclined." Eisenhower, *Mrs. Ike*, 235.

42. Eisenhower Library, http://www.eisenhower.archives.gov/All_About_Ike /Speeches/1953%20Inaugural_Address.pdf., accessed 25 January 2011. Paragraphing added.

43. Allen, "Peace, Prosperity and Prime Time TV," 255.

44. Ibid., 261.

45. Ibid., 251.

46. Eisenhower Library, "1953 Presidential Inauguration." Available from http://www .eisenhower.archives.gov/all_about_ike/Presidential/1953Inaugural/1953_Inauguration .html, accessed 12 February 2010.

47. Oral history with Clare Boothe Luce, OH# 220, Columbia University Oral History Project, DDEPL, 8–14; Allen, "Peace, Prosperity and Prime Time TV," 237.

48. Oral history with Clare Boothe Luce, OH# 220, Columbia University Oral History Project, DDEPL, 8–14, 237.

49. Ibid.

50. Ibid., 238–39. When Eisenhower discussed church membership with Billy Graham during the presidential campaign, Graham specifically suggested several Presbyterian churches in Washington, including the National Presbyterian Church. Eisenhower to Cliff Roberts, 29 July 1952, in Louis Galambos et al., *The Papers of Dwight David Eisenhower*, vols. 12–13, NATO *and the Campaign of 1952* (Baltimore: Johns Hopkins University Press, 1989), 1284–85. Eisenhower also received a letter from his friend Cliff Roberts, chairman of the Augusta National Golf Club, saying that southern voters might be able to support a candidate that did not belong to a church.

51. "The President's Church Attendance—1956," Ann Whitman File, Eisenhower Library; Smith, *Faith and the Presidency*, 541n16.

52. "The President's Appointments," January–December 1957. Available online at http://www.eisenhower.archives.gov/Research/Digital_Documents/Digital_ Documents.html, accessed 28 May 2011.

53. Smith, *Faith and the Presidency*, 225.

54. "The Presidency: The Camp David Conference," *Time*, 5 October 1959. Available from http://www.time.com/time/magazine/article/0,9171,894236-2,00.html, accessed 31 December 2009.

55. Marshall E. Newton, "Eisenhower Views His Job as a Test," *New York Times*, 4 May 1948, quoted in Smith, *Faith and the Presidency*, 221.

56. James Penton, *Apocalypse Delayed: The Story of Jehovah's Witnesses* (Toronto: University of Toronto Press, 1997), 71. "Religion Is a Snare and a Racket" is the title of a lecture given by Joseph F. Rutherford, second president of what became the Jehovah's Witnesses.

57. Bergman, "Why President Eisenhower Hid His Jehovah's Witness Upbringing."

58. Allen, "Peace, Prosperity and Prime Time TV," 255.

59. Ira Chernus, *Apocalypse Management: Eisenhower and the Discourse of National Security* (Stanford: Stanford University Press, 2008), 241.

60. Allen, "Peace, Prosperity and Prime Time TV," 266 and 267n80.

61. Ira Chernus, *General Eisenhower*, 309n29.

62. Bergman, "The Influence of Religion on President Eisenhower's Upbringing," 97.

63. Ann Whitman to E. S. Whitman (n.d.) July 1953, Eisenhower Library.

64. Edwin Gaustad and Leigh Schmidt, *The Religious History of America* (San Francisco: Harper, 2002), 341; Mark A. Noll, *History of Christianity in the United States and Canada* (Grand Rapids, Mich.: W. B. Eerdmans, 1992), 347.

65. David Eisenhower with Julie Nixon Eisenhower, *Going Home to Glory: A Memoir of Life with Dwight D. Eisenhower, 1961–1969* (New York: Simon & Schuster, 2010), 108.

66. Bergman, "The Influence of Religion on President Eisenhower's Upbringing," 101.

67. Eisenhower, *Going Home to Glory*, 108–9.

68. Ibid., 107.

69. Ibid., 179.

70. Robert Wuthnow, *After Heaven: Spirituality in America since the 1950s* (Berkeley: University of California Press, 1998), 6–8.

71. Gallup Poll #539, 16 November 1954, Poll questions retrieved 25 January 2011 from Gallup Brain database.

72. Chernus, *Apocalypse Management*, 233; Samuel Lubell, *Revolt of the Moderates* (New York: Harper, 1956), 4.

73. Clifton E. Olmstead, *History of Religion in the United States* (Englewood Cliffs, N.J.: Prentice-Hall, 1960), 592.

74. Reinhold Niebuhr, interview by Mike Wallace, 27 April 1958. Available from http://speakingoffaith.publicradio.org/programs/niebuhr-rediscovered/wallace.shtml, accessed 12 February 2010.

75. Eisenhower, *Going Home to Glory*, 105–6.

76. Ibid., 106–7.

77. Ibid., 141.

78. Ibid.

79. Perret, *Eisenhower*, 607.

80. Michael Korda, *Ike: An American Hero* (New York: Harper, 2007), 723.

81. The dean was Francis Sayre, grandson of President Woodrow Wilson.

82. Quotation taken from Felix Belair Jr., "Eulogy by Nixon Calls Eisenhower Giant of His Time," *New York Times*, 31 March 1969, 1.

83. "Train Bearing Eisenhower's Body Heads for Kansas," *New York Times*, 1 April 1969, 31.

84. Interview with Vernon Walters in Perret, *Eisenhower*, 608.

# John F. Kennedy

1. Jim Bishop, *A Day in the Life of President Kennedy* (New York: Random House, 1964).

2. Kelly Whitmann, "Joseph P. Kennedy, Sr." Available from http://www.essortment .com/all/josephkennedys_ravv.htm, accessed 9 February 2009.

3. Edward Kennedy, *True Compass* (New York: Twelve, 2009), 56.

4. Ibid., 29, 56.

5. Lawrence Leamer, *The Kennedy Men: 1901–1963* (New York: William Morrow, 2001), 53.

6. Charles Spaulding, quoted in Nigel Hamilton, *JFK: Restless Youth* (New York: Random House, 1992), 510.

7. Christopher P. Anderson, *Jack and Jackie: Portrait of an American Marriage* (New York: William Morrow, 1996), 31. Arthur Krock, Box 8, Nigel Hamilton Oral History.

8. Kennedy ended the affair himself, leaving Swanson with financial losses because of it. Her third husband (she was married six times) divorced her because of the affair.

9. Kennedy, *True Compass*, 479.

10. Doris Kearns Goodwin, *The Fitzgeralds and the Kennedys: An American Saga* (New York: St. Martin's Griffin, 1991), 144.

11. Rose Fitzgerald Kennedy, *Times to Remember* (Garden City, N.Y.: Doubleday, 1974), 520–21.

12. Ted Schwarz, *Joseph P. Kennedy: The Mogul, the Mob, the Statesman, and the Making of an American Myth* (Hoboken, N.J.: John Wiley & Sons, 2003), 49.

13. Skeptics have attributed the honor to the family foundation's gift of $2.5 million a year earlier to a favorite church charity of Francis Cardinal Spellman of New York,

whose influence with the Vatican exceeded that of any other American archbishop. See Geoffrey Perret, *Jack: A Life Like No Other* (New York: Random House, 2001), 205.

14. Kennedy, *Times to Remember*, 521.

15. Thomas Maier, *The Kennedys: America's Emerald Kings* (New York: Basic Books, 2003), 255.

16. Interview with John White, quoted in Hamilton, *JFK*, 434.

17. For more about Kathleen Kennedy, see Lynne McTaggart, *Kathleen Kennedy: Her Life and Times* (Garden City, N.Y.: Dial Press, 1983).

18. Schwarz, *Joseph P. Kennedy*, 220.

19. Maier, *The Kennedys*, 306–7.

20. Sally Bedell Smith, *Grace and Power* (New York: Ballantine Books, 2006), 267.

21. Richard D. Mahoney, *Sons and Brothers: The Days of Jack and Bobby Kennedy* (New York: Arcade, 1999), 10.

22. Perret, *Jack*, 205.

23. Maier, *The Kennedys*, 539. George Cabot Lodge, son of the patrician Henry Cabot Lodge, was the Republican opponent.

24. Leamer, *The Kennedy Men*, 171–72.

25. Diary of John F. Kennedy, 1 July 1937 to 3 September 1937, John F. Kennedy Presidential Library and Museum, Boston, Massachusetts.

26. Michael O'Brien, *John F. Kennedy: A Biography* (New York: Thomas Dunne, 2005), 80.

27. Robert Dallek, *An Unfinished Life: John F. Kennedy, 1917–1963* (New York: Little, Brown, 2003), 59.

28. Quoted in Dallek, *An Unfinished Life*, 59. Dallek's footnote reads: "CBS transcribed interview in the JFKL audio-visual archive." Ibid., 723.

29. Ibid., 59.

30. Herbert S. Parmet, *Jack: The Struggles of John F. Kennedy* (New York: Dial Press, 1980), 31, 41–59.

31. Henry James, quoted in Hamilton, *JFK*, 357.

32. Ibid., 419.

33. Ibid. Italics added.

34. Ibid., 471.

35. Ibid., 474.

36. Interview with Frank Waldrop, in ibid., 440.

37. Dallek, *An Unfinished Life*, 84.

38. Goodwin, *Fitzgeralds and the Kennedys*, 635.

39. Ibid.

40. Hamilton, *JFK*, 406.

41. Jerry Blaine, *The Kennedy Detail* (New York: Simon and Schuster, 2010), 26.

42. Bedell Smith, *Grace and Power*, 128. Max Jacobson was the physician.

43. Ibid., 440.

44. Jan Pottker, *Janet and Jackie* (New York: St. Martin's Press, 2001), 79.

45. Bedell Smith, *Grace and Power*, 73, 514.

46. Ibid., 74.

47. Pottker, *Janet and Jackie*, 108, 204.

48. Blaine, *The Kennedy Detail*, 105.

49. Bedell Smith, *Grace and Power*, 512.

50. Jackie Kennedy to Harold Macmillan, 31 January 1964. Harold Macmillan Archive, Bodleian Library, Oxford University, quoted in Bedell Smith, *Grace and Power*, 37.

51. Jerry Blaine, email message to author, 11 June 2011.

52. Marion "Oatsie" Leiter, quoted in Bedell Smith, *Grace and Power*, 36–37.

53. Quoted in Donald Spoto, *Jacqueline Bouvier Kennedy Onassis: A Life* (New York: St. Martin's Press, 2000), 61.

54. J. Randy Taraborrelli, *Jackie, Ethel, Joan: Women of Camelot* (New York: Grand Central, 2000), 330.

55. Pottker, *Janet and Jackie*, 129–30.

56. The summary comes from James Hennesey, *American Catholics* (New York: Oxford University Press, 1983), 251–52. The words summarize the teachings of an influential work by Father John A. Ryan on public policy widely used as a textbook in Roman Catholic colleges and seminaries in the postwar period. As of 1960, this official Vatican policy on church and state was still operative in such Roman Catholic countries as Spain and Portugal.

57. John C. Bennett, "A Protestant Look at American Catholicism," *Christianity and Crisis*, August 1958.

58. Theodore C. Sorensen, *Kennedy* (New York: Harper & Row, 1965), 19.

59. "Remarks of Senator John F. Kennedy at American Society of Newspaper Editors," 21 April 1960. Transcription of speech in John F. Kennedy Pre-Presidential Papers at the John F. Kennedy Library and Museum, Boston, Massachusetts.

60. "Address of Senator John F. Kennedy to the Greater Houston Ministerial Association," John F. Kennedy Presidential Library and Museum. Available from http:// www.jfklibrary.org/Historical+Resources/Archives/Reference+Desk/Speeches/JFK /JFK+Pre-Pres/1960/Address+of+Senator+John+F.+Kennedy+to+the+Greater +Houston+Ministerial+Association.htm, accessed 15 June 2009.

61. Jerry Blaine, *The Kennedy Detail*, 17.

62. Bedell Smith, *Grace and Power*, xix.

63. Arthur M. Schlesinger Jr., *A Thousand Days: John F. Kennedy in the White House* (Boston: Houghton Mifflin, 1965), 207.

64. Blaine, *The Kennedy Detail*, 21.

65. Bedell Smith, *Grace and Power*, 192. Original source: Louchheim Journal, 22 December 1963, Katie S. Louchheim Papers, Library of Congress (1957–1963).

66. Bedell Smith, *Grace and Power*, 244. Originally found in Richard Kluger, *The Paper: The Life and Death of the New York Herald Tribune* (New York: Knopf, 1986), 629.

67. Bedell Smith, *Grace and Power*, 381.

68. Ibid., xxi.

69. Interview with Elizabeth Burton, quoted in Bedell Smith, *Grace and Power*, 149–50.

70. Hans Slomp, *European Politics into the Twenty-first Century* (Westport, Conn.: Praeger, 2000), 89.

71. Elaine Sciolino, "Questions Raised About a Code of Silence," *New York Times*, 17 May 2011.

72. "The Cardinal and Jackie," *Time*, 1 November 1968; Pottker, *Janet and Jackie*, 276. Similarly, Richard Nixon's home Quaker church discussed disfellowshiping him for his six years of support of the Vietnam War while president but ultimately decided against it. See H. Larry Ingle, "Milton Mayer, Quaker Hedgehog," *Quaker Theology* 8 (2003): n.p.

73. Helen Chavchavadze, quoted in Bedell Smith, *Grace and Power*, 170.

74. Ronald Kessler, *In the President's Secret Service* (New York: Crown, 2009), 11. The stories in this book of revelations of Secret Service agents are similar to those of the *National Enquirer*. Many of the stories do, however, expand upon what historians already know from many other sources. In the words of one reviewer, Seymour M. Hersh's 500-page *The Dark Side of Camelot* (Boston: Little Brown & Company, 1997) "holds up to the available light in strict chronological order just about every report, claim, rumor or telltale clue of . . . his numerous one-time, part-time, sometime and longtime sexual partners." See Thomas Powers, "The Sins of a President," *New York Times*, 30 November 1997. Thomas Reeves, *A Question of Character* (New York: Random House, Inc., 1997), contains similar accounts of Kennedy's affairs.

75. Kessler, *In the President's Secret Service*, 11.

76. Ibid., 12.

77. Ibid.

78. Charles Bartlett, quoted in Bedell Smith, *Grace and Power*, 170; Chuck Spalding, quoted in Leamer, *Kennedy Men*, 407.

79. Bedell Smith, *Grace and Power*, 426.

80. David Talbot, *Brothers: The Hidden History of the Kennedy Years* (Glencoe, Ill.: Free Press, 2007), 135. This book contains the account of Hoover's memos to the attorney general.

81. Gail Collins, "An Affair to Remember," *New York Times*, A21, 2 July 2009. The hotel was probably the luxurious Carlyle, where Kennedy usually stayed when in New York. See Blaine, *The Kennedy Detail*, 23–29.

82. Frank Stanton, quoted in Bedell Smith, *Grace and Power*, 193.

83. Agent Clint Hill, Foreword in Blaine, *The Kennedy Detail*, xvi.

84. Blaine, *The Kennedy Detail*, 15. See also Agent Clint Hill's identical assertions about the words "worthy of trust and confidence" in Blaine, xvi.

85. Kessler, *In the President's Secret Service*, 10–11.

86. "Off-the-record," Blaine writes, "meant no press, no motorcades, and minimal police presence . . . . To the Kennedy Detail agents, 'off-the-record' meant expect the unexpected." Blaine, *The Kennedy Detail*, 10; see also 26–31.

87. Blaine, *The Kennedy Detail*, 13. In Jerry Blaine, email message to author, 11 June 2011, Blaine indicated that four agents who had been offended by Kennedy's behavior appeared on television in the late 1990s in connection with Seymour Hersh's revelatory *The Dark Side of Camelot.*

88. Kessler, *In the President's Secret Service*, 10–11.

89. Bedell Smith, *Grace and Power*, 175.

90. Sorensen, *Kennedy*, 19.

91. Cushing, Richard Cardinal, "Typewritten Manuscript of Untitled Eulogy of John F. Kennedy n.d.," Cushing Records: Series II: Speeches and Sermons: Kennedy Family, Archives, Archdiocese of Boston, Box 38, Folder 18.

92. Kenneth P. O'Donnell and David F. Powers, *Johnny, We Hardly Knew Ye* (Boston: Little, Brown, 1972), 316.

93. See Robert Dallek and Terry Golway, *Let Every Nation Know: John F. Kennedy in His Own Words* (Naperville, Ill.: Sourcebooks, 2006), 39.

94. William V. Shannon, quoted in Maier, *The Kennedys*, 372.

95. Albert Menendez, *John F. Kennedy: Catholic and Humanist* (New York: Prometheus Books, 1979), 85.

96. Cushing, "Typewritten Manuscript of Untitled Eulogy."

97. Theodore Sorensen, quoted in Maier, *The Kennedys*, 307.

98. Hamilton, *JFK*, 187.

99. Jerry Blaine, email message to author, 11 June 2011.

100. Theodore Sorensen, *Counselor: A Life at the Edge of History* (New York: HarperCollins, 2008), 75; The description "intellectual bloodbank" comes from Matthew D'Ancona, "A World Bursting at the Seams," *The Spectator*, 11 April 2007. Available from http://www.spectator.co.uk/the-magazine/features/28994/part_6/a-world-bursting-at-the-seams.thtml, accessed 9 July 2009.

101. Bedell Smith, *Grace and Power*, 257.

102. Dallek and Golway, *Let Every Nation Know*, 38.

103. *Christian Century* editor Martin Marty, quoted in Lawrence H. Fuchs, *John F. Kennedy and American Catholicism* (New York: Meredith Press, 1967), 168.

104. O'Brien, *John F. Kennedy*, 421.

105. Sorensen, *Kennedy*, 19.

106. Lem Billings, quoted in Hamilton, *JFK*, 187.

107. Kennedy's close ties to his "Irish Mafia from Boston" are well-known, but Agent Blaine declares that Kennedy also exhibited a "special" or "immediate bond" with Secret Service agents of Roman Catholic background. See Blaine, *The Kennedy Detail*, 123, 161.

108. Sorensen, *Kennedy*, 19.

109. The Dogmatic Constitution on the Church, Nos. 20 and 25, Second Vatican Council, 21 November 1964.

110. Gretchen Rubin, *Forty Ways to Look at JFK* (New York: Ballantine Books, 2005), 107.

111. Ibid.

112. Ibid.

113. Sorensen, *Kennedy*, 19.

114. Cushing, "Typewritten Manuscript of Untitled Eulogy."

115. Hamilton, *JFK*, 187.

116. Sorensen, *Counselor*, 164.

117. Sorensen, *Kennedy*, 19.

118. Sorensen, *Counselor*, 164.

119. See Peter Collier and David Horowitz, *The Kennedys: An American Drama* (New York: Summit Books, 1984), 154; Richard Reeves, *President Kennedy: Profile of Power* (New York: Simon & Schuster, 1993), 232; John McCollister, *God and the Oval Office* (Nashville: W Publishing Group, 2005), 170.

120. Dallek, *An Unfinished Life*, 470.

121. Sorensen, *Kennedy*, 19.

122. Rubin, *Forty Ways to Look at JFK*, 107.

123. Perret, *Jack*, 280.

124. Sorensen, *Kennedy*, 19.

125. Jerry Blaine, email message to author, 11 June 2011.

126. Cushing, "Typewritten Manuscript of Untitled Eulogy."

127. Bedell Smith, *Grace and Power*, 356.

128. Hamilton, *JFK*, 187; Maier, *The Kennedys*, 308.

129. Hamilton, *JFK*, 187.

130. Joseph Gargan quoted in Maier, *The Kennedys*, 308.

131. Henry James, quoted in Hamilton, *JFK*, 357–58.

132. Sorensen, *Kennedy*, 19.

133. Dallek and Golway, *Let Every Nation Know*, 38.

134. Carl Sferrazza Anthony, *The Kennedy White House: Family Life and Pictures, 1961–1963* (New York: Simon & Schuster, 2001), 92.

135. Ralph G. Martin, *A Hero for Our Time* (New York: Macmillan, 1983), 472. Martin attributes the quotation to his interview with John Sharon.

136. Mark S. Massa, "A Catholic for President?: John F. Kennedy and the 'Secular' Theology of the Houston Speech, 1960," *Journal of Church and State*, 22 March 1997. Available from http://jcs.oxfordjournals.org/content/39/2/297.extract, accessed 25 March 2011.

137. Oswald had rejected Christianity and believed instead that "the best religion is Communism," according to Kerry Thornley. Quoted in Norman Mailer, *Oswald's Tale* (New York: Random House, 2007), 397.

138. Because of his history of serious illness, Kennedy received extreme unction (a sacrament that can be repeated) several times during his life.

139. David Mehegan quotes Bundy in his review of Sally Bedell Smith's *Grace and Power*. "All the President's Friends," *Boston Globe*, 14 June 2004; Bedell Smith, *Grace and Power*, 515.

## Lyndon Baines Johnson

1. John Bullion, *Lyndon B. Johnson and the Transformation of American Politics* (New York: Longman, 2007), 13.

2. Frank Cormier, *LBJ the Way He Was* (Garden City, N.Y.: Doubleday, 1977), 255–58.

3. Mrs. Johnson's words circulated in the Williamsburg community. Liz Carpenter, Lady Bird's press secretary, was at the service and confirmed the events at Bruton Parish in an interview in June 2008.

4. LBJ to M. H. Stryker, Mayor of Williamsburg, 15 November 1967, LBJ Library.

5. LBJ to Rev. Cotesworth P. Lewis, 18 November 1967, LBJ Library. Paragraphing added.

6. George Davis, interview by Dorothy Pierce McSweeney, 13 February 1969, University of Texas Oral History Project, LBJ Library.

7. The story is found in 1 Kings 22:8–28 and in Chronicles 18:7–27.

8. Charles Peters, *Lyndon B. Johnson* (New York: Times Books, 2010), 9.

9. LBJ quoted in ibid., 2.

10. George Reedy quoted in ibid., 3.

11. Eric F. Goldman, *The Tragedy of Lyndon Johnson* (New York: Alfred A. Knopf, 1969), 299; Ronnie Duggar, *The Politician* (New York: W. W. Norton, 1982), 76.

12. Robert A. Caro, *The Years of Lyndon Johnson: The Path to Power* (New York: Alfred A. Knopf, 1982), 91–92.

13. Robert Dallek, *Lone Star Rising: Lyndon Johnson and His Times, 1908–1960* (New York: Oxford University Press, 1998), 53.

14. Caro, *Years of Lyndon Johnson*, 91–92. Duggar, *Politician*, 87.

15. The plaque commemorating Johnson's baptism declares that it occurred either in the Pedernales River or in nearby Flat Creek.

16. Merle Miller, *Lyndon: An Oral Biography* (New York: G. P. Putnam's Sons, 1980), 24.

17. Duggar, *Politician*, 76.

18. Paul Conkin, *Big Daddy from the Pedernales: Lyndon Baines Johnson* (Boston: Twayne, 1986), 28.

19. Alfred Steinberg, *Sam Johnson's Boy: A Close-up of the President from Texas* (New York: Macmillan, 1968), 34.

20. "The White House: Three-Ring Wedding," *Time*, 5 August 1966. Available from http://www.time.com/time/magazine/article/0,9171,836134-2,00.html, accessed 24 January 2010.

21. Dallek, *Lone Star Rising*, 119; Marie D. Smith, *The President's Lady* (New York: Random House, 1964), 44–45.

22. Robert Caro, interviewed by "Weekend America," 4 March 2008. Available from http://weekendamerica.publicradio.org/display/web/2008/03/14/spitzer_lbj/, accessed 1 February 2011.

23. Claudia Alta Taylor Johnson, *A White House Diary* (New York: Holt, Rinehart and Winston, 1970), 254. Entry from 19 March 1965.

24. Liz Carpenter, interview by author, June 2008.

25. Conkin, *Big Daddy from the Pedernales*, 194.

26. Johnson, *A White House Diary*, 43. Entry from 12 January 1964.

27. Joseph A. Califano Jr., *The Triumph and Tragedy of Lyndon Johnson: The White House Years* (New York: Simon & Schuster, 1991), 334–35.

28. Quoted in Michael Davie, *LBJ: A Foreign Observer's Viewpoint* (New York: Ballantine Books, 1966), 69–73.

29. Cormier, *LBJ the Way He Was*, 121.

30. Hal K. Rothman, *LBJ's Texas White House: "Our Heart's Home"* (College Station: Texas A&M University Press, 2001), 100; Lady Bird Johnson, *A White House Diary*, 25; Cormier, *LBJ the Way He Was*, 255–58.

31. Interview with Wunibald Schneider, 26 July 1979, LBJ Library Oral History Collection.

32. Rothman, *LBJ's Texas White House*, 100.

33. Memo from Jim Jones to LBJ, 9 June 1967, LBJ Library, White House Central Files, Subject File, Box 1, "ExRM 9/24/66-." Jim Jones served as a White House aide during the Johnson administration.

34. Robert H. Gates, interview with the author, St. Barnabas Church, October 2006.

35. Davie, *LBJ*, 69–73.

36. Ibid., 70–73.

37. Cormier, *LBJ the Way He Was*, 255–58.

38. Johnson, *Diary*, 8. Entry from 24 November 1963.

39. Bert Cooper, Church Historian, St. Mark's Episcopal Church, Washington D.C., interview by author, October 2006.

40. Ibid.

41. Johnson, *Diary*, 354. Entry from 23 January 1966.

42. Ibid., 41–42. Entry from 12 January 1964.

43. Conkin, *Big Daddy from the Pedernales*, 29.

44. Johnson, *Diary*, 203. Entry from 15 November 1964. Paragraphing added.

45. Michael Beschloss, ed., *Reaching for Glory: Lyndon Johnson's Secret White House Tapes, 1964–1965* (New York: Simon & Schuster, 2001), 390; Johnson, *Diary*, 286, 293. Entries from 10 June 1965 and 2 July 1965.

46. Liz Carpenter, Lady Bird's press secretary, commented in a June 2008 interview with the author, "I got more questions from the press on Luci's conversion than on anything else."

47. "Baptism of Fire," *Time*, 16 July 1965.

48. Technically speaking, none of these baptisms were "rebaptisms," for Roman Catholicism and much of Protestantism held that baptism was an "Indelible Sacrament"—it could be administered only once. These baptisms such as Luci's were administered in case the first baptism had in some way been faulty.

49. "3 Clerics Back Pike's Criticism of Luci Johnson's 2d Baptism," *New York Times*, 5 July 1965; "Luci Calls Her Baptism 'A Personal Matter,'" *Washington Post*, 8 July 1965.

50. Johnson, *Diary*, 239. Entry from 8 February 1965.

51. Beschloss, *Reaching for Glory*, 390; "Baptism of Fire," *Time*.

52. "The White House: Three-Ring Wedding."

53. Ibid.

54. Califano, *Triumph and Tragedy of Lyndon Johnson*, 334–35.

55. Goldman, *Tragedy of Lyndon Johnson*, 299; Conkin, *Big Daddy from the Pedernales*, 194–96.

56. Luci Baines Johnson, foreword to Thomas W. Cowger and Sherwin J. Markman, eds., *Lyndon Johnson Remembered: An Intimate Portrait of a Presidency* (Lanham, Md.: Rowman & Littlefield, 2003), xix. Paragraphing added. One plane seems to have been lost in the raid.

57. White House memorandum, 28 December 1964, LBJ Library.

58. Jack Valenti, *A Very Human President* (New York: W. W. Norton, 1975), 17–18.

59. Liz Carpenter, interview by author, June 2008.

60. Cormier, *LBJ the Way He Was*, 255–58.

61. Ibid.

62. Ibid., 169, 173.

63. Quoted in Garry Wills, *Under God: Religion and American Politics* (New York: Simon & Schuster, 1990), 185.

64. Von Hardesty and Bob Schieffer, *Air Force One* (Chanhassen, Minn.: NorthWord Press, 2003), 94.

65. LBJ to R. H. Edwin Espy, National Council of the Churches of Christ, 20 January 1969, LBJ Library.

66. Letter from LBJ to C. Ray Akin, 2 June 1967, LBJ Library.

67. LBJ to Wunibald Schneider, 2 June 1967, LBJ Library, White House Central Files, Name File, Box 125, "Schneider, Wunibald (Reverend)."

68. Interview with George Dais, 13 February 1969, LBJ Library Oral History Collection.

69. Interview with Billy Graham, 12 October 1983, LBJ Library Oral History Collection.

70. W. Marvin Watson with Sherman Markman, *Chief of Staff: Lyndon Johnson and His Presidency* (New York: St. Martin's Press, 2004), 135.

71. Valenti, *A Very Human President,* 17–18.

72. Jack Shepherd and Christopher S. Wren, eds., *Quotations from Chairman LBJ* (New York: Simon & Schuster, 1968), 173–74.

73. Valenti, *A Very Human President*, 17–18.

74. Cormier, *LBJ the Way He Was*, 255–58.

75. LBJ to Billy Graham, 22 July 1964, LBJ Library; LBJ to Billy Graham, 6 July 1967, LBJ Library.

76. A typical letter from Graham to Johnson dealing with these issues is found in the LBJ Library, 30 June 1967. A good discussion of Graham's relationship with Johnson on these issues is found in Nancy Gibbs and Michael Duffy, *The Preacher and the Presidents* (New York: Center Street, 2007), 143–54.

77. Liz Carpenter, interview by author, June 2008.

78. Gibbs and Duffy, *Preacher and the Presidents*, 123. Graham also discusses the incident in his 12 October 1983 interview in the LBJ Library Oral History Collection.

79. Robert Dallek, *Flawed Giant: Lyndon Johnson and His Times, 1961–1973* (New York: Oxford University Press, 1998), 602.

80. Jan Jarboe Russell, *Lady Bird: A Biography of Mrs. Johnson* (New York: Scribner, 1999), 304–5.

81. Ibid.

82. Peters, *Lyndon B. Johnson*, 157, 155–58.

83. Ibid., 160.

84. Ibid., 161.

85. Sally Bedell Smith, *Grace and Power: The Private World of the Kennedy White House* (New York: Random House, 2004), 530.

86. Ibid., 139.

87. Clarke Newlon, *LBJ: The Man from Johnson City* (New York: Dodd, Mead, 1964), 113–14.

88. Doris Kearns Goodwin, *Lyndon Johnson and the American Dream* (New York: St. Martin's Press, 1976), 8.

89. Watson, *Chief of Staff*, 132.

90. Valenti, *A Very Human President*, 17–18.

91. "Protestants: A Worshipper in the White House," *Time*, 6 December 1968. Available from http://www.time.com/time/printout/0,8816,844670,00.html#, accessed 12 December 2009.

92. Cormier, *LBJ the Way He Was*, 255–58.

## Richard M. Nixon

1. Richard Nixon, *In the Arena: A Memoir of Victory, Defeat, and Renewal* (New York: Simon & Schuster, 1990), 88.

2. Larry Ingle, "Richard Nixon: Exemplary 20th Century Quaker," 21 May 2001. Available from http://www.pendlehill.org/Lectures%20and%20Writings/MNL May_21_2001.htm, accessed 2 June 2008.

3. Ibid.

4. Nixon, *In the Arena*, 89.

5. See Jonathan Aitken, *Nixon: A Life* (London: Weidenfeld and Nicholson, 1993), 43.

6. Aitken, *Nixon: A Life*, 33.

7. Margaret Macmillan, *Seize the Hour* (London: John Murray Publishers, 2006), 14–15.

8. Deborah Hart and Gerald S. Strober, *The Nixon Presidency: An Oral History of the Era* (Washington, D.C.: Brassey's, 2003), 38.

9. See Aitken, *Nixon: A Life*, 54; and Stephen E. Ambrose, *Nixon* (New York: Simon & Schuster, 1987), 57.

10. Lance Morrow, *The Best Years of Their Lives: Kennedy, Johnson, and Nixon in 1948: The Secrets of Power* (New York: Basic Books, 2005), 31. The debating coach was Mrs. Clifford Vincent.

11. Ambrose, *Nixon*, 57.

12. The Whittier High School reports that Nixon's transcript includes no class rank.

13. All quotations from John Sayle Watterson, *The Games Presidents Play: Sports and the Presidency* (Baltimore: Johns Hopkins University Press, 2006), 232.

14. Interview with Frank Gannon, 9 February 1983. Available from http://www.libs.uga.edu/media/collections/nixon/nixonday1.html, accessed 2 June 2008.

15. Ibid.

16. Interview with Frank Gannon. Seven years later, in his *In the Arena* (89), Nixon repeats his doubts about the physical resurrection of Jesus.

17. Aitken, *Nixon: A Life*, 55.

18. Ambrose, *Nixon*, 58; Aitken, *Nixon: A Life*, 57.

19. Nixon, *In the Arena*, 89.

20. Monica Crowley, *Nixon in Winter* (New York: Random House, 1998), 358.

21. *Encyclopedia of World Biography*, 2nd ed., s.v. "Nixon, Richard."

22. *American Weekly*, Box 4, "The Richard Nixons," Richard Nixon Library and Birthplace Foundation, Yorba Linda, California.

23. Greg Mitchell, *Tricky Dick and the Pink Lady* (New York: Random House, 2005), 170.

24. Quoted in Erwin F. Gellmen, *The Contender* (New York: Simon & Schuster, 2007), 270.

25. Quoted in Gellmen, *Contender*, 270.

26. Garry Wills, *Nixon Agonistes* (Boston: Houghton Mifflin, 1970).

27. Molly Ivins, "Nixon: Man and Record," *San Francisco Chronicle*, 27 April 1994.

28. "Senator Nixon's Checkers Speech." Full text available from http://www.watergate.info/nixon/checkers-speech.shtml, accessed 2 March 2010.

29. The speech gained its name because Nixon declared that he would never return Checkers, a cocker spaniel that a supporter had given to his two daughters. "And you know, the kids like all kids love the dog, and I just want to say this right now that regardless of what they say about it, we're gonna keep him."

30. Martin Weil and Eleanor Randolph, "Richard M. Nixon, 37th President, Dies," *Washington Post*, 23 April 1994.

31. "Transcript of Nixon's News Conference on His Defeat by Brown in Race for Governor of California," *New York Times*, 8 November 1962.

32. Statistics can be found at http://www.archives.gov/research/military/vietnam-war/casualty-statistics.html, accessed 23 February 2011.

33. Lewis B. Puller Jr., *Fortunate Son* (New York: Bantam Books, 1993), 192–212.

34. Richard G. Hutcheson Jr., *God in the White House: How Religion Has Changed the Modern Presidency* (New York: Macmillan, 1988), 83.

35. Randall E. King, "When Worlds Collide," *Journal of Church and State* 39, no. 2 (Spring 1997): 273–95.

36. Crowley, *Nixon in Winter*, 350–51.

37. King, "When Worlds Collide."

38. Michael Granberry, "The Western White House in San Clemente," *Los Angeles Times*, 27 April 1994. Available from http://articles.latimes.com/1994-04-27/news/ss-51101_1_la-casa-pacifica-western-white-house-watergate-tapes?pg=2, accessed 26 February 2010.

39. Gibbs and Duffy, *The Preacher and the Presidents*, 172.

40. William Martin, *With God on Our Side* (New York: Broadway Books, 1997), 41.

41. William Martin, *A Prophet with Honor: The Billy Graham Story* (New York: William Morrow, 1991), 356.

42. Martin, *Prophet with Honor*, 357.

43. Ibid.

44. Walter Isaacson, *Kissinger: A Biography* (New York: Simon & Schuster, 2005), 599.

45. Hutcheson, *God in the White House*, 83; "U.S. Reaction: The People Take It in Stride," *Time*, 19 August 1974. Available from http://www.time.com/time/magazine/article/0,9171,942984-4,00.html, accessed 15 June 2008.

46. Martin, *Prophet with Honor*, 435.

47. Ibid.

48. A certain amount of legerdemain is inevitably associated with the term "balanced budget."

49. Watterson, *Games Presidents Play*, 320.

50. Nixon gives his views of the Watergate scandal in such books as his *In the Arena*, 33–43. In his *Nixon: A Life*, Aitken attempts to challenge the "righteous certainty that Nixon got what he deserved" (467–528).

51. The girlfriend was Ola Florence Welch; the debating partner was Kenny Ball. Their memories as well as Aitken's assessment of the college-aged Nixon are found in Aitken, *Nixon: A Life*, 11–15.

52. Gibbs and Duffy, *Preacher and the Presidents*, 59. Eisenhower made the comment to his secretary.

53. Anthony Summers and Robbyn Swan, *The Arrogance of Power: The Secret World of Richard Nixon* (New York: Viking, 2000), 101.

54. R. W. Apple Jr., "The 37th President, Richard Nixon, 81, Dies," *New York Times*, 23 April 1994.

55. Ann Whitman, quoted in Gibbs and Duffy, *Preacher and the Presidents*, 59.

56. Hart and Strober, *Nixon Presidency*, 40.

57. Isaacson, *Kissinger: A Biography*, 599.

58. "Funeral Services of Mrs. Nixon," Richard Nixon Foundation. Available from http://www.nixonlibraryfoundation.org/index.php?src=gendocs&link=PNfuneral, accessed 24 July 2008.

59. Ibid.

60. D. Michael Lindsay, *Faith in the Halls of Power: How Evangelicals Joined the American Elite* (Oxford: Oxford University Press, 2007), 34–35.

61. Aitken, *Nixon: A Life*, 338.

62. Ibid.

63. Interview with Frank Gannon, 9 February 1983.

64. Aitken, *Nixon: A Life*, 55.

65. Ambrose, *Nixon*, 139.

66. Charles W. Colson, *Born Again* (Old Tappan, N.J.: Chosen Books, 1976), 45.

67. Ambrose, *Nixon*, 139.

68. Joe Gandelman, "Nixon Tape Release Further Soils Nixon's Soiled Reputation," *The Moderate Voice*, 11 December 2010. Available from http://themoderatevoice .com/94713/nixon-tape-release-further-soils-richard-nixons-soiled-reputation/.

69. Ambrose, *Nixon*, 139.

70. Weil and Randolph, "Richard M. Nixon, 37th President, Dies."

71. Ibid.

## Gerald R. Ford

1. Cannon Notes on Armbrister Interview, 1988–94, folder "Notes on the Armbrister Interviews (1–200)," Box 2, James M. Cannon, Gerald R. Ford Library, Ann Arbor Mich.

2. Ibid.

3. Gerald R. Ford, *A Time to Heal: The Autobiography of Gerald R. Ford* (New York: Harper and Row, 1979), 48. All biographies contain some material about Ford's mother's divorce. A brief but detailed account can be found in Robert A. Wilson, ed., *Character above All: Ten Presidents from FDR to George Bush* (New York: Simon & Schuster, 1995), 148.

4. Ford, *A Time to Heal*, 45.

5. Quoted in James Cannon, *Time and Chance: Gerald Ford's Appointment with History* (New York: HarperCollins, 1994), 47. Ford legally changed his name in 1935. His stepfather's middle name was originally spelled "Rudolff."

6. Ford, *A Time to Heal*, 46.

7. Nancy Gibbs and Michael Duffy, "The Other Born-Again President?" *Time*, 2 January 2007. Available from http://www.time.com/time/printout/0,8816,1573304,00 .html, accessed 31 December 2008.

8. Ford, *A Time to Heal*, 46.

9. Hutcheson, *God in the White House: How Religion Has Changed the Modern Presidency*, 92.

10. Bonnie Angelo, *First Mothers: The Women Who Shaped the Presidents* (New York: Morrow, 2000), 149.

11. Ford, *A Time to Heal*, 84.

12. Ibid., 51.

13. Watterson, *The Games Presidents Play*, 247.

14. Ford, *A Time to Heal*, 51. Watterson, *Games Presidents Play*, 247.

15. Cannon Notes on Armbrister Interview, 1988–94, folder "Notes on the Armbrister

Interviews (201–400)," Box 2, James M. Cannon, Gerald R. Ford Library; Watterson, *Games Presidents Play*, 248.

16. Ford, *A Time to Heal*, 57–59.

17. Ibid., 58.

18. Quoted in Cannon, *Time and Chance*, 40. Ford's mentor at the firm was Julian Amberg.

19. Cannon, *Time and Chance*, 51.

20. Ibid., 92–93, 102.

21. See letter from Gerald R. Ford to C. Leslie Glenn, 24 October 1974, folder "PP 13 8 Religious Affiliations," Box 199, White House Central Files, Gerald R. Ford Library.

22. James M. Cannon Notes, 1989–97, folder "Notes on Armbrister Interviews (pages 1501–1600)," Box 2, James M. Cannon, Gerald R. Ford Library.

23. James M. Cannon Notes, 1989–94, folder "Notes on Armbrister Interviews (pages 1501–1600)," Box 2, James M. Cannon, Gerald R. Ford Library.

24. Marjorie Hyer, "Episcopalian Ford Serious on Religion," *Washington Post*, 7 December 1973.

25. Ibid.

26. Hutcheson, *God in the White House*, 91.

27. Tip O'Neill, *Man of the House* (New York: Random House, 1987), 324.

28. A 1960s Roman Catholic translation employing introductions, footnotes, and modern language, the Jerusalem Bible renders the Hebrew proper name of God as "Yahweh."

29. Letter, Ron Nessen to Steve P. Gaskins Jr., 8 August 1975, folder "RMI Bibles," Box 1, White House Central Files, Gerald R. Ford Library; James M. Cannon Notes, 1989–94, folder "Notes on Armbrister Interviews (pages 1001–1100)," Box 2, James M. Cannon, Gerald R. Ford Library.

30. Barrie Doyle and James C. Hefley, "The New President: Prayer and a Quiet Faith," *Christianity Today* 18 (30 August 1974): 1297; James M. Cannon Notes, 1989 97, folder "Notes on Armbrister Interviews (pages 1501–1600)," Box 2, James M. Cannon, Gerald R. Ford Library.

31. Doyle and Hefley, "New President," 1297.

32. Gerald R. Ford, "Gerald R. Ford's Remarks on Taking the Oath of Office as President," 9 August 1974. Available from http://www.ford.utexas.edu/library/speeches /740001.htm.

33. Doyle and Hefley, "New President," 1297. The quotations come from Albert Quie of Minnesota and John Dellenback of Oregon, respectively.

34. Gibbs and Duffy, "Other Born-Again President."

35. Doyle and Hefley, "New President," 1297. The rector was the Reverend William

L. Dols. Laura A. Kiernan, "Throng Sees Fords at Church," *Washington Post*, 19 August 1974, A2.

36. Gerald R. Ford, "Granting Pardon to Richard Nixon," Presidential Proclamation, White House, Washington, D.C., 8 September 1974.

37. Mayo Mohs, "The Theology of Forgiveness," *Time*, 23 September 1974.

38. Ford, "Granting Pardon to Richard Nixon."

39. "The Administration: The Fallout from Ford's Rush to Pardon," *Time*, 23 September 1974.

40. "Jerald F. ter Horst, Press Secretary to the President: Files, 1974," Gerald R. Ford Library.

41. "The Pardon: Questions Persist," *Time*, 28 October 1974.

42. Randall Balmer, *God in the White House: A History* (New York: HarperOne, 2008), 77.

43. "Another White House Either-Or Dilemma," *Christian Century*, 25 September 1974, 867. Punctuation changed; italics and paragraphing added.

44. Robert Watson and Anthony Eksterowicz, *The Presidential Companion: Readings on the First Ladies* (Columbia: University of South Carolina Press, 2003), 63.

45. James M. Cannon Notes, 1989–94, folder "Notes on Armbrister Interviews 9 pages 1001–110," Box 2, James M. Cannon, Gerald Ford Library.

46. Letter, Marba S. Perrott to Mrs. Jeanette Hirsch, 12 January 1976, folder "Religious Matters," Box 5, Elizabeth O'Neill Files, Gerald R. Ford Library.

47. Betty Ford, *The Times of My Life* (New York: HarperCollins, 1978), 205, 95, 102, 268.

48. Chip Berlet, "Religion and Politics in the United States: Nuances You Should Know," *PRA Public Eye Magazine*, Summer 2003. Available from http://www.publiceye.org/magazine/v17n2/evangelical-demographics.html#7e, accessed 2 February 2011.

49. Interview with James Darlack of the Goddard Library, Gordon-Conwell Theological Seminary, 14 July 2008.

50. Gerald R. Ford, "An Appreciation," in Billy Zeoli, *God's Got a Better Idea* (Old Tappan, N.J.: Fleming H. Revell, 1978), 10.

51. Article, "A New Billy Visits Ford's White House," n.d., folder "Zeoli, Rev. Billy (1)," Box 2, Gordon Vander Till Papers 1970–76, Gerald R. Ford Library, n.p.

52. Article, "Billy Z: God's Man in the Locker Room," January 1974, folder "Zeoli, Rev. Billy (1)," Box 2, Gordon Vander Till Papers 1970–76, Gerald R. Ford Library, n.p.

53. Frank Deford, "Reaching for the Stars," *Sports Illustrated*, 3 May 1976.

54. Ibid.

55. Karen Peterson, "'Rev. Billy': The Down Home Evangelist in the White House," *Chicago Tribune*, 29 April 1975.

56. Gerald R. Ford, "An Appreciation," 8, 10.

57. Hutcheson, *God in the White House*, 95.

58. Martin, *A Prophet with Honor*, 461–63.

59. Ibid.

60. Ibid.

61. During the 1964 campaign, Graham's father-in-law and his daughter, Anne, publicly endorsed Goldwater. Conservative evangelicals besieged Graham with telegrams urging him to endorse the Republican candidate as well. Fearful of such an endorsement, Lyndon Johnson invited the evangelist and his wife to stay at the White House during the last weekend before the election. A good discussion of Graham's dilemma in 1964 can be found in Balmer, *God in the White House*, 55–56.

62. Martin, *Prophet with Honor*, 461–63.

63. Gibbs and Duffy, "Other Born-Again President."

64. Gerald R. Ford, "Remarks of Gerald Ford after Taking the Oath of Office as Vice President," 6 December 1973. Available from: http://www.ford.utexas.edu/library/speeches/731206.htm, accessed on 3 February 2011.

65. Peter Baker, "In State Funeral, a Farewell to Ford," *Washington Post*, 3 January 2007.

66. Jon Meacham, "The Quality of His Mercy," *Washington Post*, 7 January 2007.

67. Senator Jennings Randolph of West Virginia, quoted in "Gerald Ford: Prayer and Quiet Faith," *Christianity Today*, 28 December 2006.

68. Richard Stern, "Patriotic Ritual," *New Republic*, 2 January 2007.

69. Unless otherwise indicated in specific quotations, all descriptions and events from the period of mourning and several funerals of Gerald Ford come from the coverage given by the following newspapers: *Grand Rapids Press*, 2 January 2007; *New York Times*, 3 January 2007; *Detroit News*, 3 January 2007; *Detroit News*, 3 January 2007; *Washington Post*, 3 January 2007; *Grand Rapids Press*, 4 January 2007; *Washington Post*, 4 January 2007.

## *James Earl Carter Jr.*

1. Jimmy Carter, *Sharing Good Times* (New York: Simon & Schuster, 2004), 5.

2. Jimmy Carter, *A Remarkable Mother* (New York: Simon & Schuster, 2008), 26.

3. Jimmy Carter, *Always a Reckoning* (New York: Crown, 1994), 99.

4. Jimmy Carter, *An Hour before Daylight: Memories of a Rural Boyhood* (New York: Simon & Schuster, 2001), 122.

5. Jimmy Carter, *Turning Point* (New York: Times Books, 1992), 16.

6. Carter, *Turning Point*, 17; Frye Gaillaird, *Prophet from Plains* (Athens: University of Georgia Press, 2007), 7.

7. Betty Glad, *Jimmy Carter, in Search of the Great White House* (New York: W. W. Norton, 1980), 31.

8. Carter, *Remarkable Mother*, 197.

9. Ibid., 81, 88.

10. Glad, *Jimmy Carter*, 34.

11. Carter, *An Hour before Daylight*, 111.

12. Quoted in Peter G. Bourne, *Jimmy Carter* (New York: Scribner, 1997), 29.

13. Carter, *An Hour before Daylight*, 261.

14. Carter, *Remarkable Mother*, 27–29.

15. Ibid.

16. Ibid., 31.

17. Carter, *An Hour before Daylight*, 265.

18. Ibid., 266. Variations of this quotation appear in other books, such as in Harold Gullan, *Faith of Our Mothers: The Stories of Presidential Mothers from Mary Washington to Barbara Bush* (Grand Rapids, Mich.: Wm. B. Eerdmans, 2001), 316.

19. Carter, *An Hour before Daylight*, 268. Paragraphing added.

20. Carter, *Remarkable Mother*, 203.

21. Kenneth E. Morris, *Jimmy Carter: American Moralist* (Athens: University of Georgia Press, 1996), 51.

22. Carter, *An Hour before Daylight*, 219.

23. E. Brooks Holifield, "The Three Strands of Jimmy Carter's Religion," *New Republic*, 5 June 1976, 16.

24. Carter, *An Hour before Daylight*, 255.

25. Jimmy Carter, "Letter from President Jimmy Carter," *Georgia Tech Alumni Magazine*, Fall 1977, 23.

26. Morris, *Jimmy Carter: American Moralist*, 95.

27. Ibid., 101.

28. Jimmy Carter, *Living Faith* (New York: Times Books, 1996), 22.

29. Carter, *Turning Point*, 19.

30. Kevin Mattson, *What the Heck Are You Up To, Mr. President?* (New York: Bloomsbury, 2009), 23–24.

31. Carter, *Turning Point*, 23; Jimmy Carter, "Race Lessons Learned Early," *Spokane Daily Chronicle*, 11 June 1976.

32. Morris, *Jimmy Carter: American Moralist*, 118.

33. Carter, *Living Faith*, 120.

34. Gaillard, *Prophet from Plains*, 26.

35. Morris, *Jimmy Carter: American Moralist*, 142.

36. Ibid., 141.

37. Glad, *Jimmy Carter*, 99.

38. Ibid., 108.

39. Carter, *Sharing Good Times*, 45.

40. Carter, *An Hour before Daylight*, 264.

41. Carter, *Sharing Good Times*, 45–47.

42. Carter, *Living Faith*, 202–3, 208.

43. Glad, *Jimmy Carter*, 110.

44. Ibid.

45. Carter, *Living Faith*, 218–19.

46. "James Earl Carter: Life before the Presidency," Miller Center of Public Affairs, University of Virginia. Available from http://millercenter.org/academic/americanpresident/carter/essays/biography/2, accessed 17 March 2010.

47. E. Stanly Godbold, interviewed in *American Experience*, "The Presidents: Jimmy Carter," PBS, 1995.

48. Jimmy Carter, inaugural address, Atlanta, Georgia, 12 January 1971. Available from www.jimmycarterlibrary.gov/documents/inaugural_address.pdf, accessed 10 January 2009.

49. Quoted in Glad, *Jimmy Carter*, 180.

50. Glad, *Jimmy Carter*, 182.

51. "DEMOCRATS: Taking Jimmy Seriously," *Time*, 1 December 1975. Available from http://www.time.com/time/magazine/article/0,9171,913765-2,00.html, accessed 7 February 2011; Julian E. Zelizer, *Jimmy Carter* (New York: Times Books/Henry Holt, 2010), 35–36.

52. "Inauguration Day, 1977: Heralding a New Spirit," *Christianity Today*, 4 February 1977, 50–51.

53. Carter, inaugural address.

54. Nancy Gibbs and Michael Duffy, "Billy Graham: 'A Spiritual Gift to All,'" *Time*, 31 May 2007. Available from http://www.time.com/time/nation/article/0,8599,1627139,00.html, accessed 17 March 2010.

55. Gibbs and Duffy, *The Preacher and the Presidents*, 250.

56. Russell Chandler, "Graham Warns of Voting on Religion Basis," *Los Angeles Times*, 11 August 1976.

57. Gibbs and Duffy, *Preacher and the Presidents*, 251; Amy Sullivan, *The Party Faithful: How and Why Democrats Are Closing the God Gap* (New York: Scribner, 2008), 8.

58. Marjorie Hyer, "The Church for Carter?" *Washington Post*, 1 August 1976. See also Janis Johnson, "First Baptist First in Church Race," *Washington Post*, 21 January 1977. These articles include details about Carter's search for a church.

59. Ellen Parkhurst, interview with the author, 16 June 2010.

60. Janis Johnson, "President's Daughter Immersed in Heated Pool," *Washington Post*, 7 February 1977. "Pastor Baptizes Amy Carter in Immersion Rite," *Los Angeles Times*, 7 February 1977.

61. "Jimmy Carter's Church Attendance as President," Carter Library. Available from http://www.jimmycarterlibrary.org/documents/jec/church.phtml, accessed 17 March 2010.

62. Smith, *Faith and the Presidency*, 300.

63. Marjorie Hyer, "Graham Praises Carter Witnessing for Christ," *Washington Post*, 8 December 1980.

64. Paraphrased from Bourne, *Jimmy Carter*, 368.

65. O'Neill, *Man of the House*, 314.

66. Jimmy Carter, *White House Diary* (New York: Farrar, Straus and Giroux, 2010), 284–85.

67. Ibid., 361.

68. Ibid., 339.

69. Samuel Ichiye Hayakawa quoted in "The Nation: Ceding the Canal—Slowly," *Time*, 22 August 1977; Bourne, *Jimmy Carter*, 382.

70. Richard G. Hutcheson Jr., "Jimmy Carter's Moral Presidency," *Christian Century*, 21 November 1979, 1161.

71. George F. Will, "Is Carter Carrying a Big Stick? No, It's Just a Big Umbrella," *Los Angeles Times*, 10 April 1980.

72. John Anderson quoted in Alan Baron, "Probing the Wreckage of the Rescue Effort," *Los Angeles Times*, 27 April 1980.

73. Zelizer, *Jimmy Carter*, 107.

74. Ralph de Toledano, "The Inexcusable Failure in Iran," *Ludington Daily News*, 8 May 1980. Paul H. Elovitz's "Presidential Responses to National Trauma: Case Studies of G. W. Bush, Carter, and Nixon," *Journal of Psychohistory* 36, no. 1 (Summer 2008): 44–48, argues that Carter's handling of the Iranian hostage crisis stemmed from self-defeating tendencies deriving from his childhood.

75. Quoted in Frances Fitzgerald, *Cities on a Hill: A Journey through Contemporary American Cultures* (New York: Simon & Schuster, 1981), 29. Cf. Balmer, *God in the White House*, 98.

76. Resolution on Abortion, sbc Resolutions, June 1971. Available from http://www .sbc.net/resolutions/amResolution.asp?ID=13, accessed 19 June 2010. The term "messenger" signifies the Baptist teaching that no Christian can delegate his or her authority.

77. W. Barry Garrett, "What Price Abortion?" *Christianity Today*, 2 March 1975, 565. Cf. Balmer, *God in the White House*, 95; and Randall Balmer, *Thy Kingdom Come: An Evangelical's Lament* (New York: Basic Books, 2006), 12–13.

78. Quoted in Garrett, "What Price Abortion?" 565. Cf. Balmer, *God in the White House*, 94; and Balmer, *Thy Kingdom Come*, 12–13.

79. All quoted resolutions of the Southern Baptist Convention on abortion are available from http://www.johnstonsarchive.net/baptist/sbcabres.html, accessed 19 June 2010.

80. Richard Land quoted in Dwayne Hastings, "Analysis: sbc Sets the Record Straight on Convention's Abortion Stance," *Baptist Press*, 19 June 2003.

81. Dick Clark of Iowa was the senator.

82. Jimmy Carter, *Our Endangered Values* (New York: Simon & Schuster, 2005), 32.

83. Carter, *Our Endangered Values*, 33.

84. Zelizer, *Jimmy Carter*, 4.

85. Carter, *Remarkable Mother*, 197.

86. Somina Sengupta, "Carter Sadly Turns Back on National Baptist Body," *New York Times*, 21 October 2000.

87. Richard Fausset, "For Jimmy Carter, a More Personal Mission," *Los Angeles Times*, 1 February 2008.

88. Jimmy Carter, interview with Larry King, *Larry King Live*, CNN, 2 November 2005.

89. Jimmy Carter on "Moral Crisis: Fundamentalists Share Blame for Chasm in America," *The Early Show*, CBS, New York, 9 November 2005.

90. Holifield, "The Three Strands of Jimmy Carter's Religion."

91. Quotations from Jimmy Carter to Ursula Niebuhr, 1 August 1976, PR II, Box PR-47 WHCF-Subject File, Carter Library.

92. Carter, *Living Faith*, 25.

93. Bourne, *Jimmy Carter*, 171.

94. Southern Baptist Convention, *Faith and Message*, Section 18: The Family. Available from http://www.sbc.net/BFM/bfm2000.asp, accessed 19 March 2010.

95. Fausset, "For Jimmy Carter, a More Personal Mission."

96. Gayle White, "Carter Cuts Ties to 'Rigid' Southern Baptists," *Atlanta Constitution-Journal*, 20 October 2000.

97. Charles Colson, "The Gospel of Oppression? Jimmy Carter on Religion," 23 July 2010, Crosswalk.com. Available from http://www.crosswalk.com/news/commentary/11606448/, accessed 15 June 2010.

98. "Frequently Asked Questions," Cooperative Baptist Fellowship of Georgia. Available from http://www.cbfga.org/about/frequently-asked-questions.html, accessed 10 January 2009.

99. Taken from a statement by the Interim Steering Committee of the Cooperative Baptist Fellowship, the words appear in the discussion of the Bible found in Walter B. Shurden, *The Struggle for the Soul of the SBC* (Macon, Ga.: Mercer University Press, 1993), 309–14.

100. The Carter Center Home Page. Available from http://www.cartercenter.org/index.html, accessed 7 February 2011.

101. Maggie Fick, "Sudan Is Last Battleground as Carter Fights Guinea Worm," *Washington Post*, 12 January 2011.

102. Gunnar Berge, presentation speech of the Norwegian Nobel Committee, Oslo, 10 December 2002. Available from http://nobelprize.org/nobel_prizes/peace/laureates/2002/presentation-speech.html, accessed 19 March 2010.

103. Carter, *Our Endangered Values*, 185.

104. Zelizer, *Jimmy Carter*, 4.

105. Jimmy Carter, "Nobel Lecture," Oslo, 10 December 2002. Available from http://nobelprize.org/nobel_prizes/peace/laureates/2002/carter-lecture.html, accessed 19 March 2010.

# Ronald Wilson Reagan

1. Ron Reagan, *My Father at 100* (New York: Viking, 2011), 12–13.

2. Letter, Ronald Reagan to Mrs. Warne, ca. 1967, in Kiron K. Skinner et al., *Reagan: A Life in Letters* (New York: Simon & Schuster, 2003), 276.

3. Letter, Ronald Reagan to Dorothy D. Conaghan, ca. 1976 in Skinner, *Reagan*, 256.

4. Paul Kengor, *God and Ronald Reagan: A Spiritual Life* (New York: Harper Perennial, 2005), 152.

5. Anne Edwards, *Early Reagan* (New York: William Morrow, 1987), 26.

6. Reagan, *My Father at 100*, 84.

7. Garry Wills, *Reagan's America* (New York: Doubleday, 1987), 12ff; Richard V. Pierard and Robert D. Linder, *Civil Religion and the Presidency* (Grand Rapids, Mich.: Academie Books, 1988), 259.

8. John Crabtree, quoted in "Dixon Remembers Reagan as a Good Kid," *Daily Chronicle*, 21 August 1980.

9. "Ronald Reagan's Roots: A Portrait of a Potential President," *The Star*, 17 June 1980.

10. Lou Cannon, *Reagan* (New York: G. P. Putnam's Sons, 1982), 27. In *My Father at 100*, 58, Ron Reagan declares that Jack served as treasurer of the Roman Catholic church in Tampico, Illinois, "probably in lieu of regularly attending mass." The tradeoff between attending Mass and holding such an office seems strained.

11. Edwards, *Early Reagan*, 34. The anecdote comes from Neil Reagan, who cited his mother as its source. According to Edwards, Jack's response actually referred to his having forgotten to tell Nelle that Neil would have to be raised Roman Catholic, not to his having forgotten that Neil needed to be baptized.

12. Cannon, *Reagan*, 27. The story is also told in Nancy Reagan, *My Turn: The Memoirs of Nancy Reagan* (New York: Random House, 1989), 106.

13. Writers usually state that Wilson was of Scots-Irish heritage, but Ron Reagan found her mother's background to be English. Ron Reagan, *My Father at 100*, 36.

14. Edwards, *Early Reagan*, 32.

15. Ibid. Ron Reagan, *My Father at 100*, 50.

16. Ron Reagan, *My Father at 100*, 50.

17. Ibid., 61.

18. Kengor, *God and Ronald Reagan*, 28.

19. Ron Reagan, *My Father at 100*, 50

20. Ronald Reagan, *An American Life* (New York: Simon & Schuster, 1990), 56.

21. Kengor, *God and Ronald Reagan*, 28ff, lists Reagan's many activities at the First Christian Church.

22. Ronald Reagan, *An American Life*, 56.

23. Ibid., 32.

24. Kengor, *God and Ronald Reagan*, 33.

25. Ronald Reagan, interview by Stephen Vaughn, October 1989, in Kengor, *God and Ronald Reagan*, 36.

26. Kengor, *God and Ronald Reagan*, 37.

27. Wills, *Reagan's America*, 18.

28. Watterson, *The Games Presidents Play*, 278–79.

29. Edwards, *Early Reagan*, 99.

30. Ronald Reagan, *An American Life*, 75.

31. Ibid., 145–46.

32. Michael Reagan, "Stories of Faith: Ronald Reagan, Mikhail Gorbachev," Beliefnet. com, 2011, http://www.beliefnet.com/Faiths/storiesoffaith/ReaganandGorbachev.aspx, accessed 14 February 2011.

33. Ronald Reagan, "My Faith," *Modern Screen*, June 1950, 38.

34. Ibid., 37–38. Paragraphing added.

35. John Patrick Diggins, *Ronald Reagan* (New York: W. W. Norton, 2007), 79.

36. Nancy Reagan, *My Turn*, 68.

37. Frances Spatz Leighton, *The Search for the Real Nancy Reagan* (New York: Macmillan, 1987), 9–10.

38. Ronald Reagan, *An American Life*, 319.

39. Nancy Reagan, *My Turn*, 75.

40. Lawrence Jones, "Reagan's Religion," *Journal of American Culture* (Winter 1985): 59–70.

41. James Richardson to author, 23 June 2008.

42. Rob Moll, "Pastoring a Wounded President: Interview with Louis Evans," *Christianity Today*, 22 June 2004.

43. Smith, *Faith and the Presidency*, 332.

44. Ronald Reagan, *The Reagan Diaries*, vol. 1, *January 1981–October 1985*, ed. Douglas Brinkley (New York: HarperCollins, 2009), 72.

45. Dinesh D'Souza, *Ronald Reagan: How an Ordinary Man Became an Extraordinary Leader* (New York: Free Press, 1997), 213.

46. Ronald Reagan, *An American Life*, 399. In *My Turn*, 258, Nancy Reagan says that she and her husband "started to help raise funds to build a simple wooden chapel at Camp David."

47. Jack A. Gertz to Edwin Meese III, 16 March 1982, attached to Edwin Meese III to Gertz, 16 March 1982, ID #062980, RM, WHORM: Subject Files, Ronald Reagan Library. A former journalist and a Reagan appointee to the National Commission for Employment Policy, Gertz was then executive director of public affairs and media relations at AT&T.

48. Nancy Reagan, *My Turn*, 258.

49. Ibid., 111–12.

50. Ibid.

51. Ron Reagan, *My Father at 100*, 7–8.

52. William E. Pemberton, *Exit with Honor: The Life and Presidency of Ronald Reagan* (Armonk, N.Y.: M. E. Sharpe, 1997), 10.

53. Michael K. Deaver, *Behind the Scenes* (New York: William, Morrow, 1987), 82–83. This anecdote has not been authenticated. The current members and staff of Emmanuel Episcopal Church in Middleburg, Virginia, know the story, but none observed the incident. The rector of the church who presided at the service has died and had no wife. At the time, the church had no curate who might have assisted at the service. Peter Lee, then bishop of the Episcopal diocese of Virginia, knows the story well but also has no authentication for it. In 1987, Deaver was convicted on three counts of perjury for lying about his later work as a lobbyist to a congressional subcommittee and to a federal grand jury. But Deaver's book was published before Reagan left the presidency, and neither Nancy Reagan nor the White House denied the story.

54. Ronald Reagan to Sister Mary Ignatius, 26 November 1984, in Skinner, *Reagan*, 280.

55. Michael Reagan, "Stories of Faith: Ronald Reagan, Mikhail Gorbachev."

56. Ron Reagan, *My Father at 100*, 8.

57. Gibbs and Duffy, *The Preacher and the Presidents*, 268. Michael Reagan reports that his father said the same thing to him shortly after the shooting. Michael Reagan, "Stories of Faith: Ronald Reagan, Mikhail Gorbachev."

58. Gibbs and Duffy, *Preacher and the Presidents*, 268.

59. Michael Reagan, "Stories of Faith: Ronald Reagan, Mikhail Gorbachev."

60. Skinner, *Reagan*, 277.

61. Nancy Reagan, *My Turn*, 18–19; Moll, "Pastoring a Wounded President."

62. Moll, "Pastoring a Wounded President."

63. Kengor, *God and Ronald Reagan*, 75–80.

64. Ibid.

65. Skinner, *Reagan*, 276–77.

66. D'Souza, *Ronald Reagan*, 210–11.

67. J. Anthony Lukas, "The Rapture and the Bomb," *New York Times*, 7 August 1985.

68. Richard N. Ostling, Michael P. Harris, and James Castelli, "Religion: Armageddon and the End Times," *Time*, 5 November 1984.

69. Gibbs and Duffy, *Preacher and the Presidents*, 265.

70. Ibid., 281.

71. Martin, *A Prophet with Honor*, 499.

72. Gibbs and Duffy, *Preacher and the Presidents*, 282–83.

73. Ibid., 281.

74. Smith, *Faith and the Presidency*, 349–52.

75. Sam Donaldson, in Adriana Bosch, *Reagan: An American Story* (New York: TV Books, 1998), 187. Capitalization changed.

76. William E. Smith and Bruce W. Nelan, "South Africa: Reagan's Abrupt Reversal," *Time*, 16 September 1985.

77. Lindsay, *Faith in the Halls of Power*, 32.

78. Donald T. Regan, *For the Record: From Wall Street to Washington* (New York: Harcourt Brace Jovanovich, 1988), 342–43.

79. Smith and Nelan, "South Africa."

80. The list comes from Smith, *Faith and the Presidency*, 328. The quotation appears in "Scrapping the Moral Majority," *Time*, 26 June 1989.

81. Rowland Evans and Robert Novak, "Belted in the Bible Belt," *Washington Post*, 4 July 1980.

82. Patti Davis, *Home Front* (New York: Crown, 1986) and *The Way I See It* (New York: Putnam Adult, 1992), portrayed the Reagan family as seriously dysfunctional. Similar stories are found in Michael Reagan's *On the Outside Looking In* (New York: Kensington, 1988) and in Ron Reagan's *My Father at 101*. For a study of the family by a nonmember, see Anne Edwards, *The Reagans: Portrait of a Marriage* (New York: St. Martin's Press, 2003).

83. Ron Reagan, *My Father at 100*, 8–9.

84. Steven V. Roberts, "White House Confirms Reagans Follow Astrology, Up to a Point," *New York Times*, 4 May 1988.

85. Edwards, *The Reagans*, 68.

86. Nancy Reagan, *My Turn*, 45.

87. Cannon, *Reagan*, 385.

88. Regan, *For the Record*, 367.

89. Nancy Reagan, *My Turn*, 48.

90. "Nancy Reagan's Astrologer," *Time*, 16 May 1988, 25.

91. Nancy Reagan, *My Turn*, 49.

92. Roberts, "White House Confirms."

93. "Carroll Righter Dies; Hollywood Astrologer," *New York Times*, 4 May 1988.

94. Steven V. Roberts, "Not a Slave to the Zodiac, Reagan Says," *New York Times*, 18 May 1988; Nancy Reagan, *My Turn*, 134.

95. "Carroll Righter Dies."

96. Ronald Reagan, *Where's the Rest of Me?* (New York: Dell Publishing, 1981), 249.

97. Roberts, "White House Confirms."

98. Nancy Reagan, *My Turn*, 105.

99. Lindsay, *Faith in the Halls of Power*, 31.

100. O'Neill Jr., *Man of the House*, 396.

101. Ibid., 396, 434.

102. Ibid., 401.

103. Ibid., 408.

104. Ibid., 403.

105. Ibid., 428.

106. Alan Brinkley, *The Unfinished Nation*, concise 5th ed. (Boston: McGraw Hill, 2008), 932.

107. Steven F. Hayward, *The Age of Reagan: The Conservative Counterrevolution, 1980–1989* (New York: Crown Forum, 2009), 477.

108. Brinkley, *Unfinished Nation*, 908.

109. See, for example, Daniel J. Mitchell, "The Truth about Tax Rates and the Politics of Class Warfare," 5 March 2001. Available from http://www.heritage.org/research/reports/2001/03/the-truth-about-tax-rates-and-the-politics-of-class-warfare, accessed 22 February 2011; Michael J. Mandel, "Reagan's Economic Legacy," 21 June 2004. Available from http://www.businessweek.com/magazine/content/04_25/b3888032_mz011.htm, accessed 22 February 2011.

110. Jonathan Weisman, "Reagan Policies Gave Green Light to Red Ink," *Washington Post*, 9 June 2004.

111. Michael Schaller, *Reckoning with Reagan: America and Its President in the 1980s* (New York: Oxford University Press, 1992), 70.

112. Hank Plante, "Ronald Reagan & AIDS: A Legacy of Silence," *San Francisco Examiner*, 6 February 2011. Available from http://www.examiner.com/city-buzz-in-san-francisco/ronald-reagan-aids-a-legacy-of-silence, accessed 15 February 2011.

113. Edmund Morris, "Did Reagan Have Alzheimer's in Office?" *Newsweek*, 31 January 2011, 31.

114. Ron Reagan, *My Father at 100*, 7.

115. Whether Reagan displayed Alzheimer's while in office remains an ongoing controversy. Ron Reagan maintains that while his father did not display recognizable symptoms during his second term, he was nevertheless in the early stages of the disease. Citing his frequent observations of the president, as well as the consistent lucidity of Reagan's

nightly diary entries, Edmund Morris (Reagan's official biographer) claims that Reagan showed no signs of the disease until a severe fall after he left office. See Ron Reagan, *My Father at 100*, 217–19; Edmund Morris, "Did Reagan Have Alzheimer's in Office," *Newsweek*, 31 January 2011, 31.

116. George Bush, "Eulogy for Ronald Reagan," 11 June 2004, Washington, D.C. Available from http://www.americanrhetoric.com/speeches/patrickbuchanan1992rnc.htm, accessed 14 February 2011.

117. Letter, Ronald Reagan to the Reverend and Mrs. Ben H. Cleaver, 4 January 1973, in Skinner et al., *Reagan: A Life in Letters*, 276. Kengor also cites this quotation in *God and Ronald Reagan*, 27.

## George Herbert Walker Bush

1. Jeffery A. Engel, *The China Diary of George H. W. Bush: The Making of a Global President* (Princeton: Princeton University Press, 2008), 26.

2. Ibid., 80.

3. Barbara Bush, "Peking (China) Diary, 281," in Barbara Bush, *Barbara Bush: A Memoir* (New York: Charles Scribner Sons, 1994), 114.

4. Engel, *China Diary of George H. W. Bush*, 340.

5. Bush, *Barbara Bush: A Memoir*, 114.

6. Doro Bush Koch, *My Father, My President: A Personal Account of the Life of George H. W. Bush* (New York: Warner Books, 2006), 124.

7. The Bible is on permanent display at Federal Hall on Wall Street (where Washington was inaugurated). It was also used at the inaugurations of Presidents Harding, Eisenhower, and Carter. George W. Bush intended to use it at his inauguration but was prevented by rain.

8. Stephen Mansfield, *The Faith of George W. Bush* (Lake Mary, Fla.: Charisma House, 2004), 7.

9. Garry Wills, "The Republicans," *Time*, 22 August 1988, 23.

10. David Aikman, *A Man of Faith: The Spiritual Journey of George W. Bush* (Nashville: Thomas Nelson, 2005), 24.

11. Quotations from Wills, "The Republicans," 24.

12. M. W. Stackpole, "A School Church at an Academy," *Religious Education* 10, no. 6 (December 1915): 584–88. According to a 1915 description of the academy church by assistant master M. W. Stackpole, the senior class traditionally elected four fellow students to serve as deacons while the middle class elected two of its members as deacons. The student deacons served communion alongside four faculty deacons. The academy church was open to all students who brought letters of church membership from their homes and to all who "declared Christian purpose."

13. Claude Moore Fuess, *An Old New England School: A History of Phillips Academy* (Boston: Houghton Mifflin, 1917), 428.

14. Ibid., 428; Wills, "The Republicans," 24. The *Pot Pourri* for 1942 mentions Bush on 39, 80, 81, 90, 104, 106, 110, 116, 122, 128, 148, 150, 193, and 200.

15. George H. W. Bush to Dorothy Bush, n.d., 1943, in George Bush, *All the Best, George Bush: My Life in Letters and Other Writings* (New York: Simon and Schuster, 1999), 33.

16. Department of the Navy—Naval Historical Center, "Lieutenant Junior Grade George Bush, USNR," Naval History and Heritage Command, Available from http://www.history.navy.mil/faqs/faq10-1.htm, accessed 7 February 2011.

17. George Bush, "Remarks at a Prayer Breakfast in Houston," 20 August 1992, in Jim McGrath, *Heartbeat: George Bush in His Own Words* (New York: Citadel Press, 2003), 194.

18. Barbara Bush, *Barbara Bush: A Memoir*, 23. Paragraphing added.

19. Joe Hyams, *Flight of the Avenger: George Bush at War* (San Diego: Harcourt Brace Jovanovich, 1991), 1, 5–6.

20. Herbert S. Parmet, *George Bush: The Life of a Lonestar Yankee* (New York: Scribner, 1997), 69–71.

21. The George Bush Presidential Library in College Station, Texas, contains his certificate of ordination. At the bottom of this document, the following words from the Book of Church Order of the Presbyterian Church in the United States appear: "Those who fill this office ought to be blameless in life and sound in the faith. They should be men of wisdom ... and by the holiness of their walk and conversation should be examples to the flock." Donated Historical Materials; Bush, George H. W., Collection; Personal Papers; Zapata Oil File, Personal Alphabetical File; Bush Personal—First Presbyterian Church [1957–1958], G. H. W. Bush Library.

22. George Bush, *All the Best*, 82.

23. Paul Harvey, "George Bush on 'Religion,'" *Gettysburg Times*, 16 February 1989.

24. Barbara Bush, *Barbara Bush: A Memoir*, 42; Pamela Kilian, *Barbara Bush* (New York: St. Martin's Press, 2002), 43.

25. Kilian, *Barbara Bush*, 43.

26. Donnie Radcliffe, *Simply Barbara Bush* (New York: Warner Books, 1989), 119.

27. Paul Kengor, *God and George W. Bush: A Spiritual Life* (New York: HarperCollins, 2004), 3.

28. George Bush, *All the Best*, 323.

29. George Bush, letter to G. Bradford Hall, 5 March 1990, Presidential Records; White House Office of Records Management; Subject File—General; Scanned; RM (Religious Matters); G. H. W. Bush Library.

30. Donnie Radcliffe, "President Bush and the Power of Prayer," *Washington Post*, 8 January 1991.

31. Gibbs and Duffy, *The Preacher and the Presidents*, 291.

32. Ibid., 295.

33. Ibid., 296.

34. Ibid., 301; David Aikman, "Interview with Billy Graham: Preachers, Politics, and Temptation," *Time*, 28 May 1990.

35. George Bush, *All the Best*, 501; Gibbs and Duffy, *Preacher and the Presidents*, 301.

36. Parmet, *George Bush*, 476.

37. Gibbs and Duffy, *Preacher and the Presidents*, 303.

38. Statement by David Bates (ca. April 1988) in preparation for the 1988 presidential campaign. Collection of opinions by associates of George H. W. Bush in Personal Files, G. H. W. Bush Library.

39. Bush was popular within the CIA. In 1999, the CIA headquarters compound in Langley, Virginia, was officially renamed the George Bush Center for Intelligence. Vernon Loeb, "Bush Affiliation No Secret at Langley: Former Director and President Is Honored in Naming of CIA Headquarters," *Washington Post*, 27 April 1999.

40. Tom Wicker, *George Herbert Walker Bush* (New York: Viking, 2004), 50.

41. Roman Popadiuk, *The Leadership of George Bush: An Insider's View of the Forty-First President* (College Station: Texas A&M University Press, 2009), 25.

42. Senator Robert Dole, who was also a candidate in the primaries, made the comment.

43. Balmer gives the title "Listing Right" to his chapter on the Reagan and Bush presidencies. Balmer, *God in the White House*, 109–31.

44. See, for example, Bush's speech to the annual convention of the National Religious Broadcasters, an evangelical organization, on 29 January 1990, in Public Papers, G. H. W. Bush Library.

45. Balmer, *God in the White House*, 125.

46. Popadiuk, *Leadership of George Bush*, 3.

47. See, for example, Martin Luther, *Commentary on Romans*, trans. J. Theodore Mueller (Grand Rapids, Mich.: Kregel, 1976).

48. The phrasing and cadences of the speech betray the work of Bush's principal speechwriter, Peggy Noonan. George Bush, "Address before a Joint Session of Congress on the State of the Union," 29 January 1991, *Public Papers of the Presidents of the United States* (Washington, D.C.: U.S. Government Printing Office, 1991), 75.

49. Mary E. Stuckey, *Defining Americans: The Presidency and National Identity* (Lawrence: University Press of Kansas, 2004), 318.

50. George Bush, "Address on Administration Goals before a Joint Session of Congress," 8 February 1989, *Public Papers* (1989): 75.

51. George Bush, "Remarks at an Independence Day Celebration in Faith, North Carolina," 4 July 1992, *Public Papers* (1992): 1081.

52. Stuckey, *Defining Americans*, 320–21.

53. Robert Gates, *From the Shadows* (New York: Simon & Schuster, 1996), 471. Paragraphing added.

54. Ward Just, *An Unfinished Season* (New York: Mariner, 2005), 127.

55. Patrick Buchanan, Address to the Republican National Convention, 17 August 1992, Houston, Texas. Available from http://www.americanrhetoric.com/speeches/patrickbuchanan1992rnc.htm, accessed 3 March 2010.

56. Craig Unger, *The Fall of the House of Bush: The Untold Story of How a Band of True Believers Seized the Executive Branch, Started the Iraq War, and Still Imperils America's Future* (New York: Scribner, 2007), 83.

57. Wicker, *George Herbert Walker Bush*, 210.

58. They now plan to be buried in a plot at the George Bush Presidential Library and Museum in College Station, Texas.

59. Barbara Bush, *Reflections* (New York: Scribner, 2003), 89.

60. Parmet, *George Bush*, 376.

61. Killian, *Barbara Bush*, 123.

62. Parmet, *George Bush*, 376.

## William Jefferson Clinton

1. Bill Clinton, *My Life* (London: Vintage, 2005), 27.

2. Michael Takiff, *A Complicated Man: The Life of Bill Clinton as Told by Those Who Know Him* (New Haven: Yale University Press, 2010), 12. Takiff interviewed 171 people who knew Clinton from birth on. The book includes substantial background information on the president's life.

3. Ibid., 10.

4. Nigel Hamilton, *Bill Clinton: An American Journey* (New York: Random House, 2003), 23.

5. Hamilton, *Bill Clinton*, 50.

6. Paul David Leopoulos quoted in Takiff, *A Complicated Man*, 22.

7. Virginia Kelley, *Leading with My Heart* (New York: Simon & Schuster, 1994), 44.

8. Gene Weingarten, "The First Father," *Washington Post*, 20 June 1993.

9. David Maraniss, *First in His Class* (New York: Simon & Schuster, 1995), 25.

10. Takiff, *A Complicated Man*, 23–24.

11. Roy Clinton Jr. quoted in Takiff, *A Complicated Man*, 18.

12. Selwyn Raab, *Five Families: The Rise, Decline, and Resurgence of America's Most Powerful Mafia Empires* (New York: Thomas Dunne Books, 2005), 41.

13. Roy Clinton Jr. quoted in Takiff, *A Complicated Man*, 17.

14. Clinton, *My Life*, 27–28.

15. Quoted in Maraniss, *First in His Class*, 35.

16. Ibid.

17. "Remarks in a Discussion at the Ministers' Leadership Conference in South Barrington, Illinois — Interview," *Weekly Compilation of Presidential Documents* 36, 14 August 2000. Available from http://findarticles.com/p/articles/mi_m2889/is_32_36 /ai_65197888?tag=untagged, accessed 22 September 2008.

18. Clinton, *My Life*, 30.

19. Ibid., 25. Hamilton, *Bill Clinton*, 102, places the baptism on 17 October 1956, when Clinton was ten.

20. Kelley, *Leading with My Heart*, 100; ibid., 101.

21. Ibid., 70.

22. Clinton, *My Life*, 23.

23. Ibid., 40, 47.

24. Peter J. Boyer, "The Big Tent," *New Yorker*, 22 August 2005. Available from http:// www.newyorker.com/archive/2005/08/22/050822fa_fact_boyer, accessed 22 September 2008.

25. Bill Clinton, speech: Billy Graham Library Dedication, Charlotte, N.C., May 31, 2007. Available from http://www.clintonfoundation.org/news/news-media/053107-sp -cf-gn-sp-billy-graham-library-dedication, accessed 22 September 2008.

26. Takiff, *A Complicated Man*, 21 and 27.

27. Maraniss, *First in His Class*, 43; Richard L. Berke, "At Reunion, Clinton Helps in Starting School Fund," *New York Times*, 27 September 1997.

28. Takiff, *A Complicated Man*, 28.

29. Maraniss, *First in His Class*, 41.

30. Quoted in David Gergen, Matthew Cooper, and Donald Baer, "Bill Clinton's Hidden Life," *U.S. News and World Report*, 20 July 1992. Available from http://www .usnews.com/articles/news/national/2008/05/16/bill-clintons-hidden-life.html, accessed 22 September 2008.

31. Takiff, *A Complicated Man*, 35.

32. Maraniss, *First in His Class*, 51.

33. Ibid., 50, 52; Clinton, *My Life*, 71.

34. Meredith L. Oakley, *On the Make: The Rise of Bill Clinton* (Washington, D.C.: Regnery Publishing, 1994), 47.

35. Ibid., 46.

36. Kelley, *Leading with My Heart*, 164.

37. Roger Morris, *Partners in Power: The Clintons and Their America* (New York: Henry Holt, 1996), 77.

38. Maraniss, *First in His Class*, 58; Clinton, *My Life*, 76. Hentz (who still teaches at Georgetown) was not a professor at the time. A scholastic is a seminarian still prepar-

ing to become a Jesuit priest. Secular universities would have called him a "Teaching Assistant."

39. Quoted in Oakley, *On the Make*, 46.

40. David Maraniss, "Roots of Clinton's Faith Deep, Varied," *Washington Post*, 29 June 1992.

41. Takiff, *A Complicated Man*, 37.

42. David E. Rosenbaum, "The 1992 Campaign: The Draft; Clinton Could Have Known Draft Was Unlikely for Him," *New York Times*, 14 February 1992.

43. Ibid.

44. Colonel Eugene Holmes's September 1992 affidavit concerning Bill Clinton and the draft. http://www.usasurvival.org/holmes.htm, accessed 8 March 2011. Details of Clinton's involvement with the draft are found in his autobiography and in virtually all biographies of him. The information includes not only a lengthy letter to him from Colonel Holmes but also Clinton's claim that he wrote to his draft board in the summer of 1969 and asked to surrender his deferment and to be drafted "as soon as possible" (but never mailed the letter).

45. Tom W. Dillard, "Frank Durward White," *The Encyclopedia of Arkansas History and Culture*, 17 January 2009. Available from http://www.encyclopediaofarkansas.net /encyclopedia/entry-detail.aspx?entryID=125, accessed 24 December 2009.

46. Clinton, *My Life*, 239–40.

47. Ibid., 239.

48. The National Center for Public Policy Research, 2010, "Letters to Conservatives by Paul M. Weyrich." Available from http://www.nationalcenter.org/Weyrich299.html, accessed 24 January 2010.

49. President Bill Clinton speaking at the Church of the Pentecost: Asheville, N.C. ApostolicLive.com. Available from http://www.apostoliclive.com/play.php?vid=213, accessed 24 December 2009.

50. Clinton, *My Life*, 475.

51. David Maraniss, "Clinton's Faith Tempered in Crucible of Politics," *Toledo Blade*, 3 July 1992.

52. Clinton, *My Life*, 294, 354; Maraniss, *First in His Class*, 451.

53. Clinton, *My Life*, 353.

54. Shaun Casey, "The President's Religion," *Nieman Reports* 47 (22 June 1993): 34.

55. "Newsweek Article Spurs Baptist Response," *Biblical Recorder*, 6 November 1998. Available from http://www.biblicalrecorder.org/news/11_6_98/newsweek.html, accessed 28 June 2005.

56. David M. Bresnahan, "Clinton's Trouble in the Pulpit," WorldNetDaily.com, 4 September 1998. Available from http://www.worldnetdaily.com/news/article .asp?ARTICLE_ID=16701, accessed 27 June 2005.

57. Quoted in Garrett, "What Price Abortion?" *Christianity Today*, 2 March 1975, 39 [565]. See also Balmer, *God in the White House*, 94.

58. Priscilla Painton, "Clinton's Spiritual Journey," *Time*, 5 April 1993. Available from http://www.time.com/time/magazine/article/0,9171,978129,00.html?iid=chix-sphere, accessed 29 September 2008.

59. "IRS Probes Pastor's Huckabee Endorsement," msnbc.com, 13 February 2008. Available from http://www.msnbc.msn.com/id/23155264/, accessed 29 January 2010.

60. Bob Pool and My-Thuan Tran, "Pastors Test IRS Ban on Politics," *Los Angeles Times*, 29 September 2008. Available from http://articles.latimes.com/2008/sep/29/local/me-pulpit29, accessed 29 January 2010.

61. Hillary Rodham Clinton, *Living History* (New York: Simon & Schuster, 2003), 22. A Lutheran pastor, Bonhoeffer was executed in Nazi Germany in 1945, just before Allied forces reached his concentration camp. Reinhold Niebuhr was one of the leading voices in twentieth-century American Protestantism.

62. Clinton, *Living History*, 22.

63. Kathryn Joyce and Jeff Sharlet, "Hillary's Prayer: Hillary Clinton's Religion and Politics," *Mother Jones*, 1 September 2007. Available from http://www.motherjones.com/news/feature/2007/09/hillarys-prayer.html, accessed 22 September 2008.

64. Quoted in Paul Kengor, *God and Hillary Clinton: A Spiritual Life* (New York: Harper Perennial, 2008), 20.

65. Clinton, *Living History*, 22–23.

66. Kelley, *Leading with My Heart*, 190.

67. Dick Morris, *Behind the Oval Office* (Los Angeles: Renaissance Books, 1999), 144.

68. Clinton, *My Life*, 234.

69. Kengor, *God and Hillary Clinton*, 21.

70. Ibid., 61.

71. Donnie Radcliffe, *Hillary Rodham Clinton: A First Lady for Our Time* (New York: Warner Books, 1993), 102, 99.

72. Ibid., 311–12.

73. Nancy Gibbs and Michael Duffy, "Billy Graham: Hillary's Solace," *Time*, 8 August 2007.

74. Dan Balz and Ruth Marcus, "Activity Escalates, Focus Returns to Alleged Affair," *Washington Post*, 8 March 1998.

75. John M. Broader, "Greeted Warmly," *New York Times*, 28 January 1998.

76. Cal Thomas, "Graham to Clinton: Go and Sin Some More," *Orlando Sentinel*, 10 March 1998. Available from http://articles.orlandosentinel.com/1998–03–10/news/9803100466_1_forgiveness-sin-graham, accessed 1 February 2010.

77. Balz and Marcus, "Activity Escalates."

78. Thomas, "Graham to Clinton: Go and Sin Some More."

79. Gibbs and Duffy, "Billy Graham: Hillary's Solace."

80. Clinton, *My Life*, 563.

81. Kengor, *God and Hillary Clinton*, 99–100.

82. David Maraniss, *The Clinton Enigma* (New York: Simon & Schuster, 1998), 100.

83. Wayne Wold, email message to author, 31 May 2011.

84. Rex Horne, email message to author, 1 June 2011. Horne is now president of Ouachita Baptist University.

85. James M. Wall, "A Visit to the White House," *Christian Century* 110 (7 April 1993): 355.

86. Greg Warner, quoted in Painton, "Clinton's Spiritual Journey."

87. Adele M. Banks, "Carter, Clinton Meet with Baptists to Plan for New 'Covenant,'" *Washington Post*, 10 January 2007. Available from http://newsweek.washingtonpost .com/onfaith/guestvoices/2007/01/carter_clinton_meet_with_bapti.html, accessed 29 January 2010.

88. Painton, "Clinton's Spiritual Journey."

89. Paige Patterson, quoted in "Southern Baptist President Calls for Clinton's Resignation." Available from http://www.cnn.com/ALLPOLITICS/1998/09/07/southern .baptists/, accessed 29 September 2008.

90. Bresnahan, "Clinton's Trouble in the Pulpit."

91. "Testing of a President; President Clinton's Address at the National Prayer Breakfast," *New York Times*, 12 September 1998. Available from http://query.nytimes.com/gst /fullpage.html?res=9C0DE0D71731F931A2575AC0A96E958260, accessed 10 October 2008.

92. Adelle M. Banks, "Some Evangelicals Unconvinced by Clinton Contrition," Beliefnet, 2000. Available from http://www.beliefnet.com/story/37/story_3765.html, accessed 10 October 2008.

93. Wogaman, an ethicist and former seminary dean, was senior minister at Foundry Methodist Church. Campolo was a minister, professor, and author identified with the progressive wing of evangelicalism.

94. Kengor, *God and Hillary Clinton*, 173.

95. Hamilton, *Bill Clinton*, 95, attributes this quotation to Betsey Wright, Clinton's chief of staff in Arkansas.

96. Clinton, *My Life*, 51.

97. Gergen et al., "Bill Clinton's Hidden Life."

98. Tom Campbell, quoted in Ernest Dumas, ed., *The Clintons of Arkansas: An Introduction by Those Who Know Them Best* (Fayetteville: University of Arkansas Press, 1993), 49.

99. Carolyn Staley quoted in Takiff, *A Complicated Man*, 35.

100. Hamilton, *Bill Clinton*, 72.

101. Takiff, *A Complicated Man*, 3.

102. Bill Clinton, interview by Bill Hybels, 10 August 2000, quoted in Edwin S. Gaustad and Mark A. Noll, eds., *A Documentary History of Religion in America Since 1877* (Grand Rapids, Mich.: Eerdmans Publishing, 2003), 699.

103. Morris, *Behind the Oval Office*, 104.

104. Takiff, *A Complicated Man*, 198.

105. Maraniss, *First in His Class*, 451.

106. Edward Stourton, "U.S. Voters Spurn Saints and Saviours," *New Statesman* 125, no. 4307 (25 October 1996): 26.

107. Max Brantley quoted in Takiff, *A Complicated Man*, 51.

108. Matt Hadro, "Chris Matthews Slobbers over Bill Clinton While Peddling 'President of the World' Documentary," http://www.mrc.org/biasalert/2011/20110221064758 .aspx, accessed on 9 March 2011.

109. Maraniss, *First in His Class*, 451; Morris, *Behind the Oval Office*, xiv; Clinton, *My Life*, 252.

110. Maraniss, *First in His Class*, 34.

111. Agnes Varnum, "'Hope' Springs Eternal . . . Or at Least for This Election Year," International Documentary Association, n.d. Available from http://www.documentary .org/content/hope-springs-eternalor-least-election-year, accessed 6 March 2011.

112. Ibid., xiv; paragraphing added.

# George W. Bush

1. Nicholas D. Kristof, "George W. Bush's Journey: A Philosophy with Roots in Conservative Texas Soil," *New York Times*, 21 May 2000.

2. Ibid.

3. George W. Bush, *Decision Points* (New York: Crown, 2010), 5.

4. Nicholas D. Kristof, "George W. Bush's Journey: Earning A's in People Skills at Andover," *New York Times*, 10 June 2000.

5. Nicholas D. Kristof, "The 2000 Campaign: The Legacy; A Father's Footsteps Echo throughout a Son's Career," *New York Times*, 11 September 2000.

6. Bush, *Decision Points*, 20–21.

7. Kristof, "George W. Bush's Journey: A Philosophy with Roots in Conservative Texas Soil."

8. Bush, *Decision Points*, 6.

9. George W. Bush, *A Charge to Keep* (New York: William Morrow, 1999), 20.

10. Bush, *A Charge to Keep*, 19.

11. Bush, *Decision Points*, 11.

12. Kristof, "George W. Bush's Journey: Earning A's in People Skills at Andover."

13. Ibid.

14. Bush's SAT scores were 566 verbal and 640 math. When the College Board "re-centered" SAT scores in 1995, most scores rose. On today's recentered scale, Bush's SAT scores would be approximately 1270.

15. Bush, *A Charge to Keep*, 22.

16. Bush, *Decision Points*, 13.

17. Nicholas D. Kristof, "George W. Bush's Journey: Ally of an Older Generation amid the Tumult of the 60s," *New York Times*, 19 June 2000.

18. Deal Hudson, interview by the author, 1 September 2009. Hudson is director of operations at InsideCatholic.com.

19. Most biographies of George W. Bush include this episode. The words attributed to Coffin vary slightly.

20. William Sloane Coffin to Governor George W. Bush, 15 September 1998, Texas State Archives, Austin, Texas.

21. Bush, *Decision Points*, 14.

22. Warren Goldstein, *William Sloane Coffin, Jr.: A Holy Impatience* (New Haven: Yale University Press, 2004), 303.

23. George W. Bush to William Sloane Coffin, 30 September 1998, Texas State Archives, Austin, Texas.

24. Stanley A. Renshon, *In His Father's Shadow: The Transformations of George W. Bush* (New York: Palgrave Macmillan, 2004), 56.

25. Lois Romano and George Lardner Jr., "Bush: So-So Student but a Campus Mover," *Washington Post*, 27 July 1999.

26. Peter Schweizer, *The Bushes: Portrait of a Dynasty* (New York: Doubleday, 2006), 171.

27. Kristof, "George W. Bush's Journey: Earning A's in People Skills at Andover."

28. Bush, *Decision Points*, 14–15.

29. Romano and Lardner, "Bush: So-So Student but a Campus Mover."

30. Kristof, "George W. Bush's Journey: Earning A's in People Skills at Andover."

31. Bush, *A Charge to Keep*, 80.

32. Aikman, *A Man of Faith*, 63.

33. Nicholas D. Kristof, "George W. Bush's Journey: Learning How to Run," *New York Times*, 27 July 2000.

34. Kristof, "2000 Campaign."

35. Schweizer, *Bushes: Portrait of a Dynasty*, 419.

36. Kristof, "George W. Bush's Journey: Learning How to Run," 27 July 2000.

37. Kristof, "2000 Campaign."

38. Kengor, *God and George W. Bush*, 14.

39. Clifford Thompson, "George W. Bush," in *Current Biography Yearbook 2001* (New York: H. W. Wilson, 2002), 59.

40. Bush, *A Charge to Keep*, 81.

41. Bush, *Decision Points*, 27.

42. Kristof, "George W. Bush's Journey: Learning How to Run."

43. Arthur Blessitt, "The Day I Prayed with George W. Bush to Receive Jesus," Blessitt. com, http://blessitt.com/Inspiration_Witness/PrayingWithGeorgeWBush/Praying _With_Bush_Page1.html, accessed 11 March 2011.

44. Ibid.

45. Craig Unger, "How George Bush Really Found Jesus," *Salon*, http://www.salon .com/books/feature/2007/11/08/house_of_bush, accessed 11 November 2007.

46. Dan P. McAdams, "Political Bookworm," http://voices.washingtonpost.com /political-bookworm/guest_blogger/, accessed 26 March 2011.

47. Oliver Stone's film *W.* uses a fictional pastor named Earle Hudd as a composite of Blessitt, Graham, and other evangelical pastors who influenced Bush's conversion or his later religious life.

48. Bush, *Decision Points*, 31–33.

49. Bush, *A Charge to Keep*, 136.

50. George W. Bush, "Address to the Second Baptist Church," Houston, Texas, 7 March 1999.

51. Bush, *A Charge to Keep*, 132; Bush uses the term as the title for the chapter that describes how he stopped drinking.

52. Aikman, *A Man of Faith*, 79–80.

53. Ibid., 113. The business associate was Mercer Reynolds.

54. Ann Richards, *Straight from the Heart: My Life in Politics and Other Places* (New York: Simon and Schuster, 1989).

55. Bush, *A Charge to Keep*, 10.

56. Kengor, *God and George W. Bush*, 41.

57. Aikman, *A Man of Faith*, 115.

58. Bush, *A Charge to Keep*, 45.

59. Ibid.

60. Charles Wesley, "Keep the Charge of the Lord, That Ye Die Not," *Charles Wesley: A Reader*, ed. John Tyson (New York: Oxford University Press, 1989), 449. The hymn is no. 413 in the hymnbook *The United Methodist Hymnal* (Nashville: United Methodist Publishing House, 1989), which is currently used in United Methodist Churches.

61. James Robison, quoted in *George W. Bush: Faith in the White House*, DVD, directed by David W. Balsiger (Baker City, Calif.: Grizzly Adams Productions, 2004), 90 min.

62. Kristof, "George W. Bush's Journey: Learning How to Run."

63. James L. Guth, "George W. Bush and Religious Politics," *Religion and Ethics News-weekly*, 23 April 2004.

64. Statistics can be found at http://archives.cnn.com/2001/ALLPOLITICS/03/11/palmbeach.recount/, accessed 26 March 2011.

65. Richard A. Posner, *Breaking the Deadlock: The 2000 Election, the Constitution, and the Courts* (Princeton: Princeton University Press, 2001), 217.

66. Quote can be found at http://www.patrobertson.com/NewsCommentary/RabbiLapin.asp, accessed 26 March 2011.

67. Aikman, *A Man of Faith*, 139–40.

68. Hudson, interview by the author.

69. Interview with Chuck Colson by the author, 5 September 2008.

70. Daniel Burke, "A Catholic Wind in the White House," *Washington Post*, 13 April 2008.

71. Hudson, interview by the author.

72. Ibid.

73. Ibid. Hudson attributes this description to a friend of the Texas Supreme Court justice whom Miers was then dating.

74. Tony Carnes and Sarah Pulliam, "Bush's Faith-Based Legacy," *Christianity Today*, February 2009.

75. Jewish members of the White House staff included Press Secretary Ari Fleischer, speechwriter David Frum, Deputy Secretary of Defense Paul Wolfowitz, National Security Advisor Elliott Abrams, defense advisor Richard Perle, and Cheney chief of staff I. Lewis "Scooter" Libby. Michael J. Gerson and social theorist Marvin Olasky—both evangelicals—were of Jewish descent.

76. Aikman, *A Man of Faith*, 138–39.

77. The appointee was Scott Evertz, director of the office of National AIDS Policy.

78. Hudson, interview by the author.

79. David Frum, *The Right Man: The Surprise Presidency of George W. Bush* (New York: Random House, 2003), 272.

80. Kristof, "George W. Bush's Journey: A Philosophy with Roots in Conservative Texas Soil."

81. Scott McClellan, *What Happened: Inside the Bush White House and Washington's Culture of Deception* (Washington, D.C.: Public Affairs, 2008), 291.

82. Evan Thomas, "Katrina: How Bush Blew It," *Newsweek*, 19 September 2005.

83. Based upon the teachings of the church father Augustine of Hippo, Just War Theory condones wars—and then reluctantly—only when they meet rigorous quali-fications. The war must, in Augustine's words, confront "a real and certain danger" to innocent life. It must be declared by national authority. It must be waged to support

values important enough to justify the death and destruction it will cause. And it must be declared only after a nation has exhausted all other options. "My job was to give advice from a Catholic point of view," Hudson declared in an interview about his work in the White House in the months before the invasion. "So I went through the Just War Theory with a fine-toothed comb." Hudson, interview by the author.

84. McClellan, *What Happened*, 156–57.

85. Hudson, interview by the author.

86. Bush, *Decision Points*, 224–25, 238–43. Bush discusses the Iraq war in *Decision Points* on pages 223–71, 357–58, 394.

87. McClellan, *What Happened*, xiii.

88. Tara Wall, "Bush Will Be Vindicated," *CNN*, 19 January 2009. Available from http://www.cnn.com/2009/POLITICS/01/19/wall.bush/index.html, accessed 3 February 2009.

89. Doris Kearns Goodwin on *Meet the Press*, quoted in Wall, "Bush Will Be Vindicated."

90. Balsiger, *George W. Bush: Faith in the White House*. The speaker was comedian and U.S. Senator Al Franken.

91. Aikman, *A Man of Faith*, 199.

92. Kengor, *God and George W. Bush*, 164.

93. Jake Tapper, "God Is Their Copilot," *Salon*, http://www.salon.com/news/politics/feature/2000/07/07/born_again, accessed 7 July 2000.

94. Kevin Phillips, *American Dynasty: Aristocracy, Fortune, and the Politics of Deceit in the House of Bush* (New York: Penguin, 2004), 208.

95. Bob Woodward, *State of Denial* (New York: Simon & Schuster, 2007), 334–35.

96. Balsiger, *George W. Bush: Faith in the White House*.

97. Joel Rosenberg, "Flash Traffic," *World Magazine*, 6 October 2001.

98. Nicholas Kristof, "How Bush Came to Tame His Inner Scamp," *New York Times*, 29 July 2000.

## *Barack Hussein Obama*

1. Michael Barbaro, "Bloomberg, in Florida, Blasts Rumor about Rumor," *New York Times*, 21 June 2008.

2. The Pew Research Center for the People and the Press, "Obama Weathers the Wright Storm, Clinton Faces Credibility Problem." Available from http://people-press.org/report/?pageid=1277, accessed 27 March 2008.

3. Patrick Healy, "Obama Talks about His Faith", *The Caucus* (blog), *New York Times*, 26 March 2008. Available from http://thecaucus.blogs.nytimes.com/2010/09/28/obama-talks-about-his-faith-2/.

4. "Barack Hussein Obama," *Conservapedia*. Available from http://www.conservapedia.com/obama, accessed 22 April 2011.

5. Mike Huckabee, quoted in Eric Hananoki, "Huckabee: Obama Grew up in Kenya," MediaMatters.org, 1 March 2011, accessed 10 March 2011, http://mediamatters.org/blog/201103010018. In September 2010, former speaker of the House of Representatives Newt Gingrich made similar remarks, accusing Obama of "Kenyan, anticolonial behavior," although Gingrich did not refer to Obama's having grown up in Kenya. Newt Gingrich, quoted in Michael Shear, "Gingrich: President Exhibits 'Kenyan, Anticolonial Behavior,'" nytimes.com, 13 September 2010, http://thecaucus.blogs.nytimes.com/2010/09/13/gingrich-president-exhibits-kenyan-anti-colonial-behavior/, accessed 10 March 2011.

6. Conservapedia, "Obama birth certificate controversy." Available from http://www.conservapedia.com/Obama_birth_certificate_controversy, accessed 27 June 2011; Michael D. Shear, "With Document, Obama Seeks to End 'Birther' Issue," *New York Times*, 27 April 2011; Joel Achenbach, "Obama's Release of Birth Certificate Does Little to Allay Birther Fears," *Washington Post*, 27 April 2011.

7. Janny Scott, *A Singular Woman: The Untold Story of Barack Obama's Mother* (New York: Riverhead Books, 2011), 2.

8. Whitehouse.gov, "Remarks by the President." Available from http://www.whitehouse.gov/the-press-office/2011/04/27/remarks-president, accessed 27 June 2011.

9. The full "Certificate of Live Birth" can be found on http://www.whitehouse.gov/sites/default/files/rss_viewer/birth-certificate-long-form.pdf.

10. Kim Barker, "History of Schooling Distorted," *Chicago Tribune*, 25 March 2007.

11. Obama, *Dreams from My Father* (New York: Three Rivers, 1995, 2004), 50.

12. Jodi Kantor, "A Candidate, His Minister, and the Search for Faith," *New York Times*, 30 April 2007; Deborah Solomon, "All in the Family," *New York Times*, 20 January 2008.

13. Scott, *A Singular Woman*, 45.

14. Obama, *Dreams from My Father*, 19. According to relatives, Ann's mother, Madelyn Dunham, actually named the baby. Asked once by Maya why she had chosen "Stanley," Madelyn replied, "Oh, I don't know why I did that." On at least one other occasion, she explained that a leading actress of the time, Bette Davis, played a female character with the first name of Stanley in a 1942 film. Movie theaters were showing the film, *In This Our Life*, during Madelyn's pregnancy.

15. Obama, *Dreams from My Father*, 14.

16. Obama, *The Audacity of Hope* (New York: Three Rivers, 2006), 203.

17. Scott, *A Singular Woman*, 43,45. In *Dreams*, 95, Obama remembers a teenage argument when he apparently mistakenly said to his mother, "Look at Gramps. He didn't even go to college."

18. Janny Scott, "A Free-Spirited Wanderer Who Set Obama's Path," *New York Times*, 14 March 2008.

19. Scott, *A Singular Woman*, 53.

20. Tim Jones, "Barack Obama: Mother Not Just a Girl from Kansas," *Chicago Tribune*, 27 March 2007.

21. Scott, "Free-Spirited Wanderer."

22. Jones, "Barack Obama: Mother Not Just a Girl from Kansas."

23. The Rev. Peter J. Luton, quoted in Scott, *A Singular Woman*, 60.

24. Scott, *A Singular Woman*, 60.

25. Obama, *Dreams from My Father*, 17.

26. Obama, *Audacity of Hope*, 203.

27. Obama, *Dreams from My Father*, 50.

28. Scott, *A Singular Woman*, 82,83.

29. Scott, *A Singular Woman*, 83–84.

30. Obama, *Dreams from My Father*, 125–26.

31. Jones, "Barack Obama: Mother Not Just a Girl from Kansas."

32. Purdum, "Raising Obama," 318; Scott, *A Singular Woman*,142–44.

33. Jones, "Barack Obama: Mother Not Just a Girl from Kansas."

34. Purdum, "Raising Obama," 317.

35. Scott, *A Singular Woman*, 256.

36. Obama, *Dreams from My Father*, 30–31.

37. Scott, *A Singular Woman*, 100.

38. Obama, *Dreams from My Father*, 48; Scott, *A Singular Woman*, 133.

39. Scott, *A Singular Woman*, 99.

40. Scott, *A Singular Woman*, 98.

41. Barker, "History of Schooling Distorted."

42. Purdum, "Raising Obama," 320.

43. Ibid., 318; Professor Dewey was the granddaughter of the noted philosopher John Dewey.

44. Scott, *A Singular Woman*, 124.

45. Obama, *Dreams from My Father*, 42.

46. Amanda Ripley, "The Story of Barack Obama's Mother," *Time*, 9 April 2008. Available from http://www.time.com/time/nation/article/0,8599,1729524,00.html, accessed 7 February 2010.

47. Scott, *A Singular Woman*, 344–46.

48. Although Obama writes in *Dreams from My Father* that he spent two years in a Muslim school and two years in a Catholic school, reporters who have checked school records in Jakarta found that he actually spent three years in a Catholic school (1967–1970) and one year in a Muslim school (1970–1971).

49. Information on Obama's schooling in Indonesia comes from these two articles: Kim Barker, "History of Schooling Distorted," and Ariel Sabar, "Barack Obama: Putting

Faith Out Front," *Christian Science Monitor*, 16 June 2007. Available from http://www.csmonitor.com/2007/0716/p01s01-uspo.html, accessed 27 February 2010.

50. Obama, *Dreams from My Father*, 154.

51. Obama, *Audacity of Hope*, 204–6.

52. Obama, *Dreams*, 47; Scott, *A Singular Woman*, 131–35, discusses the reasons for Ann's decision.

53. Scott, *A Singular Woman*, 214.

54. Scott, "Free-Spirited Wanderer"; Scott, *A Singular Woman*, 146–47, 158.

55. Jennifer Steinhauer, "Charisma and a Search for Self in Obama's Hawaii Childhood," *New York Times*, 17 March 2007.

56. Scott, *A Singular Woman*, 266.

57. Purdum, "Raising Obama," 320.

58. Ibid., 318.

59. Steve C. Otto, e-mail message to the author, 21 March 2011. All quotations about Punahou and Hawaii from the classmate come from this e-mail.

60. Obama, *Dreams from My Father*, 60.

61. Ibid., 76

62. Ibid., 79.

63. Ibid., 86.

64. C. Serge F. Kovolseski, "Old Friends Say Drugs Played Big Part in Obama's Young Life," *New York Times*, 9 February 2008.

65. Purdum, "Raising Obama," 320.

66. Obama FAQs, Occidental College, http://www.oxy.edu/x7992.xml, accessed 10 March 2011.

67. Obama's recollections in *Dreams from My Father*; Maurice Possley's "Activism Blossomed in College," *Chicago Tribune*, 30 March 2007. Several articles that appear in the fall 2004 and winter 2008 *Occidental Alumni Magazine* provide a good discussion of Obama's two years at Occidental College.

68. Possley, "Activism Blossomed in College."

69. "Center Stage," *Occidental Magazine*, fall 2004, 26.

70. Richard Wolfe, Jessica Ramirez, and Jeffrey Bartholet, "When Barry Became Barack," *Newsweek*, 22 March 2008. Available from http://www.newsweek.com/2008/03/22/when-barry-became-barack.html, accessed 7 February 2010.

71. Obama, *Dreams from My Father*, 115.

72. Janny Scott, "Obama's Account of New York Years Often Differs from What Others Say," *New York Times*, 30 October 2007.

73. Ibid.

74. Shira Boss-Bicak, "Barack Obama '83: Is He the New Face of the Democratic

Party?" *Columbia College Today*, January 2005; Scott, "Obama's Account of New York Years."

75. Obama, *Dreams from My Father*, 120.

76. Scott, "Obama's Account of New York Years."

77. Obama, *Dreams from My Father*, 121.

78. Scott, "Obama's Account of New York Years"; Scott, *A Singular Woman*, 255–56.

79. Obama, *Audacity of Hope*, 206.

80. Bob Secter and John McCormick, "Obama Hits Chicago during 'Council Wars,'" *Chicago Tribune*, 30 March 2007.

81. Ibid.

82. Obama, *Dreams from My Father*, xvii, 141.

83. Ibid., 141.

84. Ibid.

85. Ibid.

86. Ibid.

87. Kenneth T. Walsh, "On the Streets of Chicago, a Candidate Comes of Age," *U.S. News*, 26 August 2007. Available from http://www.usnews.com/usnews/news/articles/070826/30bama.htm, accessed 16 March 2011.

88. Purdum, "Raising Obama," 321.

89. Walsh, "On the Streets of Chicago, a Candidate Comes of Age."

90. Obama, *Dreams from My Father*, 152.

91. Ibid., 161.

92. Scott, *A Singular Woman*, 272.

93. Obama, *Audacity*, 205.

94. Scott, *A Singular Woman*, 344.

95. Obama, *Audacity of Hope*, 207.

96. Sabar, "Barack Obama."

97. Obama, *Dreams from My Father*, 279–80.

98. Eli Saslow, "Obama's Path to Faith Was Eclectic," *Washington Post*, 18 January 2009.

99. Obama, *Audacity of Hope*, 206.

100. Obama, *Dreams from My Father*, 286.

101. Ibid., 280.

102. Barack Obama, "A Politics of Conscience," speech to UCC General Synod, 23 June 2007.

103. Obama, *Dreams from My Father*, 278–79.

104. Obama, "A Politics of Conscience." Another account can be found in *Dreams from My Father*, 292–95.

105. Obama, *Dreams from My Father*, 294.

106. Ibid.

107. Obama's commencement speech at the University of Notre Dame, 17 May 2009. Available from http://www.huffingtonpost.com/2009/05/17/obama-notre-dame-speech-f_n_204387.html, accessed 13 March 2011.

108. The DMin focuses not on academic specialties but rather on practical areas such as missions, evangelism, pastoral psychology, and church growth.

109. Baptists "call" (or hire) and dismiss clergy by majority vote. No higher authority can impose a pastor upon a Baptist congregation or keep one there against a congregation's will.

110. Lisa Miller, "Trying Times for Trinity," *Newsweek*, 24 March 2008. Available from http://www.newsweek.com/2008/03/15/trying-times-for-trinity.html, accessed 27 January 2010.

111. Ibid.

112. Manya A. Brachear, "Rev. Jeremiah A. Wright, Jr.," *Chicago Tribune*, 21 January 2007.

113. Jason Byassee, "Afro-centric Church," *Christian Century*, 29 May 2007, 20.

114. Ibid., 19–20.

115. Kantor, "A Candidate, His Minister, and the Search for Faith."

116. J. Bennett Guess, "Chicago's Trinity ucc." Available from http://www.ucc.org, accessed 14 March 2008.

117. Dwight Hopkins, quoted in Byassee, "Afro-centric Church," 21.

118. John M. Buchanan, "Statement on Jeremiah Wright," *Washington Post*, 3 April 2008.

119. Brachear, "Rev. Jeremiah A. Wright, Jr."

120. Dwight N. Hopkins, *Head and Heart: Black Theology: Past, Present and Future* (New York: Palgrave, 2002), 18.

121. Byassee, "Afro-centric Church," 20. Otis Moss III succeeded Jeremiah Wright as pastor of Trinity Church in 2008.

122. Byassee, "Afro-centric Church," 21.

123. David Moberg, "Obama's Community Roots," *Nation*, 16 April 2007, 18. Moberg credits Obama with the establishment of a branch of the Mayor's Office of Employment and Training in the isolated Far South Side, the removal of asbestos from most of Altgeld Gardens, and above all, the growth of the DCP into a stable, grant-getting organization that continues its work on behalf of the area today.

124. Obama, *Dreams from My Father*, 437–39.

125. Barack Obama, "A More Perfect Union," speech at Constitution Center, Philadelphia, Pennsylvania, 18 March 2008.

126. James Bone, "From Slave Cabin to White House, a Family Rooted in Black America," *Times* (London), 6 November 2008; Rachel L. Swarms and Jodi Cantor, "In First Lady's Roots, a Complex Path from Slavery," *New York Times*, 8 October 2009.

127. Christi Parsons, Bruce Japsen, and Bob Secter, "Barack's Rock: Michelle Obama," *Chicago Tribune*, 22 April 2007.

128. Scott, however, describes Michelle's family "as hardworking, churchgoing and close-knit." See Scott, *A Singular Woman*, 296. Liza Mundy's *Michelle* (New York: Simon & Schuster, 2008) discusses the controversy over Jeremiah Wright but omits any mention of the role of church in Michelle Robinson's life.

129. Lauren Collins, "The Other Obama," *New Yorker*, 10 March 2008. Available from http://www.newyorker.com/reporting/2008/03/10/080310fa_fact_collins, accessed 16 March 2011.

130. Parsons, Japsen, and Secter, "Barack's Rock."

131. Some critics claimed that Michelle Obama's senior thesis at Princeton expounded themes of black supremacy and black separatism. Ms. Obama also came under attack for referring to her husband's success in the primaries with the words, "For the first time in my adult life, I am really proud of my country." Her second sentence, more infrequently quoted, reads: "Not just because Barack is doing well, but I think people are hungry for change." Roland S. Martin, *The First: President Barack Obama's Road to the White House* (Chicago: Third World Press, 2010), 221.

132. Mundy, *Michelle*, 221.

133. Saslow, "Obama's Path to Faith Was Eclectic."

134. Lisa Miller and Richard Wolffe, "Finding His Faith," *Newsweek*, 12 July 2008. Available from http://www.newsweek.com/2008/07/11/finding-his-faith.html, accessed 27 February 2010.

135. Lisa Rogak, *Michelle Obama: In Her Own Words* (New York: Public Affairs, 2009), 124.

136. Jeremiah Wright, speech to National Press Club, Washington, D.C., 28 April 2008. This transcript can be found in typescript in "Reverend Wright at the National Press Club," *New York Times*, 28 April 2008. Available from http://www.nytimes.com/2008/04/28/us/politics/28text-wright.html?pagewanted=1, accessed 27 February 2010. It can also be found in audio form on the National Press Club's Web site at http://press.org/news-multimedia/audio/reverend-jeremiah-wright, accessed 27 February 2010.

137. Barack Obama, "I Am a Big Believer in Not Just Words, but Deeds and Works," interview by Lisa Miller and Richard Wolffe, *Newsweek*, 21 July 2008. Available from http://www.newsweek.com/2008/07/11/i-am-a-big-believer-in-not-just-words-but-deeds-and-works.html, accessed 27 February 2010.

138. Obama's platform differed from Bush's by prohibiting faith-based programs from hiring or firing staff members on the basis of religious affiliation or belief.

139. Obama, *Audacity of Hope*, 214. He repeated almost identical words in a speech in 2006 given at a conference of the evangelical social justice community Sojourners: Barack Obama, "'Call to Renewal' Keynote Address," 26 June 2006.

140. Obama, *Audacity of Hope*, 216.

141. Ibid., 218.

142. Laurie Goldstein, "Without a Pastor of His Own," *New York Times*, 14 March 2009.

143. The professor was Dwight Hopkins of the University of Chicago Divinity School. Quoted in Sabar, "Putting Faith Out Front."

144. Healy, "Obama Talks about His Faith."

145. Ted Olsen, "The Evangelical Electoral Map," *Politics Blog, Christianity Today*, 5 November 2008. Available from http://blog.christianitytoday.com/ctpolitics/2008/11/the_evangelical.html, accessed 16 March 2011.

146. Jeremiah Wright, "War on Iraq I.Q. Test," 17 March 2008; Jeremiah Wright, "War on Iraq I.Q. Test," 23 February 2003. Originally published on Trinity Web site. Currently available from http://www.mindfully.org/Reform/2003/Iraq-IQ-Test-Wright23feb03.htm, accessed 17 March 2011.

147. Joseph C. Phillips, "Bad Penny," *New Pittsburgh Courier*, 7 May 2008.

148. Jeremiah Wright, "The Day of Jerusalem's Fall," sermon, Trinity United Church of Christ, Chicago, 16 September 2001. Available from http://abcnews.go.com/Blotter/story?id=4719157&page=1, accessed 18 March 2011.

149. Jeremiah Wright, "Confusing God and Government," Trinity United Church of Christ, Chicago, 13 April 2003. Available from http://www.blackpast.org/?q=2008-rev-jeremiah-wright-confusing-god-and-government, accessed 20 March 2011.

150. Mundy, *Michelle*, 218.

151. Jodi Kantor, "Barack Obama, Forever Sizing Up," *New York Times*, 26 October 2008.

152. The statement is quoted in Miller, "Trying Times for Trinity," as well as in other publications.

153. Obama, "A More Perfect Union."

154. Ibid.

155. Ibid.

156. Philadelphia speech, 18 March 2008.

157. Quoted in Clarence Page, "Wright's Past Collides with Obama's Future," *Philadelphia Tribune*, 9 May 2008.

158. Obama, "A More Perfect Union."

159. Ibid.

160. Ibid.

161. Victoria Horsford, "What's Going On," *New York Beacon*, 1–7 May 2008.

162. Barbara Reynolds, interview by the author, 23 July 2010.

163. Jeremiah Wright, speech to National Press Club, Washington, D.C., 28 April 2008.

164. Ibid.

165. Ibid.

166. Reynolds, interview by the author.

167. Jeremiah Wright, speech to National Press Club, Washington, D.C., 28 April 2008.

168. Ibid.

169. Page, "Wright's Past Collides with Obama's Future."

170. Jeremiah Wright, speech to National Press Club, Washington, D.C., 28 April 2008.

171. Quoted in Richard Prince, "Wright Hits Black," *Afro-American Red Star*, 3 May 2008; quoted in James Wright, "A Defiant Wright Embraces the Black Church," *Afro-American Red Star*, 3 May 2008.

172. Zenitha Prince, interview by the author, 15 July 2010.

173. Mshujaa Komoyo, "The Sacrifice and Chosen Status of Rev. Dr. Jeremiah Wright," *Los Angeles Sentinel*, 5 March 2009.

174. Askia Muhammad, "Wright's Wrong, but White's Right?" *Washington Informer*, 15 May 2008.

175. Phillips, "Bad Penny."

176. Eric L. Wattree, "The Rev. Wright Is Wrong: It Is God's Will that We Use Common Sense," *Los Angeles Sentinel*, 1 May 2008. The phrase "permission slip" came from the television commentator Chris Matthews, "The Chris Matthews Show," 23 March 2008. Available from http://www.thechrismatthewsshow.com/html/transcript/index.php?selected=1&id=104, accessed 21 March 2011.

177. Garth C. Reeves, "Obama-Wright Schism," *Miami Times*, 14 May 2008.

178. Muhammad, "Wright's Wrong, but White's Right?"

179. Wattree, "The Rev. Wright Is Wrong."

180. Phillips, "Bad Penny."

181. CBS News, "Starting Gate: Worth Fighting For," 1 May 2008. Available from http://www.cbsnews.com/8301-502163_162-4061275-502163.html, accessed 27 February 2010.

182. Page, "Wright's Past Collides with Obama's Future."

183. William A. Von Hoene Jr., "Rev. Wright in a Different Light," *Chicago Tribune*, 26 March 2008; William A. Von Hoene Jr., interview by the author, 31 January 2010.

184. Ibid.

185. Ibid.

186. Jesse Hyde, "The Man Who Would Be King: Freddy Haynes Seemed a Shoo-in to Lead the NAACP. Then Obama's Ex-Pastor Came to Town," *Dallas Observer*, 12 June 2008.

187. Barack Obama, speech to press conference on Jeremiah Wright, Winston-Salem, N.C., 29 April 2008.

188. Ibid.

189. Ibid.

190. "Mr. Obama and Rev. Wright," *New York Times*, 30 April 2008.

191. Kantor, "A Candidate, His Minister, and the Search for Faith."

192. Tahman Bradley and Ferdous Al-Faruque, "Wright Sings 'Proud' Tune on Obama in DC Pulpit," ABC News, 18 January 2009.

193. Ibid.

194. Jeremiah Wright, quoted in Associated Press, "Rev. Wright, Obama 'Threw Me Under the Bus,'" 18 May 2010, available from CBS News, http://www.cbsnews.com/stories/2010/05/18/politics/main6494977.shtml, accessed 10 March 2011.

195. Clarence Earl Walker and Gregory D. Smithers, *The Preacher and the Politician* (Charlottesville: University of Virginia Press, 2009), 35.

196. Williston Walker, *The Creeds and Platforms of Congregationalism* (New York: Charles Scribner's Sons, 1893), 423–31.

197. Peter W. Williams, interview by the author, 20 March 2011.

198. Richard Allen, *The Life Experience and Gospel Labors of the Rt. Rev. Richard Allen* (Nashville: Abingdon Press, 1983), 52.

199. Leon F. Litwack, *Trouble in Mind* (New York : Alfred A. Knopf, 1998), 392.

200. Walker and Smithers, *Preacher and the Politician*, 35.

201. Martin Peretz, "Why Barack Obama Was Right Not to Repudiate His Pastor," *New Republic*, 23 April 2008, 15.

202. Buchanan, "Statement on Jeremiah Wright."

203. J. Bennett Guess, "Chicago's Trinity UCC Is 'Great Gift to Wider Church Family,'" *United Church of Christ News*, 14 March 2008.

204. Ibid.

205. Clarence E. Walker, *We Can't Go Home Again: An Argument about Afrocentrism* (New York: Oxford University Press, 2001), 44.

206. Walker and Smithers, *Preacher and the Politician*, 49.

207. Von Hoene, "Rev. Wright in a Different Light."

208. Ibid.

209. Von Hoene, interview by the author.

210. Von Hoene, "Rev. Wright in a Different Light."

211. Ibid.

212. Martin Marty, interview by the author, 31 January 2010.

213. Phillips, "Bad Penny."

214. The Baptist churches were Nineteenth Street, Shiloh, and Mount Calvary. The Methodist churches were Asbury United Methodist, Metropolitan African Methodist Episcopal, and Foundry United Methodist.

215. Jacqueline L. Salmon, "Obama Won't Choose One Church," *Washington Post*, 2 July 2009.

216. Ben Smith, "Obama Goes to Church," *Politico*. Available from http://www

.politico.com/blogs/bensmith/0910/Obama_goes_to_church.html#, accessed 13 March 2011.

217. Carol Lee, "Barack Obama Lets His Faith Show," *Politico*. Available from http://www.politico.com/news/stories/1210/46841.html, accessed 13 March 2011.

218. Ibid.

219. Amy Sullivan, "The Obamas Find a Church Home—Away from Home," *Time*, 30 June 2009; Dan Gilgoff, "White House Denies Report That Obamas Have Ended Church Search," *US News*, 29 June 2009; Adelle M. Banks, "White House Denies Report That Obama Chose Camp David Church," *USA Today*, 29 June 2009.

220. Barack Obama, quoted in "Obama: I'll Continue to Reach Out to GOP," by Mike Celizic, *Today*. Available from http://today.msnbc.msn.com/id/36096371/ns/today-today_people/#, accessed 13 March 2011.

221. Lee, "Barack Obama Lets His Faith Show."

222. Ibid.

223. "Obama's Commencement Address at Notre Dame," *New York Times*, 17 May 2009.

224. Pew Research Center, "Growing Number of Americans Say Obama is a Muslim," 18 August 2010, available from http://pewforum.org/Politics-and-Elections/Growing-Number-of-Americans-Say-Obama-is-a-Muslim.aspx, accessed 10 March 2010.

225. A number of Web sources have these words of White House aide Bill Burton. See, for example, Lee, "Barack Obama Lets His Faith Show"; see also "Sudden Surge: Obama Starts Mentioning Christian Faith Way More Often," *Democracy Forums*. Available from http://www.democracyforums.com/showpost.php?p=858759&postcount=1, accessed 13 March 2011.

226. Lee, "Obama Lets His Faith Show."

227. Ibid.

228. The presidents were Eisenhower, Kennedy, Johnson, Ford, Carter, Clinton, and both Bushes.

229. Kevin Eckstrom, interview by the author, 1 July 2011.

230. Eli Saslow and Hamil R. Harris, "Obamas Celebrate Easter in Southeast Washington," *Washington Post*, 5 April 2010.

231. Hamil R. Harris and Peter Wallsten, "Marking Holiday at Metropolitan AME, Obamas Get New Invite," *Washington Post*, 17 January 2011.

232. The presidents were Eisenhower, Johnson, Ford, Carter, Clinton, and both Bushes.

233. Salmon, "Obama Won't Choose One Church."

234. Eckstrom, interview by the author.

235. See Steve Benen, "Presidential Church Attendance Reports," *Washington Monthly*, 20 September 2010. Irregular church attendance will also do nothing to fill any gap that

may exist in the religious education of Obama's daughters. To be sure, Sasha and Malia attend Sidwell Friends (or Quaker) school, but its weekly chapel service is essentially secular. Although they may receive private religious instruction, the girls do not attend Sunday school.

236. Miller and Wolffe, "Finding His Faith."

237. Scott, *A Singular Woman*, 287.

238. Ibid.

239. Ibid., 130–31; 5.

240. Scott, *Singular Woman*, 194, 5.

241. Bedell Smith, *Grace and Power*, 257.

242. Obama, *Audacity of Hope*, 208.

243. Barack Obama, "On My Faith and My Church," *Real Clear Politics*, 14 March 2008.

244. Lisa Miller and Richard Wolffe, "Q&A: What Barack Obama Prays For," *Newsweek*, 12 July 2008. Available from http://www.newsweek.com/2008/07/11/i-am-a-big-believer-in-not-just-words-but-deeds-and-works.html, accessed 23 March 2011.

245. Sabar, "Barack Obama: Putting Faith Out Front."

246. Miller and Wolffe, "Q&A: What Barack Obama Prays For."

247. Ira Berlin, *The Making of African America: The Four Great Migrations* (New York: Viking Press, 2010).

248. "On the Road," *The Economist*, 13 February 2010.

249. Kantor, "A Candidate, His Minister and the Search for Faith"; Solomon, "All in the Family."

250. Laurie Goodstein, "Without a Pastor of His Own, Obama Turns to Five," *New York Times*, 15 March 2009. The pastor is the Rev. Eugene F. Rivers, raised in Chicago by parents who were members of the Nation of Islam.

# INDEX

Bouvier, John Vernou, III, 55

Bowman, Welbern, 7

Braden, Joan, 57

Bradlee, Ben, 68, 69

Brokaw, Tom, 141, 142

Browning, Edmond, 207

Bruton Parish Church (Episcopal), Williamsburg, Va., 76, 77, 116, 335n3

Bryan, William Jennings, 240, 311

Buber, Martin, 167

Buchanan, John, 308

Buchanan, Pat, 212, 258–59

Buchen, Phil, 127, 128

Buddhism, 210, 223, 271

Bumpers, Dale, 226

Bundy, McGeorge, 75

Bush, Barbara Pierce, 197–214; mentioned, 240, 241, 242, 256

Bush, Dorothy ("Doro"), 197–98, 205, 214, 234, 241

Bush, Dorothy Walker, 199, 205

Bush, George Herbert Walker, 197–214; and abortion, 208; achievements and criticism of administration, 209, 210–12; appointment to high government positions, 207–8, 248, 357n42; and the Bible, 198, 206, 355n7; career in oil business, 203–5, 207; character, 207, 208, 209; childhood and education, 200–201, 203, 212, 240, 243; and Chongwenmen Church, Beijing, 197–98, 234; comparison with son's career, 212–13; death of daughter Robin, 203–4, 241–42; ecumenicity of, 210, 213–14; and the Episcopal Church, 198, 199–200, 204–5, 209, 213, 214, 242; family and Connecticut background, 198–200, 213, 240, 243, 244–45; Gulf War, 206–7, 211, 213;

inaugural address, 209, 357n48; marriage, 202; military service, 201–3, 213, 246, 249; and other denominations, 88, 200, 201, 355n12; and prayer, 199–200, 202, 203, 204, 205, 207, 214; and the Presbyterian Church, 198, 203–4, 242, 356n21; presidential campaign, 209; relationship with Billy Graham and evangelicalism, 205, 206–7; and the Religious Right, 165; mentioned, 64, 88, 142, 165, 182, 196, 234, 240–50, 254, 260, 264, 320, 377n228, 377n232

Bush, George W., 240–69; and abortion, 249, 258, 260, 262; achievements and criticism of administration, 255–56, 263, 264–65, 269; advocacy of faith-based programs, 255–56, 257, 263–64; and alcohol use, 244, 246, 248, 252–53, 264, 365n51; and the Bible, 250, 252, 253, 255, 257, 260, 264, 265, 267, 355n7; business career, 246–47, 254; character, 242, 247, 252, 253, 264; childhood and education, 201, 241–48, 364n14, 364n18; controversy over acceptance into Texas Air National Guard, 248–49; conversion experience, 240, 251–52; and the Episcopal Church, 182, 242, 252, 259, 267; and evangelical tradition, 210, 212, 214, 240, 241, 242, 250–54, 255, 258, 260–61, 262–64, 267, 268, 365n47; family and Texas background, 240–41; and Iraq War, 264, 265–67, 269, 367n86; leadership of Religious Right, 165, 259, 268; marriage, 249–50, 267; and Methodism, 250, 256, 266, 267, 365n60; and personal prayer and prayer breakfasts, 251, 253,

Carter, James Earl, (*continued*)
inauguration and aversion to pomp,
154–55, 159–60; role of women in
church, 168–69; Southern Baptist
and evangelical heritage, 143, 148, 149;
support of racial integration and human rights, 144, 150–51, 153, 154, 155,
160–61, 171; theological self-education
of, 167, 171; view of presidency as
religious vocation, 160; "witnessing" of,
143, 159, 160, 171–72; mentioned, 118,
135, 186, 190, 194, 207, 228, 237, 259,
268, 296

Carter, James Earl, Sr., 143–47, 149, 150

Carter, Rosalynn Smith, 144–51; mentioned, 157, 159, 166, 169, 171

Carter, Ruth. *See* Stapleton, Ruth Carter

Cassidy, Edith, 215–17, 236

Cassidy, James, 215, 217

Cavendish, Kathleen, 48–49, 50, 53

Cavendish, William J. R., 48–49, 50

CCRC. *See* Calumet Community
Religious Conference

Certain, Robert G., 142

Chambers, Whittaker, 186

Chase, Chevy, 140

Cheney, Richard B., 249, 262, 301

Chicago, Ill., 16, 21, 66, 78, 124, 128, 135,
179, 180, 229, 230, 278, 281–319

Chongwenmen Church, Beijing, China,
197–98, 234

Christadelphians (the Brethren of
Christ), 79

Christ Church (Episcopal), Alexandria,
Va., 182,

Christ Church (Episcopal), Greenwich,
Conn., 200

Christian Church, the (Disciples of
Christ), 1, 8, 77, 80, 81, 83, 84, 85, 87,

88, 92, 98, 173–74, 176, 177, 178, 180,
187

Christian Coalition, 226, 260

Christian Reformed Church, 125, 126

Churchill, Winston, 14, 15, 22, 35

Church of England, 14, 99, 223

Church of St. Ignatius Loyola (Roman
Catholic), New York City, 55

Church of the Immaculate Conception
(Roman Catholic), Fulton, Ill., 175

civil rights, 21, 59, 70, 87, 93, 95, 97–98,
118, 145, 150, 189, 193, 199, 218, 220, 231,
237, 243, 246, 287, 293, 296

Cleaver, Ben, 177, 196

Cleaver, Margaret, 177–78

Clinton, Chelsea, 231, 234

Clinton, Hillary Rodham, 227–38; mentioned, 55, 136, 295

Clinton, Roger, Jr., 217

Clinton, Roger, Sr., 216, 217, 222, 237

Clinton, William Jefferson, 215–39;
and abortion, 227–29, 234; association with African American churches
and community, 232–33, 237, 239;
and Bible, 217, 218, 227, 236, 238;
childhood and education, 218–19,
220–25; in choir at Evergreen Chapel,
Camp David, 233; controversy over
deferment from draft, 224–25, 249,
360n44; conversion experience and
baptism, 218–19, 225–26, 359n19;
family and Arkansas background,
215–18, 236–37, 239; impeachment, 133,
238; interest in Pentecostalism, 226,
239; legal change of name, 217; marriage, 231; and Methodist and other
Protestant churches, 231, 232, 233,
234; Monica Lewinsky scandal and
other extramarital affairs, 226, 232–33,

235–36, 237, 238, 258; and Moral
Majority, 226; and New Baptist
Covenant, 234; political career, 225–
29, 231, 234, 238–39; and prayer, prayer
breakfasts, and ecumenical organizations, 221, 231, 233–34, 235–36, 237;
relationship with Billy Graham, 220,
227, 232–33; and Roman Catholicism,
219, 222, 223, 234; and Southern
Baptist churches, 215, 217, 218–19, 220,
222, 225–29, 231, 232, 235, 237; and
Southern Baptist Convention, 234–35;
mentioned, 118, 120, 133, 157, 182, 211,
244, 249, 254, 258, 259, 263, 268, 296,
315, 320

Coffin, J. Herschel, 104–5, 121

Coffin, William Sloane, 225, 244–45,
364n19

colleges and universities: Baylor
University, 5; Bennington College,
128; Calvin College, 125; Columbia
University, 33, 283, 317; Duke
University Law School, 106; Emory
University, 146; Eureka College,
177–78, 185; Georgetown University,
57, 221–24; George Washington
University, 56; Georgia Institute
of Technology, 149, 152; Georgia
Southwestern State University,
149; Gordon-Conwell Theological
Seminary, 137; Harvard Business
School, 247–48; Harvard Law School,
128, 283, 289, 292–93, 294; Harvard
University, 46, 47, 50, 51, 103, 106, 247,
248, 275–76; Hope College, 125–26;
Howard University, 36, 289, 302;
Johns Hopkins University, 26; Lane
University, 24–25; Occidental College,
282–83, 317; Oxford University,
223–24; Princeton University, 50,
54, 179, 294, 373n131; Smith College,
180; Southwest Texas State Teachers
College (Texas State University–
San Marcos), 82, 93; Stanford
Graduate School of Business, 52;
Stanford University, 61; University
of Arkansas, 224–25; University
of Hawaii, 274–77; University
of Michigan, 126; University of
Notre Dame, 193, 312; U.S. Military
Academy (West Point), 25–26, 31, 40;
U.S. Naval Academy (Annapolis),
26, 127, 146, 149, 152–53; Vassar
College, 56–57; Virginia Theological
Seminary, 130; Wellesley College, 47,
230–31; Wheaton College, 137, 139;
Whittier College, 100, 103–6, 111, 121;
Yale Law School, 127, 224–25, 231;
Yale University, 25, 55, 107, 127, 199,
203, 224–25, 231, 240, 243–50, 269

Colson, Charles, 117, 122, 134, 168–69,
255

Communism and anti-Communism, 14,
17–18, 21, 41, 42, 107–9, 117, 159, 186,
197, 198, 335n137

Congregationalism, 6, 112, 148, 198, 200,
214, 243, 281, 282, 290

Cooke, Terence, 185

Coolidge, Calvin, 6, 59

Cooperative Baptist Fellowship, 169,
349n99

Cox, Patricia Nixon, 107, 118, 120

Craig, Mark, 256, 259

creationism, 138, 165, 166, 225, 263

Criswell, W. A., 139, 164, 189, 228

Cuban Missile Crisis, 42, 59, 72

Culpeper Baptist Church, Culpeper,
Va., 231

Hollywood-Beverly Christian Church
(DOC), Los Angeles, 178
Holmes, Eugene, 224–25, 360n44
Holy Trinity Catholic Church,
Washington, D.C., 57, 60
Hoover, Herbert, 59, 112
Horne, Rex, 234, 362n84
Hot Springs, Ark., 216–21, 224, 237, 239
House Un-American Activities
Committee, 17, 108
Houston, Tex., 58, 202, 204, 205–6, 240,
242, 247, 268
Huckabee, Mike, 303
Hudson, Deal, 261, 263, 265, 266, 364n18,
366n73, 366–67n83
Huffman, John, 117
Humphrey, Hubert H., 58, 59, 87, 110,
145, 193
Hurricane Katrina, 264, 265
Hussein, Saddam, 141, 207, 211, 265, 266
Hybels, Bill, 234, 236

Iakovos, Demetrios Koukouzis, 92
Immanuel Baptist Church, Little Rock,
Ark., 225, 226–27, 234, 235
Immanuel Church-on-the-Hill
(Episcopal), Alexandria, Va., 130, 132,
136, 138, 343–44n35
Independence, Mo., 1–2, 3, 7, 8, 9, 10, 14,
16, 18, 321n1
Indonesia, 141, 270–71, 276–78, 279–80,
286, 287, 317, 318, 369–70n49
Iranian hostage crisis, 141, 161–62, 166,
348n74
Iraq War, 211, 213, 264, 265–67, 269,
367n86
Israel, 14, 15–17, 19, 122–23, 153, 160,
161–62, 170, 187, 227, 270, 290, 297,
308–9

Jackson, Jesse, 237
James, Henry, 52, 73
Jefferson, Thomas, 45, 74, 124, 186, 213
Jehovah's Witnesses (Watchtower
Society), 24, 27–31, 34, 36, 39, 40,
328n56
jeremiad form of preaching, 306
Jewish National Fund, 136
Jews/Judaism, 15–17, 41, 43, 58, 66,
90–91, 98, 115, 116, 117, 122–23, 128, 136,
155, 165, 166, 167, 218, 234, 258, 259,
262, 284, 286, 296, 366n75
John Paul II (pope), 160, 207, 266
Johnson, Lady Bird, 76–96; mentioned,
60, 136, 335n3, 337n46
Johnson, Luci Baines. See Nugent, Luci
Baines Johnson
Johnson, Lynda Bird. See Robb, Lynda
Bird Johnson
Johnson, Lyndon Baines, 76–98;
achievements and criticism of
administration, 76–78, 87, 91, 93, 94,
95, 97–98, 110, 116, 134, 145, 269; antiwar criticism from rector of Bruton
Parish Church, Williamsburg, 76–78,
116; baptism, 81; and Baptist Church,
79, 80, 81, 92, 93, 98; and Bible, 77,
79, 80, 81, 96; character, 82, 83, 92–93,
98; childhood and education, 80–82;
and the Christian Church (Disciples
of Christ), 80–81, 82, 83, 84, 85–86,
87–88, 92, 93, 94, 98; and civil rights,
87, 93, 95, 97–98, 145; controversy
over daughter Luci's baptism, 89–90;
death, 97; and Eastern Orthodoxy,
88, 92; ecumenicity of, 81, 86, 95, 98;
and Episcopal Church, 76–78, 82–83,
85–86, 87, 88, 89, 90, 91, 92, 98; extramarital affairs, 82, 93, 238;

Johnson, Lyndon Baines, (*continued*)
family and Texas background, 78–79;
lifestyle and despondency in
retirement, 96–97; and Lutheran
Church, 84, 88, 92; marriage, 82; and
other denominations, 80, 81, 83, 84,
86, 92; personal fear of damnation,
81, 95–96; and prayer, 91, 94, 96;
preference for liturgical churches,
88–89, 91; relationship with Billy
Graham, 86, 88, 94, 95–96, 345n61;
religious background of family,
79–80, 95; and Roman Catholicism,
84–85, 88, 89–91, 92, 94, 95, 98; and
the Vietnam War, 76–77, 78, 87, 91,
92, 93, 94, 95, 97, 269; mentioned,
110, 116, 117, 134, 140, 145, 154, 182,
224, 238, 269, 320, 377n228,
377n232
Johnson, Sam Houston, 79, 83, 88
Johnson, Samuel Ealy, Jr., 78–80
Jones, Don, 229–30
Just War Theory, 265–66, 366–67n83

Kelley, Virginia Blythe Clinton, 215–16,
217, 219
Kellman, Jerry, 284–85, 286, 287, 293
Kennebunkport, Maine, 199, 205, 248,
252
Kennedy, Anthony, 262
Kennedy, Caroline, 45, 57
Kennedy, Edward, 46, 47, 49–50, 59, 110,
162
Kennedy, Ethel Skakel, 49
Kennedy, Eunice. *See* Shriver, Eunice
Kennedy
Kennedy, Jacqueline Bouvier, 45–74;
mentioned, 136
Kennedy, Jean. *See* Smith, Jean Kennedy

Kennedy, John F., 45–75; achievements
of administration, 59; assassination,
56, 57, 75, 83, 87, 182; and Bible, 53,
68; childhood and education, 50–52;
culture of Washington changed by,
59–61; election to Congress and
Senate, 54, 57; extramarital affairs of,
52–53, 61–65, 69, 74, 110, 238, 332n74,
332n81; family background, 45–50;
funeral, 136; lack of basis for controversy, 74–75; lifelong poor health
of, 54, 67, 75, 110, 335n138; marriage,
54–55, 57, 69; military service, 52–54;
national controversy over Roman
Catholic faith of, 12, 13, 58–59, 74,
110, 310; and other denominations,
51, 54, 66, 70, 73; and prayer, 46, 48,
67, 70, 72; presidential candidacy and
election, 57–59, 109–10, 112; public assumptions about faith of, 45,
65–66, 67; public practice of Roman
Catholicism and private doubt and
indifference toward, 49, 50, 51–53, 57,
58–59, 67–75, 261, 319, 320, 377n228;
relationship with Billy Graham,
70–71, 95, 110; religious background
of inner circle, 66–67; religious views
compared with those of Deistic James
Monroe, 73–74; Secret Service and
press, discretion of, 59, 63, 64–65,
67–69, 72, 332n74; mentioned, *ix*, 45,
94, 112, 118, 159, 192, 199, 223, 258, 310,
319, 320, 335n138, 377n228
Kennedy, John F., Jr., 57
Kennedy, Joseph P., Jr. ("Joe Jr."), 49, 50
Kennedy, Joseph P., Sr., 45, 46–47, 48,
50, 51, 52, 53, 54, 72
Kennedy, Kathleen. *See* Cavendish,
Kathleen

Reagan, Ronald, Jr. ("Ron"), 173, 183, 185, 195, 350n10, 354–55n115
Reagan, Ronald Wilson, 173–96; and abortion, 164; achievements and criticism of administration, 163, 182, 188–89, 193–95, 196; Alzheimer's disease, 185, 187, 196, 354–55n115; assassination attempt on, 181–82, 183, 185, 186, 190–91, 352n52; and astrology, 190–92, 193; and the Bible, 176, 179, 180, 186, 187; character, 173, 183; childhood and education, 176–77; and the Christian Church (Disciples of Christ), 173–74, 176–77, 178, 185, 187, 193, 196; death and funeral, 196; and evangelicalism, 173–74, 187, 189–90; family and Illinois background, 173, 174–76, 192; as governor of California, 164, 181, 183; in Hollywood, 178, 183, 190, 192, 193; and the Iranian hostage crisis, 162; irregular church attendance, 178, 181–85, 186, 196, 320; marriages of, 178, 185, 189; personal theology, 174, 178–79, 185–87, 193; and prayer, 176, 178, 179, 185, 186, 188; and the Presbyterian Church, 180, 181, 185, 186; relationship with Billy Graham, 181, 187–88, 190; and the Religious Right, 165, 189, 268; revival of presidential ceremony, 160; and Roman Catholicism, 179, 185, 193; unfamiliarity with services of Episcopal Church, 184–85, 352n53; mentioned, 123, 162, 165, 168, 208, 213, 234, 250, 260, 268, 320
Rebozo, Bebe, 112, 113, 119
Reed, Ralph, 260
Reformed Church in America (Dutch Reformed), 112, 125, 126
Regan, Donald T., 191

Rehnquist, William, 262
Religious Right, the, 165, 259, 268, 296
Reynolds, Barbara, 299, 301
Rice, Condoleezza, 260, 267
Richards, Ann, 254
Richardson, Adam, 315
Righter, Carroll ("the gregarious Aquarius"), 192
River Brethren (Brethren in Christ), 24, 25, 26–27, 28, 29, 34, 39, 40
Rivers, Eugene F., 378n250
Robb, Lynda Bird Johnson, 89, 91
Robbins, Kenneth, 179
Roberts, Clifford, 327n50
Roberts, John, 262
Roberts, Oral, 41
Robertson, Pat, 93, 165, 189, 209, 268
Robinson, Craig, 294
Robinson, Michelle. *See* Obama, Michelle Robinson
Robison, James, 165, 189, 253, 257
Rodham, Dorothy Howell, 229
Rodham, Hillary. *See* Clinton, Hillary Rodham
Rodham, Hugh, 229
*Roe v. Wade*, 135, 163–65, 227–28
Roman Catholicism, 1, 8, 10, 28, 38, 41, 43, 80, 84–85, 88–95, 98, 107–12, 155, 164–67, 174–79, 185, 188–89, 193, 198, 206, 213–23, 228, 234, 244, 258, 262–66, 271, 279, 283–86, 292, 296, 305–7, 331n56, 337n48. *See also* Kennedy, John F.
Roosevelt, Eleanor, 14, 55, 136
Roosevelt, Franklin Delano, 14, 19, 20, 22, 33, 59, 61, 65, 98, 118, 159, 193, 198
Ross, Brian, 302
Rove, Karl, 241, 247, 255, 257, 262
Rumsfeld, Donald, 262

Russell, Charles Taze, 27
Ryan, John A., 331n56
Ryan, Thelma Catherine ("Pat"). *See*
   Nixon, Thelma Ryan ("Pat")

San Clemente, Calif., 113
Sayre, Francis, 90, 329n81
sbc. *See* Southern Baptist churches,
   members, and Convention
Scalia, Antonin, 262
Schiavo, Terry. *See* Terry Schiavo case
Schlesinger, Arthur, 59–60, 68
Schneider, Wunibold W., 84, 85, 94
Second Vatican Council, 58, 69, 90, 222
secular humanism, 164, 271, 320
Shriver, Eunice Kennedy, 48, 74
Sinatra, Frank, 60
Skull and Bones secret society, 199, 203,
   244, 246
Smith, Alfred E. (Al), 45, 66, 80
Smith, Jean Kennedy, 48
Smith, Joseph, III, 1–2, 321n1
Social Gospel movement, 188, 230, 237
Soetoro, Ann. *See* Sutoro, Ann Dunham
   Obama
Soetoro, Lolo, 276, 277, 278, 279, 280
Soetoro, Maya Kassandra, 271, 277, 280,
   281, 318, 320, 368n14
Sorensen, Ted, 54, 58, 67, 68, 69, 70, 71,
   73
Sotomayor, Sonia, 262
Southern Baptist churches, members,
   and Convention, 2, 5, 8, 19–20, 79,
   80, 81, 92, 136, 138–39, 140, 143, 144,
   148–49, 154, 155, 158, 159, 160, 163–64,
   166–69, 174, 189, 213, 215, 218, 222, 223,
   226–28, 234–35, 237, 257, 260, 261,
   296, 348n76
Spann, Gloria Carter, 145–46, 147

Spaulding, Chuck, 66, 68
Spellman, Francis, 329–30n13
St. Aidan's Catholic Church, Brookline,
   Mass., 50
Stalin, Joseph, 4, 14, 17, 22
St. Ann's by the Sea Episcopal Church,
   Kennebunkport, Maine, 200, 252
Stapleton, Ruth Carter, 146, 152
St. Barnabas Episcopal Church,
   Fredericksburg, Tex., 85
St. Columba's Episcopal Church,
   Washington, D.C., 205
St. Dominic's Chapel (Roman Catholic),
   Washington, D.C., 91
Stebes, Joseph, 223
Stevens, John Paul, 141
Stevenson, Adlai, 87, 212
St. Francis Xavier Catholic Church,
   Stonewall, Tex., 84, 94
St. John's Episcopal Church, Lafayette
   Square, Washington, D.C., 14, 133,
   182, 205, 209, 259, 311, 313, 314, 316
St. Margaret's Episcopal Church, Palm
   Desert, Calif., 141
St. Mark's Episcopal Church, Grand
   Rapids, Mich., 126, 129
St. Mark's Episcopal Church, San
   Antonio, Tex., 82
St. Mark's Episcopal Church,
   Washington, D.C., 87
St. Martin's Episcopal Church, Houston,
   Tex., 204–5, 242
St. Matthew's Cathedral (Roman
   Catholic), Washington, D.C., 72, 75,
   89
St. Patrick's Cathedral (Roman
   Catholic), New York City, 57
Strauss-Kahn, Dominique, 62
Sukarno (Kusno Sosrodihardjo), 276

Walker, Lucretia Wear, 198

Wallace, David, 8

Wallace, Elizabeth Virginia ("Bess"). *See* Truman, Bess

Wallace, Madge Gates, 8, 16

Walters, Cora, 219

Warren, Bill, 129

Warren, Earl, 42

Warren, Elizabeth Anne Bloomer. *See* Ford, Betty

Washington, George, 182, 198

Washington National Cathedral (Episcopal), 44, 83, 87, 90, 141, 142, 196, 259

Watchtower Society. *See* Jehovah's Witnesses

Watergate scandal: and Billy Graham, 117, 138, 156; and Ford, 130–31, 138, 140; and G. H. W. Bush, 208; and Nixon, 116–17, 118, 130–31, 140, 341n50; mentioned, 133, 154

Wead, Doug, 206, 254, 260

Wee Kirk o' the Heather Church, Glendale, Calif., 178

Welch, Laura. *See* Bush, Laura Welch

Welch, Ola Florence, 341n51

Wentworth-FitzWilliam, Peter, 48–49

Wesley, Charles, 256, 365n60

Wesley, John, 230

Westmoreland Congregational Church, Bethesda, Md., 112

Weyrich, Paul, 226

White, Frank D., 225

White, John, 48, 53

White Citizens Council (Sumter County, Calif.), 150, 220

Whittier, Calif., 100, 101, 106, 111–12, 118, 121

Willow Creek Community Church, South Barrington, Ill., 234

Wilson, Woodrow, 90, 154, 167, 329n81

Wogaman, J. Philip, 233, 236, 362n93

Wright, Jeremiah, 288–310. *See also* Obama, Barack Hussein

Wyman, Jane, 178–79, 190

Yarborough, Ralph, 245

Yorba Linda, Calif., 99, 123

Young, Solomon, 2

Zeoli, Billy, 137–38

## GEORGE H. SHRIVER LECTURE SERIES IN RELIGION IN AMERICAN HISTORY